Antique Trader's

COUNTRY AMERICANA
PRICE GUIDE
2ND EDITION

EDITED BY
KYLE HUSFLOEN

Published by
Antique Trader Books, A Division of

**krause
publications**

700 E. State Street • Iola, WI 54990-0001
Telephone: 715/445-2214
Web: www.krause.com

Please, call or write us for our free catalog of antiques and collectibles publications.
To place an order or receive our free catalog, call 800-258-0929.
For editorial comment and further information,
use our regular business telephone at (715) 445-2214.

Library of Congress Catalog Number: 99-68142
ISBN: 0-87341-895-6

Printed in the United States of America

EDITOR'S NOTE

What is "country Americana?" That is a tricky question since the term implies that only artifacts made and used in rural America should be included. Of course, much of what is collected today as "country" was mass-produced in cities and has now become lumped under the general collecting title of "country" because these items reflect our yearning for the charm and nostalgia of the "good old days."

In deciding what to include in this general guide, my staff and I went over long lists of possible collecting categories which might fall under the heading of 'country-related.' It wasn't always easy to decide what should be included and what not, but in the end we felt it made sense to try and focus in on a diverse range of topics which reflected a wide range of collecting tastes. With only 448 pages to work with, we had to limit somewhat what could be included but we hope you'll find our selections of interest and value.

The collecting of "country Americana" has a long and fascinating history with its real roots stretching back to the Centennial Exhibition of 1876 when "colonial" American artifacts were displayed and caught the fancy of many of the thousands of visitors to Philadelphia that year. Not long after, Colonial Revival furniture was being produced and by the 1890s there was a dedicated core of collectors, mostly in the New England region, who were scouring the countryside for furniture, glass, china, and other artifacts which they felt reflected the historic charm of early American life. By the 1920s "Colonial Revival" was really 'hot,' and major manufacturers mass-produced all types of furniture and decorative accent pieces with an 'antique' appeal. The 1920s also saw the growth of major Americana collections by such notables as Wallace Nutting, Henry Ford and Henry duPont Winterthur and many of their collections of the finest early American antiques now reside in museums. The average collector could settle for less expensive and simpler pieces for their homes. During the Depression, when prices for antiques fell, many Americans decorated with "country" items out of simple necessity but as times improved by the late 1930s rooms full of "pumpkin pine" furniture, accessorized with old bottles and decorative old china showed up in many popular mass-market magazines as well as the growing number of specialty publications aimed specifically at the burgeoning antiques collecting market.

The "country look" continued to be popular with a certain segment of the antique-loving public right through the 1940s to the 1970s, but what seems to have spurred the most recent craze for all things with a country "look" was the publication in the early 1980s of books specifically aimed at the home decorating market where page after page of color photos showed off charming groupings of baskets, woodenwares, primitive furniture and even newer "handcrafted" items. Although that frenzied period of gathering nearly anything and everything may have ebbed, there will most certainly always continue to be an interest in and demand for the wide range of antiques and collectibles which harken back to simpler times and add colorful appeal to any domestic setting, rural or urban.

Here's wishing you good luck and great enjoyment in your pursuit of your favorite category of "country Americana!"

Kyle Husfloen, Editor

CONTENTS

ACKNOWLEDGMENTS

This book was made possible only through the combined efforts of the staff of Antique Trader Books and the generous efforts of a number of specialist collector and authorities. My staff and I were most fortunate to receive the enthusiastic support and input of a large number of people whose particular knowledge of certain categories has ensured that they will provide you, the reader, with the broadest, most in-depth and accurate overview of these collecting fields. A special note of thanks goes to Tom Porter of Garth's Auctions, Delaware, Ohio, who prepared our special introductory feature. Garth's, as many of you are aware, is one of the premier auction houses today specializing in the sale of all type of country antiques and collectibles. We appreciate Mr. Porter's willingness to share some insights gathered during his career as auctioneer and collector.

Below we list, by category, the names of the many folks who unselfishly shared of their time and knowledge to provide special introductions, price listings and photographs for the following chapters covering the world of "Country Americana."

Further listings and addresses of color clubs are included in a special appendix at the back of this book.

GENERAL CATEGORIES

Bootjacks
Harry A. Zuber
Houston, TX

Bottle Openers
Charles Reynolds
Reynolds Toys
2836 Monroe St.
Falls Church, VA 22042

Cash Registers
William Heuring
Hickory Bend Antiques
2995 Drake Hill Rd.
Jasper, NY 14855

Christmas Collectibles
Robert Brenner
Princeton, WI

Cookbooks
Barbara DePalma
Deer Park Books
27 Deer Park Rd.
Gaylordsville, CT 06811

Farm Collectibles
Philip Whitney
303 Fisher Rd.
Fitchburg, MA 01420-1548

Kitchenwares

General
Carol Bohn
KOOKS (Kollectors of Old Kitchen Stuff)
Mifflinburg, PA 17844

Coffee Mills
Mike White, Editor
The Grinder Finder
P.O. Box 483
Fraser, CO 80442

Egg Beaters
Don Thornton
Beat Books
1345 Poplar Ave.
Sunnyvale, CA 94087

Graniteware
Jo Allers
Cedar Rapids, IA 52410

Juice Reamers
Bobbie Zucker Bryson
Tuckahoe, NY

Laundry Room Items

Irons
David Irons
223 Covered Bridge Rd.
Northampton, PA 18607

Jimmy & Carol Walker
Iron Talk
P.O. Box 68
Waelder, TX 78959-0068

Lighting Devices

Aladdin Lamps
Thomas W. Small
201 Hemlock Lane
Meyersdale, PA 15552

Kerosene Lamps
Catherine Thuro-Gripton
Toronto, Canada

Gerry Bloxam
Newmarket Century House Antiques
150 Lorne Ave.
Newmarket, Ontario Canada L3Y 4J7

**Lightning Rod Balls and
Weathervanes & Roof Ornaments**
Phil Steiner
Weather or Knot Antiques
15832 So. C.R. 900 W.
Wanatah, IN 46390

Sewing Adjuncts
Beth Pulsipher
Prairie Home Antiques
240 N. Grand
Schoolcraft, MI 49087

Stoves
Clifford Boram
Antique Stove Information
Clearinghouse
417 No. Main St.
Monticello, IN 47960

Tobacciana
Tony Hyman
Treasure Hunt Publications
P.O. Box 3028
Pismo Beach, CA 93488

Tools
Martin & Kathy Donnelly
P.O. Box 281
Bath, NY 14810

Tramp Art
Clifford Wallach & Michael Cornish
277 W. 10th St.
New York, NY 10014

Windmill Weights
Richard S. Tucker
Argyle Antiques
406 Country Club Rd.
Argyle, TX 76226

CERAMICS

Blue & White Pottery
Stephen E. Stone
18102 East Oxford Dr.
Aurora, CO 80013

Flow Blue & Mulberry
Ellen Hill
Mulberry Hill South
655-10th Ave., N.E., Apt. 5
St. Petersburg, FL 33701

Pennsbury Pottery
Susan N. Cox
800 Murray Dr.
El Cajon, CA 92020
amial: antiqfever@aol.com

Red Wing Pottery
Charles W. Casad
Monticello, IL

Stoneware
Vicki & Bruce Waasdorp
P.O. Box 434
Clarence, NY 14031

Watt Pottery
Dennis M. Thompson
P.O. Box 26067
Fairview Park, OH 44126

PHOTOGRAPHY CREDITS

Bootjacks
Harry A. Zuber

Bottle Openers
Charles Reynolds

Cash Registers
Hickory Bend Antiques

Ceramics

Blue & White Pottery
Stephen E. Stone, Aurora, Colorado

Pennsbury Pottery
Susan N. Cox
Lucile Henzke, Texas
Laura DeMerchant, San Diego,
California
Photos from the collection of George
Fedele, Newport Avenue Antiques
Mall, 4836 Newport Avenue, San
Diego, California

Red Wing
Charles W. Casad
Stanley Baker, Minneapolis,
Minnesota
Gail DePasquale
Woody Auction Service, Douglass,
Kansas
Dorothy Beckwith, Platteville,
Wisconsin

Christmas Collectibles
Robert Brenner

Coffee Mills
Michael White

Graniteware
Jo Allers

Kerosene Lamps
Ken Bell, Ontario, Canada

Kitchen Collectibles
Carol Bohn
Don Simmons

Laundry Room Items Irons
Carol & Jimmy Walker

Tobacciana
Tony Hyman

Watt Pottery
Dennis M. Thompson
Fairview Park, Ohio

Windmill Weights
Richard S. Tucker

For permission to use photographs and listings for various categories, we wish to extend thanks to the following auction houses:

Aldefers
Hatfield, PA

Christie's
New York, NY

Collector's Sales and Service
Middletown, RI

Copake Country Auction
Copake, NY

DeFina Auctions
Austinburg, OH

Garth's Auctions
Delaware, OH

Gary Guyette - Frank Schmidt, Inc.
West Farmington, ME

Gene Harris Antique Auction Center
Marshalltown, IA

Glass Works Auctions
East Greenville, PA

Green Valley Auctions
Mt. Crawford, VA

Grunewald Antiques
Hillsborough, NC

International Toy Collectors Assoc.
Athens, IL

Jackson's Auctions
Cedar Falls, IA

James Julia
Fairfield, ME

Lee Vines
Hewlett, NY

Marlyn Margulis
Cherry Hill, NJ

Northeast Auctions
Portsmouth, NH

Pacific Glass Auctions
Sacramento, CA

Robert G. Jason-Ickes
Olympia, WA

Skinner, Inc.
Bolton, MA

Sotheby's
New York, NY

Susan Eberman
Bedford, IN

Temples Antiques
Eden Prairie, MN

Tradewinds Antiques
Manchester-by-the-Sea, MA

Wolf's Auctioneers and Appraisers
Cleveland, OH

INVESTING IN ANTIQUES—THE GOOD, THE BAD AND BLACK SATIN GLASS

By Tom Porter of Garth's Auctions, Delaware, Ohio

Carolyn and I bought our first antique in 1957. We were newlyweds living in Maryland. I was a private in the Army and making $22.00 a week. Carolyn, a registered nurse working for a federally funded children's hospital, made $121.00 a week. We thought we were making a lot of money and could afford the best, until we went to look at new furniture. We needed a dining room table. The price of the new one that we liked was $900.00. After we recovered from sticker shock, we started wandering through antiques shops. We found an inlaid cherry Hepplewhite drop-leaf table for $125.00. We sold it 15 years, four kids and five moves later for $350.00. Little did we know that with the purchase of that table we were investing in our future.

These pieces were sold at Garth's in early 1999. In the background, a painted poplar game board in old red with green and yellow striping and black squares, applied edge, 20" sq., $1,073. On the table, left, a pine sewing box, probably Shaker, with whittled conical legs, one nailed drawer and open well and top compartment w/finials and eyelets for thread, 8 x 10 " plus handle, $275, right, an early hardwood coffer with peaked hinged top, chip-carved decoration, and old scrubbed finish, probably German, some damages, 9 x 13 ",10 "h., $440. The table is a country Chippendale tavern table with a curly maple base and pine top and apron, traces of old brown paint, 18th c., 26 x 36 ", 24 " h., $2,530. Under the table is a stoneware ovoid jug with a brushed cobalt blue "3" and the impressed label "N. White, Utica," mid-19th c., 15 " h., $358.

Bottom line, we became interested in antiques because we couldn't afford anything else. We stayed interested in antiques because we recognized quality and appreciated craftsmanship, as well as individualistic expression of styles. Not to mention the practicality and functionality of certain items. Of course we came to admire and collect the weird, the colorful, the curiousq—items that don't have a thing to do with practicality and functionality but, perhaps most important to us, are fun.

In 1962, we met Garth Oberlander. By that time, Garth had been holding auctions for about 10 years, but had been a dealer for 25. Carolyn and I subsidized our growing family by "picking" and we went to Garth's auctions to learn more about antiques and what they were worth. Garth was always willing to educate. And boy, did we learn. We were lucky enough to join Garth in business in 1967. He remained our partner, mentor, and friend until his death in 1973. Whenever we are asked to evaluate past trends, current values and future growth of the antiques market, Carolyn and I continue to follow Garth's Golden Rules.

Sold at Garth's in early 1999, this grouping was highlighted by an English Chippendale mahogany fall-front writing desk with fitted interior and four graduated drawers. With replaced brasses and hinges and some repairs it sold for $1,210. On top is a grouping of Rockingham-glazed pottery. The two pie plates sold together for $193 while the platter and oval dish brought $171. The Old Sleepy Eye blue and white pitcher, 8" h., had stains, crazing and a short hairline and brought $100. In front, the early leather fire bucket featured an old dark brown patina and worn black and white painted label, 13 " h., it brought $314.

This country-style open stepback pewter cupboard was walnut with red and blue repaint and board and batten doors below. It had been cut down from a one-piece flat wall cupboard and sold at Garth's in 1999 for $440. Featured with it were various pieces of pewter. A three-piece grouping with a communion goblet marked "Sheldon & Feltman, Albany," a mug and a jar with a tight fitting lid sold for $88. The pewter basin on the top shelf carried the touch mark of Samuel Hamlin, Jr. or Sr. and brought $385. Below on the left is a 13 "d. charger with the eagle touch or Thomas Badger of Boston, $468 and 13 " d. made in England (indistinct mark), $275. The six round-bowled pewter spoons were of late manufacture and went for $121. In the lower front is a very large 18 " d. European charger, very worn, which still brought $770.

RULE NUMBER ONE: BUY WHAT YOU LIKE

Invest in antiques like you invest in a relationship. Take time to learn about what you like. Ask questions. Get comfortable. Grow. Don't assume anything.

In the mid-1960s I was just sure that black satin glass was going to be the hottest thing since sliced bread. I didn't particularly like the stuff, buy hey, if it was going to make me the next John Paul Getty, why not try to corner the market? Let me tell you, I bought and bought and bought. To this day, there has never been a strong market for black satin glass. So, I was stuck with a lot of something that I didn't even like. And I lost money. Since then, Carolyn and I have bought what appealed to us. We haven't always made money on our choices, but who can put a monetary value on enjoyment?

The low cradle with turned finials shown here was of pine and hardwood with an old dark brown finish. The bottom was replaced and it had repairs and sold for $193. In front of it are two turned wood mortars and pestles, which sold together for $83. The carved hardwood cookie board featuring a standing 18th century man on one side and a lady on the other, 7 3/8 x 17", made $275. In the lower front , a primitive pair of wood and wrought-iron ice skates with old worn leather straps and old blue repaint sold for $55. Above is a hexagonal "penny" rug with colored wool circles appliqued to a feed sack burlap back, 24 " w., it reached $358. All these sold at Garth's in early 1999.

RULE NUMBER TWO: THE BEST GETS BETTER

Buy the best that you can afford.

When an especially great piece of furniture or an exemplary item in any category would go across the auction block, Garth would say, "Buy the best and here it is...don't be sorry tomorrow that you didn't bid today." Truly great pieces get better with time and with any luck increase in value.

The attractive Federal chest of drawers is inlaid cherry and features four long graduated drawers with rope-spiral inlaid banding around each drawer and on the apron, inlaid escutcheons and paneled ends. It does have replaced oval brass pulls and some repairs and replacements but dates from the early 19th century and sold at Garth's in 1999 for $2,255. On top is a paneled ironstone china pitcher, 10" h., the Aurora pattern with a dark blue floral transfer highlighted in colored enamels. It brought $248. The three-piece ironstone tea set with a black transfer-printed floral decoration, mid-19th c., brought $248.

RULE NUMBER THREE: BUYING STOCK ISN'T AS FUN AS BUYING ANTIQUES

I'd rather sit on a Windsor chair than sit on a stock.

I buy antiques that make me smile. For me, that is a quality of life investment because I have yet to see a Brink's truck following a hearse. This philosophy isn't for everyone, but it works for us. Carolyn and I decided many years ago that we were going to invest in antiques instead of stocks. We couldn't afford to do both. Investing in antiques satiated our buying habit, furnished our home and brought us countless hours of enjoyment. Selling the antiques that we collected put our four daughters through college and kept Uncle Sam satisfied.

Buying antiques as investments isn't unlike playing the stock market, however. There is risk involved. Sometimes you win, sometimes you lose. But how often does a losing stock certificate make you grin?

This dramatic Jacquard coverlet features a central medallion of oak leaves and acorns flanked by a large angel at each corner and all within a wide floral border. In red, blue, green, brown and natural white it measures 72 x 80" and had some wear, stains and fringe loss. It sold at Garth's in 1999 for $220.

RULE NUMBER FOUR: IF YOU AREN'T MAKING MISTAKES, YOU AREN'T DOING ENOUGH

Read. Listen. Watch. Buy. Learn.

Nobody's perfect. Mistakes are inevitable. But Carolyn and I have found that even mistakes can be invaluable. Once you invest your hard-earned money into an antique, conjecture becomes reality — your reality. Once you have lost money in an antique you bought, for whatever reason, you tend not to make the same mistake again. Consider your mistakes as a tuition payment in your "continuing antiques education." Every successful antiques dealer and collector I know has invested a lot of money into their continuing education — learning from their bad investments has made them successful.

At the left is a Federal country-style corner washstand in pine with a mellow refinishing, early 19th c., overall 39" h., $550. Above it is a small charcoal drawing on paper with a scene of Mt. Vernon and an indistinct date and initials in the corner, held in an old grained beveled frame, 19th c., 12 3/8 x 16 ",$440. In front of the washstand is a pair of early brass ring-turned andirons, $303. At the right is an early sampler in silk thread on homespun linen featuring alphabets, birds, flowers, trees & the inscription "Hannah Campaion Aged 10 years, Ochiltee 1826," $578, which hangs above one of six Classical mahogany and mahogany veneer side chairs with a scroll-carved crest and vase-form splat, ca. 1830, the set $495. This grouping was sold at Garth's in early 1999.

RULE NUMBER FIVE: HINDSIGHT IS 20/20

The antiques industry is self-perpetuating; just like people, things get older by the day. Unfortunately, that does not mean they automatically become more valuable.

Trends in the antiques market are created when a group of people decide that something is desirable. American Indian artifacts were extremely popular in the 1970s; prices dropped in the 1980s and just recently have begun to rise. Prices for Shaker furniture were stronger in the late '80s than they are currently.

Some trends remain the same and many antiques are economically accessible. It is still consistently possible to buy antique furniture and accessories more reasonably than it is to purchase new furniture and accessories. Have you visited Ethan Allen lately?

As for future trends? I wish I knew. Who would have thought that a PEZ candy container would be worth 400 times the original value? And why hasn't black satin glass ever taken off?

Which brings me back to Rule Number One.

The Federal mahogany drop leaf table with turned and reeded legs and brass casters, early 19th c., 20 x 42" closed, sold for $880. On top are a large chalk cat with original grey paint and black stripes, some wear and touch-up, 12 " l., $440, and a smaller similar cat, 6" l., also $440. Hanging above are a large water-color theorem on paper of a basket of colorful fruit in an old frame, 16 x 20 ", $715, and a small water-color on paper full-length portrait of a gentleman in a top hat, initialed "MM" and in an eglomisé matte and giltwood frame, 10 x 13", $385. All of these sold at Garth's in 1999.

BASKETS

The American Indians were the first basket weavers on this continent and, of necessity, the early Colonial settlers and their descendants pursued this artistic handicraft to provide essential containers for berries, eggs and endless other items to be carried or stored. Rye straw, split willow and reeds are but a few of the wide variety of materials used. The Nantucket baskets, plainly and sturdily constructed, along with those made by specialized groups, would seem to draw the greatest attention to this area of collecting.

Berry, splint-sided, wide slightly flaring spaced splints joined at the rim & base by narrow tin rims, traces of red, pint, 4 1/4" d., 3 7/8" h., pr. **$303**

Bushel basket, woven splint, oval w/nailed rim & handle, stamped "Genoa Apple Basket," old patina, 12 1/2 x 20 1/2", 8" h. **165**

Bushel basket, splint stave construction, deep rounded sides joined at the top by a bentwood band, small bentwood handles, old dark red, 19" d., 11" h. **385**

Bushel basket, woven splint, deep rounded sides w/a wrapped rim & bentwood rim handles, old patina, 23" d., 13" h. (some wear & damage) **358**

Bushel basket, splint stave construction, the deep rounded sides of slightly spaced staves joined at the top by a bentwood band, small wire rim handles w/turned wood grips, old patina, 22 1/2" d., 15 1/2" h. **193**

"Buttocks" basket, woven splint, 38-rib construction, bentwood handle, 6 x 6 1/4", 2 3/4" h. (wear, stain & some damage) **165**

"Buttocks" basket, woven splint, 22-rib construction, deep sides w/wrapped rim & slender bentwood handle, good old patina, 7 1/4 x 7 1/2" h. plus handle (minor damage) **215**

"Buttocks" basket, 37-rib construction, woven splint w/bentwood handle, marked "Ohio State Fair 1938," old patina, 8 1/2 x 9 1/2", 4 3/4" h. **303**

"Buttocks" basket, woven splint, 22-rib construction, deep sides w/wrapped rim & slender bentwood handle, good patina w/dark brown color, 11 x 12 1/2", 6" h. plus handle **220**

"Buttocks" basket, woven splint, 16-rib construction w/wrapped rim & center bentwood twig handle w/Eye of God design, 12 x 14", 6 1/2" h. plus handle **105**

"Buttocks" basket, woven splint, 36-rib construction, good old patina, 10 3/4 x 9 1/2", 7" h. plus bentwood handle (some damage) . **495**

"Buttocks" basket, tightly woven splint, 40-rib construction, boat-shaped w/incurved ends, twisted twig center handle, old finish, 10 1/2 x 17", 8" h. plus handle (minor damage) **325**

"Buttocks" basket, woven splint & cane, 18-rib construction, long oval form w/wrapped rim, center bentwood handle w/Eye of God design, 16 x 20", 8" h. **193**

Large "Buttocks" Basket

"Buttocks" basket, woven splint, greyish patina, some damage, 10" d., 12" h. plus bentwood handle (ILLUS.) **149**

"Buttocks" sewing basket, woven splint, 22-rib construction, wrapped rim & center bentwood handle, worn cloth lining, 6" d., 4" h. plus handle.. 110

Cheese basket, woven splint, shallow round form w/wrapped rim & overall large honeycomb design, 9" d. 358

Fruit basket, woven splint, round w/tapering sides, wrapped rim w/open rim handles, good patina, 16 1/2" d., 11" h. 231

Half basket, woven splint, 17-rib construction, pocket-form w/flat back & rounded front, bentwood fixed handle, 5 1/2" w., 4 1/2" h. plus handle 138

Herb Drying Basket

Herb drying basket, woven splint, round, wrapped rim w/open rim handles, good patina, 21" d., 6 1/4" h. (ILLUS.)........................... 248

Laundry basket, woven splint, deep round sides tapering in to a base band, the wide wrapped rim w/small rim bentwood handles, bottom signed in Gothic letters "Harvard 1916," old patina, 22" d., 9" h. (rim wrap incomplete, some splint damage).............................. 303

Laundry basket, woven splint, rectangular bottom w/deep swelled sides & oblong wrapped rim, end-to-end hinged bentwood handle w/interesting laced end detail, old patina, 15" l..................................... 138

Laundry basket, woven wicker, oblong w/wrapped rim & rim handles, attributed to Zoar, Ohio, 26 1/2 x 32" (some damage) 220

Market basket, woven splint, rectangular w/upright sides, fanned ribbing, wrapped rim, center bentwood handle, natural patina, 11 1/2 x 17''', 6 1/2" h. plus handle (some damage) 110

Market basket, woven splint, deep rectangular sides w/radiating ribs & rounded bottom ends, wrapped rim, bentwood center handle, old patina, 9 1/2 x 14", 7" h. 149

Market Basket

Market basket, woven splint, rectangular w/upright sides, fanned ribbing, wrapped rim, center bentwood handle, 15 1/2 x 26",10" h. plus handle (ILLUS.) 209

"Melon" basket, woven splint, 11-rib construction, end-to-end bentwood handle w/diamond design at each end, good patina, 10 1/2" d., 6" h. plus handle (some damage).......... 176

Nantucket basket, finely woven splint, round, 19th c., 7 1/4" d., 3" h. (minor losses to basket & lashing)...................................... 1,150

Nantucket basket, splint ribs & cane weaving w/whip-wrapped rim & swivel bentwood handle w/brass attachment, turned wooden base, faded ink inscription on bottom, old patina, 7 x 7 1/2", 3 1/4" h. plus handle.. 1,045

Nantucket basket, tightly woven splint, wide rounded form w/a narrow wrapped rim & bentwood swing handle, remnants of paper label, early 20th c., 8 3/8" d., 4 3/8" h. **1,265**

Nantucket basket, finely woven splint, round, w/paper label on base reading "I was made on Nantucket Island I am strong and stout Don't lose or burn me I'll never wear out," S.P. Boyer, 7 1/2" d., 4 1/2" h. **2,645**

Nantucket Basket

Nantucket basket, tightly woven splint, wide rounded form w/a narrow wrapped rim & bentwood swing handle, early 19th c., imperfections, 13 3/4" d., 9 7/8" h. (ILLUS.) **1,265**

Peach basket, woven splint staves, wide thin staves in a woven diamond design forming the slightly tapering deep cylindrical sides, thin bentwood base & rim bands, old brown patina, 14 1/2" d., 11 1/2" h. **193**

"Picket fence" basket, tapering cylindrical form constructed of spaced fence-like picket slats w/rounded tops, joined by a galvanized metal band around the base & a wire ring around the top, old patina, 16" d., 10" h. **248**

Pie basket, cov., round lattice construction w/slender slats forming the sides, interior band & thin rim band w/scalloped edge, removable interior shelf, plywood bottom, 11 1/2" d. **578**

Pie basket, cov., cylindrical oval lattice sides composed of thin wood lattice w/central interior band & thin, scalloped rim band, double bentwood swing handles at center of rim, removable interior shelf, plywood bottom, 15 1/2" l. **468**

Storage basket, woven splint, deep oval sides w/four small bentwood rim handles, two at each side, lined w/burlap stenciled w/a label "C.H.H.," 19 x 25", 9" h. (minor damage) **303**

Storage Basket

Storage basket, woven splint, deep rectangular sides w/wrapped rim & center bentwood handle, red, blue & natural, 10 1/2 x 17", 10 1/2" h. plus handle (ILLUS.)...................... **77**

Storage basket, cov., honeycomb design openwork woven splint, cylindrical sides w/flat fitted cover, 11" d. (damage, hole) **138**

Storage basket, cov., woven wicker, a deep bulbous oval body w/a deep fitted top & two large wrapped swing handles, natural finish, ca. 1920, 17" l. **86**

Utility basket, woven splint, 64-rib construction, flat bottom w/rounded sides & wrapped ri mw/small bentwood end handles, good patina, 15 " d., 5 3/4" h. (some wear & damage) **193**

Utility basket, woven splint, round, wrapped rim & center handle, good

patina, 8 1/2" d., 6" h. plus handle
(ILLUS.) **330**

Small Utility Basket

Utility basket, woven splint, deep
round cylindrical sides w/a
wrapped rim & bentwood handle,
old patina, 12" d., 6" h. plus handle   **138**

Utility basket, woven splint, deep
cylindrical sides w/narrow wrapped
rim, slender bentwood swivel
handle, worn red exterior paint,
9 1/2" d., 6 3/4" h. **330**

Utility basket, woven splint, deep
round tapering sides w/small
wrapped bottom band & wide
round wrapped top band, high
bentwood handle, good patina,
10 1/4 x 11 1/2", 7" h. plus handle.   **110**

Utility basket, woven splint, slightly
tapering deep round sides
w/wrapped rim & slender bentwood
swing handle, overall worn blue
paint, 11" d., 7 1/4" h. (some
damage) **402**

Utility basket, woven splint,
cylindrical sides w/33-rib
construction, overhead bentwood
handle, good color, 12" d., 7 1/2" h.
plus handle **220**

Utility basket, woven splint,
cylindrical sides wwrapped rim &
swivel bentwood handles, good old
dark patina, 12 x 13", 7 1/2" h.
(damage in bottom) **220**

Utility basket, woven splint,
cylindrical sides w/33-rib
construction & narrow wrapped
rim, high angular overhead
bentwood handle, good color,
13" d., 7 3/4" h. plus handle **138**

Utility basket, woven splint, round
cylindrical sides w/a heavy
wrapped rim & bentwood handle,
grey scrubbed patina, 15" d., 8" h.
plus handle **193**

Utility basket, woven splint, deep
rounded rectangular form
w/wrapped rim & bentwood swing
handle, old greyish patina,
9 1/2 x 13", 8 1/4" h. plus handle
(wear, damage) **138**

Work basket, woven splint, wide
shallow openwork round form
w/small rim handles, flaking heavy
green paint, 11" d. **385**

BOOTJACKS

The Bootjack is a utilitarian device used to remove a boot, and often an American art form at the same time. As with so many everyday items created in the 19th and early 20th centuries, the way something looked was as important to its creator as its use. United States patent records from 1790 to 1873 indicate the first patent for a bootjack was issued April 6, 1852 to Saris Thomson of Hartsville, Massachusetts (Patent #8865). Normally, the bootjack has been produced from cast iron or wood and ranges from extremely fine casting and carvings to crude ones-of-a kind.

As with so many collectible items bootjacks are heavily reproduced, especially crickets and "Naughty Nellies"—castings are lightweight and of a poor quality. Prices on early fine castings and carvings have risen steadily in the last five years but prices for the more common varieties are still reasonable.

Cast iron, model of a cricket w/original paint, decorated in brown, red, blue & yellow on a black ground, ca. 1900 .... **$125**

Cast iron, traveling-type, pivoting arms fit size of heel, cut-out vine design, style pat'd. Oct. 29, 1867 by "A. P. Seymour, Hecla Works, N. Y.," 8 3/4" open, 5 1/8" closed .. **95**

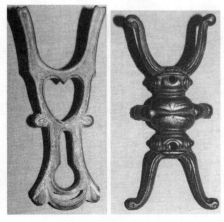

From left: Bootjack with Heart & Keyhole Cut-Outs and Double-ended Beetle

Cast iron, forked end w/heart & keyhole cut-outs, some gold & white paint, 9 3/8" (ILLUS.) **175**

Cast iron, advertising, original gold paint, geometric & scroll design w/embossed words "Use - Musselmans - Bootjack - Plug - Tobacco," early 20th c., 9 1/2" **165**

Cast iron, figural, double-ended beetle, 9 1/2" (ILLUS.) **270**

Cast iron, figural female weightlifter holding barbell w/rope & rings in her outstretched arms, late 19th c., 10" **1,000**

Cast iron, figural "Naughty Nellie" w/hands away from her head, painted gold, date unknown, crude casting, 10" **600**

Cast iron, figural Devil w/painted white horns & arms, cut-out circular eyes & triangular nose above a painted red mouth & cut-out stomach, w/some original paint, ca. 1880-90, 10 1/2" **300**

Cast iron, figural "Naughty Nellie" w/original paint, late 19th c., 10 1/2" **650**

Cast iron, figural mermaid w/outstretched arms lying atop green seaweed, w/original paint, ca. 1900, 11" **500**

Cast iron, model of a stag head above scroll design, ca. 1880, 11". **650**

Cast iron, Victorian scroll design, ca. 1900, 11" **450**

Cast iron, double-ended w/half-circles in middle & quarter moon each end, early 20th c., 11 1/4" (ILLUS.) **175**

Cast iron, figural "Naughty Nellie" w/head slightly turned to left, w/original red paint, fine detail, paint worn, 11 1/2" **300**

Cast iron, model of a steer head, marked "101 Ranch" below w/Pat. Pend. on underside, ca. 1910, 11 1/2" **700**

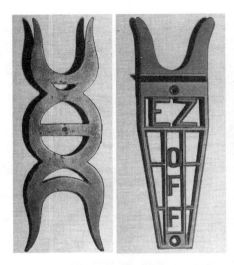

From left: Double-Ended Bootjack with Half-circles and EZ-OFF Bootjack

From left: Double-Ended "A. M. Mitchell" Bootjack and wrought-iron Bootjack with Hearts

Cast iron, w/cut-out letters "EZ" above word "OFF," nicely cast, 11 1/2" (ILLUS.).............................. 250

Cast iron, double-ended, cut-out floral design w/"A. M. Mitchell" on one side & "Charleston, ILL." on reverse, 11 5/8" (ILLUS.)............... 350

Cast iron, model of the Tree of LIfe w/unusual vulture heads, cut-out heart at base, ca. 1890, 11 3/4" ... 200

Cast iron, elaborate floral & scroll designs w/inverted heart in center & hole at bottom, ca. 1880-90, original red paint, 12 1/4".............. 300

Cast iron, embossed lettering "Wittier's" above & "American Centennial Boot Jack - 1876" around a cut-out star, above another star circled by "Hyde Park" all above "Mass - 1776," 13" 450

Cast iron, model of a pair of upside-down dress boots above two scrolls, ca. 1870s, 13" 450

Cast iron, model of a snail, date unknown, 13" 125

Cast iron, U-form end & heavy shaped frame w/three stylized hearts, Pennsylvania, unique, 13" (ILLUS.) 750

Cast iron, cut-out scroll design w/cut-out wording "DOWNS & CO" in center ('N,' '&' 'S' in reverse), date unknown, 13 1/2" 200

Cast iron, double-ended w/triangles in center, Pennsylvania, early 20th c., 13 1/2" (ILLUS.) 150

Cast iron, fancy raised stylized floral design w/heart at bottom, 14" (ILLUS.) 300

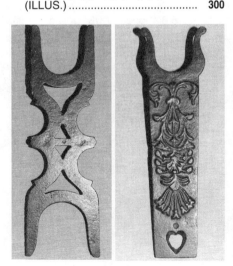

From left: Double-Ended Bootjack with Triangles and Floral Design & Heart Bootjack.

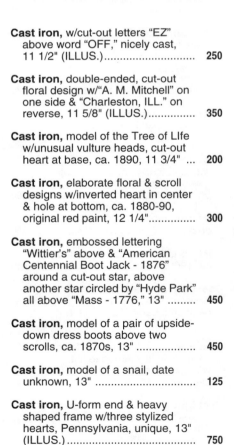

Cast iron, cut-out lettering "BOSS," ca. 1880s, 15" **400**

Cast iron, undulating hairpin-form, Pennsylvania, probably unique, early 20th c., 17" (ILLUS.) **350**

Cast iron, closed loop at the top to hold both boot & heel, cut-out wagon wheel in center, ca. 1880, 20 1/2" **350**

Wooden, folding-type, hand-carved pistol, brass hinges & pins, ca. 1860-70, 10" **350**

Wooden, walnut, folding ladies' legs w/pointed toes, brass hinges & pins, ca. 1860-70, 10" **350**

Wooden, folding-type, long narrow boards w/brass hinges & pins, possibly Shaker, ca. 1870-80, 10 1/2" **300**

Wooden, lady's-leg style, hinged brass fittings & boot strap pulls inset inside, early 20th c., 12" (ILLUS. of two views) **900**

Wooden, flattened board beetle-form incised w/scrolls & a shield w/initials "W.L.," Victorian, 13" (ILLUS.) **175**

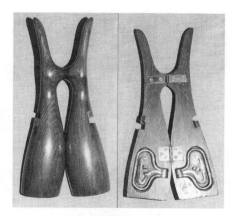

Wooden Lady's Leg Bootjack

Wooden, tapering board w/incised Pennsylvania Dutch folk art designs including a star, pinwheel & heart, initials "R.T.," at bottom, late 19th - early 20th c., Pennsylvania, 13 1/4" (ILLUS.) **300**

Wooden, folding-type, w/closed loop, w/original label "Folding Boot-Jack - Wheeler Case & Co." pat'd. Dec. 7, 1869, Utica, New York, 23" open, 14 3/4" closed **200**

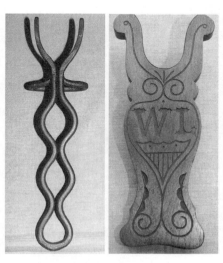

From left: Hairpin-Form Pennsylvania Bootjack and Beetle-form Board Bootjack

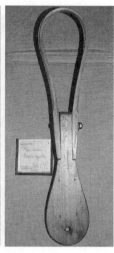

From left: Pennsylvania Folk Art Bootjack Wooden Wheeler Case Co. Patent Model Folding Bootjack

Heart-Shaped Wooden Bootjack

Wooden, slender design w/small
  hole at bottom, original red paint
  w/black pinstriping, ca. 1850, 16" .   **250**

Wooden, folding-type, w/closed loop,
  original patent model for Wheeler
  Case Co., 22 3/4" (ILLUS.)........... **1,000**

Wooden, large heart-shaped loop at
  the top, fork at opposite end,
  25 1/2" (ILLUS.)............................   **125**

Wooden & cast iron, mechanical,
  spring-operated mechanism,
  oblong wood platform on iron base,
  ca. 1900, 13 1/2" **125**

BOTTLE OPENERS

Before the turn of the century, the crown cap for bottled drinks was invented and immediately there was a need for a bottle cap remover or bottle opener.

There are many variations of openers, some in combination with other tools, others are utilitarian with fancy handles. Perhaps the most important type of bottle opener today is the figural bottle opener. There are 22 classifications or types of figural bottle openers, with Type 1 being the most important and sought after by collectors. Figures for openers include people, animals, birds, pretzels, keys, etc. Wall-mount openers are mostly faces of people or animals with the opener located in or near the mouth.

The important early producers (ca. 1940-50) of iron and pot-metal (zinc) figural openers were Wilton Products, John Wright Inc., Gadzik Sales and L & L Favors. Figural openers were made primarily as souvenirs from vacation spots around the country.

Today, new original figural openers are produced in limited numbered editions and sold to collectors. Manufacturers such as Reynolds Toys have produced over 40 different figural bottle opener editions since 1988. There are two clubs for bottle opener collectors: Figural Bottle Opener Collectors (F.B.O.C.) and Just For Openers (J.F.O.). J.F.O. is a club primarily for beer opener collectors, but includes collectors of figural openers, corkscrews and can openers. The numbers used at the end of the entries refer to Figural Bottle Openers Identification Guide, a new book printed by F.B.O.C.

Bottle Openers By Type

Type 1— Figural bottle openers, free-standing or in natural position or wall-mounted, the opener an integral part of the figure.

Type 2— Figural openers with corkscrew, lighter or nutcracker, etc.

Type 3— Figural openers, three-dimensional on both sides but do not stand.

Type 4— Figural openers with loop openers an integral part of design.

Type 5— Figural openers with a loop inserted in the casting process. The loop or opener is not part of the casting process.

Type 6— Same as Type 5 with an added can punch.

Type 7— Same as Type 5 with an added corkscrew or lighter.

Type 8— Flat, back not three-dimensional, loop part of casting.

Type 9— Same as Type 8, loop inserted in the casting process.

Type 10—Same as Type 8 with a corkscrew.

Type 11—Openers are coin or medallion shape, one- or two-sided, with an insert or cast integral loop opener. (These are very common.)

Type 12—Figural stamped openers, formed by the stamping process (steel, aluminum, or brass).

Type 13—Extruded metal openers.

Type 14—Johnny guitars or figural holders. Johnny Guitars are figures made of wood, shells, string, etc.; they have a magnet that holds a stamped steel (Type 12) opener; figural holders or display holders are cast holders that have a clip that holds one or two cast figural openers.

Type 15—Church keys with a figure riveted or cast on the opener. Some do not have a punch key.

Type 16—Figural church-key openers with corkscrew.

Type 17—Decorated church-key openers (church-key loop or wire loop openers with names and jewels attached).

Type 18—Base opener (opener molded in bottom as integral part).

Type 19—Base opener added (opener added to bottom by brazing or soldering).

Type 20—Base-plate opener (opener screwed in base of figure).

Type 21—Wooden openers/Syroco openers (metal insert, cast stamped or wire type).

Type 22—Knives, hatchets, scissors, etc., with openers

Rarity
A—Most Common
B—Difficult
C—Very difficult
D—Very hard to find
E—Rare to Very Rare (few known)

FIGURAL (FULL DIMENSIONAL)

TYPE 1

All-American, cast iron, figure of a man in an orange football jersey w/the letters "Z B T" across his chest, standing on base marked "Joe Alexander," rarity E, 4 1/4" h., F-38 (ILLUS.) **$600-950**

Alligator & boy w/hands up, cast iron, figural group of black boy w/his hands raised above his head,

*All-American
Bottle Opener*

being bitten in the behind by an
alligator, rarity B, 2 1/4" h., F-134
.... **150-250**

Alligator w/boy, cast iron, figural
group of black boy being bitten in
the behind by an alligator, rarity B,
3" h., F-133 .... **75-150**

Aviator, aluminum, figure of pilot
dressed in brown flight suit &
goggles w/his right hand raised,
rarity B, 3 3/4", N-591 (ILLUS.).. **45-90**

Bar wolf, cast iron, rarity C, 9 1/2",
F-149 .... **150-250**

Barking at the moon, aluminum,
figural group, a barking brown &
white dog sitting at the base of a
crescent moon, 2" h., N-529 ..... **45-110**

Bear, baby, aluminum, model of baby
bear wearing a red top, blue pants
& holding a cap in his hand, rarity
C, 3" h., N-562 .... **45-90**

Bear, mama, aluminum, model of
mama bear wearing a yellow &
green dress, rarity C, 4" h., N-561 **45-90**

Bear, papa, aluminum, model of
papa bear wearing a blue jacket,
red vest & grey pants, rarity C,
4 5/8" h., N-560 .... **45-90**

Bear at fence, aluminum, model of a
bear standing at a fence marked
"FIGURAL - BOTTLE -
OPENERS," rarity B, 4 5/8" h.,
N-582 .... **75-150**

Beer drinker, cast iron, figure of a
portly man wearing a hat, blue shirt
& brown pants holding a beer mug,
rare, 5 1/2" h., F-192 (ILLUS.) ... **1,500+**

Bicycle FBOC 1990, aluminum,
model of a gold bike on a base
marked "FBOC," 2 5/8" h., N-572 **45-90**

Billy goat, cast iron, figure of a goat
w/head tilted back, rarity C,
2 3/4" h.. F-74 .... **150-250**

Bird's Birch Beer, aluminum, model
of a grey bird perched atop a
branch, the bird marked "BIrd's,"
the branch marked "Birch Beer,"
3" h., N-574 .... **45-90**

Black horse, aluminum, model of a
rearing horse, rarity A, 3 3/4" h.,
N-584 .... **50-75**

Buffalo, aluminum, 2" h., N-595 .. **50-75**

Caddy, cast iron, figure of a black
boy wearing a red shirt, black
pants & red shoes, holding a golf
bag w/clubs & resting his hand on

*Aviator Bottle
Opener*

*Beer Drinker
Bottle Opener*

Cathy Coed Bottle Opener

Cool Penguin Bottle Opener

Father Christmas Bottle Opener

a white sign that reads "19," rarity D, 5 7/8" h., F-44 .... **350-550**

Canvasback duck, cast iron, colorfully painted duck w/red head & neck & a yellowish white body, 1 13/16" h., F-107 .... **75-150**

Cathy Coed, cast iron, figure of a young woman wearing a yellow hat, blue V-neck blouse, short flared yellow skirt & black Mary Jane-type shoes, standing on a base marked "Women's Weekend," rarity E, 4 5/16" h., F-39 (ILLUS.)............................ **1,200+**

Chili pepper '93, cast iron, model of a red chili pepper, rarity B, 5 7/8" h., N-658 .... **75-150**

Cockatoo, cast iron, colorfully painted, 3" h., F-121 .... **100-225**

Cocker Spaniel, cast iron, model of dog w/white body & brown ears, neck & hind end, standing w/one foot raised, rarity A, 2 3/4" h., F-80 .... **75-110**

Cool penguin, zinc, model of walking penguin wearing a top hat, rarity C, 4" h., (ILLUS.)............................ **150-250**

Cowboy w/cactus, pot metal, figural group of cowboy wearing cowboy

hat & plaid shirt clutching a cactus, rarity D, 4 5/8" h., F-23 .... **350-650**

Crystal beetle, pot metal & crystal, model of a beetle w/cut-crystal circular body w/metal legs & head, rare, 4 3/8" .... **550+**

Devil, aluminum, figure of Devil dressed in red robes holding pitch fork, rarity B, 4" h., N-563 .... **100-150**

Dodo bird, cast iron, model of a bird w/black body, colorful markings on wings, head & an orange beak, rarity E, 2 13/16", F-122 .... **450-650**

Dolphin, aluminum, model of stylized goldfish green dolphin w/tail curled over its head, 4" h., N-616 .... **75-150**

Donkey, aluminum, w/3" ears, rarity D, 3 3/8" h., F-59 .... **350-550**

Donkey, brass, base marked "Norwood," rare, 4 1/8" h. .... **550+**

Donkey, brass, body of donkey marked "Phila. - 1948," rarity D, 3 3/4" h. .... **500+**

Donkey, cast iron, figure of standing donkey w/white teeth, rarity D, 3 1/2" l, N-613 (ILLUS.) **250-350**

Standing Donkey Bottle Opener

*Freddie Frosh
Bottle Opener*

Dragon, cast iron, model of dragon w/open mouth, arched back & curled tail, rarity E, 5" h. .... **550+**

Dumbbell, cast iron, rare, 4 5/8", F-220 .... **550+**

Elephant, cast iron, model of walking elephant w/mouth open & trunk raised, rarity D, 4 1/4" l., N-616   **1,200+**

Elephant, cast iron, rarity E, 3 1/4", F-47 .... **450-650**

Eskimo ice, aluminum, figural group of Eskimo dressed in a parka holding the leash of the dog sitting in front of him, 3" h., N-575 .... **50-90**

Father Christmas, aluminum, rarity C, 4 1/2" h., N-558 (ILLUS.) **150-250**

Father Time, aluminum, figure of Father Time dressed in grey robe, holding a sickle & an hour glass, rarity B, 4 3/4" h., N-599 (Illus.) . **75-150**

Flying fish, aluminum, model of a trout atop a wave, rarity B, 4 3/4" h., N-656 .... **75-150**

Freddie Frosh, cast iron, model of young man w/his hands in his pockets wearing a beanie-style cap, sweater w/Greek letter across the front, standing on a green base, rarity D, 4" h., F-37 (ILLUS.) **450-650**

Goat, cast iron, model of seated goat, rarity A, 4 5/16" h., F-71 .. **60-100**

Gobbler, aluminum, model of gold-painted turkey w/stern look on his face, wearing suit w/arms crossed, 3" h., N-625 .... **45-75**

Good luck, aluminum, model of a hand in the form of a fist w/forefinger overlapping thumb, wrist marked "Good Luck," rarity A, 3 3/4" h., N-624 .... **50-75**

Grass skirt Greek, cast iron, figure of a black boy wearing a grass skirt, clutching a sign that reads "Phi Gamma Delta - Fiji Island Party - '53," rarity D, 5" h., F-43 .... **650+**

Heart in hand, cast iron, model of an up-turned hand w/a cut-out heart in the palm, rarity E, 4 1/4" h., F-203 .... **350-550**

Hunting dogs, aluminum, model of two dogs, one chocolate brown & one light brown, 2" h., N-587 .... **50-75**

Indian chief, aluminum, figure of chief wearing full headdress, standing w/legs spread & hands on hips, 5" h., N-598 .... **50-75**

Iroquois Indian, cast iron, figural, aluminum, rarity A, 4 3/4", F-197   **50-75**

Key (large), stainless steel, marked "Powell - White - Star Valves - are - Closers," rare, 9" l. **300-400**

Lady in kimono, cast iron, stylized figure of woman wearing a kimono, entire figure is black except for the red sash & light brown hat, rarity D, 3 7/8" h., N-580 .... **200-300**

Lady in the wind, aluminum, figure of woman wearing royal blue dress & hat, she is leaning into the wind clutching her hat, 4" h., N-598 .. **50-75**

Lamppost drunks, cast iron, figural, common, 4 1/8" h., F-1, 2, 11.... **10-25**

Lion hoop, cast iron, model of a lion jumping through hoop, 3 5/8" l., N-576 .... **250-350**

Mademoiselle lamp/sign, cast iron, rarity A, 4 1/2", F-10 .... **50-75**

Male nude w/garment, brass, rarity E, 2 7/8" h., F-24 (Illus.)............. **200-300**

Mexican w/cactus, cast iron, figural group of Mexican wearing sombrero, sitting beside cactus, rarity E, 2 7/8" h., F-24 (ILLUS.)............................ **550-750**

Mighty Musky, cast iron, rarity B, 6 1/8" l., N-659 .... **75-150**

Miner, FBOC '95, cast iron, figure of miner wearing blue pants, yellow shirt & brown hat holding pan & pick on base marked "FBOC 1995," rarity A, 4 1/8", N-670 (ILLUS.) **50-75**

Missouri mule, bronze, model of stylized kicking mule, rarity A, 2 7/8" h., N-551 .... **50-75**

Monkey, cast iron, model of seated monkey, 2 5/8" h., F-89 .... **250-300**

Mother goose, aluminum, figure of woman in a green dress & white apron holding a goose, rarity A, 3 3/4" h., N-573 .... **50-75**

Motorcycle rider, aluminum, figural group of man riding motorcycle wearing a red helmet, goggles, white shirt & brown pants, rarity B, 2 3/4" h., N-588 .... **75-150**

New Year baby, aluminum, figure of baby New Year holding a parrot & wearing a black top hat, diaper & sash marked "1989," 4 5/8" h., N-567 .... **75-100**

Nude on swan iron, brass, rarity B, 6 5/8" h. (ILLUS.) **75-150**

Nude w/wreath, chrome, female nude w/raised arms & spread wings, rarity B, 5 3/16", F-173 .. **75-150**

Old pal, aluminum, model of a dog w/head turned & paw raised, rarity B, 2 3/4" h., N-570 .... **45-90**

Oriental clown, aluminum, figure of Oriental man w/hands in pockets dressed in brown, black & red clown suit, rarity C, 4 3/8" h., N-559 (ILLUS.) **90-110**

Mexican with Cactus Bottle Opener

Miner Bottle Opener

Nude on Swan Bottle Opener

Oriental Clown Bottle Opener   *Parrot on Perch Bottle Opener*   *Sammy Samoa*
Bottle Opener

Owl, bronze, model of a stylized owl sitting on a branch, rarity A, 2 7/8" h., N-552 .... **50-75**

Owl, cast iron, rarity E, 2", F-127 .. **350-550**

Paddy the Pledgemaster, cast iron, figure of a young man wearing a blue sweater & white pants holding a paddle marked "Phi Kappa Pi," standing on a base marked "Dinner Dance '57," 3 7/8" h., F-41 .... **300-350**

Palm tree, cast iron, rarity B, 4 9/16", F-21 .... **90-200**

Parrot, FBOC, 1987, cast iron, model of a colorful parrot on black perch, rarity A, 5 1/2" h., F-108c **50-75**

Parrot, large, cast iron, rarity A, 5 1/2" h., F-108 .... **50-75**

Parrot on perch, cast iron, figure of yellow, blue, green & red parrot on elaborate perch, rarity E, 4 5/8" h., F-114 (ILLUS.) **450-700**

Patty Pep, cast iron, figure of young woman wearing a red cap & coat & a brown skirt, buttons of coat marked w/Greek letters, on a base marked "Pledge Dance '57," rarity E, 4" h., F-36 .... **1,200+**

Pelican, cast iron, model of a pelican w/orange eyes, 3 3/8" h., F-131 .... **250-350**

Pelican, cast iron, model of a pelican w/up-turned orange beak, 4" h., F-130 .... **75-150**

Pelican w/flat head, cast iron, model of pelican w/black head, colorful body & yellow beak, rare, 3 7/16" h., like F-129 .... **550+**

Polar bear, aluminum, model of polar bear standing on its hind legs holding a brown stick, rarity C, 3 3/4" h., N-557 .... **90-125**

Pretzel, cast iron, black, marked "Hauenstein Beer," rarity D, 2 7/8" w., F-231 .... **250-350**

Pretzel, cast iron or aluminum, rarity A, 3 3/8" w., F-230 .... **50-75**

Pumpkin head, aluminum, figure of a person w/pumpkin head wearing black robe, rarity B, 4 1/4" h., N-565 .... **75-150**

Red Riding Hood, aluminum, figure of Red Riding Hood holding a basket w/the wolf at her feet, 4" h, N-568 .... **50-75**

Rhino, cast iron, rarity E, 4", F-76 .... **350-550**

*Uncle Same
Bottle Opener*

Rooster, cast iron, 4" h., F-100 ...   **75-100**

Rooster, cast iron, rarity A, 3 1/8" h.,
F-97 ....   **50-75**

Rooster (large), cast iron, tail down,
rarity B, 3 3/4" h., F-98 ....   **75-150**

Rooster (tail down), cast iron, rarity
B, 3 3/4" h., F-99 ....   **550+**

Sailor, aluminum, cast iron, painted,
rarity D, 5 7/8", F-18 ....   **350-700**

Sammy Samoa, cast iron, figure of a
native wearing leaves, rare, 4
5/16" h., F-39 (ILLUS.) **950-1,500**

Sawfish, cast iron, 5" l., F-157 .....   **350-550**

Sea gull, cast iron, model of a sea
gull on a brown perch, 3" h., F-123
....   **50-75**

Sea horse, cast iron, 4" h.,
F-140 ....   **75-150**

Setter dog, cast iron, model of a dog
w/front paw raised & straight tail,
rarity A, 2 1/2" h., F-79 ....   **60-90**

Shoe, aluminum, rarity C, 3 3/4" h.,
F-209 ....   **150-250**

Skeleton, aluminum, rarity B,
4 7/8" h., N-566 ....   **75-150**

Skunk, cast iron, 2" h., F-92c **150-250**

Steering wheel, brass, rarity A,
2 7/8", F-225 ....   **50-75**

Straw hat/sign, FBOC 15th, cast
iron, figural group of man clutching

sign post that reads "F.B.O.C. 15th
Conv.," rarity A, 3 7/8" h., N-618   **50-75**

Swimmer, aluminum, rare, 3 1/4",
F-195 ....   **850+**

Teen girl, cast iron, figure of a teen-
aged girl lying on her stomach
w/her chin in her hands & her feet
in the air, wearing black pants,
white shirt & a red ribbon in her
blond hair, 2" l, N-577 ....   **250-350**

Top hatter, bronze, model of stylized
bird wearing a top hat, rarity A,
2 1/2" h., N-606 ....   **50-75**

Totem pole, aluminum, rarity B,
3 3/4" h., N-573 ....   **45-90**

Uncle Sam, figural group of Uncle
Sam clutching sign post w/sign that
reads "Uncle Sam," 1 of 13, rarity
D, 3 7/8" h., N-580 (ILLUS.) **250-350**

WALL MOUNT

TYPE 1

Amish man, cast iron, w/long beard
wearing Amish-style hat, rare,
4 1/8" h., F-422 ....   **1,900+**

Bear head, cast iron, 3" h, F-426..   **150-250**

Beer drinker, cast iron, model of
older man wearing cap, white shirt
& orange vest holding a mug of
beer, surrounded by cast-iron
frame w/banner at the bottom
marked "Spencer Brewing Co. -
Lancaster, Pa.," rarity E, 6 3/8" h.,
F-406 ....   **550-850**

Black face, aluminum, black face
wearing bow tie w/mouth open to
reveal white teeth, rare, 5" h., F-
401 (ILLUS.) ....   **650+**

Black face, cast iron, black face
w/red mouth & hole in the ears,
marked "Crowley," 4" h., F-404 .....   **550+**

Boy winking, cast iron, freckle-faced
winking boy w/two large front teeth,
rare, 3 7/8" h., F-418 ....   **550+**

Bronze pirate, pirate head wearing a
red scarf on his head, an eye patch
& holding a knife between his
teeth, 5" h., N-512 ....   **75-150**

Bulldog, cast iron, rarity B, 4" h.,
F-425 ....   **75-150**

Clown head, cast iron, model of a clown head w/orange hair, red nose & mouth wearing red-polka-dotted tie, 4 1/2" h., F-417 .... **75-150**

Coyote, cast iron, gold-painted, rare, 3 1/2" h., F-429 .... **850+**

Double-eye, cast iron, four-eyed bald-headed man, rarity A, 3 7/8" h., F-414 (ILLUS.) **50-75**

Florida Pipe & Foundry, cast iron, four-eyed black woman w/red hair & lips, wearing bonnet that reads "Florida Pipe & Foundry," rare, 4 1/8" h., F-410 .... **550+**

Four-eyed man, cast iron, four-eyed man w/mustache, rarity B, 3 15/16" h., F-413 .... **75-150**

Hanging drunk, cast iron, figure of a man dressed in a black tuxedo & top hat, holding bottle in left hand w/right hand outstretched, rarity B, 5" h., F-415 (ILLUS.) **75-150**

Miss Four Eyes, cast iron, four-eyed woman w/brown hair, red lips & gold earrings, rarity B, 3 3/4" h., F-408 (ILLUS.)........................... **50-75**

Miss Two Eyes, zinc, two-eyed woman w/short hair & hoop earrings, rarity C, 3 3/8" h., F-409 .... **150-250**

Moon, aluminum, smiling & winking black painted moon face w/silver painted eyebrows, eyes, nose, cheeks, teeth & chin, rarity B, 3 1/2" h., N-664 .... **75-150**

Norwegian, cast iron, man wearing blue cap w/gold tassel, rarity D, 5 3/4" h., N-579 (ILLUS.) **350-700**

Sun, aluminum, orangish red-painted smiling sun w/black eyebrows, rarity B, 4" h, N-663 .... **75-150**

Teeth, brass, model of teeth & gums marked "Bottle Chops," rarity B, 3 1/4" w., F-420B **75-150**

From left: Black Face Bottle Opener, Double-eye Wall Bottle Opener, Wall Mount Hanging Drunk Opener

From left: Miss Four Eyes Wall Mount Opener, Norwegian Wall Mount Opener, Uncle Sam Wall Mount Opener

Uncle Sam, cast iron, head of Uncle Sam w/red & white painted top hat & white painted hair, eyebrows, teeth & bow tie, rarity B, 6 1/8" h., N-537 (ILLUS.) **75-150**

TYPE 2

Old Snifter, zinc, turns head & corkscrew comes out **125**

Old Snifter, zinc, w/lighter & corkscrew **275**

TYPE 3

Dachshund, Wilton Flats, cast iron, three-dimensional but does not stand **50-100**

Donkey, Wilton Flats, cast iron, three-dimensional but does not stand **50-100**

Elephant, Wilton Flats, cast iron, three-dimensional but does not stand **50-100**

Fish, Wilton Flats, cast iron, three-dimensional but does not stand **50-100**

Scottie Dog, Wilton Flats, cast iron, three-dimensional but does not stand **50-100**

TYPE 4

Drunk, Wilton, cast iron, three-dimensional drunk wearing black top hat & suit, w/loop top **65**

Mermaid, cast iron, three-dimensional, marked "Chiquita," loop tail **110**

TYPE 8

Gemini, zinc, flat back **20**

Lobster, cast iron, flat back, red, claws serve as loop **35**

Mad Man, zinc, flat back, depicts man bending at the knees w/hands clasped, legs serve as loop **75**

TYPE 9

Mermaid, lead & steel, depicts mermaid w/tail curled under, her upraised arms holding loop, loop inserted in casting process **45**

Pretzel, large, lead & steel, top of pretzel holds loop, loop inserted in casting process **150**

Winston Churchill, aluminum & steel, shows Churchill in front of hand giving a victory sign, fingers of hand hold loop, loop inserted in casting process **90**

From left: Coin in Holder Opener, Coins Bottle Opener, Medallion Bottle Opener

Axes Bottle Openers   *Shield & Knight Opener*   *Butler Bottle Opener*

TYPE 11

Coin in holder, stainless steel &
bronze, bronze coin in rectangular
holder, loop cut out at top (ILLUS.)   20

Coins, cast iron, three Oriental coins
joined together w/loop cut out of
top coin (ILLUS.)   15

Medallion, bronze, two-sided, w/loop
at top (ILLUS.)   10

TYPE 12

Ax, stamped steel & wood,
rectangular wood handle, opener
cut out of blade (ILLUS. left).........   10

Ax, stamped steel & wood, thin
rounded wood handle, opener cut
out of blade (ILLUS. right)   10

Fist, stamped steel, w/opener cut out
of palm, wrist reads "Kung-Fu"   12

Foot, stamped steel, w/opener cut
out of the ball of the foot, marked
"Goon"   12

Football, stamped steel, w/opener
cut out of top, small medallion at
bottom reads "Clearwater"   12

TYPE 13

Shark, aluminum, mouth serves as
opener, marked "Ocean City, MD,"
attached to key ring   3

TYPE 14

Bar & patrons, bar holds two figural
openers shaped as patrons   75-150

Golf bag & caddie, golf bag holder
holds figural caddie opener   75-150

Johnny Guitars, figures of old
people w/magnets that hold Type
12 openers, each.......................   45-75

Shield & knight, shield holds figural
knight opener (ILLUS.)   75-90

TYPE 15

Cat, attached to church key-type
opener, depicts green cat
w/crossed arms   25

Girl, attached to church key-type
opener, girl w/long hair & large red
bow on top of head   25

Violin case, attached to church key-
type opener, case marked
"Beethoven's fifth"   25

TYPE 20

Horse's head, zinc, base plate
opener screwed in bottom 35

TYPE 21

Butler, Syroco, wearing black suit &
white apron, holding green bottle,
metal opener attached to head
inside body (ILLUS.)...................... 90

Clown, Syroco, wearing white outfit
w/blue collar, metal opener
attached to head inside body 350

Figure, wooden, figure of bird,
Danish 10-30

Figure, wooden, figure of golfer
w/wooden golf club serving as
opener, Danish 10-30

Figure, wooden, figure of Viking
w/beard & holding shield, horned
hat serves as opener, Danish ... 10-30

War-time Wooden Opener

Man by lamppost, wooden, carved,
figure of man w/suitcase standing
next to lamppost, music box in
suitcase, metal opener attached to
head inside body 225

Man in tuxedo, Syroco, wearing top
hat, metal opener attached to head
inside body 90

Wooden, metal opener attached,
marked "War-time Bottle Opener-
With nail-head under cap, pull
up...your bottle is open!," World
War II era (ILLUS.) 90

BOTTLES

BITTERS

(Numbers with some listings below refer to those used in Carlyn Ring's For Bitters Only.*)*

African Stomach Bitters, cylindrical w/applied top, smooth base, dark amber, 9 5/8" h. **$88**

African Stomach Bitters - Spruance, Stanley & Co., cylindrical w/applied mouth, dark amber, 9 5/8" h. (cleaned) **132**

Allen's (Dr.) Stomach Bitters - Pittsburgh, PA, cylindrical w/tall neck & applied mouth, aqua, 12 1/4" h. **330**

Appentine Bitters Bottle

Appentine Bitters (under) Geo. Benz & Sons, St. Paul, Minn., w/"Pat. Nov. 23, 1897" on base, square, scrolls along sides of label panel, medium amber, 8 1/4" h. (ILLUS.) **385**

Arabian Bitters - Lawrence & Weichselbaum, Savannah, Ga., rectangular w/paneled sides & applied sloping collar, ca. 1870, medium amber, 9 3/4" h. (some light inside stain) **242**

Dr. Bell's Liver - Kidney Bitters

Bell's (Dr.) Liver - Kidney Bitters, square w/beveled corners, applied sloping collar mouth, pale greenish aqua, 9" h. (ILLUS.) **105**

Brown's Celebrated Indian Herb Bitters - Patented 1868, figural Indian Queen, yellowish amber, rolled lip, 12 1/8" h. **660**

Digestine Bitters, rectangular, sample size, ringed lower neck & tooled mouth, medium amber, 3 1/2" h. (lightly cleaned) **853**

Doyle's - Hop - Bitters - 1872, around sides of sloping shoulder, square w/paneled sides w/raised clusters of hop berries & leaves, yellow w/green tone, 9 5/8" h. **275**

Drake's Plantation Bitters - Patented 1862, cabin-shaped, five-log, deep chocolate amber, 10" h. (ILLUS.) **220**

Drake's (S T) - 1860 - Plantation - x - Bitters - Patented - 1862, cabin-shaped, six-log, golden honey amber, 10" h. (D-105) **116**

Drake's (S T) 1860 Plantation x Bitters - Patented 1862, cabin-shaped, six-log, light to medium yellowish olive, 10" h., D-108 (ILLUS.) **3,080**

*From left: Drakes Plantation Bitters Bottle,
Rare Drake's Plantation Bitters*

**Drake's (S T) - 1860 - Plantation -
x - Bitters - Patented - 1862,**
cabin-shaped, six-log, medium
copper puce, 10" h. (D-105) 231

**Drake's (S T) 1860
Plantation x Bitters - Patented
1862,** cabin-shaped, six-log,
medium reddish puce, 10" h.
(D-105) 156

**Drake's (S T) - 1860 - Plantation -
x - Bitters - Patented - 1862,**
cabin-shaped, six-log, strawberry
puce, 10" h. (D-105) 251

**Fish (The) Bitters - W.H. Ware,
Patented 1866,** figural fish, dark
amber, 11 1/2" h. 225

**German Balsam Bitters, W.M.
Watson & Co., Sole Agents for
U.S.,** square w/applied tapering
collar, rare opaque blue, 9" h.
(ILLUS.) 825

Greeley's Bourbon Bitters, barrel-
shaped, ten rings above & below
center band, medium smoky olive
green, 9 3/8", G-101 (ILLUS.)....... 1,155

**Henley's (Dr.) Wild Grape Root IXL
Bitters,** cylindrical w/applied rim,
aqua, 12" h. (slight haze).............. 121

**Henley's (Dr.) Wild Grape Root IXL
Bitters,** cylindrical w/applied rim,
teal blue, 12" h. (minor interior
stain)... 1,100

**Henley's (Dr.) Wild Grape Root IXL
Bitters,** cylindrical w/applied rim,
yellowish green, 12" h. (minor
interior stain)................................. 2,090

**Henley's (Dr.) Wild Grape Root -
IXL (in oval) Bitters,** cylindrical
w/tall neck & applied mouth,
smooth base, deep aqua,
ca. 1870, 12 1/8" h. (light spots of
stain)... 88

**Herb (H.P.) Wild Cherry Bitters,
Reading, Pa.,** cabin-shaped,
square w/cherry tree motif & roped
corners, paper label reading "H.P.
Herb Wild Cherry Bark Bitters,"
99% of label, medium 7-Up green,
8 7/8" h. (ILLUS.)........................... 5,060

*From left: Rare German Balsam Bitters
Bottle, Greeley's Bourbon Bitters*

*From left: Rare h.P. Herb Wild Cherry
Bitters, Moffat Phoenix Bitters*

Hertrichs Bitter, Einziger Fabrikant, Hans Hertrich Hof Gesetzlich Geschutzt, footed ball-shaped w/tall ringed neck, applied double collar, deep olive green, 9" h. 385

Lacour's Bitters - Sarsapariphere, cylindrical w/ringed rim & sunken side panels, amber, 9" h. 935

Langley's (Dr.) Root & Herb Bitters, J.O. Langley, proprietor, cylindrical, deep amber, 6" h. 121

Lash's Kidney and Liver Bitters - The Best Cathartic and Blood Purifier, square w/paneled sides & applied sloping collar, deep red amber, 8 3/4" h. (few haze spots).. 187

Lediard's Celebrated Stomach Bitters, square w/beveled corners, applied sloping double collar mouth, medium bluish green, ca. 1865-70, 9 1/2" h. (lightly cleaned)...................................... 743

Litthauer Stomach Bitters (paper label), Hartwig, Kantorowicz, Posen, Germany, square case gin shape, milk glass, 99% of label, 9 1/2" h. 132

Mishler's Herb Bitters - Table Spoon Graduation (ruler marker) - Dr. S.B. Hartman & Co. - 40 Med. Doses, embossed on base "Stoeckels Grad. Pat. Feb. 6 '66W. McC. & Co. No. 2," square, strawberry, 9" h. (lightly cleaned) .. 385

Mishler's Herb Bitters - Table Spoon Graduation (ruler marker) - Dr. S.B. Hartman & Co. - 40 Med. Doses, embossed on base "Stoeckels Grad. Pat. Feb. 6 '66W. McC. & Co. No. 2," square, medium peach or topaz, 9" h. 523

Moffat (John) - Phoenix Bitters - New York - 1-Dollar, rectangular w/beveled corners, medium olive amber, 1/2 pt., 5 3/8" h.(ILLUS.).... 908

National Bitters - Patent 1867, figural ear of corn, medium amber, "Patent 1867" on base, applied mouth, 12 5/8" h. (ILLUS.) 303

From left: National Bitters Ear of Corn Bottle, Nibol Kidney and Liver Bitters, Peruvian Bitters with Monogram

Nibol Kidney and Liver Bitters, square, 100% paper label reading "Nibol Tonic Laxative," w/contents, amber, 9 1/2" h. (ILLUS.).............. 176

Old Sachem - Bitters - and - Wigwam Tonic, barrel-shaped, ten-rib, deep cherry puce, 9 1/2" h. 660

Old Sachem - Bitters - and - Wigwam Tonic, barrel-shaped, ten-rib, deep reddish puce, 9 1/2" h. 440

Peruvian Bitters - "W & K" monogram in shield, applied top, smooth base, orangish red amber, 9 1/8" h. (ILLUS.)........................... 231

Pharazyn (H.) Phila. Rights Secured, figural Indian Queen w/raised shield, golden amber 990

Roback's (Dr. c.W.) - Stomach Bitters - Cincinnati, O., barrel-shaped, yellow amber w/olive tone, some light inside haze, minor scratches on label panel, 9 3/8" h. (ILLUS.) 743

Rose's (E.J.) Magador Bitters For Stomach, Kidney & Liver - Superior Tonic, Cathartic and Blood Purifier, rectangular w/beveled corners & tooled lip, medium amber, ca. 1900, 8 3/4" h.   83

From left: Roback's Stomach Bitters, Rare Royce's Sherry Wine Bitters

Royce's Sherry Wine Bitters, rectangular w/beveled corners & rounded shoulders, applied sloping collar, aqua, 8" h. (ILLUS.) **1,705**

Sahl'burgh, PA, rectangular w/indented side panels, rounded shoulders, applied sloping collar, root beer amber, 10 1/4" h............ **3,960**

Solomon's Strengthening & Invogorating Bitters - Savannah, Georgia, square, crudely applied top, cobalt blue, 9 5/8" h. (lightly cleaned, tiny potstone in side)... **715**

Tippecanoe (birch bark & canoe design), h.H. Warner & Co., cylindrical, "Rochestr N.Y." on base, applied disc mouth, amber, 9 1/4" h. **121**

Townsend's (Old Dr.) Magic Stomach Bitters, New York, rectangular w/indented panels, applied sloping collar, medium bluish green, 10" h. (shallow chip on side of lip) **963**

Uhler's Purifying & Strengthening Bitters, Philada., rectangular w/indented side panels, applied sloping mouth, aqua, 7 7/8" h. (overall stain, spider crack) **143**

Warner's Safe Bitters (design of safe), Rochester, N.Y., "A. & d. h.C." on base, rectangular w/rounded shoulders, applied mouth, medium amber, 7 1/2" h. **605**

Wheeler's - Berlin - Bitters - Baltimore, hexagonal, applied mouth, pontil, yellowish green citron, 9 1/2" h. (light exterior cleaning) **5,500**

Rare Dr. Wonser's Bitters Bottle

Wonser's (Dr.) U.S.A. , Indian Root Bitters, cylindrical w/applied mouth, ringed neck, ribbed shoulder, amber, 3/4 qt., 11" h. (ILLUS.) **6,600**

Woodcock Pepsin Bitters, Joseph c. Schroeder Co., St. Louis, MO. U.S.A., wide rectangular form w/rounded shoulders, 90% original paper labels on front & back, clear, ca. 1900, 8" h. **187**

FLASKS

Flasks are listed according to the numbers provided in American Bottles & Flasks and Their Ancestry *by Helen Mc-Kearin and Kenneth M. Wilson.*

Chestnut, plain body, sheared lip, brilliant yellow green, Midwestern, ca. 1820-30, 5 1/2" h. (small patch of exterior wear) **358**

Chestnut, twenty-four vertical ribs, sheared & inward-rolled rim, medium amber, Midwestern, ca. 1820-30, 5 1/2" h. **330**

Chestnut, twenty broken ribs swirled to the left, small slender neck w/sheared lip, yellow olive, Midwestern, ca. 1820-30, 7 3/8" h. **3,850**

Rare Chestnut Flask

"Washington" - "Jackson"
Flask

Chestnut, "grandfather" type, twenty-four broken ribs swirled to the right, sheared lip, deep reddish amber, Midwestern, ca. 1820-30, 8 1/4" h. (some milky inside stain) **990**

Chestnut, "grandfather" type, twenty-four ribs swirled to the left, sheared lip, golden amber, Midwestern, ca. 1820-30, few spots of inside haze, 8 3/8" h. (ILLUS.) **3,850**

GI-11 - Washington bust below branches - American eagle w/head turned right & body curving, sunrays above eagle's head & 13 small stars, horizontal beading w/vertical medial rib, deep bluish aqua, pt. **550**

GI-114 - Draped bust of Byron facing left - Draped bust of Scott facing right, vertically ribbed edges, dark amber, half pint (some inside stain) **176**

GI-114 - Draped bust of Byron facing left - Draped bust of Scott facing right, vertically ribbed edges, medium olive green, half-pint (some highpoint wear) **253**

GI-24 - "Washington" above bust - Taylor bust below "Bridgeton" [star] New Jersey," vertically ribbed sides, pale greenish aqua, pt. **110**

GI-26 - Washington bust - American Eagle w/shield w/eight vertical & two horizontal bars on breast, head

turned to right, aqua, qt. (highpoint wear, spotty inside stain) **105**

GI-31 - "Washington" above bust - "Jackson" above bust, yellow amber w/olive tone, pt. **176**

GI-34 - "Washington" above bust - "Jackson" above bust, vertically ribbed edges w/heavy medial rib, yellowish amber w/slight olive tone, pinhead flake on outer lip, bold impression, half-pint (ILLUS.) **385**

GI-40a - Washington bust below "The Father of His Country" - Taylor bust, "Gen Taylor Never Surrenders," smooth edges, applied double collared lip, aqua, pt. **66**

GI-55 - Washington bust w/short queue & plain toga - Taylor bust , w/collar decoration missing, smooth edges, medium pale bluish green, pt. **440**

GI-71 - Taylor bust (facing left) w/"Rough and Ready" below - Ringgold bust (facing left) w/"Major" in semicircle above bust & "Ringgold" below bust, heavy vertical ribbing, aqua, pt. **165**

GI-80 - "Lafayette" above bust & "T.S." & bar below - "DeWitt Clinton" above bust & "Coventy C-T" below, horizontally corrugated edges, medium yellow olive w/amber tone, pt............................. **605**

GI-94 - "Where Liberty Dwells is My Country - Benjamin Franklin" over bust of Franklin - "Dyottville Glass Works Philadelphia - T.W. Dyott, M.D." over bust of Dyott, aqua, pt. **385**

GI-97 - Franklin bust obverse & reverse, vertical ribbing, pale greenish aqua, qt........................... **160**

GII-1 - American Eagle on oval, head turned to right obverse & reverse, horizontally beaded edges w/narrow vertical medial rib, sheared lip, open pontil, aqua, pt. . **275**

GII-126 - American Eagle w/shield above laurel wreath, obverse & reverse, smooth edges, light pink amethyst, half pint **715**

GII-143 - American Eagle w/plain shield in talons & pennants in beak, calabash, four-flute edges, medium green, qt. **495**

GII-53 - American Eagle w/shield & furled flag - "For Our Country," wide bands of vertical edge ribbing, aqua, pt............................. **143**

GII-63 - American Eagle below "Liberty" - inscription in five lines "Willington - Glass - Co - West Willington - Conn.," smooth edges, deep amber w/olive tone, half pint. **231**

GII-63 - American Eagle below "Liberty" - inscription in five lines

From left: American Eagle Flask, "Success to the Railroad" Flask

"Willington - Glass - Co - West Willington - Conn.," smooth edges, deep bluish green, half pint **1,540**

GII-63 - American Eagle below "Liberty" - Willington Glass Co., smooth edges, applied lip, dark amber, half pint............................. **143**

GII-64 - "Liberty" above American Eagle w/shield facing left on leafy branch - "Willington - Glass - Co - West Willington - Conn," smooth sides, olive green, pt. (tiny lip flake) **121**

GII-79 - American Eagle above oval obverse & reverse, edges w/single vertical rib, deep olive amber, qt. (ILLUS.) **275**

GII-81 - American Eagle above oval inscribed "Granite - Glass Co." obverse - reverse the same except inscription "Stoddard - NY," narrow vertical edge rib, sheared lip, tubular pontil, olive amber, pt. **209**

GII-86 - American Eagle above oval obverse & reverse, vertically ribbed edges, medium olive amber, half pint... **143**

GIII-14 - Cornucopia with Produce & curled to right - Urn with Produce, vertically ribbed edges, deep bluish green, half pint **358**

GIV-18 - Masonic Arch, pillars & pavement w/Masonic emblems - American Eagle without shield on breast, plain oval frame below "KCCNE" inside, smooth edges w/single rib, medium yellowish amber, pt. **220**

GIV-19 - Masonic Arch, pillars & pavement w/Masonic emblems - American Eagle without shield on breast, plain oval frame below "KCCNE" inside, smooth edges w/single rib, some design elements such as trowel, skull & beehive missing, yellowish amber green, pt. **204**

GIV-20 - Masonic arch, pillars & pavement w/Masonic emblems - American Eagle w/"KCCNC" in oval frame below, single vertical edge rib, medium yellowish amber, lots of seed bubbles, pt. **176**

GIV-43 - Masonic six-point star w/eye of God in center all above "A D" - six-point star w/arm in center all above "GRJA," sheared lip, vertical edge ribs, olive amber, pt. 198

GIX-1 - Scroll w/two six-point stars obverse & reverse, vertical medial rib, long neck w/sheared lip, graphite pontil, deep yellowish green, qt. (slight inside stain, small spot of interior lip roughness) 825

GIX-10b - Scroll w/six-point stars, a small one in upper space & medium sized one in lower space obverse & reverse, vertical medial rib, dark olive amber, pt. 660

GIX-11 - Scroll w/two eight-point stars obverse & reverse, tubular pontil, aqua, pt. (slight inside haze)   88

GV-10 - "Railroad" above horse-drawn cart on rail & "Lowell" below - American Eagle lengthwise & 13 five-point stars, vertically ribbed edges, plain lip, pontil, olive green, half pint (very minor lip flakes)....... 198

GV-5 - "Success to the Railroad" around embossed horse pulling cart - similar reverse, plain lip, vertically ribbed edges, medium moss green, light inside stain, pt. (ILLUS.) 385

GV-6 - "Success to the Railroad" around embossed horse pulling cart obverse & reverse, w/"Success" above scene, sheared lip, pontil, olive green w/dark striations, pt. 242

GVI-5 - "Corn for the World" above large ear of corn - Monument w/"Baltimore," crude pebbly glass, golden yellowish amber, qt. (ILLUS.) 1,600

GVIII-10 - Sunburst w/twenty-nine triangular sectioned rays, center raised oval w/"Keen" reading from top to bottom on obverse & reverse, yellowish olive green w/amber tone, half pint (some heavy highpoint wear) 231

GVIII-14 - Sunburst w/twenty-one triangular sectioned rays, obverse & reverse, sunburst centered by ring w/a dot in middle, deep yellowish green, half pint (small iridescent inside lid bruise) 413

GVIII-18 - Sunburst w/twenty-four rounded rays obverse & reverse, horizontal corrugated edges, open pontil, sheared lip, light olive green, half pint.............................. 440

GVIII-28 - Sunburst w/sixteen rays obverse & reverse, rays converging to a definite point at center & covering entire sides, horizontally corrugated edges, light yellow green, half pint (some wear) 413

GVIII-29 - Sunburst in small sunken oval w/twelve rays obverse & reverse, panel w/band of tiny ornaments around inner edge, sides around panels w/narrow spaced vertical ribbing, light bluish green, 3/4 pt. 259

"Corn for the World" Flask

From left: Rare Sunburst Flask, Spring Tree - Summer Tree Flask

GVIII-7 - Sunburst w/twenty-four rounded rays flanked by a small circle on each side, obverse & reverse, horizontal corrugated edges & stepped lower neck, yellowish olive amber, pt. (ILLUS.) **1,380**

GVIII-8 - Sunburst w/twenty-eight triangular sectioned rays, obverse & reverse, center raised oval w/"KEEN" on obverse & w/"P & W" on reverse, yellowish olive amber, pt. **440**

GVIII-8 - Sunburst w/twenty-eight triangular sectioned rays obverse & reverse, center raised oval w/"KEEN" reading from top to bottom on obverse & "P & W" on reverse, sheared lip, open pontil, dark olive green, pt. **440**

GX-15 - Summer Tree - Winter Tree, smooth edges, applied double lip, smooth base, deep aqua, pt. (inside haze) **66**

GX-18 - Spring Tree (leaves & buds) - Summer Tree, smooth edges, light inside haze, deep bluish green, qt. (ILLUS.) **1,705**

GX-19 - Summer Tree - Winter Tree, smooth edges, deep bluish aqua, qt. **110**

GX-19 - Summer Tree - Winter Tree, smooth edges, yellow w/olive tone, qt. **1,540**

GX-4 - Cannon framed by "Genl Taylor Never Surrenders," grapevine frame around "A Little More Grape Capt Bragg," vertically ribbed sides, copper color, pt. **4,950**

GXI-26 - "For Pike's Peak" above a small miner w/tools above oval reserve - American Eagle above oval reserve, aqua, half pint **143**

GXI-50 - "For Pike's Peak" above prospector w/tools & cane - Hunter shooting stag, plain edges, root beer amber, pt. **990**

GXII-13 - Clasped hands above oval w/"L.F. & Co." all inside shield w/"UNION" above - American Eagle above frame

w/"Pittsburgh Pa.," yellow w/strong olive tone, qt. **1,210**

GXII-18 - Clasped hands above oval, all inside shield - American Eagle w/plain shield above oval frame, base w/"L & W" inside disc-shaped frame, medium amber, pt. **187**

GXII-41 - Clasped hands above oval all inside shield w/"Union" above shield - Cannon, medium lime green, pt. (some overall inside milky stain) **798**

GXII-43 - Clasped hands above square & compass above oval w/"Union" all inside shield - American Eagle, calabash, greenish aqua, qt........................... **138**

Rare "Flora Temple" Flask

GXIII-21 - "Flora Temple" above figure of a horse over "Harness Trot 219 3/4," plain reverse w/original round paper label reading "Salt River Bourbon Whiskey Distilleries, Jefferson County Kent'y...," rare w/label, applied shoulder handle, smoky copper, pt. (ILLUS.) **1,925**

GXIII-35 - Sheaf of Grain w/rake & pitchfork crossed behind sheaf - "Westford Glass Co., Westford Conn," smooth edges, applied double collar w/large spillover, olive amber, pt. (slight inside stain) **143**

GXIII-35 - Sheaf of Grain w/rake & pitchfork crossed behind sheaf - "Westford Glass Co., Westford

Conn," smooth edges, reddish
amber, half pint.............................. 165

GXIII-38 - Sheaf of Wheat w/rake &
pitchfork crossed behind it - star,
yellowish olive, qt. (minor inside
content stain)................................. 688

GXIII-39 - Sheaf of Grain above
crossed rake & pitchfork - large
five-pointed star, smooth edges,
applied double lip, deep green, pt. 1,210

GXIII-48 - Anchor between fork-
ended pennants inscribed
"Baltimore" & "Glass Works" -
Sheaf of Grain w/crossed rake &
pitchfork, yellowish amber, qt. 935

GXIV-7 - "Traveler's Companion"
arched above & below stylized
duck - eight-pointed star, smooth
sides, medium amber, half pint 578

Pitkin, thirty-six broken ribs swirled to
the left, sheared lip, deep root beer
amber, ca. 1820-30, 6 1/4" h......... 413

Pitkin, thirty-two ribs swirled to the
right, sheared lip, olive green,
ca. 1790-1810, 7 1/4" h. 853

INKS

Cathedral, master size, six Gothic
arch panels, cobalt blue, ABM lip,
smooth base marked "Carter's,"
ca. 1920, some inside stain,
9 3/4" h. (ILLUS.)........................... 99

*From left: Carter's
"Cathedral" Master Ink,
Master "Carter's" Ink Bottle*

Cylindrical, master-size, deep
bluish green, applied sloping
double collar w/pour spout, smooth
base, 98% front & back original
illustrated Carter's paper labels,
ca. 1870-80, 8" h.
(ILLUS.) 358

Domed w/central neck, 12-sided
form, deep olive amber, sheared
lip, base pontil, 2" h. 660

Figural, blown-molded head of Ben
Franklin w/neck curving upward,
aqua, sheared lip, smooth base,
2 3/4" h. (small flake on edge of
base) 209

House-shaped w/central neck,
aqua, marked "S.I. - Comp.,"
tooled mouth, smooth base,
2 3/4" h. 132

Igloo-form w/side neck, deep
purple, sheared lip, smooth base,
2" h. 1,375

Igloo-form w/side neck, reddish
amber, ground lip, smooth base
2" h. 242

Rare "Teakettle" Inkwell

Teakettle-type fountain inkwell
w/neck extending at angle from
base, deep cobalt blue, ground lip,
smooth base, original brass neck
ring & hinged lid, 2" h. (ILLUS.) 660

Teakettle-type fountain inkwell
w/neck extending at angle from
base, double dome-form body,
lime green opaque, polished lip &
base, possibly Boston & Sandwich
Glass Co., 2" h. 880

Teakettle-type fountain inkwell
w/neck extending up at angle
from base, white porcelain
w/multi-colored floral decoration on

Rare "Turtle" Ink Bottle

Unusual "J.S. Dunham" Ink

each panel, original brass hinged lid, 2 3/8" h. **633**

Turtle-form, paneled sides, light yellow w/green tint, embossed letters on panels "J - & - I - E - M," sheared lip, smooth base, 1 3/4" h. (ILLUS.) **825**

Twelve-sided w/central neck, aqua, embossed around panels "J.S. Dunham - St. Louis," rolled lip, open pontil, 2 7/8" h. (ILLUS.) **385**

Twelve-sided w/central neck, light ice blue, embossed around sides "Titcomb's Ink Cin.," rolled lip, base pontil, 2 7/8" h. (lightly cleaned) **358**

Umbrella-type (16-panel cone shape), deep yellowish root beer amber, rolled lip, open pontil, possibly Stoddard glassworks, 2 1/4" h. **440**

Umbrella-type (6-panel cone shape), light bluish green, rolled lip, open pontil, 2 1/2" h. **149**

Umbrella-type (8-panel cone shape), bright lime green, rolled lip, smooth base, 2 5/8" h. (lightly cleaned).. **468**

Umbrella-type (8-panel cone shape), deep amber, sheared lip, smooth base w/pontil, probably New Hampshire, 2 1/2" h.............. **187**

Umbrella-type (8-panel cone shape), deep olive amber, sheared lip, base pontil, New England, 2 1/2" h. **132**

Umbrella-type (8-panel cone shape), medium emerald green, rolled lip, base pontil, 2 1/2" h. **209**

Umbrella-type (8-panel cone shape), sapphire blue, molded on four panels "B - B - & - Co.," deep olive amber, sheared lip, base pontil, New England, 2 1/2" h. rolled lip, base pontil, 1 3/4" h. (overall light haze) **770**

Umbrella-type (8-panel cone shape), straight lower panels, aqua, marked "Harrison's Columbian Ink," rolled lip, base pontil, 2" h..................................... **154**

Umbrella-type (8-panel cone shape), yellowish olive w/amber tone, rolled lip, open pontil, 2 3/8" h. **330**

PICKLE BOTTLES & JARS

Amber, six-sided cathedral-type, tooled mouth, smooth base, ca. 1880-1890, 13 3/8" h. **1,265**

Apple green, four-sided cathedral-type w/Gothic windows, applied mouth, smooth base, ca. 1855-1865, light to medium apple green, 10 7/8" h. **440**

Aqua, lobe-sided, iron pontil, "W.K. Lewis & Co." **475**

Aqua, square w/applied top, double neck ring & shoulder scrolling, iron pontil, embossed "W. d. Smith, N.Y.," lots of whittle **750**

Aqua, cathedral shape, rolled lip, double neck ring tapering to fishtail shoulder scroll, iron pontil, embossed "Albany Glass Works," ca. 1850-1860, 8 5/8" h. 990

Aqua, square w/double neck ring, shoulder scrolling, obverse & reverse diamond panel embossing, W. d. Smith, N.Y., ca. 1839-1959, 8 3/4" h. 700

Aqua, six-sided cathedral-type w/Gothic windows, rolled lip, open pontil, marked "T. Smith & Co." around shoulder, ca. 1850-1860, 9 1/2" h. 688

Aqua, square, rolled lip w/tapering shoulder collar, iron pontil, embossed "64 oz. William - Underwood - & Company - Boston," ca. 1850-1860, 12 1/2" h. 187

Bluish-green, four-sided cathedral-type w/Gothic windows, rolled lip, iron pontil, ca. 1855-1865, 11 3/4" h. 1,265

Citron, four-sided Cathedral-type, four Gothic arches, ringed wide applied neck, ca. 1855-65, 11 5/8" h. (ILLUS.)........................ 468

Deep aqua, Cathedral-type, four Gothic arches w/ornate finials, wide ringed neck w/rolled lip, ca. 1855-65, 11 3/4" h. 253

Deep bluish aqua, rectangular w/paneled sides & wide applied

From left: Cathedral-type Pickle Jar, Ribbed Amber Pickle Jar, Skilton Foote & Cos. Pickle Bottle

mouth, marked "Anchor Pickle And Vinegar Works," smooth base marked "H.N. & Co.," ca. 1880, 8" h. (potstone on one side w/small radiations)...................................... 44

Emerald green, four-sided cathedral-type w/Gothic arch windows, rolled lip, iron pontil, ca. 1850-1860, 11 1/2" h. 2,530

Emerald green, four-sided cathedral-type w/Gothic arch windows, rolled lip, smooth base, ca. 1860-1870, 13 3/4" h. 143

Green (deep to medium), square w/applied top, two neck rings & vertically ribbed, open pontil, ca. 1839-1859, 7 1/2" h. 1,700

Greenish aqua, square w/two rings & vertical ribs on neck, rolled lip, iron pontil, embossed "W.D.S. N.Y.," ca. 1855-1865, 7 3/4" h. 198

Greenish-aqua, paneled body w/petal-style embossing on shoulder & base, rolled lip, ca. 1855-1865, 10 5/8" h. 330

Medium amber, square heavily ribbed sides w/rounded corners & wide applied mouth, tiny flake inside lip, ca. 1855-70, 8 1/4" h. (ILLUS.) 231

Teal blue, cathedral-shaped, rolled lip, double neck ring tapering to fishtail shoulder scroll, iron pontil, embossed "J McCollick & Co New York," ca. 1850-1860, 8 5/8" h...... 1,650

Yellow green, round, rolled lip, pontil-scarred base, ca. 1850-1860, embossed "Wm. Numsen & Sons Baltimore," 9 1/4" h............... 330

Yellow olive, round w/tooled mouth, smooth base, embossed "Skilton Foote & Co. S Trade [motif of monument] Mark Bunker Hill Pickles" on body, "Onions, from Skilton, Foote & Co., Bunker Hill Pickles" on 100% original label, 7 3/8" h. 176

Yellow w/amber tone, square w/cathedral panels, tooled mouth, smooth base, 98% original label marked "Arrow Brand Pickles, J. J. Wilson Chicago," ca. 1880-1900, 8 5/8" h. 358

Yellow w/olive amber tone,
"Bunker Hill Pickles" w/embossed monument, 6 1/2" h., Twilight Rose patt. 140

Yellowish amber, cylindrical w/wide applied mouth, "Skilton Foote & Cos Bunker Hill Pickles" w/trademark, professionally cleaned, 7 3/4" h. (ILLUS.) **55**

WHISKEY & OTHER SPIRITS

Beer, "Bay View Brewing Co., Seattle, Wash. - Not To Be Sold," cylindrical w/applied mouth & original marked porcelain stopper & wire bail, medium olive green, ca. 1890, 11 3/4" h. (wire bail broken) **303**

Beer, "C. Conrad & Co's Original Budweiser U.S. Patent No. 6376," cylindrical w/lady's-leg neck & applied mouth, aqua, 9 1/4" h. (lightly cleaned) **99**

Beer, "Gambrinus Brewing Co., G.B. Co., Portland, Or.," cylindrical w/lady's-leg neck & tooled mouth, "S.B. & G. Co." on smooth base, amber, ca. 1890, some inside stain, tiny "peck" mark on shoulder, 11 1/4" h. (ILLUS.) **33**

Beer, "Golden Gate Bottling Works, Trade (design of bear drinking from stein) Mark, San Francisco," cylindrical w/tooled top & original wire bail & porcelain stopper, medium yellow amber, ca. 1900, 7 3/4" h. (ILLUS.) **55**

From left: Gambrinus Brewing Co. Bottle, Golden Gate Beer Bottle, Early Rainier Beer Bottle

From left: Red Wing Brewing Co. Beer Bottle, Rare Dallimores Brandy Bottle, Kiderlen Celebrated Old Gin

Beer, "Rainier Beer, Seattle, U.S.A.," cylindrical w/lady's-leg neck & tooled lip, amber, fragments of original foil wrapper on neck, ca. 1900, 5 1/2" h. (ILLUS.) **66**

Beer, "Red Wing Brewing Co., Red Wing, Minn.," embossed wording, attached porcelain stopper, amber, rare, 15" h. (ILLUS.) **95**

Bourbon, "Cutter (J.H.) Old Bourbon A.P. Hotaling & Co., Portland, O.," tapering flask form w/applied mouth, smoky clear, pt. (small pressure ding on top, stained) **330**

Brandy, "Dallimores - Celebrated - Brandy - 130 Broome St. - N.R. Broadway - New York," paneled cylinder w/applied straight double collar, small flake at base of one panel, ca. 1845-55, deep olive green, 7 1/8" h. (ILLUS.) **2,860**

Cognac, "Cognac - W. & Co." (in seal), squatty bulbous tapering to a cylindrical neck w/applied mouth & neck handle, ca. 1860-70, medium amber, 5 3/4" h. **660**

Gin, "Kiderlen Rotterdam Celebrated Old Gin," barrel-shaped, tooled mouth, light olive green, crack down from lip, 8 1/2" h. (ILLUS.) ... **176**

Mead, "Champagne Mead," eight-sided cylinder w/applied blob top, smooth base, greenish blue (few dings at bottom corners)................ **110**

*Van Brunt's Aromatic
Schnapps*

*Early Zanesville Bottle
with Handle*

Schnapps, "Udolpho Wolfe's
Aromatic Schnapps, Schiedam,"
rectangular w/beveled corners,
applied sloping collar mouth, olive
green w/amber tone, 9 3/8" h. **77**

Schnapps, "Van Brunt's Aromatic
Schnapps, Schiedam," square
w/beveled corners, applied sloping
collar, deep olive green, some
inside stain, 10" h. (ILLUS.)........... **132**

Spirits, club-form, tall neck w/applied
rim, swirled broken-rib design,
yellow olive, Midwestern, ca. 1820-
30, 8 1/8" h. **4,400**

Spirits, free-blown mallet-form, pontil
w/deep kick-up, applied string lip,
deep olive amber, England,
ca. 1730-45, 8" h. **440**

Spirits, free-blown onion-form w/tall
neck & applied string lip, pontilled
base, medium yellowish olive
green, Europe, ca. 1715-30,
6 7/8" h. **143**

Spirits, globular, short neck w/rolled
rim, applied strap handle w/end
crimp, twenty-four ribs swirled to
the left, medium amber, Zanesville,
Ohio, ca. 1820-30, V-shaped
stress crack from end of handle,
6 1/2" h. (ILLUS.)......................... **4,620**

Spirits, globular, tall neck w/rolled
rim, twenty-four ribs swirled to the
left, unusual wide neck, yellow
w/strong olive tone, Midwestern,
ca. 1820-30, 7 3/8" h. **1,018**

Spirits, globular, tall ribbed neck,
broken-rib patt., rolled lip,
Midwestern, ca, 1820, medium

amber, 7 1/2" h. (some milky inside
stain)... **8,250**

Spirits, globular, plain body w/tall
neck, rolled rim, medium yellowish
amber, Midwestern, ca. 1820-30,
7 7/8" h. **275**

Spirits, globular, tall neck w/rolled
rim, twenty-four ribs swirled to the
left, medium amber, Midwestern,
ca. 1820-30, 8" h. **468**

Spirits, club-form, tall neck w/applied
rim, twenty-four broken ribs swirled
to the right, medium sapphire blue,
Midwestern, ca. 1820-30, 8 1/4" h. **8,525**

Spirits, globular, tall neck w/rolled
lip, twenty-four ribs swirled to the
left, lots of bubbles, yellowish
amber, Midwestern, ca. 1820-30,
9 5/8" h. **577**

Whiskey, "Binninger's Regulator, 19
Broad St., New York" around
molded clock face, 100% paper
label on reverse w/printed clock
face & same inscription, applied
double collar, medium amber, 6" h. **2,315**

Whiskey, "C.A. Richards & Co., 99
Washington St., Boston," square
w/beveled corners, reversed "Ns"
in molded text, applied sloping
collar, deep reddish amber,
9 1/2" h. **94**

Whiskey, "Chestnut Grove
Whiskey, c.W.," chestnut flask-
shaped w/applied neck handle,
applied mouth, medium amber,
8 7/8" h. (ILLUS.)........................... **154**

*Chestnut Grove
Whiskey Flask*

Whiskey, "Clinch & Co. Liquor
Dealers, Grass Valley," coffin flask,
applied sloping mouth, clear, half
pint... **303**

Whiskey, "Davy Crocket Pure Old
Bourbon, Hey, Grauderholz & Co.,
S.F. Sole Agents," cylindrical w/tall
neck & tooled mouth, ca. 1900,
medium orangish amber, 12" h. **110**

Rare E.G. Booz Whiskey Bottle

Whiskey, "E.G. Booz's Old Cabin
Whiskey - 1840 - E.G. Booz's Old
Cabin Whiskey - 120 Walnut St.,
Philadelphia," cabin-shaped,
straight roof, overall milky inside
stain, deep amber, 7 5/8" h.
(ILLUS.) **3,300**

Whiskey, "From Wine House Liquors
& Cigars Reno, Nev.,"
pumpkinseed flask, clear,
half pint... **1,540**

Whiskey, "G.W. Huntington" (on
applied seal), cylindrical w/wide
rounded shoulder w/seal, applied
sloping collar, ca. 1855-65,
medium bluish green, 11 3/4" h..... **468**

Whiskey, "Gaines (W.A.) Old Crow
Whiskey, The Capital, Cheyenne,
Wyo.," flask-shaped w/neck screw
threads, clear, half pint **264**

Whiskey, "Gilmor & Gibson,
Importers, Baltimore" (on applied
seal), cylindrical w/wide rounded
shoulder, tall neck & applied
sloping collar, ca. 1870-80, red
amber, 9 3/4" h. **303**

Whiskey, "Melczer & Co. (Jos.)
Wholesale Liquor Dealers San
Francisco, Cal.," flask w/applied
tapering mouth, clear, half pint **99**

Whiskey, "Mohawk Pure Rye
Whiskey, Patented Feb. 11, 1868,"
figural Indian queen w/shield,
rolled lip, golden amber, 12 5/8" h. **2,315**

Whiskey, "Old Bourbon Castle
Whiskey - F. Chevalier & Co., Sole
Agents," cylindrical w/tall neck &
tooled lip, medium orangish amber,
12" h. **231**

Whiskey, "Old Monongahela, C
(sheaf of wheat) H, Rye Whiskey,"
cylindrical w/wide rounded
shoulder w/seal, appled sloping
collar, ca.1865-75, olive amber,
9 1/2" h. **330**

Whiskey, "Old Velvet Brandy, S.M. &
Co." (on applied seal w/necklace),

Silkwood Whiskey Bottle

conical w/tall neck & applied
double collar, internally ribbed,
ca. 1855-70, medium amber,
9 7/8" h. **688**

Whiskey, "Peerless (in script)
Whiskey [in banner], Wolf, Wreden
Co. Sole Agents, S.F.," cylindrical
w/tall neck & tooled lip, medium
orangish gold, 11 7/8" h. **440**

Whiskey, "Potts & Potts - Atlanta,
Ga." (on applied seal), cylindrical
w/tall neck w/applied sloping
double collar, medium amber,
ca. 1870, 9 1/2" h. **264**

Whiskey, "R.B. Cutter, Louisville,
KY," ovoid w/applied mouth &
handle, partial paper label on
reverse w/"Woodbury, New
Jersey," golden amber, 8 3/4" h. ... **413**

Whiskey, "Silkwood Whiskey,
Laventhal Bros., San Francisco,
Cal.," cylindrical w/swirled ribs at
base of the tall neck w/tooled lip,
amber, ca. 1900, 11 3/8" h.
(ILLUS.) **154**

Whiskey, "Sontaw's Old Cabinet
Whiskey" (one applied seal),
cylindrical w/sloping applied
mouth, medium amber, 8 3/8" h.
(cleaned) **183**

BOXES

Band box, wallpaper-covered
cardboard, oval, the flat fitted top &
sides covered in a paper w/a
design of large shaded arches,
19th c., 6 5/8" l., 2 3/4" h.
(minor wear) **$546**

Band box, wallpaper-covered
cardboard, oval w/deep sides &
narrow fitted cover, the sides w/a
scenic landscape w/figures, trees
& a building in brown, black &
white on a dark blue ground,
building titled "Castle Garden,"
signed "Joel Post" in ink, 23" l.
(ILLUS.) **3,300**

Bentwood, round w/fitted flat cover,
lapped seams, old green paint,
7 1/2" d. (nail rust) **314**

Book-form, carved wood, w/a slide
top, chip-carved borders on the
covers surrounding a high-relief
male on one side & female on the
other, the binding deeply carved
w/a name & date "Michel Thomas
1759," very minor losses, 3 5/8" h.
(ILLUS.) **1,610**

Bride's box, pine bentwood, oval
w/deep fitted cover, the sides
w/original polychrome decoration
of large stylized flowers on a brown
ground, the flat cover w/a large
figure of a woman, laced seams,
Europe, late 18th - early 19th c.,

Early Book-form Box

10 1/4 x 16 3/4" (some edge
damage w/repair & touch-up) **495**

Bride's box, pine bentwood, oval,
deep fitted cover, the sides w/the
original detailed polychrome floral
decoration on a blue ground, the
flat cover w/a polychrome scene of
a youth pushing a girl on a swing
w/a German inscription, partial
decal on lid "Nederland...," laced
seams, Europe, 19th c., age
cracks in cover, 12 x 18 3/4"
(ILLUS.) **2,035**

Rare Large Band Box

Fancy European Bride's Box

Candle box, hanging-type, painted poplar, a low scalloped crestboard w/two metal hanging loops above a hinged rectangular top opening to the storage well, staple hinges, old worn bluish green paint, 4 1/2 x 10 1/4", 4 1/2" h. (repaired split in back board) **198**

Chart box, painted pine & poplar, rectangular hinged top on a dovetailed box w/applied base, original grain paint in brown & tan, lettered "R.E.B.," probably Cape Cod, Massachusetts, first half 19th c., 12 3/4 x 48", 11" h. **489**

Collar box, printed cardboard, oval w/flat fitted top, the border of the top printed to resemble large tacks, the side printed w/a rectangular reserve showing two early men's collars & the advertising "E. Stone No. 116 1/2 William-Street New York," 19th c., 13" l., 5" h. (wear, minor losses) **575**

Document box, painted & decorated poplar, rectangular w/deep hinged cover w/central brass bail handle & iron hasp & lock on the front, the cover opening to a well & lidded till, the exterior decoration w/ochre painted on a red ground, gilt initials "G.W.S.," American, 19th c., very minor wear, 9 1/2 x 18", 8 1/4" h. (ILLUS.) **1,150**

Glass box, metal mounts w/hinged cover, round, cobalt blue enameled on the cover w/a winter farm scene in white, brown & tan, the sides w/white enameled swag & dot bands, late 19th c., 3" d., 2 1/4" h. (ILLUS.) **165**

Decorated Document Box

Glass Box with Landscape on Cover

Scroll-decorated Blue Glass Box

Italian Micromosaic Jewelry Box

Glass box, gilt-metal mounts w/hinged cover, squatty rounded body in sapphire blue decorated w/small white & yellow enameled blossoms, the flattened domed cover w/large white & yellow daisy-like flowers w/yellow leaves above a white grass ground, 3 3/8" d., 3" h. **175**

Glass box, gilt-metal rim & footed base, hinged cover, the cover decorated w/white enamel leafy scrolls & small dot blossoms, the sides w/delicate white enamel scroll band, late 19th c., 4 3/8" d., 4" h. (ILLUS.) **225**

Jewelry box, Micromosaic, rectangular casket-form, gilt-metal beaded framework & pierced bird & foliate feet, the sides & top each set w/micromosaic landscape scenes of Roman ruins, stamped "C. Roccheggiani, Roma, Italy," late 19th c., 5 x 6", 4" h. (ILLUS.) . **4,830**

Pipe box, painted cherry, shaped & pierced backboard joining cutout sides & front w/thumb-molded drawer & turned knob on molded base, old red paint, New England, last half 18th c., 5 1/6 x 6 x 20 1/2" **4,025**

Storage box, burl veneer, rectangular w/hinged cover, the interior w/old gold paint w/sponged colors & mirror in cover, 5 1/4" l. (some veneer damage) **193**

Storage box, cov., round bentwood w/copper tacks in seam, flat fitted cover & arched bentwood swing handle, old varnish finish, 13 1/2" d., 6 1/2" h. plus handle (some renailing) **193**

Storage box, cov., round bentwood w/side seam & flat fitted cover, old black paint, 7" d. (minor edge damage) **275**

Storage box, cov., painted wood, dovetailed construction w/molded base, original yellow grain-painted surface, probably Mid-Atlantic States, early 19th c., 8 3/4 x 11 3/4", 9 3/4" h. (interior w/later red paint, repair to base).... **316**

Storage box, cov., round bentwood w/lapped seams w/steel tacks, flat fitted cover, wire bail handle w/turned wood hand grip, old patina, 10 1/2" d. **83**

Storage box, painted & decorated pine, dovetailed case w/hinged cover, old brown graining on a white ground, 19th c., 16" l. (wear, edge damage) **193**

Storage box, painted pine, a narrow top shelf above a molded slant-lift lid opening to a single compartmented interior, dovetailed case w/applied molding, original worn salmon red paint, New England, 18th c., 16 1/2 x 25 1/2", 17 1/2" h. (ILLUS.) **5,175**

Early Painted Pine Storage Box

Painted & Decorated Wood Box

Wall box, pine, the wide & high backboard topped by a flat disk pierced w/a hanging hole above sharply sloping edges to flat sides above a narrow, shallow projecting base box w/shaped sides, the reverse inscribed w/a three-masted sailing ship, old refinish, New England, late 18th c., 3 3/8 x 9 3/4", 17 3/4" h. (minor cracks & losses) **690**

Wood box, painted & decorated pine, rectangular hinged flat top w/breadboard end lifts above a deep nailed box, decorated w/old mustard yellow paint w/a polychrome scroll-painted decoration on the front (added later), New England, 1830s, paint wear on top, 16 x 29", 23" h. (ILLUS.) **805**

BUTTER MOLDS & STAMPS

While they are sometimes found made of other materials, it is primarily the two-piece wooden butter mold and one-piece butter stamps that attract collectors. The molds are found in two basic styles, rounded cup-form and rectangular box-form. Butter stamps are usually round with a protruding knob handle on the back. Many were factory-made items with the print design made by forcing a metal die into the wood under great pressure, while others had the design chiseled out by hand. An important reference book in this field is Butter Prints and Molds, *by Paul E. Kindig (Schiffer Publishing, 1986).*

Chicken & house mold, cased carved wood w/scene of house & large chicken, hinged sides, 4 1/2 x 10" **$193**

Cow stamp, hardwood, carved design of a cow & tree, old weathered finish w/age cracks, turned one-piece handle, 4 1/4" d.   **163**

Eagle & Star Stamp

Eagle & star stamp, round, carved hardwood w/center design of large eagle w/open wings & star near head, one piece turned handle, old patina, age crack, 4" d. (ILLUS.) ...   **289**

Eagle & stars "lollipop" stamp, square, pine w/primitively carved spread-winged eagle in center w/stars in arc above head, old patina, minor age cracks, 8 1/2" l. .   **275**

Flower & Heart Stamp

Flower & heart stamp, rectangular w/rounded ends, carved pine w/deeply cut stylized flower above a double heart, soft worn patina, 3 3/8 x 6 1/8" (ILLUS.) **523**

Flowers & initials stamp, rectangular, pine w/carved stylized pot of flowers w/"H.M." in a cross-hatched design, "1823" carved on back, old patina, 2 5/8 x 4" **165**

Heart & star stamp, rectangular, carved wood w/"The Union" above a large double heart & stars, old scrubbed finish, added tin hanger, 3 1/8 x 5" **358**

Hearts Stamp

Hearts stamp, round, hardwood, carved lines dividing surface into four sections, each containing a carved heart w/cross-hatching, zipper-notched border band, old patina, square self handle, 4 3/4 x 4 7/8" (ILLUS.) **440**

Man on horseback/floral stamp, oval, carved wood, one side w/man on horseback, initials & dated "1684," the reverse w/basket of flowers & "1684," old patina, 5 1/4 x 5 1/2" (wear & deep fissures) **743**

Pomegranate w/foliage, round cased, good patina, case stamped "Pat. Apr. 17, 1866," 4 3/4" d. **138**

Tulip Stamp

Tulip stamp, round, carved poplar w/stylized deep cut tulip in center, carved star on each side at top & one at bottom, zipper-notched border band, old patina, one-piece turned handle, 4 7/8" d. (ILLUS.) **413**

Carved Tulip Stamp

Tulip stamp, rectangular, carved pine, stylized tulip, old patina, added tin hanger, 3 x 4 7/8" (ILLUS.) **248**

Tulip stamp, round, poplar w/primitively carved tulip & leaves, self handle dated "1796," initials worn away, old black finish, attributed to Ephrata, Pennsylvania, 4 1/2 x 5" **550**

C

Blue & White Pottery. Apple Blossom Water Cooler

CANES & WALKING STICKS

Carved Whalebone Canes

Carved Narwhal whalebone presentation cane, tapered silver knob handle decorated in a sailor's knot pattern, a band of bright-cut flowers in diamonds & beaded edge, the top w/Scottish coats of arms of crowned lion rampant, upper ribbon banner inscribed "pro regein tyrannos," lower ribbon inscribed "Victoria Velmors," edge ring inscribed "W.S. McDonnall 11 Blackford Road," above a paneled shaft w/diamond & ring-turned carving, continuing to spiral twist, a turned ring then tapering shaft, presented to Captain Duff of the Royal Navy, tip missing, pre-1836, 37 1/2" l. (ILLUS. left) **$2,530**

Carved softwood walking stick, fist-carved handle above a shaft carved in low-relief w/a snake wrapping around the sides, branded inscription "A.M. Gregg, Dec. 3, 1891, Waufpgy, Pike Co. Ohio," old worn crusty finish, 34 1/4" l. (some edge damage) **165**

Carved stag horn & malacca presentation cane, natural smooth round stag horn knob handle, carved as a scallop shell above a silver collar inscribed "Bryant P. Tilden to John Callender," full bark malacca shaft w/two silver oval eyelets terminating in a very long 8 1/4" brass & iron ferrule, American, ca. 1775, 35 3/4" h. **2,310**

Carved walrus tusk & whalebone cane, handle in the form of a lady's leg, above tapering shaft inset w/two baleen spacers, 19th c., 34 3/4" l. (minor age crack, slight warping).. **920**

Three Ivory Canes

Carved walrus tusk & whalebone cane, octagonal handle w/ebony spacer, tapering shaft w/octagonal carving continuing to sailor's knots & spiral turning continuing to a fluted column, ring turnings & diamond points, 19th ca., age cracks, 35 1/2" l. (ILLUS. center).. **2,645**

Carved whale ivory & whalebone cane, the ring-turned knopped handle w/traces of red sealing wax, top w/mother-of-pearl inlaid disk, baleen spacer, hexagonal top third of shaft inset w/abalone diamonds & dots & ring turnings continuing to round tapering form, 19th c., damage to spacer, tip end of shaft missing & broken, missing one diamond inlay, minor age cracks, warping, 31 1/4" l. (ILLUS. left) **748**

Carved whale ivory & whalebone cane, the L-shaped ivory handle carved in the form of a Victorian lady's leg w/high button shoe & black stocking w/scalloped edge above a long cylindrical plain silver collar w/whalebone shaft twist-carved & tapering to a smooth end in a plated copper ferrule, probably sailor-made, ca. 1860, 34 1/2" l........................ **1,320**

Carved whale ivory & whalebone cane, handle carved in the form of an eagle's head w/inset eyes, baleen spacers, one w/a silver ring, above a round tapering shaft, 19th c., 34 3/4" l. (one eye missing, minor age cracks)........... **2,530**

Carved whale ivory & whalebone cane, carved Turk's-head knot handle above the shaft w/spiral decoration extending midway then round tapering & inset w/baleen spacers, 19th c., minor cracks, slight warping, 35 1/4" l. (ILLUS. right) **1,073**

Carved whale ivory & whalebone cane, carved spiral knob handle w/four baleen spacers above a tapering round shaft, 19th c., age cracks, 36 3/4" l. (ILLUS. right w/Narwhal cane)........................... **403**

Carved whale ivory & whalebone cane, L-shaped two-part handle decorated in a jockey motif of cap, horseshoe & stirrup above a paneled to round shaft, 19th c., 38" l. (repair, missing spacer, slight warping).. **345**

Carved whale ivory & whalebone walking stick, w/polyhedron handle inlaid w/ebony dots resembling a die, above a tapering shaft inset w/ebony & metal spacers, 19th c., 34 3/4" l. (crack beneath the knob, one dot missing) **1,093**

Carved whalebone & white ivory walking stick, w/Turk's-head knot handle above a spiral carved tapering shaft, decorated w/a carved ivory woven ring & a single

carved baleen spacer, 19th c., 34 1/2" l. (slight warping) **2,645**

Carved wood cane, the handle carved in the form of an antelope's head w/glass eyes, polychrome highlights, 19th c., 37" l. (minor cracks)...................... **230**

Ivory & Hardwood Walking Stick

Elephant ivory & hardwood walking stick, carved ivory head of a young girl wearing a large silver bonnet above a ribbed silver collar, the shaft of mahoganized hardwood w/horn ferrule, probably England, ca. 1880, 35 1/2" l. (ILLUS) **3,740**

Elephant ivory & hardwood walking stick, Art Nouveau style handle, beautifully carved ivory depicting flowing design of broad leaves & a fully opened blossom

w/delicate stem carved through-
and-through above a smooth silver
collar on ebonized hardwood shaft
w/horn ferrule, possibly France,
ca. 1900, 36" l............................... **2,420**

**Elephant ivory & malacca walking
stick,** a finely carved ivory hand
w/a braided ring cuff, holding a
knotted branch, small flat
mushroom-shaped top, braided
silver collar on a stopped malacca
shaft w/white metal & iron ferrule,
probably American, ca. 1850,
35 3/4" l. **1,155**

Glass cane, blue w/shepherd's crook
handle, twisted white
striping w/smooth rounded point,
probably American, ca. 1890,
43 1/2" l. **330**

Ivory, brass & wood cane, the
angled ivory handle carved in the
form of a lady's leg wearing a
brass boot, brass ferrule &
hardwood shaft, 35" l. **403**

Ivory & hardwood cane, angled
ivory handle w/finely detailed
carved ivory full-bodied fox w/glass
eyes, depicted in a crouched
position, bushy tail fully extended,
teeth bared & ears laid back,
ebonized hardwood shaft w/thin
decorated gilt collar & horn ferrule,
probably England, ca. 1890, 36" l. **4,290**

Metal & exotic wood cane, the
crook handle decorated at the
shoulder in the form of relief-
molded knight's head w/metal
helmet elaborately decorated & a
coat of mail protecting his throat &
chest, two winged dragons flow
from the back of his head onto the
handle, shaft of tropical zebrawood
w/a worn white metal
ferrule, small Continental
hallmarks, early 20th c., 33 1/4" h. **770**

Metal & snakewood cane, Art
Nouveau style, silver figural duck
fashioned in a half crook, the head
of a duck depicted emerging from
smooth flowing leaves, lightly
figured snakewood shaft w/worn
horn ferrule, Continental hallmarks,
perhaps Vienna, ca. 1900, 34" l.
(some denting at top of
handle) **880**

Metal & snakewood walking stick,
tapering cylindrical handle of
English sterling decorated in
C-scrolls w/smooth unmarked
shield on the side, finely figured
snakewood shaft w/horn ferrule,
hallmarked London, England,
1892, 37 3/4" l. (areas of insect
damage) **550**

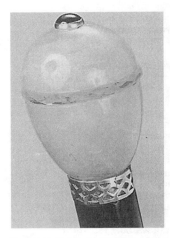

Quartz & Hardwood Walking Stick

Quartz & hardwood walking stick,
egg-shaped rose quartz handle
encircled by a faceted rock crystal
ring w/cabochon garnet set in
silver inlaid on top above a silver
collar reticulated w/small
diamond openwork, ebonized
hardwood shaft w/horn ferrule,
probably England, early 20th c.,
36" l. (ILLUS.) **990**

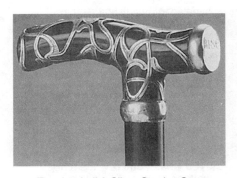

Tortoiseshell & Silver Overlay Cane

Tortoiseshell & hardwood cane,
gently curved tortoiseshell handle

decorated w/openwork silver
overlay w/smooth silver end cap
initialed & dated "1905," above
sterling silver collar hallmarked
London, England, 1905,
ebonized hardwood shaft w/horn
ferrule, 35 3/4" l. (ILLUS.)............. **1,100**

Wooden folk art walking stick,
carved man's head forms handle,
painted brown, black, red, yellow &
orange, 20th c., 42" l. (ILLUS.)...... **165**

Wooden & metal walking stick, the
handle cast in English sterling as a
finely detailed full figural owl
w/glass eyes perched atop a
stump, hallmarked London,
England, 1887, rosewood shaft
w/worn brass & iron ferrule, 37" l.. **1,210**

Wooden walking stick, carved black
man's head forms handle, good
detail w/glass eyes, black-grained
shaft, 35" l. (some wear to head)... **330**

Wooden walking stick, curved top
carved & painted to resemble a
diamond-back rattlesnake in brown
w/gold & black diamonds, inset
glass eyes, 37" l. **193**

Folk Art Walking Stick

CASH REGISTERS

The brass cash register, invented to prohibit employees from stealing the day's profits, was certainly never meant to be a cherished antique, passed down from generation to generation for display in one's home. However, the quality of the mechanisms in these machines, as well as the timeless beauty of their ornate cases, make it easy to understand why this one-time common business machine has become such a sought-after and coveted antique.

Antique cash registers are typically priced according to scarcity and demand. Prices of antique brass cash registers are usually consistent throughout the country. These prices are meant as only a guide, what you could reasonably expect to pay at an antiques shop or show, or from a private collector. The prices quoted would be for a basic model, complete register which works and has no missing or broken parts, in good to excellent condition. Missing or broken pieces can significantly add to your investment should you wish to return the register to its original condition. Added features such as original top sign, clock, lights, electric motor, multiple drawers, documentation, or other uncommon factory options can signif-

icantly add to the value of the cash register.

National Cash Register Company of Dayton, Ohio, was the major manufacturer of cash registers, therefore it stands to reason that most of the registers available today were produced at one of their factories. Other companies did make registers, but there are so few of them available today that it is impossible to give pricing for specific models; therefore only the company is listed. Certain cash registers are quoted only as "rare." These machines are known to exist, but in such small quantities that it is difficult to assign a fair dollar value.

Of course, when appraising a register to purchase, you must consider the value of your enjoyment of the piece and all price guides are disregarded.

—William J. Heuring

NATIONAL COUNTER-TOP CASH REGISTERS

Model No. 0, narrow-scroll case
(ILLUS. right) **$8,000**

Model No. 0, wide-scroll case....... **10,000**

Model No. 1, extended base **8,500**

NCR Model 0 and NCR Models 130

NCR Model 2 w/Wood Case

Model No. 2, inlaid wood case
(ILLUS.) **3,500**

NCR Model 4

Model No. 4, fine-scroll case
(ILLUS.) **3,000**

Model No. 4, inlaid wood case......... **6,000**

NCR Model 2

Model No. 2, narrow scroll case
(ILLUS.) **1,800**

Model No. 3, inlaid wood case **3,500**

Model No. 3, narrow-scroll case...... **1,800**

Model No. 3, wide-scroll case **2,500**

NCR Model 5

Model No. 5, fine-scroll case on
original shipping crate (ILLUS.) **2,500**

Model No. 6, extended base, fine-
scroll case **6,000**

NCR Model 30

NCR Model 313

Model No. 6, extended base, fleur-de-lis case **3,500**

Model No. 7, fine-scroll case **1,200**

Model No. 7, fleur-de-lis case.......... **1,000**

Model No. 8, fine-scroll case **1,200**

Model No. 8, fleur-de-lis case.......... **1,000**

Model No. 9, fine-scroll case **1,200**

Model No. 9, fleur-de-lis case.......... **1,000**

Model No. 11, cast-iron case........... **1,800**

Model No. 12, fine-scroll case **1,800**

Model No. 13, cast-iron case............ **800**

Model No. 14, cast-iron case............ **800**

NCR Model 63 w/Top Sign

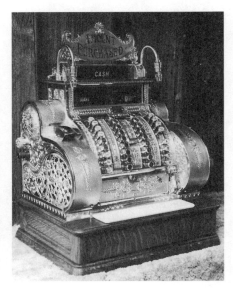

NCR Model 442

Model No. 30, fine-scroll case
(ILLUS.) 3,000

Model No. 30, inlaid wood case ...... **RARE**

Model No. 35, fine-scroll case 1,200

Model No. 35, fine-scroll case (early) 3,500

Models No. 35 through 49,
dolphin case, each 800

Models No. 35 through 49,
Renaissance case, each 1,000

Model No. 50, dolphin case 800

Model No. 50, Renaissance case.... 2,200

Model No. 52, dolphin case 1,600

Model No. 63, cast-iron case, w/top
sign (ILLUS.) 800

Model No. 63, early combination
ring-up 4,500

Model No. 64, cast-iron case............ 800

Model No. 71, scroll case 1,800

Model No. 79, empire case 800

Model No. 79, scroll case 1,800

Model No. 87, empire case 800

Models No. 129 or 130, Art
Nouveau case (brass), each
(ILLUS. center) 1,500

Models No. 129 or 130, Art
Nouveau case (cast-iron), each ... 1,000

Models No. 129 or 130,
Bohemian case (cast iron), each
(ILLUS. left) 2,000

Models No. 210 or 211, each.......... 1,600

Models No. 215 or 216, each.......... 1,500

Models No. 224 or 225, each........... 900

Models No. 312 or 313, each (ILLUS
of Model 313) 900

Models No. 316 or 317, each........... 900

Models No. 322, 323, 326 or 327,
(extended base), each................. 1,600

Models No. 324 or 325, each.......... 900

**Models No. 332, 333, 334, 336, 342,
343, 346, 347, 348, 349, 356, or
359,** each..................................... 700

Models No. 410, 415, 416, or 420,
each.. 800

Models No. 441, 442, or 451, each
(ILLUS. of Model 442) 800

Models No. 500 through 599,
counter top-style, multi-drawer,
each... 1,600

Models No. 500 through 599, single
drawer, each................................ 1,200

Models No. 711 or 717, each.......... 200

Models No. 1054 or 1064, each....... 600

NATIONAL FLOOR MODELS

NCR Floor Model 572

Models No. 500 through 599, floor
model, brass case atop set of
wood drawers, each (ILLUS. of
Model 572) 3,500

OTHER MANUFACTURERS:

American Cash Register Model 50

American cash registers
(ILLUS. of Model 50) **1,000-3,000**

CERAMICS

BLUE & WHITE POTTERY

The category of blue and white or blue and grey pottery includes a wide variety of pottery, earthenware and stoneware items widely produced in this country in the late 19th century right through the 1930s. Originally marketed as inexpensive wares, most pieces featured a white or grey body molded with a fruit, flower or geometric design and then trimmed with bands or splashes of blue to highlight the molded pattern. Pitchers, butter crocks and salt boxes are among the numerous items produced but other kitchenwares and chamber sets are also found. Values vary depending on the rarity of the embossed pattern and the depth of color of the blue trim; the darker the blue, the better. Some entries refer to several different books on Blue and White Pottery. These books are: Blue & White Stoneware, Pottery & Crockery by Edith Harbin (1977, Collector Books, Paducah, KY); Stoneware in the Blue and White by M.H. Alexander (1993 reprint, Image Graphics, Inc., Paducah, KY); and Blue & White Stoneware by Kathryn McNerney (1995, Collector Books, Paducah, KY).

Baking dish, embossed Peacock patt., round w/heavy egg-and-dart-molded rim over gently curved sides, 9" d. **$800**

Basin, embossed Apple Blossom patt., 9" d. **185**

Batter jar, cov., printed Wildflower patt., 7" d., 8" h. .... **300+**

Bean pot, cov., marked "Boston Bean Pot," 10" d., 9" h. **450**

Beer cooler, cov., embossed Elves patt., includes spigot, 14" d., 18" h. **725**

Bowl, 3" d., miniature, heavy dark blue rim band .... **40+**

Bowl, 4" d., 2" h., berry/cereal, plain w/pale blue rim band **55**

Bowl, 4" d., 2" h., embossed Flying Bird patt., w/advertising **450**

Bowl, 4" d., 2" h., miniature, heavy blue rim band .... **50+**

Bowl, 4 1/2" d., 2 1/2" h., embossed Reverse Pyramids patt. **65-75**

Bowl, 4 1/2" to 14" d., embossed Pineapple patt., ten sizes, price ranges .... **174 up**

Bowl, 6" to 12" d., embossed Greek Key patt., ranges .... **100-170+**

Bowl, 7" d., embossed Beaded Rose patt. **150**

Bowl, 7 1/2" d., 2 3/4" h., embossed Apricot with Honeycomb patt......... **135**

Bowl, 7 1/2" d., 5" h., embossed Reverse Pyramids patt. **90-100**

Bowl, 9" d., 4" h., embossed Daisy Roaster .... **250+**

Bowl, 9 1/2" d., 3 3/4" h., embossed Apricot with Honeycomb patt......... **185**

Bowl, 9 1/2" d., 4 1/2" h., embossed Gadroon Arches or Pedal Panels patt. **175**

Bowl, 10" d., 5" h., embossed Heart Banded patt. **135**

Bowl, 10 1/2" d., 5 1/2" h., embossed Diamond Point patt. **170**

Bowls, embossed Cosmos patt., nesting-type, depending on size, each **65-275**

Bowls, embossed Ringsaround (Wedding Ring) patt., six sizes, ranges **85-225**

Bowls, embossed Scallop patt., 6" d., 3 1/2" h., 8" d., 3 1/2" h., 9 1/2" d., 5" h., nesting type, depending on size, each **85-125**

Bowls, printed Wildflower patt., 4" to 14" d., nesting-type, the set.......... **350+**

Brush vase, embossed Bow Tie (Our Lucile) patt., w/rose decal, 5 1/2" h. **115**

Butter crock, cov., embossed Cow
and Fence patt., 7 1/4" d., 5" h. ...... **625+**

Butter crock, cov., embossed Cows
and Columns patt., 2 lbs. to 10 lbs.,
ranges .... **425-650+**

Butter crock, cov., embossed Daisy
and Basketweave patt., 7" d.,
6 3/4" h. .... **300+**

Butter crock, cov., embossed Daisy
and Trellis patt., 6 1/2" d., 4 1/2" h.   **225**

Butter crock, cov., embossed
Diffused Blue with Blocks patt.,
7 1/2" d., 5 1/2" h. **125**

Dragonfly & Flower Butter Crocks

Butter crock, cov., embossed
Diffused Blue with Inverted
Pyramid Bands patt., 6" d., 4" h. ... **125+**

Butter crock, cov., embossed
Dragonfly and Flower patt., large,
8" d., 5" h. (ILLUS. right)............... **345**

Butter crock, cov., embossed
Dragonfly and Flower patt., small,
rare (ILLUS. left)........................... **500**

Butter crock, cov., embossed Grape
and Leaves Low patt., 6" d., 5" h... **250**

Butter crock, cov., embossed
Lovebird patt., 6" d., 5" h. **750**

Butter crock, cov., embossed
Peacock patt., w/bail handle, 1 lb.,
4" h. **1,000**

Butter crock, cov., embossed Indian
patt., 2 lb....................................... **650**

Butter crock, cov., stenciled, 2 lb..... **245+**

Butter crock, no cover, embossed
Indian patt., 2 lb. .... **600+**

Butter crock, no cover, embossed
Indian patt., 3 lb. .... **650+**

Butter crock, cov., stenciled, 5 lb..... **258**

Butter pot, cov., printed Wildflower
patt., four sizes, each .... **150+**

Basketweave & Morning Glory canisters

Canister, cov., embossed
Basketweave & Morning Glory
(Willow) patt., "Beans," average
5 1/2" to 6 1/2" h. .... **325+**

Canister, cov., embossed
Basketweave & Morning Glory
(Willow) patt., "Coffee," average
5 1/2 to 6 1/2" h. (ILLUS. top left) .. **325+**

Canister, cov., embossed
Basketweave & Morning Glory
(Willow) patt., "Crackers" or
"Raisins," average 5 1/2 to
6 1/2" h., each. .... **625+**

Canister, cov., embossed
Basketweave & Morning Glory
(Willow) patt., "Salt," "Rice," or
"Cereal," average 5 1/2 to
6 1/2" h., each (ILLUS. of Salt,
upper right w/Coffee) .... **475+**

Canister, cov., embossed
Basketweave & Morning Glory
(Willow) patt., "Sugar," average
5 1/2 to 6 1/2" h. (ILLUS. bottom
with Coffee & Salt) .... **325+**

Canister, cov., embossed
Basketweave & Morning Glory
(Willow) patt., "Tea," average 5 1/2
to 6 1/2" h. .... **325+**

Canister, cov., wooden cover,
printed Snowflake patt., six
various in set, 5 3/4" d., 6 1/2" h.,
each.. **235**

Bead & Rose Chamber Pot

Chamber pot, cov., embossed Open
Rose and Spear Point
Panels patt., 9 1/2" d., 6" h. .... **300+**

Chamber pot, cov., printed
Wildflower patt., 11" d., 6" h. .... **250+**

Chamber pot, open, embossed
Bead & Rose patt., 9 1/2" d., 6" h.
(ILLUS.) .... **250+**

Cider cooler, cov., w/spigot, 13" d.,
15" h. **425**

Coffeepot, cov., Diffused Blue patt.,
oval design,11" h. (ILLUS.)........... **1,700**

Coffeepot, cov., embossed
Bull's-eye patt. .... **2,000+**

Cold fudge crock, w/tin lid & ladle,
marked "Johnson Cold Fudge
Crock," 12" d., 13" h. .... **300+**

Diffused Blue Coffeepot

Cookie jar, cov., embossed
   Basketweave & Morning Glory
   (Willow) patt., marked "Put Your
   Fist In," 7 1/2" h. **625**

Flying Bird Cookie Jar

Cookie jar, cov., embossed Flying
   Bird patt., 6 3/4" d., 9" h.
   (ILLUS.) .... **1,250+**

Cuspidor, embossed Sunflowers
   patt., 9 3/4" d., 9" h. .... **200+**

Custard cup, embossed Fishscale
   patt., 2 1/2" d., 5" h. .... **100+**

Custard cup, embossed Peacock
   patt., 2 7/8" h. (ILLUS. right) **545**

Ewer, embossed Apple Blossom
   patt., large,12" h. **450**

Ewer, embossed Banded Scroll patt.,
   7" h. .... **275+**

Ewer, embossed Bow Tie (Our
   Lucile) patt., w/rose decal, 11" h.   **175**

Ewer, Small Floral Decal
   (Memphis patt.), 7" h. .... **365+**

Ewer & basin, embossed Apple
   Blossom patt., the set .... **700+**

Ewer & basin, embossed Feather &
   Swirl patt., ewer 8 1/2" d., 12" h.,
   basin 14" d., 5" h., the set **550**

Foot warmer, signed by Logan
   Pottery Co. .... **250+**

Iced tea cooler, cov., w/spigot,
   Maxwell House, 13" d., 15" h..... **325**

Jardiniere, embossed Apple
   Blossom patt., 6" h. (ILLUS.) **495**

Jardiniere & pedestal base,
   embossed Tulip patt., jardiniere
   7 1/2" h., pedestal 7" h., the set
   (ILLUS.) .... **1,500+**

Measuring Cup & Pitchers

Tulip Pattern Jardiniere & Pedestal

Match holder, model of a duck,
5 1/2" d., 5" h. .... **250+**

Measuring cup, embossed Spear
Point and Flower Panels patt.,
6 3/4" d., 6" h. (ILLUS. top) **450**

Meat tenderizer, printed Wildflower
patt., 3 1/2" d. at face .... **370+**

Milk crock, cov., w/bail handle,
embossed Lovebird patt., 9" d.,
5 1/2" h. .... **600+**

Mixing bowl, embossed Flying Bird.
patt., 8" d. .... **340+**

Mouth ewer, embossed Bow Tie
(Our Lucile) patt., 8" h. .... **275+**

Mug, Diffused Blue patt., banded
design, w/advertising..................... **300+**

Mug, embossed Cattail patt., 3" d.,
4" h. .... **130+**

Apricot Pattern Pitcher

Mug, embossed Columns and
Arches patt., rare, 4 1/2" h. .... **350+**

Mug, embossed Flying Bird patt.,
3" d., 5" h. **225**

Capt. John Smith & Other Pitchers

Mug, embossed Grape Cluster in
Shield patt., 12 oz.......................... **195**

Mug, printed Wildflower patt.,
4 1/2" h. .... **200+**

Mustard jar, cov., 3" d., 4" h........ **200+**

Pitcher, 10" h., 7" d., embossed
American Beauty Rose patt. **425**

Pitcher, 8" h., embossed Apricot
patt., 5 pt. (ILLUS.) **265**

Pitcher, embossed Bands and
Rivets patt., 1 gal............................ **275+**

Pitcher, embossed Bands and
Rivets patt., 1 pt. .... **285+**

*Basketweave &
Morning Glory Pitcher*

Pitcher, 9" h., 6 1/2" d., embossed
Basketweave & Morning Glory
(Willow) patt., tankard-type
(ILLUS.) .... **255+**

Columns & Arches Pitcher & Mug

Pitcher, 6 1/4" h., 6 3/4" d.,
embossed Capt. John Smith &
Pocahontas patt., (ILLUS. bottom
right) .... **350+**

Pitcher, 8" h., embossed Castle patt.
.... **325**

Pitcher, 10" h., 8 1/2" d., embossed
Cherry Cluster with Basketweave
patt. .... **325+**

Pitcher, 9" h., embossed Columns &
Arches patt. (ILLUS. w/mug) .... **600+**

Pitcher, 9" h., 6 1/2" d., embossed
Cosmos patt., (ILLUS. left
w/American Beauty Rose pitcher) . **415+**

Daisy Cluster Pattern Pitcher

Pitcher, 8" h., 8" d., embossed Daisy
Cluster patt. (ILLUS.).................... **700+**

Pitcher, 8" h., embossed Eagle patt.   **650**

Lovebirds Pattern Pitcher

Pitcher, embossed Grape Cluster in
Shield patt., 4 pt. .... **450+**

Pitcher, embossed Grape Cluster in
Shield patt., 5 pt. .... **475+**

Pitcher, 9" h., 5 1/2" d., embossed
Iris patt. (ILLUS. right w/measuring
cup) .... **400+**

Pitcher, 8 1/2" h., 6" d., embossed
Leaping Deer patt. **400**

Pitcher, 8 1/2" h., 5 1/2" d.,
embossed Lovebirds patt. (ILLUS.) **450+**

*Old Fashioned
Garden Rose Pitcher*

Pitcher, 7" h., 7" d., embossed Old
Fashioned Garden Rose patt.,
(ILLUS.) .... **400+**

Pitcher, 9 1/2" h., 5 3/4" d.,
embossed Pine Cone patt.
(ILLUS.) **625**

Pitcher, 8 1/2" h., 6" d., embossed
Shield patt. (ILLUS. center w/Capt.
John Smith pitcher) .... **475+**

Pitcher, 8 1/2" h., 6" d., embossed
Standing Deer with Fawn patt. **275**

Pitcher, 8" h., 4" d., embossed Tulip
patt.,(ILLUS. left w/measuring cup
& Iris pitcher) .... **350+**

Pitcher, 9" h., embossed Windmill &
Bush patt. .... **400+**

Pine Cone Pattern Pitcher

Pitcher, 8" h., printed Acorn patt.
(ILLUS. top w/Apple Blossom
ewer) **300**

Pitcher, 9" h., 8" d., printed Dutch
Farm patt. .... **250+**

Pitcher, 7 1/2" h., 4" d., printed
Wildflower patt. .... **275+**

Pitcher, embossed Cherry Band
patt., w/advertising, various sizes,
ranges **375-475**
Pitcher, embossed Plume patt.
(ILLUS. left w/Apple Blossom
ewer) .... **350+**

Rolling pin, printed Wildflower patt.,
large .... **300+**

Small Wildflower Rolling Pin

Rolling pin, printed Wildflower patt., small (ILLUS.)................................ **375+**

Salt box, cov., Blue Band patt., 5" d., 6" h. .... **130+**

Salt box, cov., Diffused Blue patt., 6" d., 4" h. .... **130+**

Salt box, cov., embossed Daisy patt., 6" d., 6 1/2" h. **235**

Salt box, cov., embossed Flying Bird patt., 6 1/2" d., 6" h. (ILLUS. left w/Lovebird butter crock) .... **550+**

Salt box, cov., embossed Raspberry patt., 5 1/2" d., 5 1/2" h. **200**

Salt box, cov., embossed Waffleweave patt. .... **230+**

Salt box, cov., plain **100**

Salt box, cov., printed Wildflower patt., hinged wooden cover, 6" d., 4 1/2" h. .... **170+**

Salt jar, embossed Polar patt., 11" d., 13 1/2" h. .... **750+**

Soap dish, printed Wildflower patt., 3 5/8" w., 5 1/4" l. .... **275+**

Stein, embossed Grape with Leaf Band patt., 5" h. .... **125+**

Stewer, cov., embossed Basketweave & Morning Glory (Willow) patt., 4 qt .... **275+**

Stewer, cov., printed Wildflower patt., 4 qt. .... **285+**

Teapot, cov., spherical body w/row of relief-molded knobs around the shoulder, inset cover w/knob finial, swan's-neck spout, shoulder loop brackets for wire bail handle w/turned wood grip, blue Swirl patt., 6" d., 6" h. ((ILLUS.) .... **800+**

Tobacco jar, cov., embossed Berry Scrolls patt., 5" d., 6 1/2" h. .... **300+**

Umbrella stand, embossed Two Stags patt., solid blue, 21" h. ..... **1,000+**

Waste jar, cov., embossed Basketweave & Morning Glory (Willow) patt., 9 1/2" d., 12 1/2" h. **350+**

Water cooler, cov., barrel-shaped w/slightly oversized domed cover, the front w/an embossed panel of polar bears surrounded by ornate scrolls highlighted in dark blue, grotesque head at bung hole & spigot near base, the back w/embossed flowers, 13 3/4" h. plus cover (small cover chips) .. **495**

Apple Blossom Water Cooler

Water cooler, cov., embossed Apple Blossom patt., w/spigot, 13" h. (ILLUS.) **1,000**

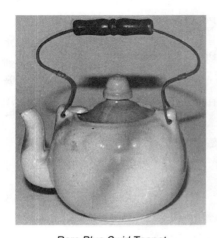

Rare Blue Swirl Teapot

Water cooler, embossed Polar Bear in Medallion patt. w/"Ice Water," cylindrical w/molded rings at the rim & base, bung hole near base, 15 1/4" h. (no cover or spigot) .. **385**

FLOW BLUE

Amoy Water Pitcher

Flow Blue ironstone and semi-porcelain was manufactured mainly in England during the second half of the 19th century. The early ironstone was produced by many of the well known English potters and was either trans-fer-printed or hand-painted (Brush stroke). The bulk of the ware was exported to the United States or Canada.

The "flow" or running quality of the cobalt blue designs was the result of introducing certain chemicals into the kiln during the final firing. Some patterns are so "flown" that it is difficult to ascertain the design. The transfers were of several types: Asian, Sce-nic, Marble or Floral.

The earliest Flow Blue ironstone patterns were produced during the period between about 1840 and 1860. After the Civil War Flow Blue went out of style for some years but was again manufactured and exported to the United States beginning about the 1880s and continuing through the turn of the cen-tury. These later Flow Blue designs are on a semi-porcelain body rather than heavier ironstone and the designs are mainly florals.

AMERILLIA (Podmore Walker & Co., ca. 1840s-50s)
Plate, 7 1/2" d. $70

Platter, 16" 600

AMOY (Davenport, dated 1844)
Creamer, 6 1/2" h. 300

Cup & saucer, handled 195

Pitcher, water, 12" h., rare body style (ILLUS.) 1,500

Plate, 7 1/2" d. 75

Plate, 8 1/2" d. 85

Plate, 9 1/2" d. 120

Plate, 10 1/2" d. 165

Platter, 12" 250

Platter, 16" 450

Platter, 18" 650

Soup plate w/flanged rim, 10" d. 200

Sugar bowl, cov. 375

Vegetable bowl, open, 8" l. 595

Waste bowl, "double bulge" style 325

ANEMONE (Minton, ca. 1860)
Plate, 8 1/2" d. 95

Plate, 9 1/2" d. 125

Platter, 14", oval 400

Anemone Covered Vegetable Bowl

Vegetable bowl, cov., footed (ILLUS.) 400

ARABESQUE (T.J. & J. Mayer, ca. 1845)
Creamer, Classic Gothic style, 6" h..   500

Plate, 7 1/2" d. 150

Plate, 10 1/2" d. 195

Soup plate w/flanged rim, 10" d. 185

Sugar bowl, cov., Classic Gothic
   style 595

Teapot, cov., Classic Gothic style 800

ARGYLE (W.H. Grindley & Co., ca. 1896)
Butter dish, cov., w/drainer.............. 600

Cup & saucer, handled 110

Pitcher, 1 1/2 pt. 425

Plate, 7" d. 65

Plate, 8" d. 75

Plate, 9" d. 85

Plate, 10" d. 95

Platter, 14" l. 275

Vegetable bowl, open, medium 185

ATHENS (C. Meigh, ca. 1845)
Cup & saucer, handleless................ 225

Plate, 7 1/2" d. 95

Plate, 10 1/2" d. 125

Punch cup (ILLUS.) 145

Athens Punch Cup

CARLTON (S. Alcock, ca. 1850)
Plate, 8 1/2" d. 130

Plate, 9 1/2" d. 140

Platter, 14"...................................... 300

Soup plate w/flanged rim, 10" 150

Carlton Vegetable Bowl

Vegetable bowl, cov., ca. 1850
   (ILLUS.) 400

CASHMERE (Francis Morley, ca. 1845)
Coffeepot, cov., octagonal,
   9 1/2" h. 1,925

Cup & saucer, handleless............... 300

Mug, 3 1/2" h..................................... 400

Plate, 7 1/2" d. 100

Plate, 8 1/4" w., paneled, set of 13
   (one w/spider crack, one w/flake).. 935

Plate, 9 1/2" d. 175

Plate, 10 1/4" d., paneled, set of 4.... 715

Plate, 10 1/2" d. 200

Soup plate w/flanged rim,
   10 3/4" w., scalloped edges, set of
   7 1,375

Soup plate w/flanged rim, 10" d. 235

CASHMERE (Morley & Ashworth, ca. 1859-62)
Platter, 13 3/4 x 17",
   scalloped edge 880

CHAPOO (John Wedgwood, ca. 1850)
Creamer, 6 1/2" h. 350

CHAPOO (John Wedgwood, ca. 1850)
Cup & saucer, handleless................ 135

Plate, 10 1/2" d. 155

Soup plate w/flanged rim, 10" d. 165

CHINESE (Dimmock, ca. 1845)
Platter, 18", well & tree-type (ILLUS.) 700

CHUSAN (J. Clementson, ca. 1840)
Creamer, 6" h. 250

Plate, 7 1/2" d. 125

Plate, 9 1/2" d. 145

Platter, 14" l. 350

Vegetable bowl, open, 8" l. 200

COBURG (J. Edwards, ca. 1850)
Cup & saucer, handleless 150

Plate, 8 1/2" d. 135

Plate, 10 1/2" d. 155

Platter, 16" 300

CONWAY (New Wharf Pottery, ca. 1891)
Sugar bowl, cov. 200

Vegetable bowl, open, oval 150

DOROTHY (Johnson Bros., ca. 1900)
Plate, 8" d. 65

Plate, 9" d. 75

FLORAL
(Laughlin Art China Co., ca. 1900)

Floral Tyg

Tyg, three-handled (ILLUS.) 350

FLORIDA (W.H. Grindley, ca. 1891)
Cup & saucer, handled 170

Plate, 7" d. 100

Plate, 8" d. 125

Chinese Platter

GAUDY (Brushstroke, ca. 1850)

Gaudy Relish Dish

Relish dish, w/polychrome (ILLUS.)   195

GAUDY
(Mellor Venables & Co., ca. 1840)
Creamer, Classic Gothic shape........   250

Sugar bowl, cov., Classic Gothic
shape...   450

Gaudy Teapot

Teapot, cov., Classic Gothic shape
(ILLUS.)...   900

GINGHAM FLOWERS
(Brushstroke, ca. 1845)
Cup & saucer, handleless...............   220

Plate, 7 1/2" d.   175

Plate, 9 1/2" d. (ILLUS.)...................   200

Platter, 14" l.....................................   350

GOTHIC (J. Furnival, ca. 1850)
Plate, 8 1/2" d.   145

Gingham Flowers Plate

Plate, 9 1/2" d.   165

Soup plate w/flanged rim, 10"   175

GRAPE & BLUEBELL
(Brushstroke, ca. 1850)
Plate, 8" d.   150

Soup plate w/flanged rim, 10 1/2" ..   175

HONG KONG (C. Meigh, ca. 1845)
Cup & saucer, handleless................   165

IRIS (Arthur Wilkinson - Royal Stafford-shire Potteries, ca. 1907)
Plate, 5 3/4" d.   15

Plate, 9" d.   30

Platter, 13" l......................................   90

Vegetable bowl, cov., 7 1/2" d.   180

JAPAN (T. Fell & Co., ca. 1860)
Pitcher, 8" h......................................   400

Platter, 16" l.   350

LA BELLE
(Wheeling Pottery, ca. 1900)
Bowl, large, helmet-shaped..............   375

Cracker jar, cov., 7 1/2" h................   600

Cup & saucer, handled   195

Dessert dish, fancy   155

Mug, chocolate   400

Pitcher, 7 1/2" h...............................   450

LORNE (W.H. Grindley, ca. 1900)
Cup & saucer, handled 125

Plate, 7" d. 75

Lorne Plate

Plate, 10" d. (ILLUS.) 100

Platter, 12", oval 150

Dinner service: six 10" d. dinner
plates, ten 9" d. luncheon plates,
thirteen cups & ten saucers, one
each sauce dish, gravy boat & cov.
vegetable dish; each marked, the
set (minor stains, several chips)... 1,210

LUCERNE
(New Wharf Pottery, ca. 1891)
Plate, 9" d. 85

Vegetable bowl, cov. 150

MANHATTAN
(Johnson Bros., ca. 1895)
Plate, 9" d. 90

Sugar bowl, cov. 245

MANILLA
(Podmore, Walker & Co., ca. 1845)
Creamer, Primary shape, 6" h. 350

MARGUERITE
(W.H. Grindley, ca. 1891)
Plate, 7" d. 60

Plate, 9" d. 85

MELBOURNE (W.H. Grindley, ca. 1891)
Plate, 9" d. 95

Platter, 16" l. 200

MENTONE (Johnson Bros., ca. 1900)

Mentone Teapot

Teapot, cov. (ILLUS.) 600

NANKIN (Davenport, ca. 1850)
Cup & saucer, handleless 200

Plate, 10 1/2" d. 195

Vegetable bowl, open, rectangular,
8" l. 250

NON PARIEL
(Burgess & Leigh, ca. 1891)
Plate, 9" d. 100

Soup plate, 8" d. 130

NORMANDY
(Johnson Bros., ca. 1900)
Cup & saucer, handled 150

Plate, 7" d. 90

Plate, 8" d. 100

Plate, 9" d. 120

Soup plate, 8" d. 135

OREGON (T.J. and J. Mayer, ca. 1845)
Creamer, pumpkin shape 350

Plate, 7 1/2" d. 130

Plate, 10 1/2" d. 195

Platter, 12" l. 350

Platter, 14" l. 400

Sugar bowl, cov., pumpkin shape.... 450

Teapot, cov., pumpkin shape............ 650

OSBORNE (Ridgways, ca. 1905)
Egg cup, large 130

Plate, 7" d. 65

Plate, 9" d. 85

PELEW (E. Challinor, ca. 1850)
Pitcher, water, 9" h. 800

Plate, 7 1/2" d. 130

Plate, 10 1/2" d. 175

Teapot, cov., pumpkin shape 650

ROSE (W.H. Grindley, ca. 1893)
Plate, 7" d. 55

Plate, 9" d. 75

ROXBURY (Ridgway, ca. 1910)
Bowl, berry 50

Vegetable bowl, open 150

SCINDE (J&G Alcock, 1839-46)
Cup & saucer, handleless 225

Scinde Gravy Boat

Scinde Punch Cup

Gravy boat w/undertray, Full Panel
Gothic style (ILLUS.) 375

Plate, 7 1/2" d. 160

Plate, 10 1/2" d. 225

Punch cup (ILLUS.).......................... 175

SPINACH
(Libertas, Brushstroke, ca. 1900)

Spinach Bowl

Bowl, 5" d. (ILLUS.) 95

Plate, 9" d. 85

STRAWBERRY
(J. Furnival, Brushstroke, ca. 1850)
Cup & saucer, handleless 200

Plate, 7 1/2" d. 150

Plate, 9 1/2" d. (ILLUS.) 175

Platter, 14" l. 450

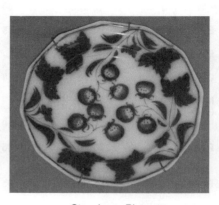

Strawberry Plate

TEMPLE (Podmore, Walker & Co.)
Relish dish, shell-shaped................ 300

Soup plate w/flanged rim, 10" d. 165

TONQUIN (J. Heath, ca. 1850)
Creamer, full panel Gothic style, 6" h. 300

Cup & saucer, handleless................ 195

Plate, 9 1/2" d. 145

Soup plate, 10" d............................. 165

Sugar bowl, cov., full panel Gothic
   style... 450

TOURAINE (H. Alcock & Co., ca. 1898 or Stanley Pottery, ca. 1898)
Plate, 7" d. 70

Plate, 8" d. 75

TROY (C. Meigh, ca. 1840)
Plate, 8 1/2" d. 175

Plate, 10 1/2" d. 195

Soup plate w/flanged rim, 10" 200

WAVERLY
(J. Maddock & Son, ca. 1891)
Plate, 7" d. 65

Plate, 8" d. 75

Vegetable bowl, open 110

WHAMPOA (Mellor Venables, ca. 1840)
Teapot, cov., Primary shape............. 795

HISTORICAL & COMMEMORATIVE WARES

Numerous potteries, especially in England and the United States, made various porcelain and earthenware pieces to commemorate people, places and events. Scarce English historical wares with American views command highest prices. Objects are listed here alphabetically by title of view.

Most pieces listed here will date between about 1820 and 1850. The maker's name is noted in parentheses at the end of each entry.

Albany, New York platter, long-
   stemmed roses border,
   16 3/4 x 20", Jackson (glaze wear) **$690**

Almshouse, New York plate, floral
   & scroll border, dark blue, 10" d.,
   Andrew Stevenson (small blister,
   light stains, small chips on table
   ring) 385

American Views, Boston and Bunker Hill platter, flowers, moss
   & leaves border, purple, 16" l.,
   Thomas Godwin (crazing, glaze
   imperfections, minor staining) 374

Arms of New York plate, flowers &
   vines border, dark blue, 10" d., T.
   Mayer (wear, scratches w/pinpoint
   flakes)... 440

Arms of Rhode Island plate, flowers
   & vines border, dark blue, 8 5/8" d.,
   T. Mayer (worn w/scratches) 385

Arms of South Carolina plate,
   florals & vines border, dark blue,
   7 1/2" d., T. Mayer (rim wear, small
   flakes on table ring) 550

Baltimore & Ohio Railroad, level (The) plate, shell border, dark
   blue, 10 1/8" d., E. Wood (stains,
   minor roughness on table ring)...... 990

Baltimore & Ohio Railroad, level (The) soup plate, shell border,
   dark blue, 10" d. (E. Wood) 953

Battery, New York (Flagstaff Pavilion) plate, vine leaf border,
   dark blue, 7 1/8" d., R. Stevenson
   (wear, scratches)........................... 220

Battle of Chapultepec plate,
   9 1/2" d., Texian Campaign series,
   symbols of war & a "goddess-type"
   seated border, green, Shaw (light
   facial wear) 532

Boston and Bunker's Hill platter,
   19" l., well & tree, Catskill Moss
   series, bunches of moss on a
   network of moss, light blue
   (Ridgway) 420

Boston Harbor sugar bowl, flowers,
   foliage & scrolls border, spread-
   winged eagle w/shield in
   foreground w/Boston harbor in
   background, 5 7/8" h., Rogers
   (some exterior edge wear &
   pinpoints, inner flange of bowl & lid
   chipped, chip on finial, lid is slightly
   undersize)...................................... 1,155

Boston Mails...Ladies Cabin platter, border medallions of steamships & two views of "Acadia" & "Columbia," light blue, 16" l., Edwards (minor staining, knife marks) 259

Boston State House dinner service: 29 dinner plates, 19 luncheon plates, 11 soup plates, four bread & butter plates, 10 platters (one w/a pierced inset), a cov. soup tureen, ladle & undertray, four cov. sauce tureens & three undertrays, four cov. serving dishes, a square center bowl; dark blue, Rogers, the set (some w/staple & other repairs, minor cracks, chips & staining).. 14,950

Boston State House pitcher, 5 3/4" h., Rose Border series, fully opened roses w/leaves border, dark blue, Stubbs (half the spout w/old restoration, slightly discolored) 202

Boston State House plate, floral border, dark blue, unmarked, 8 1/2" d., Wood (minor wear) 193

Boston State House soup plate, floral border, dark medium blue, 10" d. (Wood) 364

Boston State House tile, rectangular, floral border, dark medium blue, 6" l., Minton (several very minor flakes along rim) 190

Capitol, Washington (The) cake plate, footed, Beauties of America series, flowers within medallions border, dark blue, 10 1/2" d., 2 1/2" h., Ridgway (few hard-to-find internal hairlines & minor stain) 3,080

Capitol, Washington (The) plate, shell border, dark blue, 7 1/2" d. (E. Wood) 715

Capitol, Washington (The) plate, vine border, dark blue, 10" d., Stevenson (flake on table ring) 550

Capitol, Washington (The) plate, vine border, embossed white rim, dark blue, 10 1/8" d., Stevenson (minor wear) 413

Castle Garden, Battery, New York platter, trefoil separated by knobs border, dark blue, 18 1/2" l., Wood (minor wear & scratches, small flake) 2,915

Chief Justice Marshall, Troy plate, shell border, dark blue, 8 1/2" d., E. Wood (minor edge wear) 495

City Hall, New York plate, flowers within medallions border, dark blue, 9 7/8" d. (Ridgway) 330

City of Albany, State of New York plate, shell border, dark blue, 10 1/4" d., E. Wood (minor scratches) 660

City of Montreal platter, 18" l., well & tree, flowers border, light blue, Davenport (professional restoration to hairline from rim half way into center) 672

Columbia College, New York plate, acorn & oak leaves border, medium blue, 6 3/8" d., R. Stevenson (flake at table ring & pinpoints on rim) 385

Columbia College, New York plate, floral & scroll border, dark blue, 7 1/2" d., Andrew Stevenson (rim chip) 660

Commodore MacDonnough's Victory plate, irregular shells border, dark blue, 10 1/8" d., Wood (minor wear, light scratches) 605

Dam & Water Works (The), Philadelphia (Sidewheel Steamboat) soup plate, fruit & flowers border, dark blue, 9 3/4" d., Henshall, Williamson & Co. (wear) 660

Dam & Water Works (The), Philadelphia (Stern Wheeler Steamboat) plate, fruit & flower border, dark blue, 10" d., Henshall, Williamson & Co. (chips on table ring, some wear & scratches) 660

Detroit platter, 18 3/4" d., Cities series, groups of flowers & scrolls border, dark blue, Davenport (professional repair of line through left part of transfer) 2,800

Entrance of the Erie Canal into the Hudson at Albany plate, floral

border, dark blue, 10" d., E. Wood
(minor wear, pinpoint flakes, spider
crack).. 880

Exchange, Baltimore plate, fruit &
flowers border, dark blue, 10" d.
(Henshall, Williamson & Co.)......... 440

Fair Mount Near Philadelphia bowl,
spread-eagle border, dark blue,
9 1/4" d., Stubbs (wear, light
crazing, chip on table ring, several
shallow chips on beaded rim)........ 550

Fair Mount Near Philadelphia plate,
spread-eagle border, dark blue,
10 1/4" d., Stubbs (minor
scratches)...................................... 275

**From Fishkill, Hudson River
platter,** Picturesque Views series,
birds, flowers & scrolls border,
black, 15 1/2" l.,Clews (light wear
on face, seen only when tilted)...... 476

**Great Fire, City of New York,
Burning of Coenties Slip plate,**
fire engines & eagles border, light
blue, unknown maker, 8" d. (wear
& small edge flakes)...................... 385

Harvard College plate, acorn & oak
leaves border, dark blue, minor
roughness on table ring, 10" d.,
(Stevenson & Williams) 275

Hospital, Boston plate, vine border,
dark blue, 8 1/2" d., Stevenson &
Williams (wear & scratches) 289

**Landing of General Lafayette at
Castle Garden, New York, 16
August 1824 plate,** floral & vine
border, dark blue, 10 1/4" d., Clews
                                                          432

**Landing of General Lafayette at
Castle Garden, New York, 16
August 1824 platter,** floral & vine
border, dark blue, 15 1/4" l., Clews
(small edge flakes) 1,760

**Landing of General Lafayette at
Castle Garden, New York, 16
August 1824 wash bowl,** floral &
vine border, dark blue, 12 1/8" d.,
4 1/2" h. Clews (wear, chip on
table rim, two rim hairlines) 1,210

**Landing of the Fathers at
Plymouth, Dec. 22, 1620 plate,**
pairs of birds & scrolls & four

medallions w/ships & inscriptions
border, dark blue, 6 1/2" d. (E.
Wood)... 173

**Landing of the Fathers at
Plymouth pitcher,** pairs of birds &
scrolls & four medallions w/ships &
inscriptions border, medium blue,
6 1/2" h., Wood (minor chips, star
crack, glaze wear) 345

**Mitchell & Freeman's China and
Glass Warehouse, Chatham
Street, Boston plate,** foliage
border, dark blue, 10 1/4" d.,
Adams (very minor wear) 1,100

**Mount Vernon, The Seat of the
Late Gen'l. Washington cup &
saucer,** large flowers border, dark
blue, maker unknown, 5 1/2" d.,
2 1/2" h. (light wear on saucer,
small chip on foot of cup) 364

**Mount Vernon, The Seat of the
Late Gen'l. Washington sugar
bowl,** large flowers border, dark
blue, 5 7/8" h., unknown maker
(chips & rim hairlines, lid may be
mismatched)................................. 1,155

Nahant Hotel, Near Boston plate,
spread-eagle border, dark blue,
8 7/8" d. (Stubbs)......................... 413

**Narrows from Fort Hamilton (The)
platter,** 17 1/2" l., American
Scenery series, long-stemmed
roses border, black, Ridgway (light
wear) 308

Near Fishkill, Hudson River plate,
flowers & birds border, black,
10 1/4" d., Clews (minor glaze
rubs) 99

Near Fishkill plate, flowers & scrolls
border, dark blue, 7 3/4" d. (Clews) 248

**New York From Brooklyn Heights
plate,** flowers between leafy scrolls
border, dark blue, 10 1/4" d.,
Stevenson (minor wear & chip on
table ring) 1,485

**Niagara Falls From the American
Side platter,** shell border, dark
blue, 14 7/8" l., Wood & Sons
(wear, scratches)......................... 2,640

**Octagon Church, Boston fruit
bowl,** footed & handled, reverse

w/"Bank, Savannah" & "Exchange, Charleston," dark blue, Beauties of America series, J. & W. Ridgway, 10" d., 5" h. (minute glaze chips, very minor firing crack on one handle) 1,495

Octagon Church, Boston soup plate, flowers within medallions border, dark blue, 9 3/4" d. (Ridgway) 385

Park Theatre, New York soup plate, acorn & oak leaves border, dark blue, 10" d., Stevenson & Williams (pinpoint flakes on table ring) 385

Pass in the Catskill Mountains plate, shell border, circular center, dark blue, 7 1/2" d., E. Wood (minor wear) 193

President's House, Washington plate, four medallion - floral border, purple, 10 3/8" d. (E. Wood) 248

Shepherd Boy Rescued platter, six-point star w/birds & flowers border, dark blue,12 5/8" l., Clews (staining, knife marks, glaze chips)   115

State House, Boston gravy boat, flowers within medallions border, dark blue, 6 1/2" l., Ridgway (minor stains at interior pinpoints) 330

State House, Boston platter, spread-eagle border, dark blue, 14 5/8" l., Stubbs (minor scratches, spider crack) 1,045

States series oval dish, border w/names of fifteen states in festoons separated by five or eight-point stars, center scene of castle w/flag, boats in foreground, dark blue, crazing & light stains, 11 3/4" l., Clews (ILLUS.) 1,540

States series pitcher, border w/names of fifteen states in festoons separated by five-point stars, center scene of castle w/flag, boats in foreground, dark blue, unmarked, 9 3/4" h. (small edge flakes on rim, handle & spout, minor wear & shallow flake on bottom) 2,530

States series plate, building, sheep on lawn, border w/names of fifteen states in festoons separated by five-point stars border, dark blue, 8 3/4" d., Clews (rim w/area of glaze flakes, stain)........................ 303

Rare Texian Campaigne Compote

Oval States Series Dish

Table Rock, Niagara plate, shell border - circular center, dark blue, 10 1/8" d., E. Wood (minor wear & scratches) 413

Texian Campaigne - Battle of Palo Alto compote, battle scene center, symbols of war & a "goddess-type" seated border, light blue, 5 1/2" h., 10 1/4" d., Shaw (ILLUS.) **2,800-3,000**

Transylvania University, Lexington plate, shell border, dark blue, 9 1/4" d., Wood (wear)............... **385**

United States Hotel, Philadelphia plate, 10" d., foliage w/grotto center border, dark blue, Tams (large in-the-making spider to left of ladies)...................................... **532**

View of Governor's Island Soup Plate

View of Governor's Island soup plate, floral & scroll border, dark blue, minor wear & small flakes w/crow's foot hairline, 10 3/8" d., Stevenson (ILLUS.) **2,475**

View of Trenton Falls—Three People Rock plate, shell w/circular center w/trailing vine around outer edge of center border, dark blue, 7 3/4" d., Wood (light wear)..................................... **280**

Washington plate, flowers & scrolls border, dark blue, 7 3/4" d. (Clews) **385**

Washington Standing at Tomb, scroll in hand cup & saucer, dark blue, saucer 6 1/2" d., E. Wood

(minor chips, staining, transfer imperfections) **454**

Water Works, Philadelphia plate, acorn & oak leaves border, dark blue, 10 1/8" d. (Stevenson & Williams)...................................... **605**

Winter View of Pittsfield, Massachusetts open vegetable dish, vignette views & flowers border, dark blue, 12 1/2" l., Clews (minor wear w/some glaze wear on edges) **1,870**

Winter View of Pittsfield, Massachusetts plate, vignette views & flowers border, dark blue, 6" d. (Clews) **230**

IRONSTONE

The first successful ironstone was patented in 1813 by c. J. Mason in England. The body contains iron slag incorporated with the clay. Other potters imitated Mason's ware and today much hard, thick ware is lumped under the term ironstone. Earlier it was called by various names, including graniteware. Both plain white and decorated wares were made throughout the 19th century. Tea Leaf Lustre ironstone was made by several firms.

GENERAL

Bowl, scalloped rim, all-white, ca. 1870, h. Burgess **$95**

Bowl, 7 1/2" d., 4"h., "Amherst Japan" patt., pedestal-based bowl, garden scene w/orange flowers, blue & green leaves, lots of gold trim **185**

Bowl, 12 5/8" d., 4 3/4" h., Imari-style colorful decoration, England, 19th c. (spider crack in base, gilt & enamel wear)............................. **201**

Bread plate, Fuchsia shape, all-white **18**

Chamberpot, cov., Prairie shape, all-white, J. Clementson **125**

Chamberpot, cov., Cable & Ring shape, all-white, 9 1/2" d. **22**

Coffeepot, cov., Fuchsia shape, all-white, J. & G. Meakin 300

Creamer, Britannia shape, all-white, Powell & Bishop 115

Creamer, Senate shape, all-white, Maddock & Gater 65

Creamer, Shamrock, Thistle & Rose shape, all-white, ca. 1870s, Powell & Bishop 135

Creamer, Staffordshire, all-white, Maddock & Son 110

Cup, handleless, coffee, Ceres shape, all-white, Elsmore & Forster   50

Cup, handleless, Columbia shape, all-white 27

Cup, handleless, octagonal, all-white   28

Cup, handleless, tea, Ceres shape, all-white, Elsmore & Forster 34

Cup plate, all-white, G. Phillips 18

Cup plate, all-white, Longport 18

Cup & saucer, Ceres shape, all-white, Elsmore & Forster 55

Cup & saucer, handleless, all-white, h. Alcock 48

Cup & saucer, handleless, Boote's 1851 Octagon shape, all-white 65

Cup & saucer, handleless, "gaudy" free-hand Seaweed patt. in underglaze blue w/red & green enamel 83

Cup & saucer, handleless, "gaudy" free-hand Urn patt. in underglaze blue w/red, pink & green enamel... 275

Cups, Fuchsia shape, handled, all-white, very small, set of 4 120

Cups & saucers, handleless, red transfer scene, impressed "Pearl China W.R. & Co.," five sets (minor wear & stains).............................. 204

Cups & Saucers, Stylized Tulip shape, handleless, all-white, E. Challinor, 5 sets (one saucer crazed) 245

Dessert service: pr. of two-handled sauce tureens, covers & underplates, one scallop-edged rectangular compote, pr. of scallop-edged rectangular serving dishes, pr. of scallop-edged oval serving dishes, pr. of oval serving dishes & twelve 9 1/8" d. dessert plates; hand-colored decoration of vase issuing flowers on a stand opposite a pierced rock issuing flowers on a blue plateau, framed with a border of floral & trelliswork panels & a shaped gilt-edged rim, impressed "Mason's Patent Ironstone China," factory marks, one sauce tureen cover w/large rim chip, one dessert plate w/central crack & two w/large rim chips, minor wear to gilding, the set (ILLUS. of part).............................. 3,220

Ironstone Sauce Tureens with Underplates

Mason's Ironstone Dinner Plate

Dinner service: oval platter, eighteen 10 1/4" d. dinner plates; each printed & colored in the center w/large vase of flowers flanked by four precious objects within a cobalt & gilt scroll frame edged w/iron-red & green lappets, pale yellow ground border reserved w/flowers & foliate scrolls within a lustrous brown edged rim, aubergine printed factory marks & red painted pattern number 2240, ca. 1840-60 (ILLUS. of part)......... **2,587**

Dinner service: four nested platters, well & tree platter, cov. soup tureen w/undertray, twenty-two dinner plates, twenty-four soup plates, fifteen 7 3/4" d. luncheon plates; Imari-style floral decoration, 77 pcs. (some staple repairs, minor cracks, chips, staining)................. **2,300**

Dish, oval, Tracery shape, all-white, Johnson Bros., 6 1/4" l. **20**

Ewer, Ceres shape, all-white, Turner & Goddard..................................... **175**

Ewer, Hawthorne's Fern shape, all-white, John Hawthorne.................. **125**

Ewer, Panelled Pod shape, all-white, J. & G. Meakin, 11 1/2" h............... **175**

Ewer, Hyacinth shape, all-white, Hope & Carter, 12 1/2" h. **225**

Ewer, Lily of the Valley shape, all-white, J. Hughes, 12 3/4" h............ **225**

Honey dish, Girard shape, all-white, Ridgway Bates & Co. **25**

Honey dish, Sharon Arch shape, all-white, ca. 1861 .... **18**

Mold, Grape Clusters shape, all-white, Davenport, large **78**

Mold, Pineapple shape, all-white, oval, medium size......................... **75**

Mold, Sheaf of Wheat shape, all-white, unmarked **88**

Pitcher, milk, Senate shape, all-white, T. & R. Boote **60**

Pitcher, milk, 5 1/4" h., Oriental transfer-printed design w/polychrome enamel & snake handle, marked "Mason's" **248**

Pitcher, 7" h., Gothic shape, all-white **68**

Pitcher, 9 3/4" h., "gaudy" blue transfer floral design w/red & green enamel, snake handle, marked "Mason's Patent Ironstone China" **275**

Pitcher, 10" h., all-white, J. Maddock & Son.. **175**

Pitcher, 10" h., Aurora patt, blue transfer-printed w/polychrome enameling (minor edge wear)........ **248**

Pitcher, 11 1/2" h., Memnon shape, all-white, J. Meir & Son.................. **235**

Plate, 7 1/2" decagonal, dessert, Baltic shape, all-white, registered in1855 .... **18**

Plate, 8 3/4" d., Ceres shape, all-white, Elsmore & Forster.............. **35**

Plate, Balanced Vine shape, all-white, J. Clementson **26**

Plate, Ceres shape, miniature, all-white, Elsmore & Forster.............. **55**

Plate, 7" d., Boote's 1851 Octagon shape, all-white **29**

Plate 7 3/4" d., Ceres shape, all-white, Elsmore & Forster.............. **29**

Plate, 8 1/4" d., "gaudy" free-hand Bittersweet patt. in underglaze blue w/red & green enamel w/luster, impressed "Real Ironstone" 165

Plate, 8 5/8" d., "gaudy" free-hand Strawberry patt. in underglaze blue w/red, pink & green enamel, impressed "Elsmore Forster and Co." (minor wear) 220

Plate, 8 3/4" d., Portland shape, all-white, Elsmore & Forster 36

Plate, 9 1/8" d., Boote's 1851 Octagon shape, all-white 48

Plate, 9 1/4" d., "gaudy" center decoration of floral wreath in red, blue & green surrounded by black transfer-printed & polychrome enamel rabbits, frogs & cabbages (small rim repair) 275

Plate, 9 1/2" d., Boote's 1851 Octagon shape, all-white 35

Plate 9 5/8" d., Ceres shape, all-white, Edward Pearson 30

Plate, 9 5/8" d., Chinese shape, all-white 34

Plate, 9 3/4" d., "gaudy" center floral decoration in underglaze blue w/red, pink & green enamel w/luster (stains & some wear) 275

Plate, 9 3/4" d., Paris shape, all-white, John Alcock.......................... 26

Plate, 10" d., center scene of chick & butterfly w/motto around rim, black transfer-printed w/polychrome enamel, marked "Staffordshire England" 138

Plate, 10 1/4" d., True Scallop shape, 14 sides, all-white, Edwards 36

Plate, 10 1/4" octagonal, all-white..... 55

Platter, Columbia shape, all-white, Wooliscroft...................................... 75

Platter, oval, 16" l., Ceres shape, all-white, Elsmore & Forster 85

Platter, President shape, all-white.... 95

Platter, oval, 11" l., Tracery shape, all-white, Johnson Bros. 50

Platter, 15 3/4" l., Wheat in the Meadow shape, all-white, Powell & Bishop 112

Platter, 16" l., Boote's 1851 Octagon shape (good condition)................. 150

Platter, 16" l., Oriental black transfer-printed scene w/red enamel & worn gilt, marked "Mason's" '........ 50

Gaudy Ironstone Platter

Platter, 16 1/2" l., "Amherst Japan" patt., "gaudy" blue transfer floral decoration w/red & yellow enameling, impressed "Improved Stone China" (ILLUS.) 358

Platter, 18 1/4" l., Leaf & Crossed Ribbon shape, all-white, Livesley, Powell & Co..................................... 145

Platter, 18 1/4" l., Scalloped Decagon shape, all-white, registered in 1858, Davenport (light bull's eye on edge of rim) 165

Platter, 13 1/4 x 18 1/4", Tiny Oak & Acorn shape, all-white, J. W. Pankhurst 135

Platter, 13 1/2 x 18 1/4", Bordered Hyacinth shape, all-white, W. Baker & Co. 135

Platter, 21 1/8" l., decorated w/a central scene of a pavilion & pagoda in a garden of large floral blooms, iron-red & underglaze blue, framed within a border of angular panels & pendant flowers within a shaped rim, mid-19th c., crown & ribbon factory mark printed in brown, Mason (small rim chips & fritting to underside) 575

Platter, 22 1/4" l., "gaudy" polychrome floral enameling w/underglaze blue, Staffordshire (minor flaking).............................. 770

Platter, 24" l, wide oblong form w/angled corners, well-&-tree-type, "gaudy" style, transfer-printed dark blue Imari-style floral decoration in center w/stylized floral border decorated in polychrome enamel (ILLUS.) 633

Punch bowl, dark blue transfer-printed decoration w/lattice & scrollwork, scalloped rim, RN 298859, England, 19 1/4" d., 9 1/2" h. 605

Sauce dish, Boote's 1851 shape, round, all-white 6

Saucer, Atlantic "A" shape, all-white, registered in 1858, T. & R. Boote .. 28

Saucer, Boote's 1851 Octagon shape, round, all-white 35

Shaving mug, all-white 48

Soap slab, all-white, A. Shaw.......... 35

Soup ladle, all-white, line design around handle, unmarked 150

Soup plate, Mocho shape, all white, T. & R. Boote, 8 1/2" d.................. 14

Soup plate, Boote's 1851 shape, all-white, 9 1/4" octagonal 55

Soup plate all-white, 9 3/8" d., Pankhurst 36

Soup plate, Paris shape, all-white, John Alcock, 9 3/4" d..................... 45

Soup plate, President shape, all-white, 9 3/4" d............................... 45

Soup plate, Bellflower shape, all-white, John Edward, 10" d. (some wear) 46

Soup plate w/flanged rim, "gaudy" free-hand Blackberry patt. in underglaze-blue w/red & yellow enamel w/luster, impressed "Walley Paris White Ironstone," 9 5/8" d. 220

Soup plate w/shields, all white, J. W. Pankhurst................................. 36

Soup tureen, cov., Berlin Swirl shape, all-white, 8 3/4 x 12" 110

Sugar bowl, cov., Athens patt., black transfer w/some blue, Wm. Adams & Sons, 7 3/4" h. (stains & crazing) 193

Sugar bowl, cov., Athens shape, all-white, Wedgwood 135

Sugar bowl, cov., Wheat & Clover shape, all-white, Tomkinson Bros. & Co. 110

Sugar bowl, cov., Wheat (J. F.'s), all white.. 95

Large Ironstone Platter

Syrup pitcher, cov., all-white, small,
J. & G. Meakin.............................. 48

Syrup pitcher, grape molding at top,
gold line decoration, unmarked,
9" h. 88

Tea set: cov. teapot, creamer & cov.
sugar bowl; Gothic Paneled shape
w/black transfer-printed floral
design, teapot 8 3/4" h., the set
(minor chips & hairline in lid of
sugar) 248

Teapot, cov., octagonal, all-white,
ring handle (lid has no breathing
hole) 115

Teapot, cov., Wheat shape, all-white,
W. & E. Corn 115

Toddy cup, all-white, three notches
on handle....................................... 25

Toddy cup Bellflower shape, all-
white, John Edwards 35

Toddy cup, Boote's 1851 shape, all-
white.. 38

Toddy cup, Fuchsia shape, all-white 36

Toddy cup, Pearl Sydenham shape,
all-white 40

Toddy cup, Quartered Rose shape,
all-white, Jacob Furnival............... 38

Toddy plate, "gaudy" free-hand
Blackberry patt. in underglaze-blue
& black w/red & yellow enamel
w/luster, impressed "E. Walley
Niagara Shape" w/registry mark,
6 3/4" d. (enamel on base may be
retouched) 55

Toothbrush holder w/underplate,
vertical, all-white, unmarked.......... 58

Underplate, for sauce tureen,
Panelled Berry shape, all-white..... 38

Undertray, for gravy boat, oval, all-
white, Clementson......................... 36

Undertray, for sauce tureen,
Bordered Gothic shape, all-white,
Samuel Alcock.............................. 45

Undertray, for soup tureen, Many
Panelled Gothic shape, all-white,
"Reg. September 21, 1850,"

Mellor, Venables & Co.,
12 1/2 x 15 1/2" octagonal............. 150

Vegetable dish, cov., Ceres shape,
all-white, Elsmore & Forster, 8 5/8"
oval.. 170

Vegetable dish, cov., Plain Uplift
shape, all-white, Ed. Clarke,
6 1/2 x 9" oval.............................. 68

Vegetable dish, cov., Plain Uplift
shape, all-white, J. Edwards,
7 1/2 x 9 1/4" oval........................ 78

Vegetable dish, cov., Star Flower
shape, all-white, J. W. Pankhurst,
7 x 9 1/2" oval............................... 110

Vegetable dish, cov., Sevres shape,
all-white, Dean & Stokes,
7 1/2 x 10 1/4" oval....................... 95

Wash bowl, transfer-printed Imari-
style decoration in underglaze blue
& red enamel, impressed "Mason's
Patent Ironstone China," 12" d.
(glazed-over chip back edge of lip) 110

Wash bowl, Boote's 1851 Octagon
shape, all-white, 13" d. 200

Wash bowl, Athenia shape, all-white,
J. T. Close & Co., Stoke Upon
Trent, 14" d.................................... 145

Wash bowl & pitcher, President
shape, all-white, 2 pcs.................. 375

Wash bowl & pitcher, Sydenham
patt., all-white, the set 395

Washbowl, Many Panelled shape,
12 sides, all-white, J. Alcock 125

Washbowl, Fig shape, 14 sides, all
white, 14 1/2" d.............................. 145

TEA LEAF IRONSTONE

Bone dish, crescent-shaped,
Chelsea patt., A. Meakin 40

Bone dish, plain crescent shape, A.
Meakin... 40

Bone dish, scalloped crescent
shape, A. Meakin........................... 25

Boston egg cup, Ruth Sayers
decoration...................................... 115

Butter dish, cover & insert,
Basketweave patt., A. Shaw (some
glaze wear on insert) 375

Cake plate, Bamboo patt., A. Meakin 70

Cake plate, Daisy 'n Chain patt.,
Wilkinson 190

Cake plate, Daisy patt., A. Shaw
(fine crazing, tiny edge chip) 130

Cake stand, square, low pedestal
base, handled, Square Ridged
patt., Red Cliff, ca. 1970 170

Chamber pot, cov., Lion's Head
patt., Mellor, Taylor & Co............... 175

Chamberpot, cov., Fish Hook patt.,
A. Meakin 300

Coffeepot, cov., Scroll patt., A.
Meakin... 175

Coffeepot, cov., Scroll patt., A.
Meakin... 185

Cookie jar, cov., round, Kitchen Kraft
line, gold Tea Leaf, Homer
Laughlin, ca. 1950s 175

Creamer, Bamboo patt., A. Meakin,
5 1/4" h. 195

Creamer, Cable patt., A. Shaw, 7" h.
(manufacturing flaw on lower side) 280

Creamer, Iona patt., gold Tea Leaf,
Powell & Bishop, 4 1/2" h. 70

Creamer, Square Ridged patt.,
Wedgwood (slight wear)............... 90

Cup plate, Niagara Fan patt., A.
Shaw, 4 5/8" d. 60

Cup plate, Niagara patt., A. Shaw,
4 5/8" d. 60

Cup plate, plain, A. Meakin, 3 1/2" d. 45

Cup & saucer, handled, Chelsea
patt., A. Meakin 60

Cup & saucer, handled, child's, plain
round, Wilkinson............................ 200

Gravy boat, Aladdin lamp-style,
Cumbow decoration 60

Gravy boat, Chinese patt., A. Shaw. 230

Gravy boat, Golden Scroll patt.,
Bishop & Stonier............................ 45

Ladle, soup-type, large, unmarked ... 625

Mug, hot water-type, Daisy patt.,
twelve-sided, A. Shaw 275

Oyster bowl, pedestal foot, Edwards 55

Pitcher, 6 3/4" h., Plain Round patt.,
gold Tea Leaf, J.M. & Co. (some
lustre wear).................................... 50

Pitcher, 7" h., Empress patt.,
Micratex by Adams, ca. 1960s 80

Pitcher, 7 1/2" h., milk-type, Hanging
Leaves patt., A. Shaw 375

Pitcher, 8" h., Maidenhair Fern patt.,
Wilkinson 900

Pitcher, 8" h., water-type, Lion's
Head patt., Mellor, Taylor & Co. 150

Platter, 12" l., oval, Chelsea patt., A.
Meakin... 55

Punch bowl, footed deep rounded
bowl, A. Meakin, 9" d.................... 650

Relish dish, Maidenhair Fern patt.,
Wilkinson 250

Relish dish, mitten-style, Hawthorn
patt., Wilkinson (small glaze flaw
on foot rim) 275

Sauce tureen, cover & ladle,
Maidenhair Fern patt., Wilkinson
(hairline & chip on base, small
hairline on foot)............................. 400

**Sauce tureen, cover, undertray &
ladle,** Cable patt., A. Shaw, the set
(discoloration on handle) 500

**Sauce tureen, cover, undertray &
ladle,** Fish Hook patt., A. Meakin,
plain white ladle, the set (small
inner rim chip on base) 350

Saucer tureen, cover & undertray,
Basketweave patt., A. Shaw, the
set (flake at ladle opening, under
rim flaws) 500

Serving dish, oval, Brocade patt., A.
Meakin, 7" l. (tiny discolored spot). 190

Shaving mug, Maidenhair Fern patt., Wilkinson (professional repair to outside rim chip) **500**

Soap dish, cov., Cable patt., A. Shaw (inside lid rim chip) **150**

Soap dish, cov., Square Ridged patt., Mellor, Taylor & Co............... **325**

Soap dish, cover & insert, Bamboo patt., A. Meakin **260**

Soup plate w/flanged rim, Clementson, 9" d. **70**

Soup tureen, cover, undertray & ladle, Square Ridged patt., Red Cliff, ca. 1970, the set.................... **425**

Tea set: cov. teapot, cov. sugar bowl & creamer; Empress patt., Micratex by Adams, ca. 1960s, the set.. **165**

Teapot, cov., Bamboo patt., A. Meakin... **150**

Teapot, cov., Cable patt., A. Shaw ... **250**

Teapot, cov., Daisy 'n Chain patt., Wilkinson **120**

Teapot, cov., Hanging Leaves patt., A. Shaw (slight roughness inside lid).. **600**

Teapot, cov., Simple Square patt., Wedgwood **120**

Toothbrush vase, Heavy Square patt., Clementson (some crazing, small spider crack) **350**

Vegetable dish, cov., Bamboo patt., A. Meakin, 10" l. (some glaze wear) **80**

Vegetable dish, cov., Iona patt., gold Tea Leaf, Bishop & Stonier, 12" l. . **50**

Vegetable dish, cov., oval, Basketweave patt., A. Shaw, 10 1/4" l. **230**

Vegetable dish, cov., oval, Brocade patt., A. Meakin, 10" l. **150**

Vegetable dish, cov., oval, Chelsea shape, A. Meakin........................... **120**

Vegetable dish, cov., rectangular, Bamboo patt., A. Meakin, 12" l. **90**

Vegetable dish, cov., square, Bullet patt., A. Shaw, 12" w. **95**

Vegetable dish, cov., square, Fish Hook patt., A. Meakin **120**

Vegetable dish, cov., Square Ridged patt., Mellor, Taylor & Co., 12" l..... **130**

Vegetable dish, cov., Square Ridged patt., Wedgwood, 10" l. **80**

Wash bowl & pitcher, Brocade patt., A. Meakin (spider crack in bowl).... **275**

Wash pitcher, Cable patt., A. Shaw . **170**

Wash pitcher, Daisy 'n Chain patt., Wilkinson **130**

Wash pitcher, Daisy patt., A. Shaw . **160**

Wash pitcher, Square Ridged patt., Wedgwood (small hairline in bottom) **210**

Waste bowl, Plain Round patt., T. Hughes... **40**

TEA LEAF VARIANTS

Chamber pot, cov., Morning Glory patt., Portland shape, Elsmore & Forster... **525**

Creamer, child's, Teaberry patt., Scalloped Treasure shape, Clementson **525**

Creamer, Pinwheel patt., Full Paneled Gothic shape, unmarked . **450**

Creamer, Pre-Tea Leaf patt., Niagara shape, E. Walley.............. **500**

Creamer, Teaberry patt., Heavy Square shape, Clementson........... **450**

Cup & saucer, handleless, Tobacco Leaf patt., Fanfare shape, Elsmore & Forster...................................... **120**

Gravy boat, Morning Glory patt., Richelieu shape, Wileman (wear on spout, interior small pits) **100**

Mug, Sydenham shape, lustre band trim, large, unmarked **225**

Pitcher, 7 1/8" h., milk-type, Morning Glory patt., Portland shape, Elsmore & Forster 450

Pitcher, 7 1/2" h., milk-type, Teaberry patt., Heavy Square shape, Clementson 600

Pitcher, 8" h., Lustre Scallops patt., Wrapped Sydenham shape, E. Walley (slight glaze wear, manufacturing flaw) 475

Pitcher, 9 1/2" h., Teaberry pattl., Heavy Square shape, Clementson (crazing, glaze hairline, small base nick) 500

Plate, 11" d., Teaberry patt., New York shape 50

Platter, 16" oval, Laurel Wreath patt., lustre trim...................................... 400

Relish dish, Laurel Wreath shape, lustre trim, Elsmore & Forster........ 400

Relish dish, Pre-Tea Leaf patt., Niagara shape, E. Walley (small foot rim chip)................................. 600

Relish dish, Teaberry patt., Quartered Rose shape, J. Furnival 675

Sauce tureen, cover & ladle, Laurel Wreath patt., lustre trim, plain white ladle, Elsmore & Forster, the set (ladle repair, small rim chip & spider crack).................................. 500

Soap dish, cov., Morning Glory patt., Portland shape, Elsmore & Forster (professional repair to lower rim crack)... 425

Sugar bowl, cov., Pre-Tea Leaf patt., Hyacinth shape, Cochran & Co. 550

Teapot, cov., Ceres shape, lustre trim, Elsmore & Forster 425

Teapot, cov., Chelsea Grape patt., Primary shape, unmarked, 9 1/2" h. 175

Teapot, cov., Morning Glory patt., Portland shape, Elsmore & Forstor 275

Teapot, cov., Pre-Tea Leaf patt., Niagara shape, E. Walley.............. 700

Vegetable dish, cov., New York shape, lustre & blue sprig trim (small hairline) 500

Vegetable dish, cov., oval, Tobacco Leaf patt., Elsmore & Forster 375

Vegetable dish, cov., Pomegranate patt., Prairie Flowers shape, Powell & Bishop, 9" l. 550

Vegetable dish, cov., Pre-Tea Leaf patt., Niagara shape, E. Walley..... 700

Waste bowl, Pre-Tea Leaf patt., Niagara shape, E. Walley.............. 300

Waste bowl, Teaberry patt., plain round, unmarked (some glaze wear) 195

LIVERPOOL

Liverpool is most often used as a generic term for fine earthenware products, usually of creamware or pearlware, produced at numerous potteries in this English city during the late 18th and early 19th centuries. Many examples, especially pitchers, were decorated with transfer-printed patriotic designs aimed specifically at the American buying public.

Liverpool Mug & Pitcher

Mug, tall cylindrical form, transfer-printed outdoor scene of uniformed soldier on horseback above "George Washington, Esq. General and Commander in Chief of the Continental Army in America," early 19th c., cracks, chips on base & handle, staining, 4 5/8" h. (ILLUS. left) **$2,185**

Various Liverpool Pitchers

Pitcher, 6 1/4" h., creamware, bulbous body w/wide tapering cylindrical neck & pinched spout, both sides depicting black transfer-printed decoration of an eagle, flag & two women as Peace & Plenty & a circular reserve w/the names of ten states & Boston w/the inscription "Peace, Plenty, and Independence" & under the spout "Success to the Trade of Rhode Island," restoration, minor imperfections (ILLUS. far right) **1,610**

Pitcher, jug-type, 6 7/8" h., black transfer-printed decoration, one side w/a three-masted ship under full sail, the other side w/the verse "Poor Jack," early 19th c. (staining, cracks, wear) **460**

Pitcher, jug-type, 7 1/2" h., black transfer-printed design w/one side showing the seasons of spring & autumn, the reverse decorated w/a scenic oval reserve above a related verse, framed by floral swags, scrolls & various devices, spout damage, staining, edge roughness, early 19th c. (ILLUS. right) **633**

Pitcher, jug-type, 8" h., black transfer-printed oval reserve depicting portrait busts of John Hancock & Samuel Adams w/a beehive & horn of plenty & inscribed "The Memory of Washington and the Proscribed Patriots of America, Liberty, Virtue, Peace, Justice, and Equity to All Mankind," the reverse depicts an oval w/a military scene w/hero & cannon, ships & farmers plowing in the distance & the inscription "Success to America whose Militia is better than Standing Armies. May It's Citizens Emulate Soldiers and it's Soldiers Heros...," Great

Seal of the United States beneath the spout, 19th c., restoration, chips (ILLUS. second from right).. **2,300**

Pitcher, jug-type, 8" h., transfer-decorated w/a reserve of Masons congregating & "Veritas Prevalerus," & a reserve of various Masonic & regalia designs w/"Holiness to the Lord, it is found," cracks, staining, crazing, minor glaze wear) **431**

Liverpool "Patriot" Pitcher

Pitcher, jug-type, 9 3/4" h., large oval reserve w/transfer-printed decoration of a three-masted ship flying the American flag & a spread eagle w/American shield & "The Memory of Washington and the Proscribed Patriots of America" around border, polychrome highlights, restoration, minor abrasions to transfers, early 19th c. (ILLUS.) **1,725**

Pitcher, jug-type, 9 3/4" h., one side decorated w/a black transfer-printed reserve w/a portrait of Washington surrounded by Justice, Liberty & Victory encircled by fifteen stars & the names of the fifteen states, the reverse w/a reserve of "Peace, Plenty and Independence," inscribed under the spout "Philip & Jane Gilkey," early 19th c. (base chip, minor staining, minute rim chip, rim roughness) **1,725**

Pitcher, jug-type, 10 1/8" h., one side decorated w/a black transfer-printed reserve of a three-masted sailing ship under sail flying the American flag, a reserve of Masonic designs & "United for the Benefit of Mankind," & a spreadwinged eagle w/shield, polychrome highlights, shadows of gilt trim, early 19th c. (spout chips, minor cracks, staining, transfer wear) **1,150**

Pitcher, jug-type, 10 1/8" h., one side decorated w/a black transfer-printed reserve depicting a maiden on shore waving farewell to a trio of ships, one w/American flag, captioned "Fanny's farewell. Adieu she cry'd, and waved her Lily Hand," the reverse depicts the American warship "Fanny, James Bradburn" w/polychrome decoration, Great Seal of the United States beneath the spout, early 19th c., restoration (ILLUS. second from left).......................... **1,380**

Pitcher, jug-type, 10 5/8" h., black transfer-printed decoration, one side w/a frame of entwined ribbon enclosing the names of fifteen states, signed at the base "F. Morris Shelton," the reverse w/an American three-masted ship under sail & a spread-winged eagle, polychrome highlights, early 19th c. (cracks, minor chips, staining)....................................... **805**

Pitcher, jug-type, 11 3/8" h., decorated w/three black transfer-printed Masonic reserves w/"United for the Benefit of Mankind," a reserve of a woman w/three children & "To judge with candor...," & under the spout a reserve of various Masonic

emblems & "EW," polychrome & gilt trim, early 19th c. (gilt enamel wear) **1,380**

LUSTRE WARES

Lustred wares in imitation of copper, gold, silver and other colors were produced in England in the early 19th century and onward. Gold, copper or platinum oxides were painted on glazed objects which were then fired, giving them a lustred effect. Various forms of lustre wares include plain lustre with the entire object coated to obtain a metallic effect, bands of lustre decoration and painted lustre designs. Particularly appealing is the pink or purple "splash lustre" sometimes referred to as "Sunderland" lustre in the mistaken belief it was confined to the production of Sunderland area potteries. Objects decorated in silver lustre by the "resist" process, wherein parts of the objects to be left free from lustre decoration were treated with wax, are referred to as "silver resist."

Wares formerly called "Canary Yellow Lustre" are now referred to as "Yellow-Glazed Earthenwares."

COPPER

Creamer, yellow band w/white reserves w/purple transfer-printed scene of woman & child in classical attire, polychrome enamel, 4 1/8" h. (repairs)........................... **$182**

Pitcher, 7" h., small disk foot supporting a round widely flaring rounded lower body below a short angled shoulder to the tall cylindrical neck w/an figural serpent head rim spout & angled serpent handle, the sections of the body & neck w/blue ground decorated w/applied & polychromed basket of flowers near the base & band of flowers on the neck, copper lustre bands around the foot, body & rim & copper lustre spout & handle, ca. 1840.. **413**

Pitcher, 7" h., yellow band w/white reserves & brown transfer-printed scenes of woman & children in

garden, yellow & blue enamel
(minor wear) **193**

Copper Pitcher with Badminton Players

Pitcher, 5 3/4" h., yellow band
w/white reserves w/red transfer-
printed scene of badminton players
w/blue, yellow & green enamel,
minor wear (ILLUS.) **341**

SILVER & SILVER RESIST

Creamer, jug-type, decorated
w/silver resist bands of stylized
scrolling florals, 3 3/4" h. (damage
& repair)... **121**

Mug, cylindrical, pearlware w/relief-
molded decoration, wide silver-
resist band w/leaf sprigs & red
stripes, 3 1/2" h. (small flakes) **110**

SUNDERLAND PINK & OTHERS

Pitcher, jug-type, footed wide
bulbous squatty body tapering to a
short cylindrical neck w/arched
spout, decorated w/black transfer-
printed scenes & inscribed
"Country Lad and Lass" & "Sailor's
Farewell," pink luster & polychrome
enamel (wear) **550**

Pitcher, 6 1/4" h., jug-form,
pearlware, footed bulbous ovoid
body tapering to a short neck w/rim
spout, C-scroll handle, the sides
molded w/a scene of a stag, doe &
fawn highlighted in pink lustre &
polychrome enamel on a white
ground, first half 19th c. **385**

Pitcher, 7 1/8" h., jug-type, white
reserves w/black transfer-printed &
polychrome enamel decoration of
ship, maiden & seaman &
appropriate verses, wear & minor

Jug-type Pitchers

enamel flaking, crow's foot
hairlines in bottom (ILLUS. left) **715**

Pitcher, 7 3/8" h., jug-type, pink
lustre w/grape clusters & green
enamel leaves & scrolling vines
(some wear & scratches).............. **468**

Pitcher, 7 3/4" h., jug-type,
pearlware, relief-molded
basketweave design w/flowers &
vintage, double satyr head at
spout, polychrome enamel & pink
lustre, minor wear & small chip on
spout (ILLUS. right) **660**

Sailor's bowl, interior sides
decorated w/two verses & a sailing
ship enclosed in wreath borders
w/"Lady Liberty" in the center, color
enhanced w/green & red
highlights, pink lustre bands on the
interior & exterior rims, England,
19th c., 10" d. (glaze losses, rim &
base chip).................................... **489**

MAJOLICA

*Majolica, a tin-enameled glazed pottery,
has been produced for centuries. It originally
took its name from the island of Majorca, a
source of figuline (potter's clay). Subsequently it was widely produced in England,
Europe and the United States. Etruscan
majolica, now avidly sought, was made by
Griffen, Smith & Hill, Phoenixville, Pa., in
the last quarter of the 19th century. Most
majolica advertised today is 19th or 20th century. Once scorned by most collectors, interest in this colorful ware so popular during
the Victorian era has now revived and prices
have risen dramatically in the past few years.*

GENERAL

Bowl, 12" l., footed, simple oval form
w/upright end handles modeled as

poodles peering over the bowl rim, George Jones, England, indistinct painted design number, ca. 1870. **2,070**

Candlesticks, baroque-style w/a scroll- and lobed-molded cylindrical socket above a disk drip pan above the tall shaft composed of two graduated scroll-molded or lobed knobs separated by disk rings all on a dome-topped waisted base w/S-scroll feet, in the style of Bernard Palissy, modeled by Pierre-Emile Jeannest, impressed "Minton," date code for 1876 & design number "765," 16 1/4" h., pr. **2,875**

Center bowl, figural, modeled as three figural wood nymphs supporting a free-form bowl, Europe, 19th c., 16" h. **633**

Figural Majolica Centerpiece

Center pieces, figural, the top wide round bowl modeled in a green & tan basketweave design w/a rim border band of white florettes, supported on the heads of standing bacchanalian putti, one carrying a tambourine, the other a Pan flute, standing on circular bases molded w/leaves & rockwork, impressed Minton ermine marks & date cyphers for 1860, 20" h., pr. **10,925**

Centerpiece, figural, modeled as a cherub riding a dolphin on a base of shell-form dishes & feet joined by coral & supporting a naturalistic shell, George Jones, England, molded "Copyright Reserved," old restorations throughout, ca. 1880, 16" h. (ILLUS.) **690**

Cheese keeper, cov., brown basketweave design w/circlet of pink flowers & green leaves around center, mottled brown & green base, decorated knob finial, 6 1/2" h. (small chip underside of base edge) **350**

Chestnut serving dish, a round footed dish applied w/a half-cover formed as chestnut leafage & ripe fruit, the interior glazed robin's egg blue, impressed "Minton" & date code for 1868, 11" d. **1,380**

Compote, 7 3/4" h., open, the shaped oval bowl supported by a naturalistically molded oak tree on an oval base applied w/a recumbent hound & a grouse, George Jones, impressed registry mark & indistinct painted design number, ca. 1875 .... **4,887**

Creamer, leaf-form patterned w/primroses & raised on shell feet, impressed "Minton" & dated code for 1868 & "642," 5 1/4" h. **517**

Creamer, Corn patt., 4 1/2" h. **75**

Majolica Ewer

Ewer, modeled as a shallow barrel w/flaring neck & pedestal base strewn w/grapes, shoulders applied w/four nude putti at play w/grapes, a tambourine & a goblet, the handle in the form of a crown glazed vine stem, ca. 1875, possibly Minton, some traces of restoration to upper rim & pedestal base,14 7/8" h. (ILLUS.) **805**

Garden seat, a tall waisted tapering cylindrical form w/round seat above sides molded w/relief florettes & strapwork alternating w/large cartouche-form openings, on three large tab feet, impressed Minton marks & date code for 1873, 17 1/4" h. (restorations) **1,150**

Minton Majolica Jardiniere

restorations, ca. 1860, 17 1/2" h. (ILLUS.) **3,162**

Jardiniere, compressed spherical form w/pink interior, exterior molded in relief w/insects & colorful flowers on a turquoise ground between brown glazed stalk-form borders & hooped feet, impressed "GJ" & circle factory mark, molded patent registration diamond & black painted pattern number 3393, George Jones, England, ca. 1870, 12" h. **2,645**

Jardiniere, figural, modeled as a seated Bedouin w/pipe beside a recumbent camel & jardiniere formed as a mud brick structure, all on a circular base glazed in sand color, impressed "Brown Westhead Moore & Co." w/a painted design number, ca. 1870, base 14 1/2" d. **2,875**

Minton Majolica Barrel-Form Garden Seat

Garden seat, cylindrical form molded in relief w/birds & dragonflies perched on & flying between reeds & lily pads in colors on pale blue ground between brown straw molded top & borders, interior covered in a mottled brown & green glaze, Minton, impressed year code for 1873 & registration diamond, minor chips & abrasions, 18" h. (ILLUS.) **4,600**

Jardiniere, bulbous baluster-form w/round flat rim, modeled as a Neoclassical urn applied w/lion's mask bail handles on six raised ribs ending in paw feet, decorated in yellow, white, pink & green on a robin's-egg blue ground, pink interior, Minton, England,

Jardiniere, hanging-type, modeled as a shallow bowl molded w/Neoclassical portrait medallions & scrolling foliage in Renaissance taste, in mottled glazes on a cobalt blue ground, impressed "WEDGWOOD" & letters "HM," ca. 1870, 12 1/2" d. **1,150**

Jardiniere, squatty bulbous footed base below the wide cylindrical body w/a very wide squatty bulbous shoulder tapering to a short wide flaring neck, the shoulder mounted w/winged sphinx handles in cream & yellow w/green fruited swags around the shoulder, a grotesque mask below the figural handles all on a dark cobalt blue ground, impressed Minton mark, late 19th c., 22" h. (minor glaze flaws, chip repair, firing line) **1,430**

Jardinieres & pedestals, squat wide urn-form, molded w/neoclassical friezes including a frieze of dogtooth & lotus in the Egyptian taste, & applied w/two Levantine women & two putti seated on elephant's heads, all joined by figures of nude sleeping sirens suspended in rush-woven baskets, each raised on a separate pedestal of waisted form patterned w/neoclassical friezes, in white, brown, tan & green on a dark blue ground, modeled in the style of Albert Ernst Carrier-Belleuse, impressed Minton mark & date cyphers for 1867, 26" h., pr. **46,000**

Ornate Minton Majolica Pedestal

Pedestal, columnar-form w/molded garlands, florettes, acanthus leaves & an oak leaf & acorn frieze on a cobalt blue ground, Minton mark & date code for 1876, design number 891, small repair to rim, 38" h. (ILLUS.) **5,175**

Pedestal, Louis XVI-Style, the fluted baluster-form w/a square top, elaborately molded w/acanthus leaves & formalized foliage, glazed in shades of green, blue, brown, orange & gold on a yellow ground, impressed & printed Rorstrand marks, ca. 1900, 46" h................. **2,645**

Unusual Majolica Covered Pitcher

Pitcher, cov., 13" h., tankard-type, modeled as a band of medieval merrymakers dancing around a castellated tower, the hinged cover w/a jester head knop, Minton mark & date code for 1873, design number 1231, old cracks, loss of thumbpiece (ILLUS.) **1,380**

Pitcher, 7" h., Water Lily patt., cream pebbly ground, turquoise top w/yellow rope design **265**

Pitcher, 9 1/2" h., center decoration of flowers, leaves & buds on aqua ground, large butterfly spout, cobalt rim & band at lower part of body, mauve interior **400**

Plate, 8" l., Begonia Leaf patt. **75**

Sardine box, cover & undertray, oval basket-molded box w/seaweed & rope borders, the cover molded as realistic fish, the interior glazed robin's egg blue, matching undertray, George Jones, painted design number "3517" & date letter for 1876, 9" l., the set (minor cover restoration) .. **3,450**

Vase, 36" h., floor-type, figural, modeled as a heron holding a fish in its beak & standing against a clump of leafy reeds forming a vase, impressed double fish in oval mark, Hugo Lonitz, ca. 1890 (old cracks, repair to beak tip) **9,200**

Ornate Majolica Vase

Vase, large bulbous baluster-form, a flaring pedestal base supporting a wide squatty bulbous body tapering to a short neck w/wide incurved rim band, ornate figural scrolled dragon handles from rim to shoulder, decorated w/colorful leafy scrolls, masks & a Bacchanalian scene, Italy, late 19th - early 20th c. (ILLUS.) **1,725**

Wine cooler, figural, modeled as a spirally-fluted footed urn w/a rolled, scalloped rim & large leafy swags

on each side, supported by two tritons above the round foot, impressed "Minton" & date code for 1872, design number 526, 16" h. (restorations) **4,600**

MOCHA

Mocha decoration is found on basically utilitarian creamware or yellowware articles and is achieved by a simple chemical reaction. A color pigment of brown, blue, green or black is given an acid nature by infusion of tobacco or hops. When this acid nature colorant is applied in blobs to an alkaline ground color, it reacts by spreading in feathery seaweed designs. This type of decoration is usually accompanied by horizontal bands of light color slip. Produced in numerous Staffordshire potteries from the late 18th until the late 19th centuries, its name is derived from the similar markings found on mocha quartz. In addition to the seaweed decoration, mocha wares are also seen with Earthworm and Cat's Eye patterns or a marbleized effect.

Mug, cylindrical w/narrow white & dark brown stripes, large cream band w/dark brown seaweed decoration, applied handle, chips & base hairlines, 4 5/8" h. (ILLUS. top row, left)................................ **$1,100**

Mug, cylindrical w/blue, dark brown & orange stripes, center band

Various Mocha Items

decorated w/white wavy lines & groups of dots in white slip, embossed green rim band & applied leaftip handle, stains, wear & surface chips, 6" h. (ILLUS. bottom row, left)............................ 2,970

Pitcher, 4 7/8" h., barrel-shaped w/arched spout & C-form handle, dark blue seaweed on burnt orange band w/black & white stripes, embossed green rim band & applied handle w/green leaftips, chips (ILLUS. bottom right)........... 1,870

Shaker w/domed top, footed bulbous w/tapered neck to the top, yellowware decorated w/stripes of blue, white & black, chips, 4 3/8" h. (ILLUS. top row, right) 578

Sugar bowl, footed wide cylindrical body w/small applied rim handles w/tooled ends, decorated w/balloons in orange, white & dark brown on deep cream ground w/dark brown & white stripes, no lid, wear & damage, 4" d., 3" h. (ILLUS. top row, center) 1,760

MULBERRY

Mulberry or Flow Mulberry ironstone wares were produced in the Staffordshire district of England in the period between 1840 and 1870 at many of the same factories which produced its close "cousin," Flow Blue china. In fact, some of the early Flow Blue patterns were also decorated with the dark blackish or brownish purple mulberry coloration and feature the same heavy smearing or "flown" effect. Produced on sturdy ironstone bodies, the designs were either transfer-printed or hand-painted (Brushstroke) with an Asian, Scenic, Floral or Marble design. Some patterns were also decorated with additional colors over or under the glaze; these are designated in the following listings as "w/polychrome."

Quite a bit of this ware is still to be found and it is becoming increasingly sought-after by collectors although presently its values lag somewhat behind similar Flow Blue pieces. The standard references to Mulberry wares is Petra Williams' book, Flow Blue China and Mulberry Ware, Similarity and Value Guide

and Mulberry Ironstone - Flow Blue's Best Kept Little Secret, *by Ellen R. Hill.*

ACADIA (maker unknown, ca. 1850)
Creamer, 6" h., Classic Gothic shape **$250**

Acadia Plate

Plate, 8" d. (ILLUS.) 100

AMERILLIA (Podmore, Walker & Co., ca. 1850)
Plate, 9 1/2" 85

Vegetable dish, cov. 350

ATHENS (Charles Meigh, ca. 1845)
Creamer, 6", vertical-paneled Gothic shape... 150

Pitcher, 6 paneled, 10" h. (ILLUS.)... 300

Sugar, cov., vertical-paneled Gothic shape... 200

ATHENS (Wm. Adams & Son, ca. 1849)
Plate, 8 1/2" d. 55

Soup Plate, w/flanged rim, 9" d. 90

Sugar, covered, full-paneled Gothic shape... 225

Teapot, cov., full-paneled Gothic shape... 310

Athens Pitcher

AVA (T. J. & J. Mayer, ca. 1850)
Cup & saucer, handleless,
   w/polychrome 80

Plate, 9 1/2" d., w/polychrome 75

Plate, 10 1/2" d., w/polychrome 85

Platter, 16" l., w/polychrome............. 250

Sauce tureen, cover & undertray,
   w/polychrome, 3 pcs..................... 500

**BEAUTIES OF CHINA (Mellor Venables &
Co., ca. 1845)**
Plate, 7 1/2" d., w/polychrome 65

Platter, 14" l., w/polychrome............. 225

Bochara Teapot

**Sauce tureen, cover, ladle &
   undertray,** long octagon, 4 pcs..... 675

BOCHARA (James Edwards, ca. 1850)
Creamer, 6" h., full-paneled Gothic
   shape... 150

Pitcher, 7 1/2" h., full-paneled Gothic
   shape... 170

Plate, 10 1/2" d. 75

Teapot, cov., pedestaled Gothic style
   (ILLUS.) 350

**BRUNSWICK (Mellor Venables & Co.,
ca. 1845)**
Plate, 7 1/2" d., w/polychrome 65

Platter, 16" l., w/polychrome............. 275

Relish dish, stubby mitten-shape,
   w/polychrome 125

Sugar, cov., Classic Gothic shape,
   w/polychrome 225

**BRYONIA (Paul Utzchneider & Co.,
ca. 1880)**
Cup & saucer, handled 60

Plate, 7 1/2" d. 50

Bryonia Plate

Plate, 9 1/2" d. (ILLUS.) 65

CEYLON (Charles Meigh, ca. 1840)
Plate, 9 1/2" d. 65

Plate, 10 1/2" d., w/polychrome 85

Platter, 14" l., w/polychrome............. 175

Vegetable bowl, open, small............ 125

CHUSAN (P. Holdcroft, ca. 1850)
Plate, 9 1/2" d. 80

Potato bowl, 11" d............................ 250

CLEOPATRA (F. Morley & Co., ca. 1850)
Basin & ewer, w/polychrome 750

Plate, 9 1/2" d. 70

Soap box, cover & drainer, 3 pcs. ... 250

Soup plate, w/flanged rim, 9" d. 90

COREA (Joseph Clementson, ca. 1850)
Cup & saucer, handleless................ 75

Sugar, covered, long hexagon.......... 250

Teapot, covered, long hexagon 350

COREAN (Podmore, Walker & Co., ca. 1850)
Cup & saucer, handled, large 125

Relish, mitten-shape........................ 135

Sauce tureen, cover & undertray, 3
pcs. (ILLUS.) 475

Sugar, cov., oval bulbous style 350

COTTON PLANT (J. Furnival, ca. 1850)
Creamer, 6 5/8" h., paneled grape
shape, w/polychrome 200

Cotton Plant Teapot

Teapot, cov., cockscomb handle,
w/polychrome (ILLUS.)................. 650

CYPRUS (Wm. Davenport, ca. 1845)

Cyprus Gravy

Corean Sauce Tureen

Gravy boat, unusual handle (ILLUS.) 150

Pitcher, 11" h., 6-sided...................... 250

DORA (E. Challinor, ca. 1850)
Plate, 9 1/2" d. 65

Teapot, cov., Baltic shape, brush
   stroke... 650

FERN & VINE (maker unknown, ca. 1850)

Fern & Vine Creamer

Creamer, 6" h., Classic Gothic style
   (ILLUS.) 225

Plate, 7 1/2" d. 75

FLORA (Hulme & Booth, ca. 1850)
Creamer, 6" h., w/polychrome, grand
   loop shape..................................... 150

FLORA (T. Walker, ca. 1847)
Cup & saucer, handleless................ 65

Foliage Plate

Plate, 7 1/2" d. 75

Plate, 9 1/2" d. 85

Sugar, cov., Classic Gothic shape.... 250

FLOWER VASE (T. J. & J. Mayer, ca. 1850)
Teapot, cov., w/polychrome, Prize
   Bloom shape 560

FOLIAGE (J. Edwards, ca. 1850)
Plate, 8" d. (ILLUS.) 75

GERANIUM (Podmore, Walker & Co., ca. 1850)

Geranium Plate

Plate, 8" d. (ILLUS.) 65

JARDINERE (Villeroy & Boch, ca. 1880)
Plate, 7 1/2" d. 55

Plate, 9 1/2" d. 75

Vegetable bowl, open, round........... 150

JEDDO (Wm. Adams, ca. 1849)
Cup & saucer, handleless................ 75

Relish dish, octagonal 125

Sugar, cov., full-paneled Gothic
   shape (ILLUS.) 195

Teapot, cov., full-paneled Gothic
   shape... 300

KAN-SU (Thomas Walker, ca. 1847)
Cup & saucer, handleless................ 75

Plate, 7 1/2" d. 60

Jeddo Sugar Bowl

Platter, 14" l. 250

Vegetable dish, cov., octagonal....... 375

MARBLE (A. Shaw, ca. 1850)

Marble Teapot

Teapot, cov., vertical paneled Gothic
shape (ILLUS.) 450

MEDINA (J. Furnival, ca. 1850)
Cup & saucer, handleless................ 65

Sugar, cov., cockscomb handle........ 350

NANKIN (Davenport, ca. 1845)

Marble Creamer

Creamer, 6" h., 10 panel Gothic
shape (ILLUS.) 200

Invalid feeder, large 500

MARBLE (Mellor Venables, ca. 1845)
Plate, 9 1/2" d. 75

Teapot, cov., child's, vertical paneled
Gothic.. 350

Nankin Pitcher

Pitcher, 8" h., mask spout jug
w/polychrome (ILLUS.)................. 300

Plate, 8 1/2" d., w/polychrome 75

NING PO (R. Hall, ca. 1840)
Cup & saucer, handleless................ 65

Plate, 10 1/2" d. 85

Soup plate, w/flanged rim, 10" d. 90

PARISIAN GROUPS (J. Clementson, ca. 1850)

Plate, 7 1/2" d., w/polychrome 60

Plate, 8 1/2" d., w/polychrome 70

Sauce dish, w/polychrome 65

Sauce tureen, cover & undertray, w/polychrome, 3 pcs..................... 450

PELEW (Edward Challinor, ca. 1850)

Cup & saucer, handleless, pedestalled 95

Plate, 7 1/2" d. 60

Plate, 10 1/2" d. 90

Punch cup, ring handle 100

Pelew Teapot

Teapot, cov., pumpkin shape (ILLUS.) 395

PERUVIAN (John Wedge Wood, ca. 1850)

Cup & saucer, handleless, "double bulge" (ILLUS.) 85

Teapot, cov., 16 paneled 400

Waste bowl, "double bulge" 150

PHANTASIA (J. Furnival, ca. 1850)

Creamer, 6" h., w/polychrome, cockscomb handle........................ 325

Cup plate, w/polychrome................. 95

Peruvian Cup & Saucer

Plate, 9 1/2" d., w/polychrome 85

Sugar, cov., w/polychrome, cockscomb handle........................ 400

Teapot, cov., w/polychrome, cockscomb handle........................ 650

RHONE SCENERY (T. J. & J. Mayer, ca. 1850)

Plate, 7 1/2" d. 45

Plate, 10 1/2" d. 65

Sauce tureen, cover & undertray, 3 pcs.. 500

Sugar, cov., full-paneled Gothic shape.. 200

SCINDE (T. Walker, ca. 1847)

Creamer, 6" h., Classic Gothic shape 150

Plate, 9 1/2" d. 80

Soup plate, w/flanged rim, 9" d. 90

Teapot, cov., Classic Gothic shape .. 350

SHAPOO (T. & R. Boote, ca. 1850)

Plate, 8 1/2" d. 75

Sugar, cov., Primary shape 300

Teapot, cov., Primary shape............. 450

Vegetable dish, cov., flame finial 350

TEMPLE (Podmore, Walker & Co., ca. 1850)

Cup & saucer, handled, large 95

Plate, 8 1/2" d. 55

Sugar, cov., Classic Gothic shape.... 200

Teapot, cov., Classic Gothic shape .. 350

VINCENNES (J. Alcock, ca. 1840)
Compote, Gothic Cameo shape 500

Cup & saucer, handleless,
    thumbprint 85

Plate, 7 1/2" d. 60

Plate, 10 1/2" d. 80

Vincennes Punch Cup

Punch cup (ILLUS.) 125

Soup tureen, cover & undertray,
    10-sided, 3 pcs............................ 2,000

WASHINGTON VASE (Podmore, Walker & Co., ca. 1850)
Creamer, 6" h., Classic Gothic shape 225

Cup & saucer, handleless............... 85

Plate, 10 1/2" d. 75

Soup plate, w/flanged rim, 9" d. 85

Teapot, cov., bulbous shape 495

WHAMPOA (Mellor Venables & Co., ca. 1845)
Plate, 10 1/2" d. 95

Sauce tureen, cov., long octagon
    shape, 2 pcs................................. 300

WREATH (Thomas Furnival, ca. 1850)
Ewer (ILLUS.) 295

Plate, 9 1/2" d. 85

Wreath Ewer

PENNSBURY POTTERY

In 1990, when Lucile Henzke wrote the first complete book on Pennsbury Pottery, only a small group of collectors had been amassing items from this company. Today, just a few years later, pottery enthusiasts have come to realize what a wonderful piece of Country Americana the Pennsbury owners, Henry and Lee Below (pronounced "Bello") created.

Pennsbury invoices from 1963 show that a cookie jar could be purchased for $14.00 and a bowl in the Dutch Talk pattern was selling for $4.00. Today, those same items would cost about $210.00 and $125.00, respectively. Begun in 1950, Pennsbury Pottery was established in Morrisville, Pennsylvania. The Belows named the company Pennsbury for the nearby home of William Penn. Lee had been connected with the Stangl Pottery Company of Trenton, New Jersey and was considered a talented artist-designer. She designed most of Pennsbury's folk art, the various rooster patterns and the hand-painted Pennsylvania German blue and white dinnerware. Henry, who studied pottery-making in Germany and was considered a professional in ceramic engineering and mold making, designed many of the Pennsbury shapes and managed the day-to-day office operations. Mr. Below had also been an employee at Stangl Pottery and when he decided to establish his own business, several employees at Stangl joined in his new enterprise. This probably accounts for the Pennsbury birds resembling those of Stangl. Birds were the first items produced at Pennsbury and even though they are not plentiful, they are popular with collectors today. The birds are usually marked by hand with "Pennsbury Pottery" and often the name of the bird. Many times the artist's initials or name were also included.

The most prominent and successful Pennsbury coloring was accomplished by the sgraffito technique followed with a smear-type glaze of light brown.

The bird line, dinnerware, art pieces, ashtrays, mugs, teapots, canisters, and cookie jars with finials of animals and birds, commemoratives (especially trays for railroad companies which were used as gifts for passengers), and the scarce blue and white pieces, have all found their place in the Country Americana setting for collectors today.

Pennsbury was in business seventeen years and at one time almost fifty people were working there. Mr. Below died unexpectedly in 1959 and Mrs. Below, following a long illness, died in 1968. Bankruptcy was filed in late 1970 and in April 1971 fire destroyed the pottery.

—Susan Cox

Rooster Cup & Saucer

Canister, cov., Black Rooster patt., w/black rooster finial, front reads "Flour," 9" h. **$185**

Cup & saucer, Black Rooster patt., cup 2 1/2" h., saucer 4" d. (ILLUS.)   55

Desk basket, Two Women Under Tree patt., 5" h.   75

Model of chickadee, head down, on irregular base, model no. 111, signed R.B., 3 1/2" h. 140

Mug, beer-type, Barber Shop Quartet patt.   35

Mug, beer, Amish patt., dark brown rim & bottom w/dark brown applied handle, 5" h. (ILLUS.)   38

Pie plate, Dutch Haven commemorative, birds & heart in center, inscribed around the rim "When it comes to Shoo-Fly Pie -

Commemorative Pie Plate

Grandma sure knew how - t'is the Kind of Dish she used - Dutch Haven does it now," 9" d. (ILLUS.) **125**

Commemorative Plaque

Mug w/Amish pattern

Pitcher, 5" h., Delft Toleware patt., fruit & leaves, white body w/fruit & leaves outlined in blue, blue inside **95**

Plaque w/Rooster

Amish Pattern Pitcher

Pitcher, 7 1/4" h., Amish patt. w/interlocked pretzels on reverse (ILLUS.) **105**

Plaque, commemorative, "What Giffs, what ouches you?," reverse marked "NFBPWC Philadelphia, PA 1960," drilled for hanging, 4" d. (ILLUS.) **30**

Plaque w/Pennsbury Cookie Jar

Plaque, Rooster patt., "When the cock crows the night is all," drilled for hanging, 4" d. (ILLUS.)............. **40**

Plaque, shows woman holding Pennsbury cookie jar, marked "It is Whole Empty," drilled for hanging, 4" d. (ILLUS.)................................ **35**

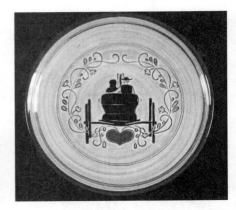

Plate w/Courting Buggy

Plaque w/Amish Couple Kissing

Plaque, Amish man & woman kissing over cow, drilled for hanging, 8" d. (ILLUS.) **87**

Plate w/Red Rooster Pattern

Plate, 10" d., Red Rooster patt. (ILLUS.) **48**

Plate w/Black Rooster Pattern

Plate, 6" d., Black Rooster patt. (ILLUS.) **25**

Plate, 8" d., Courting Buggy patt. (ILLUS.) **75**

Donkey & Clown Wall Pocket

Relish tray, Black Rooster patt., five-section, each w/different scene, Christmas-tree shape, 14 1/2" l., 11" w.. **220**

Wall pocket, donkey & clown w/dark green border, ivory center, 6 1/2" sq. **105**

RED WING

Various potteries operated in Red Wing, Minnesota from 1868, the most successful being the Red Wing Stoneware Co., organized in 1878. Merged with other local potteries through the years, it became known as Red Wing Union Stoneware Co. in 1894, and was one of the largest producers of utilitarian stoneware items in the United States. After a decline in the popularity of stoneware products, an art pottery line was introduced to compensate for the loss and this was reflected in a new name for the company, Red Wing Potteries, Inc., in 1930. Stoneware production ceased entirely in 1947, but vases, planters, cookie jars and dinnerwares of art pottery quality continued in production until 1967 when the pottery ceased operation altogether.

CONVENTION COMMEMORATIVES

Red Wing Commemorative Acid Pitcher

Acid pitcher, 1986 Red Wing Collectors Society Commemorative, maker produced 1,982 (ILLUS.) **$225**

Bowl, 1980 Red Wing Collectors Society Commemorative, maker produced 400 .... **995**

Crock, 1977 Red Wing Collectors Society Commemorative, maker produced 250 .... **2,595**

Jug, 1978 Red Wing Collectors Society Commemorative, maker produced 350 .... **2,195**

Red Wing Commemorative Miniature Jug

Jug, miniature, 1981 Red Wing Collectors Society Commemorative, maker produced 750 (ILLUS.) **445**

Mug, 1982 Red Wing Collectors Society Commemorative, maker produced 697 .... **695**

Planter, giraffe, 1995 Red Wing Collectors Society Commemorative, maker produced 8,186 .... **85**

DINNERWARES & NOVELTIES

Ashtray, wing-shaped, marked "Red Wing Potteries 75th Anniversary, 1878-1953," 7 3/8" **95**

Basket, white & green, marked "Red Wing USA #1275," 9 3/4" l. (ILLUS.) **80**

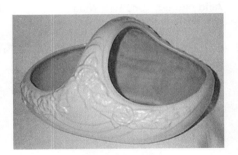

Red Wing Basket

Beverage server, cov., Tampico
  patt. 85

Bowl, cereal, Provincial patt. 8

Casserole, cov., French-style
  w/handle, Town & Country patt.,
  rust glaze, ca. 1946 165

Console bowl, Magnolia patt., 12" l. 115

Cookie jar, cov., Bob White patt....... 95

French Chef Cookie Jar

Cookie jar, cov., French Chef, blue
  on blue, Red Wing Pottery stamp
  (ILLUS.) 135

Creamer, Provincial patt. 12

Figurine, brown beaver w/football,
  signed "Red Wing Potteries, Red
  Wing, Minn.," dated 1939, very
  rare, 2 5/8" h. (ILLUS.) 175

Red Wing Figurine

Figurine, green & yellow sitting deer,
  marked "Red Wing USA #1338,"
  6" h. 110

Marmite, Village Green patt............. 9

Planter, model of a Dachshund dog,
  blue glaze, No. 1342 95

Planter, green stove, marked "Red
  Wing #765,"7 3/4" h....................... 75

Log Shaped Planter

Planter, log-shaped, white birch
  pottery, unmarked, 11" l. (ILLUS.) 85

Plate, 10" d., dinner, Provincial patt. 10

Salt & pepper shakers, Village
  Green patt., pr. 14

Trivet, Minnesota Centennial 1858-
  1958, back signed "Red Wing
  Potteries," 6 1/2" d. (ILLUS.) 95

Vase, brushed ware w/cattails,
  stamped "Red Wing Union
  Stoneware," rare, 7 3/8" h. 105

Red Wing Trivet

STONEWARE & UTILITY WARES

Bean pot, cov., white & brown glaze, w/advertising "Christmas Greetings from Christel's Cash Store, Brillion, Wisc." (ILLUS.) **105**

Bean pot, cov., white & brown glaze, w/advertising "Peterson Department Store, Clintonville, Wisc." **95**

Beater jar, spongeband, w/advertising "It Pays to Mix with Allen, Herman, Minn." **850**

Beater Jar with Advertising

Beater jar, white glaze w/blue band, w/advertising "Klatt & Stueber, Clyman, Wisc." (ILLUS.) **150**

Bowl, 5" d., paneled spongeware **280**

Bowl, 6" d., paneled spongeware, w/advertising "Muscoda, Spring Green, Boscobel, Wisc." **325**

Bowl, 8" d., paneled sides, sponged blue & red decoration **100**

Bowl, 12" d., white & blue glaze, Greek Key patt. **240**

Butter Crock, white glazed stoneware, bottom signed "Minnesota Stoneware Co.," 10 lbs. **75**

Christmas tree holder, green glaze **425**

Churn, white glazed stoneware, large wing, upside down oval stamp, 2 gal. **475**

Stoneware Churn

Churn, white glazed stoneware, large wing, oval stamp below wing, 5 gal. (ILLUS.) **350**

Churn, white glazed stoneware, large wing, oval stamp below wing, 8 gal.. **1,550**

Crock, white glazed stoneware, bottom signed "Minnesota Stoneware, Red Wing, Minn.," 8 3/4" d., 1 gal. **45**

Four Gallon Stoneware Crock

Crock, white glazed stoneware, two birch leaves, w/Union oval stamp mark, 11" d., 4 gal. (ILLUS.) **115**

Crock, white glazed stoneware, two "elephant ears," Union Oval Stamp, earred handles, 12" d., 6 gal.. **130**

Crock, white glazed stoneware, 6" wing, Red Wing oval stamp, bail handles, 15 1/4" d., 10 gal............. **135**

Crock, white glazed stoneware, small wing, Red Wing oval stamp, bail handles, 18" d., 15 gal. **115**

Crock, white glazed stoneware, Red Wing & Union oval stamp, bail handles, 20" h., 20 gal................... **121**

Fruit jar, screw-on metal lid, "Stone Mason Fruit Jar," black mark, 1 qt., ... **225**

Fruit jar, cov., Stone Mason, black label, patent date Jan. 24, 1899, "Union Stoneware" stamp, 1 qt...... **275**

Pure Leaf Lard Jar

Fruit jar, cov., Stone Mason, black label, patent date Jan. 24, 1899, "Union Stoneware" stamp, 1 gal. **750**

Red Wing Shouldered Jug

Jar, cov., Hazel Pure Food Co., white glazed stoneware, stamped "Pure

4 gal. Red Wing
jug (crock)

155.00

Blue & White Pottery
8" pitcher (peach on
front)

265.00

Workman Publishing
708 Broadway
New York, NY 10003-9555
www.workman.com

Manufactured in the United States of America

ISBN 0-7611-2407-1

Leaf Lard," wire handle, complete
with lid, 5 lbs. (ILLUS.) 245

Jug, beehive-shaped, Albany slip,
North Star stoneware, star on
base, rare, 1 qt. 285

Jug, beehive-shaped, salt glazed
stoneware, signed "Minnesota
Stoneware Company," 2 gal. 1,175

Jug, shouldered, white glazed
stoneware, 4" wing, Red Wing oval
stamp, 3 gal. (ILLUS.) 165

Jug, shouldered, white glazed
stoneware, 4" wing, Red Wing oval
stamp, 4 gal. 155

"Koverwate," (crock cover-weight
designed to keep the contents
submerged under preserving
liquid; bottom & side holes allowed
brine to come to the top), white
glazed stoneware, stamped
"Koverwate, Red Wing, Minn.," 6
gal. size 245

Stoneware Pie Plate

"Koverwate," white glazed
stoneware, stamped "Koverwate,
Red Wing, Minn.," 25 gal. size 350

Pie plate, white glazed stoneware,
signed "Minnesota Stoneware Co.,
Red Wing, Minn.," rare, 9 3/4" d.
(ILLUS.) 145

Poultry feeder jar, cov., white
glazed stoneware poultry drinking
font & buttermilk feeder, bell-
shaped, marked "Red Wing,"
complete with base, 1 gal. 145

Three Gallon Stoneware Water Cooler

Water cooler, cov., white glazed
stoneware, bailed handles, small
wing, 3 gal. (ILLUS.) 450

Water cooler, cov., white glazed
stoneware, bailed handles, small
wing, 8 gal. 475

REDWARE

*Red earthenware pottery was made in the
American colonies from the late 1600s.
Bowls, crocks and all types of utiliatarian
wares were turned out in great abundance to
supplement the pewter and handmade treenware. The ready availability of the clay, the
same used in making bricks and roof tiles,
accounted for the vast production. The lead-
glazed redware retained its reddish color
though a variety of colors could be obtained
by adding various metals to the glaze. Interesting effects occurred accidentally through
unsuspected impurities in the clay or uneven
temperatures in the firing kiln which sometimes resulted in streaks or mottled splotches.*

*Redware pottery was seldom marked by
the maker.*

Apple butter jar, bulbous ovoid body
w/applied handle & tooled lines,
brown splotches on deep orange
ground, 5" h. $578

Bowl, 5 1/4" d., 2 1/2" h., footed w/rounded sides & flat rim, dark greenish orange ground w/brown spots, bottom incised "B" (minor glaze flakes on interior) **303**

Redware Butter Churn

Bowl, 10 1/2" d., 7" h., deep sides w/light green glaze splotches, 19th c. (chips) **460**

Bust, sculpted unglazed gentleman wearing shirt, bow tie & jacket, on shaped pedestal, 19th c., 5" h. (some chips & losses) **287**

Bust of man, full bottomed wig, wheel thrown & hand-molded & tooled, brown glaze, 10" h. (minor chips) **770**

Butter churn, wooden lid & plunger, 19th c., 28" d., 26" h. (ILLUS.) **300-350**

Chamberstick, cylindrical w/saucer base & applied handle, brown & green glaze on orange ground, 3" h. (base glued) **176**

Creamer, cylindrical w/reeded base & applied handle, green & mottled brown glaze on orange ground, 2 1/8" h. (edge chips) **303**

Redware Dish

Dish, orange ground w/brown sponged rim, 6 1/2" d. (wear & chips) **440**

Various Redware Pieces

Dish, 7" d., coggled rim, greenish pinkish grey mottled glaze (small chips) 110

Dish, orange glazed interior, exterior & rim w/black patina, 7 1/2" d. (wear & hairline) 303

Dish, oblong, shallow canted sides w/flat narrow rim, orange ground w/brown & green spots, 11 3/4" l. (ILLUS.) 660

Doorstop, square form decorated w/molded starflower, yellow & brown glaze, 3 x 4 3/4 x 5" (ILLUS. center) 330

Figure of Uncle Sam, standing full-figure, polychrome, 4" h. (worn & flaked polychrome) 275

Flask, ovoid body tapering to small molded rim, deep orangeish ground w/dark brown splotches, 7" h. (wear & minor chips) 385

Flowerpot w/attached saucer, tapering cylindrical form, tooled lines at base & rim, yellow slip & mottled brown, orange & cream glaze, wear, flakes & short hairlines, 5" h. (ILLUS. left with doorstop) 358

Flowerpot w/saucer, tapering cylindrical form w/narrow rolled rim, brown running glaze on orange ground, impressed "John W. Bell, Waynesboro, Pa.," 4 3/8" h. (chips) 385

Redware Ram-form Footwarmer

Footwarmer, figural recumbent ram, 19th c., very minor chips, 6 3/4" h., 13 1/2" l. (ILLUS.) 518

Jar, bulbous ovoid body w/applied ribbed strap handle & tooled bands, brown sponging on burnt orange ground, 6" h. 165

Jar, bulbous ovoid body tapering to slightly flared rim, dark brown pattern on orangeish brown ground, 6 3/8" h. (short hairline in base, minor flakes) 275

Jar, footed bulbous ovoid body tapering to a wide slightly flaring rim, dark brown splotches on orange ground w/mottled green glaze, 7 3/8" h. (chips) 825

Jar, wide cylindrical body w/flared rim, net like pattern of dark brown over burnt orange ground, 7 1/2" h. (wear & small chips) 523

Jar, cov., wide cylindrical body w/shoulder tapering to flared rim, inset cover w/tiny cylindrical finial, dark brown daubs on greenish glaze w/mottled amber, yellow & green, 8" h. (chips) 1,485

Jar, cylindrical, greenish glaze w/amber spots & brown brushed spirals, 8 5/8" h. (wear & chips) 853

Jar, ovoid body w/strap handle, green glaze w/orange spots, 8 3/4" h. (glazed over rim hairline, chips) 220

Jar, bulbous ovoid form w/tooled lines, dark brown splotches & flecks on dark orange ground, 9 1/8" d. (wear & old chips) 220

Jar, ovoid w/shoulder handles, clear reddish brown w/black splotches, chips, 9 1/2" h. 220

Jug, globular w/ribbed strap handle & tooled lines, amber ground w/brown splotches & green mottled glaze, 3 5/8" h. 4,510

Jug, bulbous ovoid body w/applied ribbed handle, brown fleck son a metallic deep amber ground, 7 1/4" h. (wear & surface & edge chips) 193

Jug, bulbous ovoid body w/applied strap handle, dark glaze w/black splotches, 8 3/4" h (chips on base)   303

Jug, semi-ovoid body w/applied strap
handle, brown & green glaze
w/amber & brown spots, 9 1/4" h.
(minor chips).................................. 605

Redware Jug

Jug, globular w/strap handle, brown
w/orange spots, 18th c., America,
27" d., 11" h. (ILLUS.) 50-75

Jug, bulbous ovoid, brown running
glaze on deep orange ground,
glazed over handle attachment,
12" h. (wear & old chips) 110

Jug, bulbous ovoid body w/applied
strap handle, deep reddish tan,
12 1/4" d. (wear & minor glaze
flakes)... 550

Model of poodle, the seated animal
in the form of a Staffordshire
Spaniel covered in a brown glaze,
inscribed on reverse "H. McD.,"
19th c., 7 3/4" l., 7 1/4" h. (minor
losses, kiln imperfections) 173

Mold, food, fluted interior, dark brown
sponging on deep orange ground,
4 1/4" d. (hairline) 110

Mold, food, Turk's turban-style,
divided & fluted, dark brown glaze
wbrown sponged scalloped rim,
7 3/4" d. (small flakes).................. 138

Mold, food, Turk's turban-style,
swirled design w/running brown
glaze on orange ground,
impressed label "John W. Bell,
Waynesboro, Pa.," 8 3/4" d.,
4 1/8" h. (hairline) 495

Mug, footed bulbous body w/molded
ribs & applied handle, brown
sponging w/mottled green glaze on
orange ground, 3" h....................... 275

Mug, barrel form w/tooled band &
applied handle, dark brown glaze,
3 5/8" h. (chips) 121

Mug, cylindrical w/applied ribbed
handle & tooled bands, dark burnt
orange ground w/brown streaks,
4 7/8" h. (chips) 138

Mush mug, footed squatty bulbous
body w/applied ribbed handle, dark
greenish amber glaze, 3 1/2" h.
(chips).. 88

Pepper pot, waisted cylindrical base
w/top tapering sharply to
mushroom-shaped top pierced
w/holes, brown sponging on green
& light brown glaze, 5 1/2" h.......... 495

Pie plate, brown brushed & sponged
design on burnt orange ground,
7 3/8" d. (minor chips & short
hairline).. 220

Pie plate, orange glaze w/dark brown
splotches, 8 1/4" d. (ILLUS. right
with doorstop)............................. 1,155

Pitcher, 6 3/4" h., squatty ovoid body
tapering to tall slightly flared rim
w/pinched spout & applied ribbed
strap handle, brown splotches &
flecks on lighter brown ground 220

Pitcher, 7 5/8" h., bulbous ovoid
body w/tooled band, gallery rim lip,
pinched spout & ribbed strap
handle, dark brown splotches &
flecks on orange ground (wear &
chips).. 660

Pitcher, 8" h., bulbous ovoid body
w/applied ribbed handle & tooled
lines, brown flecked glaze (chips) . 193

Pitcher, 8" h., footed spherical body,
tapering cylindrical neck w/tooled
band w/reeded lip, applied C-form
handle, marbleized white, green,

brown & blue glaze w/white slip interior (chips).............................. **550**

Pitcher, cov., 9" h., wide ovoid body w/ribbed strap handle, clear glaze w/brown sponging on a red ground (lid is good fit but color varies)....... **523**

Pitcher, 10 3/4" h., wide ovoid body tapering to a flared rim w/pinched spout, ribbed strap handle, old wooden lid, clear mottled green glaze w/running daubs of yellow slip highlighted w/brown & green, brown glazed interior (minor chips) **9,900**

Pot, cov., squatty bulbous body w/flared rim, strap handle & pouring spout, dark brown sponged glaze, 5" h. (small chips & mismatched lid) **110**

Stove leveler, flaring cylindrical form w/molded top, brown splotches on orange ground, 2 3/4" h. (chips).... **176**

ROCKINGHAM WARES

The Marquis of Rockingham first established an earthenware pottery in the Yorkshire district of England around 1745 and it was occupied afterwards by various potters. The well-known mottled brown Rockingham glaze was introduced about 1788 by the Brameld Brothers and became immediately popular. It was during the 1820s that the production of true porcelain began at the factory and continued to be made until the firm closed in 1842. Since that time the so-called Rockingham glaze has been used by various potters in England and the United States, including some famous wares produced in Bennington, Vermont. However, very similar glazes were also used by potteries in other areas of the United States including Ohio and Indiana and only wares specifically attributed to Bennington should use that name. The following listings will include mainly wares featuring the dark brown mottled glaze produced at various sites here and abroad.

Loving cup, large cylindrical form on a molded base w/large C-form branch handle on each side, one side relief-molded w/a drinking scene, the other side w/a dog fight, molded vintage rim band, overall dark brown mottled glaze, 6 7/8" h. (bottom rim chips)......................... **$248**

Model of a bull, overall mottled brown glaze, 19th c., 16" l., 12 5/8" h. (minor losses, restoration) **7,475**

Rockingham-glazed Dog

Rockingham Lion

Model of a dog, seated Spaniel
facing viewer, on a thick oblong
base, free-standing front legs,
molded deer & hounds around the
base mottled dark brown glaze,
19th c., 10 1/2" h.   399

Model of a dog, seated on thick
irregular-shaped base,
freestanding front legs, mottled
dark brown glaze, wear on nose,
hairlines in front legs & small chips
on base, 10 3/4" h. (ILLUS.)   330

Model of a lion, recumbent animal
w/curly mane, on rectangular
stepped base, mottled dark brown
glaze, minor chips on base,
9 3/8" l. (ILLUS.)   880

Mugs, mottled brown & cream,
ca. 1890, 3 1/2" d., 4 1/4" h., set of
6   200

Pitcher, 9 1/2" h., footed bulbous
body w/arched spout & C-form
handle, mottled brown glaze
w/detailed relief-molded vintage &
foliage pinwheels (small chips on
spout)   413

Pitcher, 9 5/8" h., bulbous ovoid
body tapering to slightly flaring rim,
pinched spout, relief-molded
hanging game, mottled brown
glaze, figural hound handle   275

Pitcher, 10" h., gourd-form w/arched
rim spout & scrolled handle,
swirled alternate rib pattern, overall
mottled brown Rockingham glaze,
chip on base caused by stilt   504

Rockingham Teapot

Snuff jar, figural, Mr. Toby, mottled
dark brown glaze, 19th c., 4 1/8" h.
(minor glaze wear on rim)   374

Teapot, cov., footed ovoid body
w/swan's-neck spout & C-form
handle, domed cover w/bud-form
finial, mottled brown glaze w/relief-
molded scene of Rebecca at the
well, early 20th c., Ohio, 8 1/2" h.
(ILLUS.)   200

SLIPWARE

*This term refers to ceramics, primarily
redware, decorated by the application of slip,
or semi-liquid paste made of clay. Such wares
were made for decades in England and Germany and elsewhere on the Continent, and in
the Pennsylvania Dutch country and elsewhere in the United States. Today, contem-*

*Slip-Decorated Redware
Bread Tray*

porary copies of early Slipware items are featured in numerous decorator magazines and offered for sale in gift catalogs.

Bowl, 6 3/4" d., 3" h., redware, wide shallow sides w/molded edge, a band of white slip squiggle design below rim, mottled greenish glaze w/brown flecks & amber spots....... **$275**

Bowl, 14 3/4" d., 3 1/2" h., shallow, squiggly white slip decoration on dark brown glaze (wear & old edge chips)... **1,980**

Bread tray, redware, glazed oblong dish w/notched rim, decorated w/abstract patterns in yellow slip, 19th c., 11 1/2 x 18 1/2" (ILLUS.) **2,070**

Charger, redware, coggle wheel rim w/yellow slip squiggles & inscription "Pony up the Cash," attributed to Day Pottery, Norwalk, Connecticut, 14" d. (wear, hairline & old rim chips).......................... **18,700**

Dish, redware w/coggled rim, wavy lines of yellow slip w/brown & green, 6 1/2" d. (wear & surface chips)... **413**

Loaf dish, redware, rectangular w/coggle wheel rim, yellow three-quill slip decoration, 14" l. (some glaze flaking & edge chips) **715**

Loaf dish, redware, rectangular w/coggle wheel rim, yellow four-quill zigzag slip decoration in center & on each side, 14 1/4" l. (wear, glaze flakes & chips) **770**

Mold, food, Turk's turban-style, orange ground w/dark brown splotches & flecks & yellow slip rim, 9" d., 3" h. (wear & small chips)... **330**

Pie plate, w/coggled rim, three-line yellow slip decoration w/green, 7 7/8" d. (minor wear & small chip) **550**

Pie plate, w/coggled rim, yellow slip decoration highlighted in brown & green on greyish amber ground, 7 7/8" d. (wear)............................ **550**

Pie plate, redware, circular w/coggle wheel rim, three-line yellow slip decoration, 8" d. (wear, surface flakes & hairline) **385**

Pie plate, redware w/coggled rim w/three-line slip decoration, 8" d. (wear, hairline & small rim chips)... **605**

Pie plate, redware w/coggled rim, dark brown & green flecked glaze w/white slip wavy lines, attributed to Stahl Pottery, Powder Valley, Lehigh County, Pennsylvania, 8 3/8" d. (minor glaze flakes on rim) **550**

Pie plate, redware w/coggled rim, three-line yellow slip decoration, 9" d. (minor wear & old edge chips, short edge hairline)........................ **385**

Pie plate, circular, w/coggle wheel rim, redware w/wavy three-line yellow slip decoration, 9 3/4" d. (cracked) **385**

Pie plate, redware w/coggled rim, decorated w/large yellow slip bird on branch, 10" d. (wear & hairlines) **3,410**

Pie plate, w/coggled rim, yellow slip Seaweed design on blue glaze, 10 1/2" d. (minor wear, edge chips & short hairlines) **1,623**

Pie plate, redware w/coggled rim, three-line yellow slip decoration, 11" d. (wear & rim chips) **330**

Pie plate, redware w/coggle wheel rim, yellow slip flourish decoration, 12" d. (slip worn & flaked)............. **880**

Plate, 11 1/2" d., redware w/crimped rim & inscribed "Lafayette" in yellow slip w/yellow slip scrolls above & below inscription, 19th c., Pennsylvania (ILLUS.).................. **6,900**

SPATTERWARE

This ceramic ware takes its name from the "spattered" decoration, in various colors, generally used to trim pieces hand-painted with rustic center designs of flowers, birds, houses, etc. Popular in the early 19th century, most was imported from England.

Related wares, called "stick spatter," had free-hand designs applied with pieces of cut sponge attached to sticks, hence the name.

Examples date from the 19th and early 20th century and were produced in England, Europe and America.

Some early spatter-decorated wares were marked by the manufacturers, but not many. 20th century reproductions are also sometimes marked, including those produced by Boleslaw Cybis.

Creamer, bulbous body w/C-form handle & arched spout, Rose patt., free-hand flower in red, green & black in center w/blue spatter ground, 3 5/8" h. (stains flakes on table ring & chips on rim)............... **$303**

Spatterware Creamer

Creamer, bulbous body w/C-form handle & pinched spout, Peafowl patt., free-hand bird in blue, yellow & black, overall strawberry or thumbprint red, green & blue spatter, professional repair, 4" h. (ILLUS.) **5,170**

Creamer, bulbous body w/C-form handle & arched spout, Rooster

patt., free-hand bird in yellow ochre, red, blue & black, blue border, professional repair, 4 1/2" h. (ILLUS. right).................. **880**

Creamer, footed bulbous paneled body w/scrolled C-form handle & high arched spout, Peafowl patt., free-hand red, blue, green & black bird w/red spatter, 5 1/2" h. **1,375**

Creamer, footed paneled bulbous body w/arched spout & angled C-form handle, Clipper Ship patt., free-hand ship in green, red & black , blue spatter border, 5 5/8" h. (ILLUS. left) **4,840**

Cup, handleless, free-hand Gooney bird in blue, teal green, red & black, blue spatter ground (flakes on table ring) **220**

Cup & saucer, handleless, Dove patt., free-hand bird in yellow ochre, blue, green & black, blue spatter border (ILLUS.)................. **2,750**

Cup & saucer, handleless, Forget-Me-Not patt., free-hand flower in blue, red, green & black, blue spatter border in shape of six-point star on saucer, impressed anchor mark on saucer (ILLUS. bottom row, right) **3,190**

Cup & saucer, handleless, Fort patt., free-hand fort in green, black & red, blue spatter border (ILLUS. top row, center) **660**

Cup & saucer, handleless, Peacock patt., free-hand bird in yellow, blue, green, red & black, overall light

Various Spatterware Items

green spatter (ILLUS. top row, right) **1,650**

Spatterware Cup & Saucer

Cup & saucer, handleless, Peacock patt., free-hand bird in yellow, blue, green, red & black, overall lilac spatter (ILLUS. top row, left) **2,310**

Cup & saucer, handleless, Peafowl patt., free-hand red, blue, yellow & black bird w/red spatter border (minor roughness & small flakes w/chips on table rings).................. **413**

Cup & saucer, handleless, Peafowl patt., free-hand red, blue, yellow & black bird w/blue spatter border (minor edge flakes)........................ **605**

Cup & saucer, handleless, Rooster patt., free-hand blue, red, yellow & black bird on an overall blue spatter ground (ILLUS. bottom row, left) **974**

Cup & saucer, handleless, Schoolhouse patt., red, green & black, blue spatter border, scalloped border on cup, chips on saucer table ring, repair to cup (ILLUS. bottom row, center) **990**

Cup & saucer, handleless, miniature, Fort patt., green, black & red, blue spatter border **187**

Cup & saucer, handleless, miniature, Fort patt., in black, red, yellow & green, blue spatter border (minor edge wear) **550**

Pitcher, water, 10 5/8" h., tall tapering paneled body w/high arched spout & D-form handle, overall light blue spatter on white ground (chips & hairline on spout). **220**

Plate, 7 3/4" d., Peafowl patt., free-hand red, green, blue & black bird, red spatter border **839**

Plate, 8 1/4" d., Peafowl patt., blue, yellow, red & black w/purple spatter over bird's head & border (blue on breast flaked)................... **440**

Plate, 8 1/4" d., Rose patt. w/flower in red, blue, teal green & black, blue spatter ground **330**

Platter, 14 1/4" l., octagonal, w/blue transfer-printed eagle w/shield in center, blue spatter border (minor stains & faint hairlines) **880**

Sugar bowl, cov., Rooster patt., free-hand bird in yellow, blue, red & black, blue spatter border,

Spatterware Handleless Cups & Saucers

professional repair, 4 1/4" h.
(ILLUS. center with creamers)....... **880**

Teapot, cov., Gothic style paneled
design w/angled handle, swan's-
neck spout & domed cover
w/blossom finial, Peafowl patt.,
free-hand blue, yellow, green &
black bird w/red spatter ground,
7 1/8" h. (stains & small flakes, lid
w/old edge repair)......................... **880**

Teapot, cov., Gothic style paneled
tapering body w/angled handle,
swan's neck spout & domed cover
w/blossom finial, overall blue
spatter on white, 9 1/2" h. (chips) **341**

Waste bowl, Fort patt. in red, green,
black & yellow, blue spatter border,
5 3/8" d., 3 1/8" h. (wear & stains
w/pinpoint edge flakes)................ **1,155**

STICK & CUT SPONGE

Stick Spatter Shallow Bowl

Bowl, 14 1/2" d., 3" h., border
decorated w/stick spatter floral
design in red, blue, green, yellow &
purple, marked "Maastricht"
(ILLUS.) **88**

Plate, 8 3/4" d., ironstone w/blue
design stick spatter border &
purple transfer-printed eagle
w/shield, English registry mark
w/"Gem, R. Hammersley"............. **165**

Plate, 9 1/2" d., Rabbit patt., black
transfer-printed border band w/six

rabbits & three frogs trimmed in
yellow & green, free-hand
decorated center w/ring of cut-
sponge flowers & red striping **633**

Gaudy Stick Spatter Chop Plate

Plate, chop, 16 1/4" d., decorated
w/free-hand blue flowers & red &
green cut-sponge blossoms &
leaves, "Villeroy & Boch" (ILLUS.) **413**

Wash bowl & pitcher, 10 3/4" h.
pitcher, ovoid body w/arched spout
& C-form handle, center design of
large stylized four-petal flower in
red & green, overall blue sponging,
12 5/8" d. bowl w/same center
design & bordered by blue
sponging, the set (chip on back
edge of bowl rim)......................... **1,375**

SPONGEWARE

*Spongeware's designs were spattered,
sponged or daubed on in colors, sometimes
with a piece of cloth. Blue on white was the
most common type, but mottled tans, browns
and greens on yellowware were also popular.
Spongeware generally has an overall pattern
with a coarser look than Spatterwares, to
which it is loosely related. These wares were
extensively produced in England and America
well into the 20th century.*

Bank, figural pig, teal green & tan
sponging on cream ground, glaze
wear on ears & shallow flake on
one foot, 6" l. (ILLUS.) **$275**

Spongeware Pig Bank

Spongeware Mixing Bowl

Bean pot, bulbous flat-bottomed body tapering to a flat mouth, small loop handle at shoulder, wide spiral bands of blue sponging on white, marked "3 qt.," 6 1/2" h. (lid missing) 165

Bowl, 3 1/4" d., cov., miniature, flaring sides w/domed cover & button finial, wire bail w/wooden handle, blue sponging on white (hairline & chips)............................ 468

Bowl, 10 1/4" d., 5" h., blue & white w/two blue accent bands, ca. 1880, (two minor exterior rim chips) 143

Butter crock, low wide cylindrical form w/molded rim, blue on white w/blue printed "Butter" on front, 9" d., 6" h. 303

Jar, bulbous ovoid body tapering slightly to flared rim, blue on white, 4 1/4" h. (pinpoint rim flakes)......... 798

Jar, cov., ovoid w/molded rim, brown, blue & green sponging on white w/black transfer-printed label reading "Spaulding's Pure Fresh Cookies," 9 1/4" h. (chip on bottom edge) 220

Jug, semi-ovoid body w/wire bail & wooden handle, labeled "Grandmother's Maple Syrup of 50 Years Ago" & "Mfg'd by F.H. Weeks, Akron, O" on bottom, blue sponging on white, 8" h. (chips) .. 1,375

Mixing bowl, footed, deep slightly flared sides, blue sponging on white, 10" d., 5" h. (glaze wear on rim & internal hairline) 220

Mixing bowl, footed, deep flaring sides, bold repeating bands of blue

sponging on white at base & below rim w/blue strips around center, chips on foot, 11 1/4" d., 5" h. (ILLUS.) 275

Mug, cylindrical w/molded C-form handle, blue sponging on white, 3 5/8" h. (slight crow's foot in bottom) 138

Pitcher, 6" h., ovoid body w/C-form handle & pinched spout, blue on white w/brown slip interior (chips on lip & wear) 330

Pitcher, 6 1/2" h., cylindrical w/rim spout & D-form handle, olive green & white w/blue edge band (shallow chip on base)................................ 275

Pitcher, 6 3/4" h., cylindrical w/D-form handle, blue sponging on white w/center horizontal stripe (minor flake on table ring).............. 605

Blue & White Spongeware Pitcher

Pitcher, 6 7/8" h., slightly tapering cylindrical body w/rim spout & D-form handle, yellowware w/sponging in brown, green & black (wear & minor chips) 165

Pitcher, 7" h., blue & white, ca. 1880, few minor glaze flecks at interior rim (ILLUS.) 330

Pitcher, 7 1/4" h., footed bulbous nearly spherical body tapering to a wide flat flaring neck, thick C-scroll handle, overall heavy blue sponging w/a wide blue band around the bottom flanked by two white bands & two thin blue bands (small chips, hairlines) 330

Pitcher, 9" h., tall slightly tapering cylindrical body w/pinched spout & C-form handle, relief-molded rose decoration, blue sponging on white 495

Blue & White Bulbous Water Pitcher

Pitcher, 12" h., water, bulbous, blue & white w/three blue accent bands, ca. 1880, one minor glaze fleck at spout (ILLUS.) 358

Plates, 9" d. w/flanged scalloped rim, yellowware w/overall fine brown sponging, England, late 18th - early 19th c., pr. (rim chips, one w/rim repair) 440

Pot, cylindrical w/pouring spout, wire bail & wooden handle, blue on white, 5 1/4" d., 4" h. (small rim chips) 385

Ramekins/custard cups, blue on white, 3 1/4" d., 2 1/4" h. set of 6 (pieces are similar) 385

Soap dish, rectangular w/rounded corners, blue w/a bit of red sponging on white, 4 x 6 1/2" (small chips) 72

Teapot, cov., miniature, squatty bulbous body w/C-form handle, swan's-neck spout & inset cover w/blossom finial, blue on white, 4 1/8" h. (minor chips) 853

STAFFORDSHIRE FIGURES

Small figures and groups made of pottery were produced by the majority of the Staffordshire, England potters in the 19th century and were used as mantel decorations or "chimney ornaments," as they were sometimes called. Pairs of dogs were favorites and were turned out by the carload, and 19th century pieces are still available. Well-painted reproductions also abound and collectors are urged to exercise caution before investing.

Cat, seated upright animal playing a bass viol, polychrome trim & spotted fur, 19th c., 4" h. (some minor glaze wear) $86

Staffordshire Spaniel Figure

Dog, pearlware, hollow-molded, stylized creature w/head turned to the right & painted w/random patches of brown, blue & ocher, lying on a domed naturalistic base, ca. 1790-1810, 4 1/8" h. (hair crack to hind quarters) **460**

Dog, Spaniel in seated position, molded fur & chain, large copper lustre spots & trim w/painted facial details, embossed numbers on bottom, 19th c., 10" h. (ILLUS.) **225**

Staffordshire Figure of Pug

Dogs, Pug in seated position w/ears erect, yellow eyes, black & red painted facial details, wearing black collar w/gilt padlock, second half 19th c., 10 1/4" h., pr. (ILLUS. of one) **1,265**

Dogs, Spaniel seated on his haunches, looking to his right & left respectively & wearing a collar w/lock, glazed in white w/gilt highlights, w/black & pink face markings, mounted as table lamps, late 19th c., 12 1/2" h., pr. (one glass eye missing) **402**

Dogs, Whippets in standing position, each w/a rabbit in its mouth, painted in beige & red, 19th c., 11" h., pr. (minor chips) **748**

Figure group, Scottish couple standing on oval base, polychrome trim, 19th c., 7 7/8" h. (very minor chip & losses) **230**

Figure group, 'The Death of Nelson,' showing the dying admiral seated between two officers, the back modeled as his ship the Victory, polychrome decoration, rectangular base, mid-19th c. **518**

Figure of a hunter, standing on a rounded base, polychrome decoration, 19th c., 7 1/8" h. (restoration to gun) **173**

Figure of a lute player, standing on a rounded base, polychrome decoration, 19th c., 5 1/8" h. (restoration to lute, very minor chip) **115**

Figure of Dan O'Connell, minister wearing a green scarf & black coat w/gilt trim, standing beside a column covered w/blue & orange drape on a grassy oval base w/gilt title, ca. 1900, 17 1/2" h. **575**

Staffordshire Pearlware Figure of Hercules

Figure of Hercules, pearlware, muscular bearded male wearing red, yellow & black loin cloth, resting on one knee on a black marbled square base w/his head lowered as he supports a pierced pale yellow globe representing the world on his shoulders, early 19th c., possibly by Obadiah Sherrat, minute chips, 11 3/8" h. (ILLUS.) **575**

Figure of "The Lion Slayer,"
standing bearded man wearing a
Scottish kilt & feathered hat, a
dead lion beside him, polychrome
trim, 19th c., 15 3/4" h. (some worn
gilt)...................................... **220**

Horses, modeled w/right or left front
leg raised & looking straight ahead,
supported on an oval bright green
base, the animals in cream w/black
spots, mane & facial markings,
mid-19th c., 5 1/4" l., pr. **1,035**

STAFFORDSHIRE TRANSFER WARES

*The process of transfer-printing designs
on earthenwares developed in England in the
late 18th century and by the mid-19th century
most common ceramic wares were decorated
in this manner, most often with romantic
European or Oriental landscape scenes, animals or flowers. The earliest such wares were
printed in dark blue but a little later light blue,
pink, purple, red, black, green and brown
were used. A majority of these wares were
produced at various English potteries right
up till the turn of the century but French and
other European firms also made similar
pieces and all are quite collectible. The best
reference on this area is Petra Williams' book
Staffordshire Romantic Transfer Patterns -
Cup Plates and Early Victorian China (Fountain House East, 1978).*

Early Dark Blue Transfer Coffeepot

Coffeepot, cov., footed bulbous
baluster-form body w/domed
cover, long angled handle &
swan's-neck spout, overall design
of large roses & other flowers, dark
blue, small chips, ca. 1830, 11" h.
(ILLUS.)...................................... **$825**

Coffeepot, cov., footed bulbous
ovoid body w/ringed & waisted
neck w/molded rim & inset domed
cover w/knob finial, swan's-neck
spout & C-scroll handle, dark blue
transfer of an English farmyard
scene, ca. 1830, 11 1/4" h. (chips,
spider crack, finial reglued) **523**

Cup & saucer, handleless, dark blue
transfer of a boy fishing w/an
English country house in the
background, ca. 1830 (chip on
foot)... **165**

Cup & saucer, handleless, scene of
horse-drawn sleigh, dark blue,
ca. 1830 (some edge glaze flakes) **275**

Gravy boat, Winter patt., pink, 6" l. . **55**

Loving cup, wide cylindrical body
w/three loop handles, black
transfer-printed medallions
trimmed in polychrome, one titled
"Autumn," one w/the farmer's arms
& the third w/"Industry Produceth
Wealth," early 19th c., 6" h. (stains,
light crazing, spider crack in
bottom).. **220**

Pitcher, 7 1/2" h., bulbous ovoid
body w/a shoulder tapering to a
short wide flaring cupped neck
w/high arched rim spout, C-scroll
handle, decorated w/haying
scenes, green, impressed
"Adams," ca. 1840 .... **385**

Plate, 6" d., Palestine patt., pink **33**

Plate, 8" d., Canova patt., pink, T.
Mayer **50**

Plate, 8" d., Carolina patt., purple, R.
Hall **22**

Plate, 8 1/4" d., Palestine patt., pink . **39**

Plate, 8 1/2" d., Asiatic View patt.,
pink, marked "FD" **28**

Plate, 9" d., Asiatic Scenery patt.,
pink, marked "Jacksons" **50**

Plate, 9" d., Lozere patt., light blue,
Challinor **44**

Plate, 9 1/4" d., Canova patt., pink, T.
Mayer **66**

Plate, 9 1/2" d., Greek Statue patt., black 44

Plate, 10" d., California patt., light blue, J. Wedgwood 83

Plate, 10" d., Italy patt., light blue, marked "C.M. & S" 39

Plate, 10" d., lightly scalloped flanged rim, the center w/a black transfer scene of Victorian men & women riding safety-style bicycles, titled around scene "Les Sports No. 11 - Bicyclettes," dark blue floral & stem band border trim, back marked "Terre de Fer France," ca. 1900 44

Plates, 7 1/2" d., Tyrolean patt., pink, WR & Co., pr. 66

Platter, 11 5/8" l., oval, floral border w/fruit center, dark blue (light crazing, surface flake) 495

Platter, 12 3/4" l., oval, floral border w/central scene of East Indian scenery w/elephant, dark blue, impressed "Rogers," ca. 1830 (pinpoint edge flakes) 385

Platter, 14 5/8" l., oval, scrolling foliate border w/reserves of manor houses, a center reserve of game birds, dark blue, ca. 1840 (very minor rim chips & knife marks) 633

Platter, 15 1/2" l., two-color decorated, red floral border w/blue central reserve depicting a rural scene of an early train crossing an aqueduct w/a hillside village in the distance, England, late 19th c. (glaze crazing) 374

Early Staffordshire Platter

Platter, 16 1/2" l., oval, scrolling foliate border w/reserves of manor houses, a center reserve of game birds, dark blue, ca. 1840, wear & crazing (ILLUS.) 935

Platter, 17 1/2" l., oval, medium blue transfer-printed center scene of fleet of ships, wide border decorated w/shells & seaweed, John Rogers & Sons (wear & scratches, small rim chips) 1,650

Platter, 17 1/2" l., Wild Rose patt., light blue (wear & minor stains, surface flakes on back) 275

Platter, 16 1/4 x 19", decorated w/central reserve depicting an American eagle carrying a patriotic banner in flight above a distant group of sailing vessels w/rays of the rising sun in the background, scrolled foliate border, teal green, England, mid-19th c. (minor staining, glaze wear) 460

Platter, 20 1/2" l., oval, center reserve w/fruits, wide floral border, dark blue, impressed "Stubbs" (wear w/stains & scratches) 1,430

Platter, 22" l., Chinese Views patt., light blue, R & W 83

Shaving mug, Asiatic Scenery patt., light blue, 3" h. 55

Undertray, round, Italian Flower Garden patt., embossed rim & handles, 9" d. 77

STONEWARE

Stoneware is essentially a vitreous pottery, impervious to water even in its unglazed state, that has been produced by potteries all over the world for centuries. Utilitarian wares such as crocks, jugs, churns and the like, were the most common productions in the numerous potteries that sprang into existence in the United States during the 19th century. These items were often enhanced by the application of a cobalt blue oxide decoration. In addition to the coarse, primarily saltglazed stonewares, there are other categories of stoneware known by such special names as basalt, jasper and others.

Batter pail, w/bail handle, unusual cobalt blue slip-quilled tree stump design, "6" in blue script, probably Whites Utica, unsigned, ca. 1860, 6 qt., 11 3/4" h. (chips at spout & two through lines extending from rim) **$660**

Betty lamp stand, waisted cylinder w/flared foot & rim, dark greenish brown glaze, attributed to Zanesville, 3 1/2" h. (minor chips & one large chip on lip) **138**

Bottle, cylindrical body w/a conical shoulder tapering to a swelled lip w/cobalt blue trim, impressed mark "F. Gleason - 1853," 9 5/8" h. **193**

Bottle, cylindrical body w/narrow shoulder tapering to wide, slightly flared neck, brown pebble glaze w/embossed eagle, impressed label "Vitreous Stove Bottle...American Bottle Co. Middlebury, O.," lime coated interior, 5 1/4" h. **165**

Bottle, dark brown Albany slip w/matte finish, impressed label "S. Routson, Wooster, O.," 9 1/8" h. .. **605**

Bowl, ovoid w/molded rim & eared handles, brushed cobalt blue plume design front & back, blue accents on ears, attributed to Hudson Valley region of NY, ca. 1840, 3 gal., 11" h. (professional restoration to age cracks throughout & just touching the blue, some interior lime staining) **275**

Butter churn, w/eared handles, thick brushed cobalt blue paddletail design, "N.A. White & Son, Utica, NY," ca. 1885, 5 gal., 16 1/2" h. (thick blue w/silvery black cast, in making & minor surface chip at rim) **1,705**

Butter churn, swelled cylindrical form w/eared handles & short cylindrical neck, cobalt blue stenciled decorated bands curved down around the front above the label "A.P. Donagho, Parkersbug, W. Va.," late 19th c., 17 1/2" h....... **303**

Butter churn, swelled cylindrical form, slip-quilled cobalt blue top to bottom double flower, double "6"

Butter Churn w/Double Flower Design

gal. designation in blue slip-quill, includes original dasher guide, "A.O. Wittemore Havana, NY," ca. 1870, through line on back extending from rim & small line at right ear, 18" h. (ILLUS.)............... **2,750**

Butter churn, ovoid body tapering to a cylindrical neck w/molded rim & flanked by eared handles, slip-quilled cobalt blue large scrolling foliate cluster at the front, Worcester, Massachusetts, 19th c., 5 gal., 18 1/4" h. (minor chips, hairlines) **460**

Butter crock, cylindrical w/molded rim, cobalt blue stenciled label "Hamilton & Jones, Greensboro, Pa.," 6 3/8" d., 5" h. (chips) **303**

Five Gallon Cake Crock w/Dog

Cake crock, cov., cylindrical, slip-quilled cobalt blue large standing dog amid extensive ground cover, rare form & design, "West Troy Pottery," 5 gal., ca. 1880, short tight line on back & few minor interior surface chip, 13" d.,12" h. (ILLUS.) **2,750**

Crock, cylindrical w/molded rim, cobalt blue stenciled label arched at the top "Thomas Medford - Stoves - Queensware - etc. - Huntington, W. Va.," free-hand blue squiggle band at top & plain band around base, late 19th c., 8 1/4" d., 6 3/4" h. **440**

Crock, cylindrical w/molded rim & applied eared handles, slip-quilled cobalt blue stylized floral design & impressed label "Underwood & Tenney, Orange, Mass 2.," 9 1/2" h. (stains & chips) **275**

Crock, cylindrical w/molded rim & eared handles, slip-quilled cobalt blue single flower design w/signature & "2" designation inside flower, unusual, ca. 1870, "C.W. Braun, Buffalo, NY," 2 gal., 9 1/2" h. (line up from base on side & a few minor chips) **132**

Crock, ovoid w/applied & open handles, impressed & tooled design around rim, incised & blue accented double scalloped design in front, blue accents at name & handles, "S. Amboy, New Jersey," ca. 1805, almost invisible through line in front, 9 1/2" h. **2,530**

Crock, cylindrical w/molded rim & eared handles, unsigned, brushed blue swan design, ca. 1870, attributed to Pottery Works, Little West 12th St., NY, 1 gal., 7 1/2" h. (ILLUS.) **1,045**

Crock, w/molded rim & eared handles, brushed cobalt blue floral spray top to bottom, "F.B. Norton, Worcester, Mass," ca. 1870, 1 gal., 7 1/2" h (very minor design fry & stone ping on back) **198**

Crock, w/molded rim & eared handles, tornado design, "Ottman Bros. & Co., Fort Edward, NY," ca. 1870, 1 gal., 7 1/2" h. **330**

Crock, ovoid w/molded rim, blue accent stripes & gallon designation in blue brush strokes, "R.T. Williams, New Geneva, PA," ca. 1860, 1 1/2 gal., 9" h. **303**

Crock, cylindrical w/molded rim & eared handles, brushed cobalt blue flower design, "A.O. Whittemore, Havana, NY," ca. 1870, 2 gal., 8 1/2" h. (kiln burn/stack mark at base in making) **165**

Crock, w/molded rim & eared handles, simple slip-quilled flower design & "2", "Geddes, NY," ca. 1860, 2 gal., 9" h. (rim chip & short through line on back, some design fry)..................................... **143**

Cylindrical Crock w/Swan Design

"S. Hart Fulton" Crock

Crock, cylindrical w/molded rim & eared handles, slip-quilled cobalt blue chicken pecking corn on ground cover, chicken heading downhill, "New York Stoneware Co., Fort Edward, NY," ca. 1880, 2 gal., 9 1/2" h. **1,210**

Crock, cylindrical w/molded rim & eared handles, slip-quilled cobalt blue decoration of a traveler viewing a direction sign reading "11 miles to Hartford," marked by Seymour Bosworth, Hartford, Connecticut, 3 gal., 10" h. (chips, prefiring dent) **690**

Crock, cylindrical w/molded rim & eared handles, slip-quilled cobalt blue bird & stylized "3" design, "S. Hart Fulton," ca. 1877, glaze spider on back, 3 gal., 10 1/2" h. (ILLUS) **578**

Crock, cylindrical w/eared handles, brushed flower decoration w/signature, very early, ca. 1850, short lived Buffalo maker, "P. Mugler & Co., Buffalo, NY," 3 gal., 11" h. (one very minor surface chip at base) **330**

"N. Clark & Co., Mt. Morris" Crock

Crock, ovoid w/eared handles, brushed "3" & accent plume design, very uncommon maker, "N. Clark & Co., Mt. Morris," ca. 1840, few minor rim chips & minor interior

lime staining, 3 gal., 12 1/2" h. (ILLUS.) **303**

Crock, cylindrical w/molded rim & eared handles, thick brushed cobalt blue hops vine design, "J. Fisher & Co., Lyons, NY," ca. 1880, 4 gal., 11 1/2" h.............. **440**

Crock, cylindrical w/eared handles & slip-quilled cluster of grapes framed w/large leaves & vine, uncommon size for this potter, "W.A. MacQuoid & Co., Pottery Works Little West St., NY," ca. 1865, 5 gal., 12" h. (hairline at ear on right side) **1,320**

Crock, cylindrical w/molded rim & eared handles, slip-quilled cobalt blue large bird on plume design, "Reidinger & Caire, Pokeepsie, NY," ca. 1870, 5 gal., 12" h. **908**

Inkwell, figural bust of old woman wearing bonnet, tan glaze w/brown highlights, 2 1/4" h. (wear & small chips).. **275**

Jar, cov., swelled cylindrical form w/eared handles, unique cobalt blue eyedropper application to form petals on this flower design, "Clark & Co., Rochester, NY," ca. 1850, 1 gal., 9 1/2" h. (rim chip in front) **413**

Jar, ovoid body w/thick molded rim & applied eared handles, cobalt blue slip-quilled polka dot bird looking backwards, impressed label "W. Roberts, Binghamton, N.Y. 2," 9 1/2" h. **688**

Jar, semi-ovoid body w/applied shoulder handles, cobalt blue brushed floral design w/tulip on one side & flowering tree on the other, impressed "S. Bell 1/1/2," 10 1/4" h. (chips) **1,210**

Jar, cov., swelled cylindrical form w/eared handles, slip-quilled cobalt blue dancing flower design, "John Burger, Rochester," ca. 1865, 2 gal., 11" h. (stone ping on back) ... **468**

Jar, cov., eared handles, large signature design bird on plume, heavy cobalt blue w/filled body & leaves, "F.B. Norton & Co., Worcester, Mass," ca. 1870, 2 gal.,

11 1/2" h. (some design fry to thick blue) **1,100**

Jar, semi-ovoid w/molded rim & eared handles, cobalt blue stenciled label "Knox, Haught & Co., Shinnston, W.Va." above leafy sprig w/further free-hand blue leafy bands around the top & "3" at the bottom, late 19th c., 3 gal., 12 3/4" h. **1,018**

Jar, slightly ovoid w/heavy molded rim & applied eared handles, stenciled cobalt blue front label for "Williams & Reppert, Greensboro, Pa." above a free-hand "3," free-hand blue bands at top & base, late 19th c., 3 gal., 14" h. (rim chips) **248**

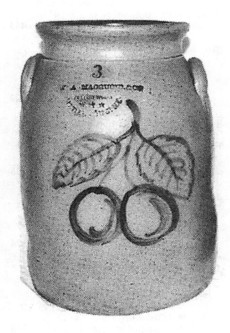

Three Gallon Jar w/Brushed Cherries

Jar, swelled cylindrical form w/eared handles, brushed cobalt blue cherries w/two large leaves & stem design & "3," marked "W.A. MacQuoid & Co. Pottery Works Little W. 12th St. NY," ca. 1870, age spiders on back, 3 gal., 14" h. (ILLUS.) **1,375**

Jar, swelled cylindrical form w/eared shoulder handles, cobalt blue brushed stylized tulip & impressed "T. Reed 3," Tuscarawas County, 14" h. (wear, short hairline & surface chips) **605**

Jar, swelled cylindrical body w/heavy molded rim & eared handles, lengthy cobalt blue stenciled label "H.L. Van Matre & Co....Manu'fd by T.P. Reppert, Greensboro, Pa." below a large free-hand "3" near the rim, late 19th c., 3 gal., 14 1/4" h. **633**

Jar, cov., eared handles, unsigned, advertising, slip-quilled w/large dotted bird on top of flower, long tail & filled wing, "Impressed Hiram Partridge & Son, #8 Court St. Indigo Paste," attributed to Crafts Factory, Whatley, Mass., ca. 1860, 4 gal., 15 1/2" h. (professional restorations to two tight lines extending from rim) **798**

Jug, miniature unglazed handled form w/Albany slip interior, pencil or pen scribed on base but difficult to make out, ca. 1870, 3" h............ **72**

Jug, unsigned, highly decorated, extremely rare, NYS origin, ca. 1870, 1 pt., 7 1/4" h. (overglazing in making) **770**

Jug, bold ovoid body tapering to a small short tooled neck, applied strap shoulder handle, impressed label "Charlestown," grey salt glaze w/olive bands, early 19th c., 10 1/4" h. (minor edge chips on base, surface chips) **220**

Jug, semi-ovoid w/blue slip-quilled cobalt blue inscription "S.F. Eagan 141 Seneca St. Buffalo N.Y.," J. Fisher, Lyons, NY, ca. 1880, 1 gal., 10 1/2" h. (glaze drip in front in making & large rust color stain on back) **132**

Jug, ovoid w/brushed flower design & very deeply incised w/double snake design, extremely rare, whimsical, "H. & G. Nash, Utica, NY," ca. 1835, 1 gal., 11" h. (minor glaze spider on back) **1,000**

Jug, semi-ovoid, brushed cobalt blue stylized floral design, 11 1/2" h. **468**

Jug, semi-ovoid w/"All Right" blue slip-quilled, ca. 1880, 1 gal., 11 1/2" h., unsigned, (quarter size base chip on side, kiln burns & dry glaze in making, glaze separation lines in handles & at base in back)   330

Jug, ovoid w/brushed decoration, "D. Roberts & Co., Utica," ca. 1828, 2 gal., 12" h. (overall staining & glaze spiders at spout)   330

Jug, ovoid w/brushed cobalt blue flower design, "N. White Utica," ca. 1840, 2 gal.,13" h. (glaze burn & stack marks in making)   275

Jug, ovoid w/faint blue brushed flower design & blue accent at name, early mark, "S. Blair, Cortland," ca. 1830, 2 gal., 13" h. (over glazing & clay discoloration in making)   176

Jug, bulbous ovoid body w/strap handle, incised figure of woman w/cross-hatched dress & chair, 13 1/2" h.   358

Jug w/Incised Cherries

Jug, ovoid w/incised leaves & blue accented cluster of cherries, blue accents at handle, rare, New York City origin, ca. 1820, unsigned, stack mark/kiln burn in making, 2 gal., 13 1/2" h. (ILLUS.)   880

Jug, semi-ovoid, slip-quilled cobalt blue "2" & "Lyons", marked "J. Fisher, Lyons, NY," ca. 1880, 2 gal., 13 1/2" h. (surface chip at spout)   715

Jug, semi-ovoid w/cobalt blue signature sunflower design, well-proportioned, "John Burger, Rochester," ca. 1865, 2 gal., 13 1/2" h. (very tight spider line on side)   908

Jug, semi-ovoid, w/slip-quilled ribbed & dotted flower design, very uncommon maker's mark, "E. Selby & Co., Hudson, NY," ca. 1850, 13 1/2" h. (some minor staining)   275

Jug, bulbous ovoid body w/applied strap handle, cobalt blue brushed foliage decoration, impressed label "G. Heiser, Buffalo, N.Y. 2.," 14" h. (stains & minor chips on base)   440

Jug, semi-ovoid w/brushed cobalt blue hops design, blue accents at handles, "Cowden & Wilcox, Harrisburg," ca. 1870, 3 gal., 14" h. (small spider on side in making)   220

Jug, semi-ovoid w/cobalt blue slip-quilled bird on foliage, scrolls, impressed "Lack & Van Arsdale, Cornwall, C-2," 14" h. (minor chips, stains)   385

Jug, ovoid, impressed w/a spread-winged eagle atop a cannon & "Charlestown," Charlestown, Massachusetts, 19th c., 14 1/2" h. (chips, kiln burns)   374

Jug, semi-ovoid w/small molded mouth & applied handle, cobalt blue brushed floral design & impressed label "Cowden & Wilcox, Harrisburg Pa 3," 3 gal., 14 3/4" h. (minor lip chips)   275

Jug, semi-ovoid w/small molded mouth & applied strap handle, cobalt blue brushed floral design & impressed label "Taunton, Mass. 2," 14 3/4" h.   220

Jug, ovoid, brushed light blue plume design, "T. Harrington, Lyons," ca. 1860, 2 gal., 15" h.   157

Jug, semi-ovoid w/thick blue slip-quilled tulip decoration, "Burger Brothers, Rochester, NY," ca. 1868, 2 gal., 15" h.................... **495**

Jug w/Wooden Stopper

Jug, w/carved wooden stopper, semi-ovoid, cobalt blue leaf & vine design, top to bottom, "Edmands & Co.," ca. 1870, stone ping & long glaze spider lines on side, kiln burn on front in making, 3 gal., 15" h. (ILLUS.) **220**

Jug, ovoid, incised & blue-trimmed flower at top, blue accents at name & handle, extremely rare mark, "P. Cross, Hartford," ca. 1805, 2 gal., 16" h. (professional restoration to age lines throughout & surface chips at the spout) **990**

Jug, tapering cylindrical body w/applied shoulder handles, cobalt blue brushed vintage below Xs & dots, impressed "4," 4 gal., 16" h. (hairlines)....................................... **303**

Jug, ovoid, two handled, cobalt blue brushed tree design, "I. Seymour Troy Factory," very early maker's mark, ca. 1810, 4 gal., 18" h. (professional restoration to freeze cracks up from base in front) **715**

Meat tenderizer, dated 1877, original handle, 9" l...................................... **110**

Milk bowl, deep slightly flaring cylindrical sides w/wide molded rim, cobalt blue stenciled label "A.P. Donaghho, Parkersburg, W.Va.," 12 3/4" d., 6 1/2" h. (professional repair, slight rim chip) **308**

Gallon Milk Pan

Milk pan, brushed cobalt blue three-leaf decoration, rim pouring lip, ca. 1850, unsigned, two minor glaze separations in making & small surface chip at rim, 1 gal., 4" h. (ILLUS.)................................. **275**

Model of a lamb, relief-molded reclining lamb, blue accents highlight ears, blue accent at the front foot, hand-incised detailed facial features, found in & attributed to Lyons, NY, ca. 1860, unsigned, extremely rare, 2" h., 2 1/2" l., ... **825**

Slip-quilled Ovoid Pitcher

Pitcher, 8 1/2" h., unglazed grey clay w/brushed brown Albany slip-quilled decoration, New Geneva Pottery, unsigned, ca. 1860, 1 qt... **853**

Pitcher, 9" h., ovoid, slip-quilled cobalt zigzag, lines & dot decoration, unsigned, probably Albany pottery, ca. 1850, surface chip at base in front and tight line at rim, on side, 1 gal. (ILLUS.)....... **523**

Pitcher, 10" h., brushed cobalt blue tulip decoration, "Burger & Lang, Rochester, NY," 1 gal., ca. 1870 (some surface wear & chips along the rim from use) **605**

Pitcher, 11" h., handled, w/three beautiful roses on front & blue accents around base and top, Pottery Works, Little West 12th Street NY, unsigned, ca. 1870, 1 gal.,.. **2,530**

Pitcher, 11 1/2" h., bulbous ovoid body w/tall cylindrical neck w/pinched rim spout & applied strap handle, colbalt blue brushed foliage design, impressed label "M. & T. Miller, Newport, Pa." (chips) **1,540**

Pitcher, 13 1/4" h., bulbous ovoid body w/a tall cylindrical neck

w/pinched rim spout, applied strap handle, brushed cobalt blue large blossoms, leafy twigs & impressed "2," 2 gal. **880**

Preserving jar, cylindrical tapering slightly to a molded rim, cobalt blue stenciled label for A.P. Donaghho, Fredericktown, Pa. above a large spread-winged eagle, 9 1/2" h....... **935**

Preserving jar, swelled cylindrical form, brushed thick cobalt blue flower design & blue accents at ears, "Penn Yan," ca. 1860, 1 gal., 9 1/2" h. (very minor surface chip at rim) **198**

Preserving jar, w/simple brushed plume design repeated four times around jar, unsigned, ca. 1860, 1 gal., 10" h. (some surface wear at rim) **143**

Preserving jar, swelled cylindrical form w/eared handles, slip-quilled cobalt blue curlicues, "Nichols & Boynton, Burlington, VT," ca. 1855, 2 gal., 10 1/2" h. **176**

Preserving jar, swelled cylindrical body w/cobalt blue stenciled

Preserving Jar with Wreath Design

Stenciled Preserving Jar

flowers & "Jas Hamilton & Co., 2,"
11" h. (crooked & hairlines) **248**

Preserving jar, cov., swelled
cylindrical form w/eared handles,
thick brushed cobalt blue wreath
design & "2," marked "T.
Harrington, Lyons," ca. 1860, 2
gal., 11 1/2" h. (ILLUS.) **633**

Preserving jar, w/original lid, eared
handles, stenciled sign of
friendship - a handshake in thick
blue, "Somerset Potters Works,"
ca. 1880, few rim chips & small
tight line over right ear, 4 gal.,
14 1/2" h. (ILLUS.) **413**

Stove leveler, flaring pedestal below
a wide cupped rim, brushed cobalt
blue leaf bands, 4 1/2" h. (hairline,
chips) **440**

Water Cooler with Bird on Plume

Water cooler, cov., slip-quilled bird
on plume design, body has blue
accented deep incised lines, "New
York Stoneware Co.," ca. 1870,
4 gal., 15 1/2" h. (ILLUS.) **1,155**

Water filter, cov., marked "Perfection
Filter Manufactured by the Central
NY Pottery Utica NY," in relief &
blue accented, opposite side
w/embossed leaf design accented
in blue, relief-molded cupids
holding banner around the name,
gargoyle handles, age line
throughout base & one very tight 3"
through line at rim, 10" h. (ILLUS.)   **688**

Ornate Salt Glazed Filter

WATT POTTERY

In July, 1922 the Watt Pottery was incorporated on the site of the old Burley Pottery in Crooksville, Ohio where it was owned and operated by the Watt family of Perry County, Ohio. It remained in business until a fire halted production in 1965.Through the 1920s and early 1930s the Watt Pottery manufactured stoneware crocks, churns, and jars. These are marked with an eagle or acorn in blue, with gallonage marked in a circle.

In 1935, the pottery dropped its stoneware line in favor of more modern ovenwares. The lightweight clay body gave the wares the necessary resilience to go from icebox to oven. In 1949, the Watt Pottery began hand-decorating its wares. The pieces were decorated by teams of three decorators and the patterns were simple in nature, with as few brush strokes as possible to allow low production costs. The bright colors against the deep cream clay give Watt Pottery its unique country appeal.

The first hand-decorated patterns are called the "Classic Patterns" and were produced from 1949 until about 1953. They are: Rio Rose, Moonflower, Dogwood, and Daisy and Crosshatch.

The patterns most sought after by today's collectors and their introduction dates are as follows: Starflower —1951; Apple—1952; Cherry—1952; Silhouette—1953; Rooster—1955; Dutch Tulip—1956; American Red Bud (Tear Drop)—1957; Morning Glory—

1958; Autumn Foliage—1959; Double Apple—1959; and Tulip—1961.

Most pieces of Watt ware are well marked. The marks are large, often covering the entire bottom of the piece. They usually consist of one or more concentric rings deeply impressed into the bottom. The words "Watt" and "Oven Ware U.S.A." are impressed as well, although some pieces have only one phrase, not both. Earlier marks featured a script "Watt" without circles. Most pieces also have the mold number impressed in the center, making identification easy. The most significant pieces which were not marked are the ice bucket (all patterns) and Apple dinner plates.

—Dennis M. Thompson

Baker, cov., Cherry patt., No. 53,
7 1/2" d. **$110**

Baker, cov., Apple patt., No. 601,
8" d. **120**

Baker, cov., Apple patt., No. 67,
8 1/4" d. **125**

Baker, cov., Autumn Foliage patt.,
No. 110, 8 1/2" d. **75**

Baker, cov., Cherry patt., No. 54,
8 1/2" d. **110**

Baker, cov., Open Apple patt., No.
110, 8 1/2" d. **295**

Baker, Apple patt., rectangular, No.
85, 9" w. **1,000**

Bean cup, Tear Drop patt., No. 75,
3 1/2" d. 2 1/4" h. **15**

Bean pot, cov., Rooster patt. **325**

Bean pot, cov., Apple patt., No. 76,
6 1/2" h. **150**

Bean pot, cov., Autumn Foliage
patt., No. 76, 6 1/2" h. **125**

Bean pot, cov., bisque, No. 76,
6 1/2" h. **10**

Bean pot, cov., Dutch Tulip patt., No.
76, 6 1/2" h. **275**

Bean pot, cov., Rooster patt., No. 76,
6 1/2" h. **350**

Bean server, individual, Autumn
Foliage patt., No. 75., 3 1/2" d. **70**

Bowl, 4" d., 1 1/2" d., Apple patt., No.
602 (ILLUS. far left) **125**

Bowl, 4 1/4" d., 2" h., Apple patt., No.
04 .... **50**

Bowl, 4 1/4" d., 2" h., Double Apple
patt., No. 04 .... **100**

Bowl, 5" d., 2" h., Apple patt., No.
603 (ILLUS. center left) **100**

Bowl, 5 1/4" d., 2 1/2" h., Tear Drop
patt., No. 05 .... **40**

Bowl, 5 1/2" d., 2" h., Reduced Apple
patt., No. 74 .... **30**

Bowl, 6" d., 2 1/2" h., Apple patt., No.
604 (ILLUS. center) **90**

Bowl, 6" d., 2 1/2" h. Tulip patt., No.
604 .... **150**

Bowl, 6 1/4" d., 2 1/4" h., Cherry
patt., No. 52 .... **35**

Watt Pottery Apple Pattern Bowls

Bowl, 7" d., 3" h., Tulip patt., No. 600 **125**

Bowl, 7" d., 3" h., Apple patt., No.
600 (ILLUS. center right) **50**

Bowl, 7 1/4" d., 3" h., Apple patt., No.
07 .... **50**

Bowl, 7 1/4" d., 3" h., Double Apple
patt., No. 07 .... **70**

Bowl, cov., 7 1/2"d., Apple patt., two-
leaf, No. 66 .... **49**

Bowl, cov., 7 1/2" d., Rooster patt.,
No. 66 .... **200**

Bowl, 8" d., 3 1/2" h., Apple patt., No.
601 (ILLUS. far right) **60**

Bowl, 8" d., 3 1/2" h., Tulip patt., No.
601 .... **125**

Bowl, 8 1/4" d., 3 1/4" h., Starflower
patt., No. 54 .... **40**

Bowl, 8 1/4" d., 3 1/2" h., Apple patt.,
No. 67 .... **50**

Bowl, 8 1/4" d., 3 1/2" h., Rooster
patt., No. 67 .... **90**

Bowl, cov., 8 1/2" d., Apple patt.,
two-leaf, No. 67 .... **140**

Bowl, 9 1/2" d., 4" h., Open Apple
patt., No. 73 .... **250**

Bowl, 10" d., 3" h., Autumn Foliage
patt., No. 106 .... **85**

Bowl, 11" d., 4" h., Starflower patt.,
No. 55 .... **40**

Bowl, 11 3/4" d., Starflower patt., No.
55, ... **110**

Bowl, spaghetti, 13" d., 3 1/2" h.,
Autumn Foliage patt., No. 39 .... **135**

Bowl, spaghetti, 13" d., 3 1/2" h,.
Dogwood patt., No. 39 (ILLUS.
back) **135**

Dutch Tulip Spaghetti Bowl

Bowl, spaghetti, 13" d., 3 1/2" h.,
Dutch Tulip patt., No. 39 (ILLUS.) . **400**

Bowl, spaghetti, 13" d., 3 1/2" h.,
Open Apple patt., No. 39 .... **800**

Bowl, spaghetti, 13" d., 3 1/2" h.,
Rooster patt., No. 39 .... **325**

Bowl, spaghetti, 13" d., 3 1/2" h.,
Starflower patt., No. 39 .... **110**

Bowl, 15" d., 3 1/2" h., Rio Rose patt. **75**

Canister, cov., Apple patt., No. 82,
5" d. **400**

Canister, cov., Starflower patt., No.
82, 5" d. **300**

Canister, cov., Dutch Tulip patt., No.
81, 6 1/2" d. **400**

Watt Pottery Spaghetti Bowl & Casserole

Assorted Watt Pottery, Autumn Foliage Patt.

Watt Pottery Canister, Rio Rose Patt.

Canister, cov., Rio Rose patt., No.
72, 7 1/4" d. (ILLUS.) 300

Canister, cov., Apple patt., No. 80,
8 1/2" d. 900

Canister, cov., Rooster patt., No. 80,
8 1/2" d. 600

Carafe, cov., Autumn Foliage patt.,
No. 115, 9 1/2" h. (ILLUS. far left) . 200

Carafe, cov., Brown banded, No.
115, 10 1/2" 350

Casserole, cov., French handled,
Pansy patt. 80

Casserole, cov., French handled,
Raised Pansy patt., No.18 135

Casserole, cov., French handled,
Rooster patt., No.18 188

Casserole, cov., four-handled, Old
Pansy patt., No. 8, 9 1/2" d.,
4 3/4" h. 50

Casserole, cov., Apple patt., No. 18,
5" d. 175

Casserole, cov., Apple patt.,
w/French handle, No. 18, 5" d. 225

Casserole, cov., Dogwood patt., No.
18, 5" d. (ILLUS. front) 125

Casserole, cov., Rooster patt.,
w/French handle, No. 18, 5" d. 200

Casserole, cov., Silhouette patt., No.
18, 5" d 25

Casserole, cov., Starflower patt., No.
18, 5" d. 90

Cheese crock, cov., Pennsylvania
Dutch Tulip patt., No. 80 700

Watt Pottery Carafe and Assorted Pitchers

Chip-n-Dip set, Autumn Foliage patt., No. 110 & 120 bowls, the set (ILLUS. center) 150

Chip-n-Dip set, Double Apple patt., No. 96 &120 bowls, the set 350

Churns, stoneware, Eagle or Acorn patt., various sizes..................... 100-150

Cookie jar, cov., "Goodies," No. 76, 6 1/2" h 150

Cookie jar, cov., Apple patt., No. 21, 7 1/2" h 400

Cookie jar, cov., Cherry patt., No. 21, 7 1/2" h. 250

Cookie jar, cov., Rio Rose patt., No. 21, 7 1/2" h. 150

Cookie jar, cov., happy/sad face, wooden lid, No. 34, 8" h. 150

Cookie jar, cov., Starflower patt., No. 503, 8" h. 350

Cookie jar, cov., Tulip patt., No. 503, 8" h. 350

Cookie jar, cov., Morning Glory patt., cream, No. 95, 10" h...................... 600

Cookie jar, cov., "Cookie Barrel," wood grain, 10 1/2" h.................... 50

Watt Pottery Policeman Cookie Jar

Cookie jar, cov., figural, Policeman, 10 1/2" h., rare (ILLUS.) 1,100

Assorted Watt Pottery, Starflower Pattern (Five-petal)

Assorted Watt Pottery, Starflower Pattern (Four-petal)

Creamer, Apple patt., two leaf, No.
62 w/advertising, 4 1/4" h. **195**

Creamer, Autumn Foliage patt., No.
62, 4 1/4" h. **159**

Creamer, Apple (three-leaf) patt., No.
62, 4 1/4" h. **90**

Creamer, Apple (two-leaf) patt., No.
62, 4 1/4" h. **150**

Creamer, Autumn Foliage patt., No.
62, 4 1/4" h. (ILLUS. left) **250**

Creamer, Dutch Tulip patt., No. 62,
4 1/4" h. **275**

Creamer, Morning Glory patt.,
cream, No. 97, 4 1/4" h.................. **400**

Creamer, Rooster patt., No.62,
w/advertising, 4 1/4" h. **195**

Creamer, Starflower patt., five-petal,
No. 62, 4 1/4" h. (ILLUS. far right) . **200**

Creamer, Starflower patt., four-petal,
No. 62, 4 1/4" h. (ILLUS. second
from left) **250**

Creamer, Tulip patt., No. 62,
4 1/4" h. **225**

Crocks, stoneware, Eagle or Acorn
patt., various sizes (ILLUS. of two)
.... **25-50**

Cruet set, cov., Apple patt., 7 1/2" h. **1,500**

Cruet set, cov., Autumn Foliage
patt., 7 1/2" h. **300**

Watt Pottery Crocks

Cup & saucer, Pansy patt. **135**

Grease jar, Autumn Foliage patt.,
No. 01, 5" h.................................... **200**

Grease jar, cov., Apple patt., No. 47,
5" h. **400**

Grease jar, cov., Starflower patt., No.
01, 5" h. **275**

Ice bucket, cov., Rooster patt. **325**

Ice bucket, cov., Autumn Foliage
patt., No. 59, 7" h........................... **200**

Ice bucket, cov., Dutch Tulip patt.,
No. 59, 7" h.................................... **400**

Ice tea keg, cov., brand name, 11" h.
(ILLUS.) **110**

Ice tea keg, cov., plain, 11" h.
(ILLUS.) **60**

Mixing bowl, Reduced Apple patt.,
deep, No. 61 .... **125**

Watt Pottery Ice Tea Kegs

Mixing bowl, Reduced Apple patt.,
Nos. 5, 6, 7, & 9, 5" to 9" d., each .   60

Mixing bowl, Morning Glory patt.,
5" d.   125

Mixing bowl, Apple patt., No. 65,
8 1/2" d., 5 3/4" h.   80

Mixing bowls, nesting, Apple patt.,
Nos. 5, 6, 7, & 9, 5" to 9" d., each .   60

Mixing bowls, nesting, Apple patt.,
ribbed, Nos. 5, 6, 7, & 9, 5" to 9" d.,
each   70

Mixing bowls, nesting, Morning
Glory patt., Nos. 6, 7, 8, & 9, 6" to
9" d., each   80

*Watt Pottery Open Apple Pattern Mixing
Bowls*

Mixing bowls, nesting, Open Apple
patt., Nos. 5, 6, 7, & 8, 5" to 8" d.,
each (ILLUS. of three)   150

Mixing bowls, nesting, Starflower
patt., Nos. 5, 6, 7, 8, & 9, 5" to
9" d., each   35

Mixing bowls, nesting, Tulip patt.,
deep, Nos. 63, 64, & 65, 6 1/2" d.,
7 1/2" d. & 8 1/2" d., each (ILLUS.)   90

Mixing bowls, nesting-type, Apple
patt., Nos. 4, 5, 6, & 7, the set   275

Mug, Apple patt., No. 121, 3" h.   175

Mug, Apple patt., No. 501, 4 1/2" h. ...   275

Mug, Autumn Foliage patt., No. 501,
4 1/2" h.   125

Pie plate, Pansy patt., cut-leaf, No.
33, 9" d.   90

Pie plate, Apple patt., No. 33,
9 1/4" d.   150

Pie plate, Rooster patt., No. 33,
9 1/4" d.   400

Watt Pottery Starflower Pie Plate

Watt Pottery Tulip Pattern Mixing Bowls

Pie plate, Starflower patt., five-petal, No. 33, 9 1/4" d. (ILLUS.) 200

Pitcher, American Red Bud (Tear Drop) patt., No. 15 85

Pitcher, Apple patt., No. 15 85

Pitcher, Rooster patt., No. 15 100

Watt Starflower No. 15 Pitcher

Pitcher, Starflower patt., No. 15 (ILLUS.) 85

Pitcher, Apple patt., No. 16 90

Pitcher, 5 1/4" h., Apple patt., No. 15   80

Pitcher, 8" h., Apple patt., w/ice lip, No. 17 225

Pitcher, 8" h., Apple patt., refrigerator, No. 69 450

Pitcher, 5 1/4" h., Autumn Foliage patt., No. 15 (ILLUS. far right) 75

Pitcher, 6 1/2" h., Autumn Foliage patt., No. 16 (ILLUS. second from right) 85

Pitcher, 8" h., Autumn Foliage patt., No. 17 (ILLUS. second from left)... 100

Pitcher, 6 1/2" h., Cherry patt., No. 16 135

Pitcher, 5 1/4" h., Cross Hatch patt., No. 15 250

Pitcher, 6 1/2" h., Double Apple patt., No. 16 200

Pitcher, 5 1/4" h., Dutch Tulip patt., No. 15 300

Pitcher, 8" h., Eagle patt., No. 17 400

Pitcher, 8" h., Morning Glory patt., No. 96 300

Watt Pottery Pitchers

Pitcher, 7" h., Raised Rose patt., old style (ILLUS. right) 225

Pitcher, 6 1/2" h., Rio Rose patt., No. 16 200

Pitcher, 7" h., Rio Rose, old style (ILLUS. left) 150

Pitcher, 8" h., Rio Rose patt., No. 17   250

Pitcher, 5 1/4" h., Silhouette patt., No. 15 200

Pitcher, 6 1/2" h., Silhouette patt., No. 16 75

Pitcher, 5 1/4" h., Starflower patt., four-petal, No. 15 (ILLUS. center) . 125

Pitcher, 6 1/2" h., Starflower patt., four-petal, No. 16 (ILLUS. second from right) 85

Pitcher, 8" h., Starflower patt., four-petal, No. 17 (ILLUS. far right) 135

Pitcher, 8" h., Starflower patt., refrigerator, No. 69 (ILLUS. far left) 500

Pitcher, 5 1/4" h., Starflower patt., five-petal, No. 15 (ILLUS. second from right) 65

Pitcher, 6 1/2" h., Starflower patt., five-petal, No. 16 (ILLUS. second from left) 85

Pitcher, 8" h., Starflower, five-petal, No. 17 (ILLUS. far left) 160

Pitcher, 8" h., Tear Drop patt., four-petal, refrigerator, No. 69 .... **500**

Pitcher, 5 1/4" h., Tulip patt., No. 15 **450**

Plate, 10" d., Moonflower patt., pink on green **75**

Watt Moonflower Plate & Platter

Plate, 10" d., Moonflower patt. (ILLUS. right)................................. **60**

Plate, 6 1/2" d., Rio Rose patt........... **20**

Platter, 15" d., Pansy patt., cut-leaf, No.31.. **90**

Platter, 15" d., Apple patt., No. 31 .... **300**

Platter, 15" d., Autumn Foliage patt., No. 31... **100**

Platter, 12" d., Cherry patt., No. 49 (ILLUS.)...

Platter, 15" d, Moonflower patt., No. 31 (ILLUS. left) **80**

Platter, 12" d., Rio Rose patt., No. 49 **75**

Watt Pottery Platter, Cherry Pattern

Platter, 15" d., Starflower patt., No. 31 .... **110**

Salt & pepper shakers, hourglass-shaped, Autumn Foliage patt., 4" h., the set (ILLUS. far right)....... **160**

Salt & pepper shakers, hourglass-shaped, Rooster patt., 4" h., the set... **375**

Salt & pepper shakers, barrel-shaped, Starflower patt., five-petal, 4" h., the set **200**

Salt & pepper shakers, hourglass-shaped, 6-petal Starflower patt., 4" h., the set **250**

Salt & pepper shakers, barrel-shaped, Tear Drop patt., 4" h., the set... **300**

Watt Pottery Teapots

Salt shaker, barrel-shaped, Cherry patt., 4" h. 85

Spaghetti bowl, 13" d., Cherry patt., No. 39... 85

Spaghetti bowl, 13" d., Starflower patt., No. 39................................ 120

Sugar bowl, cov., Autumn Foliage patt., No. 98, 4 1/2" h. (ILLUS. far left) 275

Sugar bowl, Morning Glory patt., No. 98, 4 1/4" h. 250

Teapot, cov., Apple patt., No. 505, 5" h. (ILLUS. left) 2,800

Teapot, cov., Apple (three-leaf) patt., No. 112, 6" h. (ILLUS. right) 1,500

Teapot, cov., Autumn Foliage patt., No. 112, 6" h................................ 1,000

YELLOWWARE

Yellowware is a form of utilitarian pottery produced in the United States and England from the early 19th century onward. Its body texture is less dense and vitreous (impervious to water) than stoneware. Most, but not all, yellowware is unmarked and its color varies from deep yellow to pale buff. In the late 19th and early 20th centuries bowls in graduated sizes were widely advertised. Still in production, yellowware is plentiful and still reasonably priced.

Yellowware Dog Bank

Bank, figural standing pig, marbleized glaze in brown, green

& cream, 6 1/4" l. (wear, glaze flakes)... **$83**

Bank, model of a seated dog, facing front, on a rectangular base w/coin slot, green & brown running glaze, chips on base & coin slot, 7 1/2" h. (ILLUS.) **1,045**

Beverage set: 8" h. pitcher & six 4 3/4" h. mugs; all decorated w/blue stripes at rim & base & impressed "100% Buckeye Pure," the set (slight variation in color & size, one mug w/hairline & pitcher w/small chip) **550**

Yellowware Flask and Toby Bottle

Bottle, figural standing Mr. Toby w/fiddle, crazing w/possible hairline in base, chip on hat brim, 8 1/2" h. (ILLUS. right) **715**

Bowl, 7" d., 3 1/2" h., cov., cylindrical, decorated w/blue bands & stripes (crazing & stains)........... **220**

Dish, rectangular, brown & green sponging, 8 1/2" l. (minor wear)..... **193**

Flask, decorated w/ relief-molded morning glories & an eagle, chips, 7 3/8" h. (ILLUS. left) **1,210**

Food molds, figural rabbit, 9" & 9 1/2" l., pr. (one w/hairline)........... **248**

Food molds, round w/spiral design & lady-finger rim, two 4" d., one 6" d., set of 3... **171**

Inkwell, figural dog, green & brown running glaze, 6 1/8" l. (ILLUS.) 440

Mixing bowl, footed, deep rounded sides w/rim spout, white center band w/blue seaweed decoration, flanked by narrow blue stripes, probably East Liverpool, Ohio, 9 1/4" d., 4 1/2" h. (wear, hairlines in spout & chips)............................ 468

Mixing bowls, footed, deep rounded sides w/a flared rim, wide white band beneath rim, 12" d., 5 1/2" h. & 16 1/4" d., 7 3/4" h., the set........ 330

Mug, cylindrical w/C-form handle, blue stripes w/white sanded band, 2" h. 182

Pitcher, jug-type, 5" h., strap handle & spout w/strainer, decorated w/blue stripes (flakes).................... 578

Yellowware Pitcher

Pitcher, 5 1/4" h., footed bulbous body tapering slightly to wide cylindrical neck w/flared rim, high arched rim spout & C-form ribbed handle w/leaf, light blue & white horizontal stripes around mid-body, faint hairline at base of handle (ILLUS.) 358

Pitcher, 5 1/2" h., 5 1/4" h., footed bulbous body tapering slightly to wide cylindrical neck w/flared rim, high arched rim spout & strap handle, decorated w/white bands & brown stripes 550

Pitcher, jug-type, 6 1/8" h., w/strap handle, decorated w/white bands & black stripes 688

Yellowware Pitcher

Pitcher, jug-type, 8 1/2" h., w/ribbed handle, decorated w/white band, repair on spout (ILLUS.) 550

Pitcher, 8 7/8" h., footed cylindrical body w/flared lip, ornate handle, Gothic design w/relief-molded Mary, John & Jesus, light blue cartouche label w/registry mark & "Charles Meigh, Nov 12, 1846, York Minster Jug," England 495

Soap dish, round w/drain holes, 5 5/8" d. (some wear) 550

Vegetable dish, open, oval, impressed mark "Fire Proof," 13 3/8" l. (pinpoint surface flakes) . 495

CHALKWARE

So-called chalkware available today is actually made of plaster of Paris, much of it decorated in color and primarily in the form of busts, figurines and ornaments. It was produced through most of the 19th century and the majority of pieces were originally quite inexpensive when made. Today even 20th century "carnival" pieces are collectible.

Bank, model of a pear, original red & yellow paint, replaced wooden stem, 5 1/2" h. (minor wear & chips) **$358**

Bank, "Devils Head," early Carnival-type, ca. 1950, 6 1/2" h. 61

Bank, model of a pig, "Junior Pig Bank," standing w/front legs in begging position, early Carnival-type, ca. 1940-50, 9 1/2" h. 28

Bank, model of a standing spotted pig, early Carnival-type, ca. 1950, 11" l. 55

Chalkware Indian Book End

Book ends, figural Indian chief w/headdress, kneeling on one knee, hand resting on other knee, spear by side, ca. 1940, pr. (ILLUS of one) 75

Figure group, George Washington on horse, early Carnival-type, ca. 1940, 11" h. 39

Figure of a baby, Kewpie-like, early Carnival-type, ca. 1935-45, 13" h. . 50

Figure of a black baby, Kewpie-like, early Carnival-type, ca. 1935-45, 12" h. (repaired) 110

Figure of a clown, holding balloons, early Carnival-type w/coin slot, ca. 1950, 13" h. 39

Figure of a girl, dressed in slacks, sweater & hat, early Carnival-type, ca. 1930-40, 10" h. 39

Figure of a girl, "Sailor Girl," wearing bell-bottom slacks, top w/sailor collar & sailor hat, one hand in pocket, the other near her face, early Carnival-type, ca. 1930-40, 14" h. 55

Figure of a girl, "Apache Babe," wearing jacket & slacks w/beret on the side of her head, heavy make-up, standing w/hands in pockets, early Carnival-type, ca. 1936, 15" h. 39

Figure of a girl, "Tom Boy," dressed in suit & cap, early Carnival-type, ca. 1940, 15 1/2" h. 61

Figure of a hula girl, early Carnival-type, long dark curly hair, one arm behind her head, the other hand near her face, wearing only short skirt, ca. 1947, 15" h. (repaired) 149

Figure of an Indian, seated w/drum, head band, early Carnival-type, ca. 1940-50, 12 1/2" h. 72

Figure of "Uncle Sam," early Carnival-type, white hair & beard, dark pants & light shirt, standing & rolling up one sleeve, ca. 1935, 15" h. 94

Mantel garniture, compote of fruit in circular bowl on fluted foot & square base, various fruits painted yellow, brown, red, & black, 19th c., 12 1/2" h. **2,300**

Mantel garniture, compote of fruit in circular bowl w/flaring ruffled rim on circular foot, grapes, pears, oranges & bananas painted yellow, green & orange, 19th c., 15" h. (scattered chips & wear to paint).. **1,265**

Mantel garniture modeled as a cluster of fruits & leaves on footed base, painted red, green, yellow & black w/indecipherable inscription on verso, 19th c., 14 1/4" h. (wear to paint) **3,450**

Model of a buffalo, early Carnival-type w/coin slot, ca. 1950, 10 1/2" h. **28**

Fine Chalkware Cat

Model of a cat, seated animal, old worn paint in red, black & yellow, 19th c., 9 7/8" h. (ILLUS.) **1,430**

Chalkware Sleeping Cat

Model of a cat, large reclining animal w/head down, original polychrome paint, wear & some edge damage w/touch-up repair, 12" l. (ILLUS.) .. **440**

Model of a deer, recumbent animal, old worn paint in red, black & yellow, 19th c., 5 1/2" h., pr. **935**

Model of a dog, standing w/open legs, head turned to the side, long dark ears, short tail, on a rectangular base, worn red & black paint, 7 1/2" h. **193**

Model of a ewe & lamb, recumbent animals on rectangular base, red, blue & yellow, 9 1/4" l. (very worn, repairs) **358**

Model of a gorilla, "King Kong," early Carnival-type, ca. 1930-40, 12 1/2" h. **61**

Model of a hand, holding an ear of corn for Iowa Centennial, 1838-1938, ca. 1938, 12" h. (minor losses) **28**

Model of a parrot, resting on ball plinth, old red, black & olive yellow paint, 8 1/4" h. (some wear) **743**

Model of a pig, standing on hind legs, early Carnival-type, ca. 1935, 6" h. **17**

Model of a rabbit, sitting, red, yellow & black, 5 3/8" h. (wear & scratches).................................... **550**

Model of a rooster, red, yellow, green & black, 5 3/4" h. (some color wear, stains & old repair) **715**

Model of a squirrel, seated animal holding nut in his paws, on a domed base, old red & black paint, uneven old brown varnish (minor wear) **743**

Model of an elephant, standing on hind legs, early Carnival-type, ca. 1960, 10 1/2" h. **33**

Model of compote, footed, holding fruit, old red, yellow & orange paint & brown varnish, 11" h. (some wear & possible old touch up repair) **1,100**

CHILDREN'S DISHES

During the reign of Queen Victoria, doll-houses and accessories became more popular; as the century progressed, there was greater demand for toys which would subtly train a little girl in the art of homemaking.

Berry set: master bowl & six sauce dishes; clear pressed glass, Pattee Cross patt., the set **$55**

Butter, cov., pressed glass, Drum patt., clear..................................... **145**

Butter dish, cov., clear pressed glass, Tulip & Honeycomb patt., large size **66**

Cake stand, pressed glass, Rexford patt., clear..................................... **35**

glass, American Shield patt., in a silver-plated frame w/flaring openwork foot, ring holder & central handle w/top loop centered by a small figural bird, late 19th c., the set (ILLUS. left) **121**

Castor set, four-bottle, two shakers & two bottles in clear pressed glass, Flute patt., in a silver-plated frame w/high stamped-design foot, ring holder & central handle w/a large top loop centered by a sitting girl, late 19th c., the set (ILLUS. right) **220**

Coffeepot, porcelain, embossed scroll & grape leaf design w/cobalt blue trim, Germany, 5" h............... **88**

Children's Creamer

Two Children's Castor Sets

Castor set, four-bottle, clear bottles & shaker in the clear pressed

Creamer, pressed glass, Drum patt., clear (ILLUS.) **55**

Children's Punch Set

Creamer, pressed glass,
Pennsylvania patt., clear 35

Pitcher, lemonade, pressed glass,
Oval Star patt., clear..................... 65

Punch bowl, pressed glass, Inverted
Strawberry patt., clear 65

Punch bowl, pressed glass, Oval
Star patt., clear w/gold rim............. 55

Punch bowl, pressed glass, Wheat
Sheaf patt., clear 30

Punch cup, pressed glass, Wheat
Sheaf patt., clear 8

Punch set: punch bowl & six cups;
clear pressed glass, Wheat Sheaf
patt., Cambridge, the set 121

Punch set: punch bowl & six cups;
pressed glass, Nursery Rhyme
patt., milk glass, the set (ILLUS.) .. 193

Sauce dish, pressed glass, Wheat
Sheaf patt., clear 9

Children's Spooner

Spooner, pressed glass, Hawaiian
Lei patt., Higbee mark, clear
(ILLUS.) 35

Sugar bowl, cov., clear pressed
glass, Amazon patt........................ 33

Sugar bowl, cov., Menagerie patt.,
figural sitting bear, clear 149

Sugar bowl, cov., pressed glass,
Drum patt., clear........................... 150

Sugar bowl, cov., pressed glass,
Hawaiian Lei patt., Higbee mark,
clear.. 40

Sugar bowl, cov., pressed glass,
Oval Star patt., clear..................... 30

Sugar bowl, cov., pressed glass,
Tulip with Honeycomb patt., clear . 25

Table set: cov. butter, cov. sugar
bowl, creamer & spooner; clear
pressed glass, Button Panel No.
44 patt., the set............................. 198

Table set: cov. butter, cov. sugar,
creamer & spooner; clear pressed
glass, Rexford patt., the set.......... 72

Table set: cov. sugar, creamer, cov.
butter dish & spooner; Nursery
Rhyme patt., clear, the set 220

Table set: creamer, sugar, cov.
butter, spooner & matching tray;
clear pressed glass, Hobnail
w/Thumbprint Base patt., 5 pcs..... 275

Table set, pressed glass, Oval Star
patt., clear, 4 pcs. 175

Tea set: cov. teapot, cov. sugar bowl,
creamer, two cups & saucers & two
plates; china, deep boat-shaped
bodies w/angled shoulder, domed
covers & pointed angled handles,
red transfer-printed Oriental
landscape design w/polychrome
trim, first half 19th c., teapot
3 5/8" h., the set (teapot lid bit
oversized, hairline in sugar,
hairline in one plate) 275

Tea set: cov. teapot, creamer, cov.
sugar bowl, cake plate, six cups &
saucers; porcelain, decorated
w/polychrome nursery rhyme
scenes, early 20th c., the set (one
saucer damaged) 345

Tea set: cov. teapot, creamer &
sugar bowl, waste bowl & 6 cups &
saucers; ironstone, Moss Rose
patt., 16 pcs. (teapot damaged) 220

Tumbler, pressed glass, Oval Star
patt., clear..................................... 11

Water set: pitcher & five tumblers;
clear pressed glass, Pattee Cross
patt., the set.................................. 66

Water set: pitcher & seven tumblers;
pressed glass, Nursery Rhyme
patt., clear, 8 pcs. 198

CHILDREN'S MUGS

The small sized mugs used by children first attempting to drink from a cup appeal to many collectors. Because they were made of such diverse materials as china, glass, pottery, graniteware, plated silver and sterling silver, the collector can assemble a diversified collection or single out a particular type around which to base a collection. .

Pressed glass, Beaded Column & Panel patt., clear **$15**

Pressed glass, Butterfly patt., clear   **38**

Pressed glass, Diagonal Flowered Band patt., clear **25**

Pressed glass, Grapevine with Ovals patt., clear **21**

Pressed glass, Little Bo Peep patt., clear.. **85**

Pressed glass, Little Bo Peep patt., clear, etched **65**

Pressed glass, Ribbed Forget-me-not patt., clear **23**

Pressed glass, Robin patt., amber .   **25**

Pressed glass, Scampering Lamb patt., clear **59**

Staffordshire pottery, cylindrical w/molded base & C-scroll handle, black transfer-printed design representing the month of

December w/a young girl w/a cart full of guns, drum, fiddle, doll, a British flag & a rhyme, 2 1/8" h. **61**

Staffordshire pottery, cylindrical w/molded base & C-scroll handle, black transfer-printed design representing the month of August, shows men, women & children hand-harvesting wheat w/a printed rhyme, 2 1/4" h. **77**

Staffordshire pottery, cylindrical w/molded base & C-scroll handle, blank transfer-printed design of a young girl grooming a large dog, the ground littered w/bones & a food dish, 2 3/8" h......................   **33**

Staffordshire pottery, cylindrical, blue transfer-printed sheep in front of a cottage above the words "A PRESENT FROM WASHINGTON," blue line border, ca. 1820-30, 2" h. **605**

Staffordshire pottery, cylindrical, black transfer-printed scene titled "Cornwallis Surrendering His Sword at Yorktown," pink lustre border, probably by Wood, first quarter 19th c., 2 1/16" h. (line across the base, repair to base chip damages part of the title) **413**

Staffordshire pottery, cylindrical, polychrome decorated "Keep thy Shop & Thy Shop will Keep Thee," 2 1/2" h. (hairline) **50**

CHRISTMAS COLLECTIBLES

Starting in the mid 19th Century more and more items began to be manufactured to decorate the home, office or commercial business to celebrate the Christmas season.

In the 20th century the trend increased. Companies such as Coca-Cola, Sears and others began to employ specially produced Christmas items. The inexpensive glass then plastic Christmas tree decoration began to reach into almost every home. With the end of World War II the toy market moved into the picture with annual Santa Claus parades and the children's visit to Santa to leave Christmas wish lists.

As the 21st Century approaches this trend will continue and material from earlier Christmas seasons will climb in value.

An early Christmas postcard.

Today, much excitement ripples through the air whenever anything Christmas comes up for sale, be it at an auction, estate sale, antique show, flea market or on the World Wide Web. For increasing numbers of collectors join the ranks of those who are attempting to recapture the spirit of Christmas past through their collecting. Record prices have been set for Santas, Dresden ornaments, and rare glass figurals, but beginning collectors will find multitudes of items at very inexpensive to moderate prices. Christmas collecting has a wide range of interests and prices. The past few years have seen accelerated prices in the rarer areas, stabilized in the medium to low end items, and even a reduction in price when very common items come up for sale. Even though Christmas has been celebrated for years, its celebration as a national holiday is as recent as 1891 and its unusual appeal as a collectible is, of course, much newer than that. It is in recent years that Americans have become enamored with many different collecting interests in Christmas. Christmas collecting is a vast field and a collector may amass a collection of many different things, but there are certain areas of Christmas that attract more interest than others, such as: feather trees, candy containers, paper ornaments, Dresden paper figures, wax decorations, pressed cotton creations, glass ornaments, early lighting devices, and electric bulbs.— Robert Brenner

ARTIFICIAL & FEATHER TREES

As far back as the last third of the 19th century, artificial trees have been in existence. From what can be determined, feather tree manufacturing was a cottage industry similar to the manufacture of glass tree ornaments. However, it was different in several respects. The parts for the tree—wire, wood, and berries—were factory made & the heavy wire branches were sent to cottages for wrapping. Turkey and goose feathers were the most commonly used feathers, but swan feathers also were used. Sheared trees, as we know them today, did not exist at that time and feather trees accurately reflected the *neutral appearance of live white pines. These trees are a relatively expensive collectors item, they can command prices ranging from $85.00 to $1,200.00 or more, depending on age and size. It seems to be a rule of thumb that trees are priced about $120.00 to $145.00 per foot.*

In addition to feather trees, visca trees made in America and even brush trees from the 1960s are seeing an increase in price. But aluminum trees, which appeal to the younger generation of collectors, are dramatically rising in price. Produced as early as the mid-1950s and into the late 1960s, these trees are snapped up almost as fast as they placed on sale.

Tree, green w/candleholders, square
   white base, 24" 270

Tree, white w/red berries, round red
   base, 24" 240

Tree, blue w/candleholders, square
   white base, 46" 480

CANDY CONTAINERS

Some of the earliest decorations for the Christmas tree were edibles and the containers that held these "goodies" were often used as decorations for the tree. Many cornucopias and candy containers found today are small and their appearance on the tree seems quite obvious. Candy containers in the shape of Father Christmas command the highest prices and those containers made in Germany easily command over $100.00 each. In fact, the composition and papier-mâché containers are becoming increasingly difficult to find as collectors scramble to add them to collections.

Green Tree w/red berries

Tree, green w/red berries, in round
   white base, 12" (ILLUS.)................ **$125**

Santa On Bombshell

Basket, paper, w/tinsel handle &
   Santa scrap on front 160

Boot, papier-mâché, German 40

Child, cotton, w/bisque head pushing
   papier-mâché snow ball 550

Cornucopia, paper, gold foiled cone   85

Egg, silk over pressed cardboard 160

Elf, composition, sitting on candy
   container log................................... 325

Santa, celluloid head, mesh body..... 165

Santa in car, celluloid head,
   cardboard car w/wheels 320

Santa on bombshell, composition
   (ILLUS.).. 850

Santa on Donkey, candy box
   (ILLUS.).. 185

Snow ball, cotton covered w/red
   cotton Santa on top, Japan, 4" 120

Santa on Donkey Candy Box

Various old figural light bulbs

CHRISTMAS ADVERTISING

During Victorian times, small litho-graphed prints known as trade cards were the primary form of written advertisements. These advertising cards were used for prod-ucts ranging from coffee to farm machinery. Lion Brothers and McLaughins advertised their coffee with some of the most beautiful of cards, many of which used the figure of St. Nicholas as their central theme. Along with the increased use of color in magazines, came numerous new advertisements at Christmas employing Santa Claus and other Christmas-related themes.

Biscuit tin, Kennedy w/Santa 420

Button, celluloid, Santa w/stocking .. 95

Button, celluloid, TB, 1936 45

Calendar top, blue Santa w/children 120

Candy pail, Santa, early 425

Cigar box, Santa w/toys inside cover 165

Coca-Cola, standing Santa,
ca. 1930s 210

Lion Coffee, Santa w/children
chromo 225

Snow King, stand-up Santa w/sleigh 950

Soapbox, Fairbank's 600

Trade card, Santa w/sleigh, Snow
King baking powder 95

CHRISTMAS TREE LIGHTS

FIGURAL BULBS

When Christmas trees began to be lit with electricity, a whole new area of collectibles was opened. One type of electric lamp used was the "Festoon Lamp" (sometimes referred to as "Stringer"), produced around 1895. A Festoon Lamp was a round glass globe with a carbon filament running length-wise attached to brass connectors on either end with loops for wiring them together in a series.

Around 1908, fancy figural lamps started

being imported from Germany, Austria, and Hungary. They were similar to clip-on orna-ments and some had an exhaust tip at the top; in the case of many birds, the tip was their beak. The glass had detailed molding, soft shades of paint and expressive faces making them comparable to the early European ornaments.

After World War I, Japan began to manu-facture glass figural light bulbs and soon the milk glass figural light was commonplace on American trees. Regardless of whether the lights work or not, they can easily bring more than $30.00, with the European lights being worth over $200.00.

Bubble lights, Italian miniature light sets, and matchless stars continue to set price records. The different types appeal to the younger generation of collectors.

Angel, hard plastic, painted, Japan,
ca. 1930-50s, 4 3/4" h. 12

Aviator, decorated milk glass, Japan,
ca. 1930-50s, 3" h. 65

Cat w/fiddle, milk glass, painted,
Japan, ca. 1930-50s, 3 1/2" h 28

Clown w/mask, milk glass, painted,
Japan, ca. 1930-50s, 1/2" h. 24

Dog in basket, milk glass, painted,
Japan, ca. 1930-50s, 3 1/4" h 28

Father Christmas, double-sided,
milk glass, painted, Japan,
ca. 1930-50s, 3" h. 25

Frog, milk glass, painted, Japan,
ca. 1930-50s, 2 3/4" h. 30

Jiminy Cricket, milk glass, painted,
Japan, ca. 1930-50s, Disney,
2 3/4" h. 28

King Cole, decorated milk glass 25

Lantern, milk glass, painted, snow-
laden, Japan, ca. 1930-50s,
2 1/4" h. 6

Little Orphan Annie, milk glass,
painted, Japan, ca. 1930-50s, 3" h. 60

Mickey Mouse, milk glass, painted,
Disney, Japan, ca. 1930-50s,
2 3/4" h. 30

Moon Mullins, milk glass, painted,
Japan, ca. 1930-50s, 2" h.............   50

Owl, milk glass, painted, Japan,
ca. 1930-50s, 3 1/4" h.   40

Parrot, milk glass, painted, Japan,
ca. 1930-50s, 3 3/4" h.   15

Pluto, milk glass, painted, Japan,
ca. 1930-50s, Disney, 3" h.   24

Snowman Light Bulb

Snowman, milk glass, painted,
Japan, ca. 1930-50s, 3 1/2" h.
(ILLUS.)   24

St. Nicholas w/staff, milk glass,
painted, Japan, ca. 1930-50s,
2 3/4" h.   28

ELECTRIC LIGHT BULBS

Andy Gump, milk glass   90

Ball, milk glass, red w/stars   15

Bird, brown, early European............. 120

Bubble light, oil, working.................   65

Bubble light, shooting stars 120

Santa Light Bulb

Santa, milk glass, painted, Japan,
ca. 1930-50s, 3" h. (ILLUS.)   15

Santa w/trees & toys, decorated
milk glass, regular socket, Japan,
ca. 1930-50s, 5" h.   95

Candleholders

Bulbs, C-6, Detecto 5

Clown head, milk glass 35

Cottage, milk glass, six-sided 10

Dick Tracy, milk glass 95

Dog in basket, milk basket.............. 65

Dresden, flowers, 3" 120

Dresden, dog, 5".............................. 225

Grapes, milk glass 15

Humpty Dumpty, milk glass, large
head 65

Jack-O' Lantern, milk glass 120

Lion, w/tennis racket, milk glass 50

Matchless star, single row points 45

Pig, w/bowtie, milk glass 85

Rose, clear glass, Dresden.............. 120

Rose, clear glass, small, Japan 10

Santa head, large, milk glass, 4"
(ILLUS.) 25

Smitty, milk glass 95

St. Nicholas, clear glass, early
European.. 185

Woman in shoe, milk glass.............. 65

Zeppelin, milk glass.......................... 75

Boxed set, Disney Silly Symphony .. 320

Boxed set, glass, Mother Goose
characters...................................... 285

EARLY LIGHTING DEVICES

Candles were the most popular and widely used method for illuminating the tree. Due to the fact that many fires were caused by tipping candles, balanced weight candleholders were invented. These would keep the candle standing upright, avoiding its tipping over into a branch or another ornament. The earliest and most economical were those with clay or wooden balls at the bottom. Also used as counter-balances were lead figures, heavy

glass ornaments, and soft metal ornaments.Some of the rarest Christmas candleholders include thin, fragile glass lanterns that clip onto the tree. First manufactured just before the turn-of-the-century, they were introduced as being novel alternatives to plain metal candleholders. The counter balance holders many times bring $100.00 or more with the simple clip-ons in the $1.00 to $5.00 range.

Candleholder, counterbalance, tin &
lead geometric figure at end,
several varieties (ILLUS. of four)... 120

Candleholder, counterbalance,
w/clay ball at bottom 20

Candleholder, pinch-on,
lithographed w/Father Christmas .. 185

Christmas light, glass, cranberry..... 320

Christmas light, quilted blue........... 75

Christmas light, quilted milk glass... 80

Lantern, glass, in shape of aviator
w/candle insert, clip-on................. 685

Lantern, metal w/glass panels, six-
sided... 95

Reflector, tin, American.................... 5

COOKIE MOLDS, CANDY MOLDS, & COOKIE CUTTERS

Molds and cookie cutters were often fashioned in the shape of Father Christmas. Some of the earliest of molds were created by the gingerbread bakers and lebküchen creators who were also chandlers (or wax workers). After the mid-1600s, molds were made from carved wood or molded plaster, unlike the earlier molds made of fired, unglazed clay. Candy molds were made of heavy metal and have surprisingly good detail. Even ice cream and cake molds in various Santa shapes have been found. Eppelsheimer and Co. produced pewter ice cream molds in the shape of Father Christmas in the late 1800s.Cookie cutters were at first made at home from tin and these examples of folk art are highly sought after by today's collectors. Many of these were quite large, up to 13" in length. The first ones were without handles and were awkward to use. Cutters from the 1940s and 1950s are quite interesting as many of them had quite defined shapes. Many of these molds and cutters can make interesting wall displays during the Christmas season

Bell, candy mold 60

Christmas tree, candy mold............. 65

Santa on Donkey, candy mold, two-part 295

Santas, candy mold, two rolls of 14.. 140

GAMES, PUZZLES, & TOYS

Toy collectors cross with Christmas collectors in vying for some very expensive items. With the Victorian fascination with parlor games came the inevitable manufacturing of many Christmas and Santa-related games. These were not manufactured in huge quantities since their use only seemed appropriate during a short period of the year. Wooden puzzles are also of interest to collectors because of the beautiful lithographed images of Father Christmas and later Santa Claus.Among some of the finest old toys available include cast-iron toys made by Hubley, manufactured in the early 1900s. Toys made of pressed tin were made in the Nurnberg area of Germany as early as the late 1700s. Nodders and clockwork Santas were absolutely beautiful and very few of these were saved. Paper lithography enabled the manufacturers to decorate even the most inexpensive toy with color. Especially desirable are the tin German toys such as those made after World War I because many of these survived and are available to collectors today. Those toys depicting Santa riding in mechanical cars, sleighs and airplanes are highly collectible. The tin mechanical toys manufactured in Japan from the 1930s through the 1950s have seen very dramatic price increases.

Battery-operated, Santa w/drum, eyes light up, Japan 295

Jigsaw puzzle, lantern, Santa head, American 285

Mechanical, skating Santa, Japan ... 425

Rolly poly, Santa, Schoenhut, 7" 850

Santa on top of house, 9" 310

Wind-up, celluloid Santa, Japan....... 120

Santa with Book Wind-Up Toy

Wind-up, Santa w/book, Japan (ILLUS.) 165

GREETING CARDS

Although greeting cards originated as early as 1846 in England, they did not become popular in the United States until the late 1870s. The earliest of these cards were illustrated with flowers, birds, and other such non-Christmas themes. It wasn't until the beginning of the 1920s that Santa was widely used on greeting cards. St. Nick was depicted in every conceivable style of dress and would appear in cars, airplanes, train cars, and engines and even with polar bears. His fine details of color and accessories was interpreted individually by the whims of countless artists. Since his appearance was not standardized, it is fairly simple for a collector to find unusual and interesting cards.

Fold-out, airbrush, "Xmas," 1908 15

Fold-out, five-layer nativity scene 110

Fold-out, two-layer, Angels w/nativity 60

Father Christmas Greeting Card

Fold-out, two-layer, Father
Christmas (ILLUS.)........................ **125**

Walt Disney, Mickey Mouse............. **110**

HALLMARK KEEPSAKE ORNAMENTS (1973-1976)

In 1973, Hallmark Cards introduced its new product line of Keepsake Ornaments. Adding color and variety to the present day standard glass balls, these eighteen Keepsake Ornaments quickly blossomed into a new holiday tradition and collectibles field.

The listings below represent pricing for unboxed and unpackaged Keepsake Ornaments from 1973 through 1976. Boxed and packaged ornaments will sell at a higher price.

**Adorable Adornments: Betsey
Clark,** 1975, No. QX 157-1, by
artist Donna Lee, 3 1/2" h.............. **240**

**Adorable Adornments: Drummer
Boy,** 1975, No. QX 161-1,
handcrafted, by artist Donna Lee,
3 1/2" h. **150**

Angel, 1974, No. QX 110-1, white
glass ball, 3 1/4" d. **67**

Baby's First Christmas, 1976, No.
QX 221-1, white satin ball marked
"Baby's First Christmas," dated
"1976," 3" d.................................. **100**

Betsey Clark, 1973, No. XHD 100-2,
white glass ball, depicts five girls
around Christmas tree, 3 1/4" d..... **75**

Betsey Clark series, 1976, No. QX
195-1, white glass ball marked
"Christmas 1976," 3 1/4" d............ **75**

Bicentennial Charmers, 1976, No.
QX 198-1, marked "Merry
Christmas 1976" on white glass
ball, 3 1/4" d................................. **55**

Blue Girl, 1973, No. XHD 85-2, yarn
ornament, 4 1/2" h. **25**

Chickadees, 1976, No. QX 204-1,
marked "Christmas 1976" on white
glass ball, 2 5/8" d. **60**

Colonial Children set: 1976, No. QX
208-1, depicts children making
snowman & marked "Christmas
1976" on one, children bringing
home Christmas tree & marked
"Merry Christmas 1976" on other,
white glass balls, set of 2, 2 1/4" d. **80**

Elf, 1973, No. XHD 79-2, yarn
ornament, 4 1/2" h. **28**

Happy Holidays Kissing Ball, 1976,
No. QX 225-1, red & green holly
surrounding "Happy Holidays" on
white satin ball, comes w/mistletoe,
5-6" d. **220**

Little Girl, 1973, No. XHD 82-5, yarn
ornament w/pink dress & blonde
hair, 4 1/2" h. **25**

Manger Scene, 1973, No. XHD 102-
2, white glass ball, designed scene
on dark red background, 3 1/4" h. . **85**

Mrs. Santa, 1973, No. XHD 75-2,
yarn ornament , 4 1/2" h. **25**

Norman Rockwell, 1976, No. QX
196-1, front depicts Santa resting
after travels, Santa feeding
reindeer on back, marked
"Christmas 1976," white glass ball,
3 1/4" d. 60

Norman Rockwell series, 1974, No.
QX 106-1, white glass ball, dated
"1974," depicts "Jolly Postman" &
father & son bringing home
Christmas tree, marked "Merry
Christmas 1974," 3 1/4" d. 70

Nostalgia Ornaments: Locomotive,
1975, No. QX 127-1, by artist Linda
Sickman, dated "1975," 3 1/4" d. 180

**Nostalgia Ornaments: Peace On
Earth,** 1975, No. QX 131-1, snowy
village scene, by artist Linda
Sickman, dated "1975," 3 1/4" d. 130

Raggedy Ann, 1976, No. QX 221-1,
depicts Ann hanging stockings on
fireplace, marked "Merry
Christmas 1976," white satin ball,
2 1/2" d. 50

**Raggedy Ann and Raggedy Andy
set:** 1974, No. QX 114-1, white
glass balls, set of 4, 1 3/4" d. 70

Rudolph and Santa, 1976, No. QX
213-1, front marked "Rudolph the
Red-Nosed Reindeer" w/"Merry
Christmas 1976" on back, white
satin ball, 2 1/2" d. 75

Santa, 1973, No. XHD 74-5, yarn
ornament , 4 1/2" h. 25

Santa With Elves, 1973, No. XHD
101-5, white glass ball, 3 1/4" d. 70

Snowgoose, 1974, No. QX 107-1,
white glass ball, 3 1/4" d. 70

Tree Treats: Santa, 1976, No. QX
177-1, marked "Season's
Greetings 1976," 2 3/4-3 5/8" h. ... 180

Tree Treats: Shepherd, 1976, No.
QX 175-1, marked "Season's
Greetings 1976," 2 3/4-3 5/8" h. ... 100

Twirl-Abouts: Partridge, 1976, No.
QX 174-1, partridge in pear
wreath, dated "1976," by artist
Linda Sickman, dated "1976,"
3 1/2-4" h. 145

Twirl-Abouts: Santa, 1976, No. QX
172-1, Santa in wreath, dated
"1976," by artist Linda Sickman,
3 1/2-4" h. 100

Yesteryears: Santa, 1976, No. QX
182-1, dated "1976," 2 3/4"-4" h. .. 150

Yesteryears: Train, 1976, No. QX
181-1, dated "1976," 2 3/4"-4" h. .. 155

POSTCARDS

*Santa and Christmas-related themes have
always been incorporated on postcards. The
rarest of these include the hold-to-light, silk,
mechanical and full-figured European cards.
The hold-to-lights are especially of value to
collectors because they are composed of multiple layers of cardboard, with the top layer
cut-out in strategic places, letting the light
shine through. Some cards used pieces of silk
fabric to make Santa's clothes and the rarest
of these cards are those that use colors other
than the traditional red.*

Father Christmas Holding Lantern

Father Christmas, dressed in grey-
blue suit, holding lantern up to
street sign, reads "A Merry
Christmas," Germany, B & W, No.
296 (ILLUS.) 14

Father Christmas, dressed in long
blue robe, w/children outside
house, marked "Christmas
Greetings" (ILLUS.) 20

Father Christmas Ice Skating With Children

Father Christmas, dressed in red robe, skating w/little boy on his back & holding little girl's hand, marked "Wesolych Swiat," (ILLUS.) 15

Hold-to-light, Santa w/child 240

Mechanical, Santa w/children 120

Real photo, Santa w/children 65

Santa, celluloid add-on, polycolor w/fringe 30

Santa In Sleigh, metal add-on, marked "Merry Christmas," fur trim 35

Santa riding in train w/children 35

Santa With Nimble Nicks

Santa w/Nimble Nicks, Santa in old car w/Nimble Nicks & presents, marked "Merry Christmas From Us All," Whitney Publishing (ILLUS.) .. 15

An early Christmas postcard.

Father Christmas With Children

Putz Church and Houses

Silk, Santa leaning over child in chair (ILLUS. w/introduction) 50

Silk, Santa standing w/sack of toys .. 60

St. Nicholas With Krampus

St. Nicholas w/Krampus, standing behind dish of nuts & fruit, Australia, M. M. Vienne (ILLUS.) ... 45

PUTZ (NATIVITY) RELATED MATERIALS

Animals, composition, assorted, German 25

Animals, wood, assorted, German ... 45

Church, cardboard, large, Japan (ILLUS., front) 35

Deer, celluloid, Japan, 6" 35

Figures, human, celluloid, Japan...... 65

House, cardboard, large, Japan (ILLUS. top right) 25

House, cardboard, medium, Japan (ILLUS. top left) 20

Sheep, composition head, wool
   body, 4" **120**

Trees, brush, small, Japan **8**

Trees, sponge, large, Japan **15**

SANTA FIGURES

The most valuable Santa figures are the Victorian papier-mâché items.

Papier-mâché (the combination of pulp paper, glue or paste, oil, and rosin) was pressed into two half-molds and once dry, pieces were removed, glued together, and smoothed with sandpaper. They were then sealed with varnish and painted in realistic colors. Many times beards of rabbit fur were glued on for added realism. Originally called Pelze-Nicols, they became known as Belsnickles.

Another popular version of the Santa fig-

ure used composition. These papier-mâché-type figures were dipped into liquid plaster, which dried in a very thin coat. These figures were realistically painted, paying close attention to the face and hands. They were dressed in authentic clothing and many carried branches or trees made of goose feathers. The candy containers were hidden beneath the flowing cloth skirt. There were numerous other materials also used, including: wood, wax, cotton, plaster, chalk, and metal. All of the earliest European-types command extremely high prices on the market today.

Somewhat neglected, even though they are quickly gaining in popularity, are the later cardboard Santas, made from material resembling old egg-cartons. These were copies of a more robust Santa, like those seen in Coca-Cola ads. Most had an opening in

Belsnickel Santa Figures

which candy or small presents could be inserted. They were excellent representations of our jolly American Santa Claus.

Belsnickel, Belsnickel, red, w/feather branch, 7" (ILLUS. center) 400

Belsnickel, white, w/feather branch, 11" (ILLUS. right)............................ 700

Belsnickel, blue, w/feather branch, 12" (ILLUS. left)............................. 785

Bisque, miniature, on cardboard 85

Bisque, miniature, pulling sleigh....... 160

Plaster Bank

CHRISTMAS TREE ORNAMENTS

Acorn

Standing Celluloid Santa Figures

Celluloid, standing, w/black doll, Japan, 4" (ILLUS. left) 160

Celluloid, Painted details, Irwin, 12". 290

Cotton, w/paper face, 6".................. 225

Japan, standing, paper, 4"............... 55

Japan, chenille body over cardboard, composition face, 9" 420

Plaster, bank, standing, American, 10" (ILLUS.).................................. 165

Plaster, in chimney, American, 10"... 200

Acorn, silver, ca. 1940s, "Made in the United States," 4" (ILLUS.)...... 25

Angel, small spun fiberglass decoration w/angel figure inside, ca. 1920s, 2" (ILLUS.) 30

Angel w/silver wings, Dresden-type, Germany, ca. 1880-1900s 200

Bicycle, cotton batting 200

Camel, Dresden-type Germany, ca. 1880-1900s.............................. 65

Angel Ornament

Football, Dresden-type Germany,
ca. 1880-1900s.............................. **165**

Guitar w/applied decorations,
Dresden-type, Germany, ca. 1880-
1900s... **225**

Peach Ornament

Peach, w/rough tinsel, made in
Germany, 2" (ILLUS.).................... **100**

Santa beating drum, cotton batting,
w/die cut, 4" h. **300**

DRESDEN PAPER ORNAMENTS

Banjo, three-dimensional, 3" **160**

Dresden Paper Elephant

Elephant, three-dimensional, 4"
(ILLUS.,) **520**

Elf, holding money bag, three-
dimensional, 3" **725**

Dresden Paper Elk

Elk, brown, three-dimensional, 2"
(ILLUS.,) **160**

Dresden Paper Moon

Face in quarter moon, three-dimensional (ILLUS.,) 525

Fox, brown & tan, three-dimensional, 2" 375

Goat, black & white, three-dimensional, 2" 320

Heart, gold, three-dimensional, 3" 95

Jockey on horse, three-dimensional, 3" 625

Dresden Paper Lion

Lion, three-dimensional, 2" (ILLUS.,) 195

Lobster, orange, three-dimensional, 4" 540

Monkey on branches, flat, 4" 165

Owl, tan & black, three-dimensional, 2" 410

Dresden Paper Parrot

Parrot, gold, three-dimensional (ILLUS.) 145

Pig, gold, three-dimensional, 2" 620

Rabbit, silver, three-dimensional, 3". 300

Santa, gold, three-dimensional, 4".... 190

Star, gold, flat, 3" 65

GLASS ORNAMENTS

Al Jolson head, 3 1/4" 385

Amelia Earhart, 4"........................... 245

*Automobile & Los Angeles
Zeppelin Glass Ornaments*

Automobile, red & silver, 3" (ILLUS. top) 95

Glass Ornaments of Baby & Bacchas

Baby, head, glass eyes, 2" (ILLUS.). 165

Baby, w/pacifier, in crib, 2" 360

Glass Ornaments of Baby & Bacchas

Bacchas, head, 2" (ILLUS. right)...... 420

Bear, 3".. 175

Beetle, red & gold, 2"........................ 95

Bird, game pheasant, 4".................... 320

Bird, owl, standing on clip, 4" 165

Bird, peacock, on clip, fanned spun
  glass, 4"... 50

Bird, owl, on clip, glass eyes, 5" 85

Bird, spun glass tail, 5" 25

Bird, w/berry in beak, 5" 165

Boy, whistling, w/hat & scarf, 4"........ 95

Carrot, 4" (ILLUS. right center)......... 120

Cat, w/fiddle & cap, 3"...................... 280

Cat in shoe, 4"................................. 165

Charlie Chaplin head, 3" 420

Christ Child head, 3" 180

Clown, circus, 4"............................... 35

Clown, "My Darling," 4" 70

Corn, 4" (ILLUS. right) 85

Devil head, gold, 4" 520

Dog, blowing horn, 4"........................ 210

Elephant, on ball, 3" 320

Elephant, 4".................................... 120

Fantasy ornament, bells.................. 120

Father Christmas, early, 5".............. 165

Fish, w/paper fins & tail, 4" 190

Flower, on clip, venetian dew, 3"...... 125

Frog, on toadstool, 3" 65

Grape cluster, individual grapes, 4". 40

Happy Hooligan, extended legs, 5" . 650

Horn, silver w/flowers, 4" 15

Various Glass Ornaments

Hot air balloon, angel, 4" (ILLUS. left) 160

Hot air balloon, angel, 6" (ILLUS. left) 145

Hot air balloon, Santa, 7" (ILLUS. center) 320

Indian bust, painted feathers, 4"...... 355

Indian head, on clip, 2".................... 220

Keystone Cop, extended legs, 5" 650

Kite, chenille string, 3" 520

Kugel, round, gold, 2" 35

Kugel, pear shaped, silver, 3"........... 240

Kugel, grape cluster, green, 4" 300

Los Angeles zeppelin, paper label, 4" (ILLUS. page 151)..................... 320

Mermaid, red & flesh face, 4" 400

Mrs. Santa Claus, 4" 460

Mushroom, cluster of three on clip, 4"... 60

Pear, matte finish, 4"........................ 45

Pickle, curved, 4" (ILLUS. left center) 130

Pine cone, silver, 4"........................... 5

Potato, 4" (ILLUS. left)..................... 175

Rabbit, w/carrot, 4" 85

Rose, white w/venetian dew, on clip . 110

Sailboat Tree Ornaments

Sailboat, angel scrap, 5" (ILLUS. left) 210

Sailboat, Dresden sail, 5" (ILLUS. right) 225

Santa, blue w/tree, 4"........................ 45

Santa, in basket, 4"........................... 65

Santa, on clip, 4" (ILLUS. right) 85

Santa, red w/tree, 4" (ILLUS. left) 35

Santa, below ball, 5" (ILLUS. center) 185

Snowman, w/broom, 4" 30

Songbird, on clip, 3"......................... 10

Storks, mother & baby, on clip, 5" 210

Uncle Sam, full-figure, 3"................. 525

Hot Air Balloons

Santa Ornaments

Walnut, gold, 2" 10

Witch, w/cat & broom, 4" 620

Zeppelins

Zeppelin, wire-wrapped, 5" (ILLUS. right) 310

Zeppelin, wire-wrapped, w/glass gondola, 5" (ILLUS. left) 500

ITALIAN GLASS ORNAMENTS

Alpine man, w/rope, 5" 125

Italian Glass Elf

Elf, seated, 6" (ILLUS.) 60

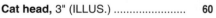

Italian Glass Cat Head

Cat head, 3" (ILLUS.) 60

Italian Glass Lamp

Lamp, 5" (ILLUS.) 55

Man in Moon, 4" (ILLUS.) 110

Italian Glass Man in Moon

Italian Glass Mouse

Mouse, playing saxaphone, 6"
(ILLUS.) 95

Italian Glass Robin Hood

Robin Hood, 6" (ILLUS.) 120

Italian Glass Wizards

Wizard, 6" (ILLUS.) 85

PAPER ORNAMENTS

Angels, w/tinsel holder, 3" 25

Angels w/Cellophane & Tinsel

Angels, w/cellophane & tinsel, 7"
(ILLUS.) 80

Santa Riding Sled

Miss Liberty, tinsel & cellophane 115

Santa, full-bodied, riding sled
(ILLUS.,) 120

Santa, full-bodied, w/tree & toys, 15"
w/tinsel 180

Santa head, w/tinsel holder, 4" 20

Star with Scrap Angel

Star w/a scrap angel, tinsel trim , 6"
(ILLUS.,) 45

Victorian children, in car w/Santa,
cellophane & tinsel trim, 6" 135

PRESSED COTTON ORNAMENTS

Angel, paper face, Dresden wings, 3" 225

Bell, blue, 3" 35

Cow, brass bell, 4" 220

Cucumber, green & yellow, 4" 95

Girl, bisque head/wool coat, w/lead
ice skates, 4" (ILLUS. left center) .. 285

Girl, paper face, 4" (ILLUS. far left) .. 200

Jockey, w/horse head, 4" 560

Man, paper crown on head, 4"
(ILLUS. center right) 320

Orange, 3" 75

Peddler, cotton fruit in pack, 4" 325

Sailor, w/cap, 4" 400

Santa, school girl, bisque, 4" 320

Victorian lady, 3" (ILLUS. far right) .. 220

SPUN-GLASS ORNAMENTS

Angel, paper on clip, w/spun glass
wings 310

Angel, in circle, 4" 70

Pressed Cotton Ornaments

Peacock, flat, elaborately painted, 5" 190

Sailboat, double sided, in circle, 5" .. 40

Santa, in circle w/comet tail, 8" 120

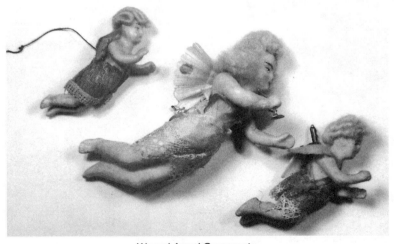

Victorian Boy Spun-Glass Ornament

Victorian boy, in circle, 5" (ILLUS.).. 55

WAX & WAXED ORNAMENTS

Angel, American, ca. 1940s, 4" 25

Angel, waxed, 4" (ILLUS. left) 120

Angel, waxed, 5" (ILLUS. right) 195

Angel, wax, 6" 240

Angel, waxed, 6" (ILLUS. middle)..... 220

Bird, in metal circle, 5" 280

Soldier, American, ca. 1940s, 4" 25

MISCELLANEOUS CHRISTMAS ITEMS

Beaded chains, glass, German, 12" 45

Fence, cast iron, painted, four-sections 400

Fence, feather w/red berries, 6 pcs. . 500

Handkerchief, family decorating tree 325

Handkerchief, Nast Santa................ 520

Mask, papier-mâché, early 1900s, German 450

Nativity set, Sunday school fold-out (ILLUS.) 40

Snow Babies figures, china, sliding down roof, each............................. 310

Snow Baby figure, china, riding polar bear 295

Tinsel, lead, National Tinsel 20

Tree stand, cast iron, Santa molded on both sides, Germany 295

Tree stand, lithographed tin, American 65

Waxed Angel Ornaments

Tree stand, wind-up, revolving, musical, early 1900s, German....... 780

MISCELLANEOUS

Advertising, pictorial die-cut counter card for Ayers Cherry, Lowell, Mass. Co., ca. 1890s..................... 400

Album, embossed, w/multiple Santas, Victorian 75

Animated elf, rubber-type head, glass eyes, cloth clothing, electric, U.S.A., 18" h................................ 600

Belsnickle, white robe covered w/glitter, early, Germany, 7 3/4" h. 600

Book, "Night Before Christmas," McLoughlin, ca. 1888 140

Cake pan, tin, Santa, 9" l. 65

Candy container, old-fashioned Santa on elephant nodder, 8 1/2" h. (some wear to flocking) ... 500

Candy container, Santa in chenille boot, Japan, 8 1/2" h. 100

Snow Man Candy Container

Candy container, Snowman, pressed board (ILLUS.) 125

Child angel, die-cut, Victorian, Germany, 11" h. 175

Christmas seals booklet, No. 80-935, Dennison Co., set of 48......... 8

Christmas tree stand, cast iron, electrified w/pointsettias & sockets for bulbs, painted 135

Christmas tree stand, cast iron, large round stand w/elves, painted 400

Costume, Santa Claus, in original box, ca. 1940 (missing beard) 45

Creche & Figures

Creche & figures, the creche made in Germany, figures made in Japan, Germany & Italy, value of figures depends on condition & where manufactured, ca. 1930s, creche price only (ILLUS.)............. 100+

Die-cut Santa Claus, air-brushed, 9 1/4" h. 85

Die-cut Santa Claus, in blue suit w/glittery & gold additions, German, Victorian, 20" h. 600

Doll, Santa Claus, composition, dressed in brown suit, snow on Santa, Germany, 30" h. 2,800

Santa Bisque Figurine

Figurine, bisque, Santa w/bag of toys, Hallmark (ILLUS.) 125

Figurine, "Nightmare Before Christmas" Santa Claus, in original box (ILLUS.) 125

Figurine, Santa Claus, celluloid, dressed in blue, in sleigh w/toys & teddy bear 125

Game, "Visit of Santa Claus," McLoughlin 500

Hanging lantern, Santa face w/glass eyes, molded composition 700

Kugel, figural ball, silver, Germany, 9" d. 200

Kugel, figural grape, bluish purple, Germany, 12" h. 600

Match cover, Santa on front cover, candle-shaped matches inside, 3 1/2" 20

Photograph, shows little boy & girl dressed in nightgowns sitting in front of Christmas tree w/toys, ca. 1910... 60

Russian Santa, white cotton batting, all-white, 18" h. 800

Salt & pepper set, ceramic, Santa Claus & Mrs. Claus, white rough spaghetti texture to represent fur,

ca. 1950s, made in Japan, 5" h., pr. (ILLUS.).................................... 50

Santa Claus & Mrs. Claus Salt & Pepper Shakers

Tinsel, metallic strand-type, U.S.A., mint in box 18

Tray, tin, oval, depicts full-figure Santa in blue suit w/toys, early tray painted by artist John Moreno in 1997 350

Tray, Coca-Cola Santa Claus, 1973, 10 3/4 x 13 1/4" (ILLUS.) 60

Tree, green bristle brush-type, on red base, simulated snow on end of

"Nightmare Before Christmas" Santa

Green Bristle Brush Tree

branches, ca. 1940s-1950s, 21" h.
(ILLUS.) **35**

Tree, feather-type, turn-of-the-
century, on decorated red base,
w/small decorations , 27" h.
(ILLUS.) .... **400+**

Feather Tree w/Decorations

Coca-Cola Santa Claus Tray

COOKBOOKS

Cookbook collectors are usually good cooks and will buy important new cookbooks as well as seek out notable older ones. Many early cookbooks were published and given away as advertising premiums for various products used extensively in cooking. While some rare, scarce first edition cookbooks can be very expensive, most collectible cookbooks are reasonably priced.

Corn Products Cook Book

"Good Things To Eat" Cookbook

Advertising, "Corn Products Cook Book," E. c. Hewitt, Karo Corn Products, NY, w/wraps, illus., 40 pp., very good (ILLUS.) **$8**

Advertising, "Good Things To Eat," Arm & Hammer, NY, 1932, w/wraps, 33 pp., very good cond. (ILLUS.) 5

Advertising, "My Favorite Chocolate Chocolate Cakes," NY, 1938, w/wraps, illus., 15 pp., very good cond. 5

Ivanhoe Foods Mayonnaise Cookbook

Advertising, "Salad Leaves or Letters to a Daughter in the City," Ivanhoe Foods, Inc. (Mayo), Auburn, NY, w/wraps, illus., 35 pp., very good cond. (ILLUS.) 6

Advertising, "The Jewett Chafing Dish with a Collection Of Recipes for Chafing-Dish Cookery," J. c. Jewett Mfg. Co., Buffalo, 1892, w/wraps, photo illus., 46 pp., excellent cond. 20

Advertising, "The Morrell Menu Maker," J. Morrell & Co., 1950, w/stiff wraps, illus., 331 pp., very good cond. 8

Brillat-Savarin, Jean A., "The Physiology of Taste," NY, 1948, revised black & gold edition, very good/very good cond. 45

Campbell, Mary M., "Betty Crocker's Kitchen Gardens," NY, 1971, Illustrated by Tasha Tudor, excellent cond. 18

Caron, Emma, "For the Discriminating Hostess," NY, 1925, privately printed, limited & signed by author, w/boards, very good cond. 25

Farmer, Fannie M., "Food and Cookery for the Sick and

Convalescent," Boston, 1915, revised w/additions, decorated hardcovers, illus., 305 pp. + ads in rear, very good cond. **20**

Fisher, M. F. K., "The Art of Eating," NY, 1954, excellent cond. **40**

Goldberg, Hymann, (formerly Prudence Penny), "Our Man in the Kitchen," NY, 1964, illus., 386 pp., w/dust jacket, very good cond. **6**

Lamberton, Gretchen I., "Nita Neighbor's Book of Jelly, Jam, Pickle and Canning Recipes," Minnesota, ca. 1920, w/wraps, 28 pp., good cond............................... **3**

Leslie, Miss, "Lady's Receipt-Book, a Useful Companion for Large or Small Families," Carey & Hart, Philadelphia, 1847, rare, good cond... **350**

Manuscript cookbook, handwritten cookbook belonging to a Julia d. Dixin, dated 1894, w/marbled boards, 56 pp., each recipe is attributed to former recipe owners, good + cond. **55**

Mellish, Katherine, "Katherine Mellish's Cookery and Domestic Management," NY, 1901, chromo illus., 987 pp., very good cond....... **325**

"Modern Priscilla Cook Book," (w/original membership certificate entitling advice & assistance from company), Boston, 1925, 352 pp., very good cond............................. **12**

Parkins, E. B., "Laurel Health Cookery...A Collection of Practical Suggestions and Recipes for the Preparation of Non-Flesh Foods," Massachusetts, 1911, very good cond... **65**

Periodical, "American Cookery," Boston, 1939, vol. XLIV, #3, original price 15 cents, (this periodical was formerly the Boston Cooking School Magazine), excellent cond. (ILLUS.) **3**

Potter, Margaret Yardley, "At Home on the Range or How to Make Friends With Your Stove," 1947, w/dust jacket, very good cond. **6**

"American Cookery" Periodical

Princess Pamela, "Princess Pamela's Soul Food Cookbook," NY, 1969, first edition, paperback, good + cond., ... **12**

Ransom, Son & Co. (D), "Ransom's Family Receipt Book," Buffalo, NY, 1899, w/wraps, 32 pp., includes almanac, good cond. **5**

Rawlings, Marjorie, "Cross Creek Cookery," NY, 1942, first edition, very good/very good cond. **75**

Rorer, S. T. (Mrs.), "Canning and Preserving," Philadelphia, 1887, 32 pp. + ads, very good cond. **30**

Underhill, Jennie E. (Mrs.), "Sunshine Cookbook," New London, CT., 1910, w/stiff wraps, 186 pp. + ads., excellent cond....... **15**

Wurdz, Gordon, "Eediotic Etiquette," NY, 1906, illus., decorative hardcover, 148 pp., good + cond. (ILLUS.) **15**

Eediotic Etiquette Book

CURRIER & IVES PRINTS

This lithographic firm was founded in 1835 by Nathaniel Currier with James M. Ives becoming a partner in 1857. Current events of the day were portrayed in the early days and the prints were hand-colored. Landscapes, vessels, sport and hunting scenes of the West all became popular subjects. The firm was in existence until 1906. All prints listed are hand-colored unless otherwise noted. Numbers at the end of the listings refer to those used in Currier & Ives Prints-An Illustrated Checklist, *by Frederick A. Conningham (Crown Publishers).*

American Country Life

American Country Life - October Afternoon, large folio, N. Currier, 1855, framed, 122, toning, a few scattered fox marks (ILLUS.)..... **$1,495**

American Farm Scenes - No. 3 (Autumn), large folio, N. Currier, 1853, framed, 133, spots of foxing (ILLUS.) 1,495
small folio, undated, framed, 396

American Fireman (The) - Rushing to the Conflict, large folio, 1858, framed, 155 (staining, cockling) **690**

American Railroad Scene - "Snowbound," small folio, 1871, framed, 187, (mottled discoloration in margins, small tear in lower edge) **3,335**

American Winter Sports - Deer Shooting "On the Shattagee," large folio, N. Currier, 1855, framed (tears, paper damage & touch-up repairs) **2,200**

Battle at Cedar Mountain, Aug. 9th, 1862 (The), small folio, undated, framed, 381 (margins trimmed w/tears & some damage) **165**

Battle of Antietam, Md., Sept. 17th, 1862 (The), small folio, undated, framed, 384 (minor edge damage & 1/4" strip added to top margin)... **292**

Battle of Antietam, Md., Sept. 17th, 1862 (The), small folio, undated, framed, 384 (stains) **165**

Battle of Chancellorsville, Va., May 3rd, 1863, small folio, undated, 395 (stains)................................. **253**

Battle of Chancellorsville, Va., May 3rd, 1863, small folio, undated, framed, 395 (minor edge wear & stains).. **286**

Battle of Chattanooga, Tenn., Novr. 24th & 25th, 1863 (The), (tears & minor stains) **275**

American Farm Scene - Autumn

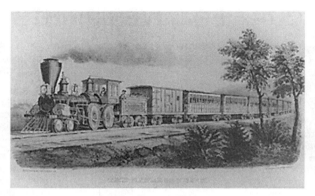

The Express Train

Battle of Corinth, Miss., Oct. 4th, 1862, small folio, undated, framed, 401 (stains & tears) 275

Battle of Fair Oaks, Va., May 31st, 1862 (The), large folio, 1862, framed, 403 (minor stains & tear) . 1,045

Battle of Fair Oaks, Va., May 31st, 1862 (The), small folio, 1862, framed, 402 (minor edge damage & stains) 270

Battle of Fredericksburg, Va., Decr. 13th, 1862, small folio, 1862, framed, 405 (stains) 286

Battle of Mill Spring, Ky., Jan. 19th, 1862, small folio, undated, framed, 412 (torn, wear & stains) 165

Battle of Pea Ridge, Arkansas, March 8th, 1862 (The), large folio, framed, 421 (minor stains, wear & top corners glued down)................ 990

Battle of Pittsburg, Tenn., April 7th, 1862 (The), small folio, 1862, framed, 423 (minor stains) 281

Battle of Pittsburg, Tenn., April 7th, 1862 (The), small folio, 1862, framed, 423 (minor stains & margin creases)....................................... 275

Battle of Sharpsburg, Md., Sept. 16th, 1862 (The), small folio, undated, framed, 429 (minor stains & edge damage)............................ 303

Battle of the Wilderness, Va., May 5th & 6th, 1864 (The), large folio, undated, framed, 435 (stains in margins & edge damage) 1,650

Bombardment and Capture of Fredericksburg, Va. Dec. 11th,

1862, small folio, undated, framed, 592 (stains & edge tears) 165

Capture of Andre (The), small folio, N. Currier, undated, framed, 806 (stains & paper damage) 83

Capture of Atlanta, Georgia, Sept. 2nd, 1864, small folio, undated, framed, 807 (tears & minor stains) 275

Clipper Ship "Lightning," large folio, N. Currier, 1854, framed, 1158 (toning, soiling, unobtrusive cockling, not examined out of frame)... 920

Cottage Life - Summer, small folio, undated, framed, 1267 (minor stains & edge damage, top edge glued down, margins trimmed) 193

Darktown Bicycle Race - The Start, small folio, 1895, 1377 523

Dis-United States (The), small folio, undated, black & white, framed, 1592 (tears, fold line & penciled in date "1861" in title) 248

Disputed Heart (A) - Claiming a Foul, large folio, 1878, 1587, framed (light toning & staining)..... 1,035

Ethan Allen and Mate and Dexter, large folio, 1867, framed 1757 (stains, edge damage & margins trimmed slightly) 770

Express Train (The), small folio, 1855, framed, 1790, (faint discoloration & pale water stains in margins) 2,070

Express Train (The), small folio, 1870, framed, 1793, few small fox marks at upper right (ILLUS.) **2,300**

Frontier Lake (The), small folio, undated, framed, 2153 (minor wear & stains, slightly trimmed) **220**

General Shields at the battle of Winchester, Va., 1862, small folio, 1862, framed, 2294 (minor stains & marginsy trimmed) **248**

Genl. Meagher at the battle of Fair Oaks, Va. June 1st, 1862, small folio, 1862, framed, 2289 (stains & repaired tears) **248**

Great East River Suspension Bridge (The), large folio, 1883, framed, 2597 (foxing, paper discoloration) **632**

Haunts of the Wild Swan (The), small folio, 1872, new curly maple frame, 3757 (foxing & minor edge damage) **303**

Henry Clay - Of Kentucky, small folio, N. Currier, 1842, framed, 2786 (minor stains & damage) **176**

Home in the Wilderness (A), small folio, 1870, framed, 2861 (minor stains & small hole in center which corresponds to knot hole in backing).. **303**

James K. Polk - Eleventh President of the United States, small folio, N. Currier, undated, framed, 3161 (stains).. **165**

Lady Woodruff, Miller's Damsel, General Darcy, and Stella, large folio, 1857, framed, 3399 (few small losses in margins, three tears in upper sheet edges, one extending into image slightly) **1,380**

Last Ditch of the Chivalry (The), medium folio, undated, black & white, framed, 3444 (stains, one covered w/white chalk & some edge damage) **138**

Lexington of 1861 (The), small folio, undated, framed, 3484 (margin stains).. **303**

Life of a Fireman (The) - The Race, large folio, 1854, framed, 3519 (ILLUS.) **1,265**

Lightning Express (The), small folio, undated, framed, 3534 (light stain & few soft handling creases) **2,760**

On the Owago, small folio, undated, 4608 (some edge damage, wear & stains).. **165**

Preparing for Market, large folio, 1856, framed, No. 4870 (toning, staining & soiling, creases, losses to corners) **1,150**

Presidents of the United States (The), small folio, N. Currier, 1844, framed, 4892 (stains, some fading & pinpoint hole) **149**

Riverside (The), medium folio, undated, framed, 5164 (edge damage & stains) **330**

The Life of a Fireman - The Race

Scenery of the Catskills, small folio, undated, old gilded frame, 5419 (minor stains).................................. 385

Season of Blossoms (The), small folio, undated, cross corner frame w/worn finish, 5448 (minor stains, margins trimmed) 248

Second Battle of Bull Run, Fought Augt. 29th, 1862 (The), small folio, undated, framed, 5452 (edge tears, fold lines & stains) 262

Siege and Capture of Vicksburg, Miss., July 4th, 1863, small folio, undated, framed, 5507 (margin stains & minor edge tears) 319

Storming of Fort Donelson, Tenn., Feb. 15th, 1862, small folio, 1862, framed, 5823 (minor stains) 190

Storming of Fort Donelson, Tenn., Feby, 15th, 1862 (The), large folio, 1862, framed, 5824 (some damage) 825

Storming of Fort Donelson (The), small folio, 1862, framed, 5822 (minor wear & stains) 248

Summer in the Woods, small folio, undated, framed, 5866 (margin stains & very minor edge damage) 358

Surrender of Cornwallis at Yorktown, Va. 1781, small folio, N. Currier, 1845, framed, 5904 (minor fading) 275

Surrender of General Lee - At Appomattox, c.H. Va., April 9th,

1865, small folio, 1873, framed 5911 (margins trimmed & damage to title).. 253

Tomb of Washington (The), small folio, undated, framed, 6108 (stains, short tears in margin)........ 138

Western Farmer's Home (The), small folio, 1871, framed, 6619 (minor stains & edge damage) 341

Winter in the Country

Winter in the Country - A Cold Morning, large folio, 1864, framed, 6736, repaired tear at left extending one inch into image, rubbed spots along left edge of image, staining in margins (ILLUS.) **10,925**

"Wooding Up" on the Mississippi, large folio, 1863, framed, several large repaired tears & losses in margins (ILLUS.) **3,450**

"Wooding Up" on the Mississippi

D

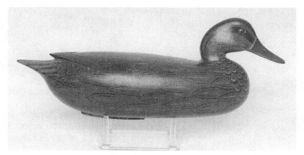

Rare New Jersey John English Decoy

Gottschalk Dollhouse

DECOYS

Decoys have been utilized for years to lure flying waterfowl into target range. They have been made of carved and turned wood, papier-mâché, canvas and metal, and some are in the category of outstanding folk art and command high prices.

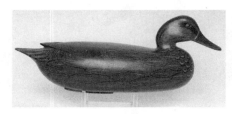

Rare New Jersey English Decoy

Black Duck, Dawson-style by John English, New Jersey, carved wood, glass eyes, original paint (ILLUS.) **$27,500**

Bluebill Drake & Hen, carved wood w/original worn paint, Maryland, 14" l., pr. **220**

Brant, by Nathan Cobb, Jr., carved & painted wood, hollow body, ca. 1880 (ILLUS.) **132,000**

Brant, swimming pose, carved wood w/old worn working paint, 20 1/2" l. (some edge damage, crack in neck at nailed repair) **253**

Canada Goose, by Harry Mitchell Shourds, carved wood, swimming position, original paint w/some wear (ILLUS.) **63,250**

Canada Goose

Canada Goose, by Phinneas Reeves, carved wood, original paint, ca. late 1800s **10,200**

Canada Goose, swimming position, carved wood w/snakey head, original realistic paint & good carved detail, signed "Canada Goose by Clem Wilding," Missouri, 31" l. (glued break in neck) **165**

Canada Goose, primitive carved wood w/white & black repaint, glass eyes, 21" l. **88**

Canvasback Drake, carved wood w/old working repaint & glass eyes, Wisconsin, 15" l. **193**

Canvasback Drake, carved wood, working paint & glass eyes, branded "Hall," 15 1/2" l. (minor wear & damage on bottom edge) **83**

Canvasback Drake & Hen, carved wood w/original worn paint, Maryland, 16" l., pr. **242**

Brant Decoy

Ceramics
Western
Stoneware
Brown + White
2 gal. crock

Bee ? crock

12 gal. crock

ANTIQUES ROADSHOW™ CALENDAR • WORKMAN PUBLISHING

Antiques Roadshow is a trademark of the BBC. Produced under license from BBC Worldwide.

Sharp's Rifle Kit

1870s. VALUE: $8,000–$12,000

This buffalo hunter's kit comes from the days when buffalo roamed freely over the Great Plains. The very heavy .45-caliber Sharp's rifle, the most desirable model for hunting buffalo, was reclaimed by the original owner from a museum in San Jose and passed on to his niece, who kept it in the family. The original cartridge tools and bullet mold that accompany the rifle add to the overall value.

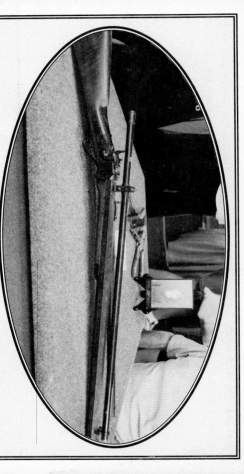

THURSDAY

JANUARY · 2002

3

Canvasback Hen, primitive, carved
wood, old working repaint,
17 3/4" l. (some damage) **138**

Early Ice Fishing Fish Decoy

Fish, carved & painted wood, wide-
pointed fish painted in green
w/orange & yellow striping, ice
fishing-type, 8" l. (ILLUS.).......... **99**

Frog, carved & painted wood,
swimming position, green w/black
spots & open red mouth, ice
fishing-type, 8" l. (ILLUS.)........... **88**

Greenwing Teal Hen, by Charles
Perdew, Illinois, carved wood,
original paint, early version......... **14,850**

Mallard Drake, cork & wood w/old
working repaint, tack eyes, base
marked "Maker Enwright, Toledo,
O.," 17" l. (some edge & shot
damage) **83**

Early Ice Fishing Frog Decoy

Mallard Drake & Hen, "1924
exhibition" by Charles Perdew,
Henry, Illinois, carved wood,
original paint & good patina, pr.
(ILLUS.) **66,000**

Mallard Hen, by Robert Elliston,
carved wood in sleeping pose,
original paint **10,450**

Merganser Drake, by Mason Decoy
Company, Detroit, Michigan,
carved wood, glass eyes, original
paint... **7,250**

Merganser Drake, carved full-bodied
solid figure painted black & white
w/orange & yellow eyes & a pale
orange bill, retains inset lead
weight, probably Maritime
provinces, 20th c. (shrinkage
cracks down underside) **805**

Pintail Drake, by Charles Walker,
carved wood, glass eyes,
w/original paint & good feather
detail (ILLUS.) **44,000**

Mallard Drake & Hen

Pintail Drake

Pintail Drake, by Elmer Crowell, Cape Cod, carved wood, glass eyes, original paint **55,000**

Ward Bros. Pintail Drake

Pintail Drake, by Ward Brothers, Crisfield, Maryland, "pinch

breasted," carved wood, glass eyes, original paint, ca. 1932 (ILLUS.) **104,500**

Teal Drake & Hen

Teal Drake & Hen, by Ward Brothers, Crisfield, Maryland, carved wood, glass eyes, original paint, pr. (ILLUS.) **38,400**

Wigeon Drake, by Joseph Lincoln, Accord, Massachusetts, carved wood, glass eyes, original paint (ILLUS.) **12,650**

Yellowlegs, by Elmer Crowell, carved wood, original paint......... **22,550**

Wigeon Drake

DOLL FURNITURE & ACCESSORIES

Victorian Doll Bed

Bed, Victorian, walnut, turned posts & balusters, 19th c., 21 x 24", 39" h. (ILLUS.) **$121**

Carriage, painted wood chassis in red w/black striping, yellow frame & wheels, black leatherette upholstery & sun shade, mid-19th c., 32" l., 27 1/2" h. (some damage & repainting) **288**

Chest of drawers, walnut, a rectangular lift-lid fitted w/two ring- and knob-turned uprights flanking an oblong lobed mirror w/arched cut-out finials, the case w/a band of half-round bobbin turning above a pair of small drawers over a long drawer all w/simple turned wood knobs, old finish, ca. 1875-85, 5 1/2 x 10", 16 3/4" h. **303**

China closet, oak, two framed glass doors opening to three shelves, two drawers below, 1930s, 12 3/4" w., 20 1/2" h. **165**

Cradle, painted poplar, rectangular w/gently canted low sides slightly arched at one end, on solid rockers, old worn green paint w/yellow striping & the name "Mollie Allen," 19th c., 10 1/4" l. (some wear) **248**

Cradle, dovetailed pine w/old brownish green sponged repaint, 13 1/2" l. (some damage) **72**

Cradle, poplar w/old red paint & yellow striping, 18 3/4" l. **209**

Cradle, dovetailed pine w/old dark grained finish, heart cut-out in foot board, 26" l. **165**

Cradle, dovetailed poplar, heart cut-outs in ends, refinished, curly maple rockers replaced, 39" l. ... **105**

Woven Wicker Doll Carriage

Doll carriage, woven wicker, the deep rounded wicker body w/a hinged wicker hood w/small triangular windows, on bent steel springs & wire wheels w/rubber rims, long upright curved metal handle w/wood grip, ca. 1920s, 24" l., 24" h. (ILLUS.) **193**

Doll carriage, wood w/steel frame, leatherized cloth top w/worn fringe, original varnish w/dark brown & yellow striping, wooden wheels, interior cushion & wallpaper trim, 36" l., 33" h. (some wear) **385**

Dollhouse, wood & fiberboard two-story bungalow, simulated grey stone & brick w/red tile roof, front, sides & back each have two framed windows w/original curtains, one window on each side second floor, full length front porch w/decorative wooden railings, three wooden steps, both sides open to reveal two small rooms in back, a large living room w/fireplace in front, wallpaper on all walls, wood textured paper on floor, original window glass, celluloid plaque on side of base marked "A. Schoenhut Co.,

Philadelphia, PA," 16 x 22", 17" h. (light wear on edges of roof & gable) **1,050**

Gottschalk Dollhouse

Dollhouse, elaborate German or Austrian villa-style, lithographed paper on wood, two-story w/blue roof, brick-like exterior & original interior papers, two rooms up & two down, separate front steps to front porch w/baluster-form posts & decorative railings, matching balconies on second floor by two front windows, Gottschalk, ca. 1870s, Saxony, tower roof missing, some paper & wood

damage, 18 5/16 x 26 1/2", 31" h. (ILLUS.) **9,200**

Dollhouse, carved oak, two-story w/mansard roof, hinged shutters, carved arches above all windows, balconies outside two second floor windows, France, on black painted stand, house 27 x 33", 40" h. (ILLUS.) **1,955**

French Carved Oak Dollhouse

Large Wooden Dollhouse

Dollhouse, wooden two-story, yellow clapboards, simulated shingle roof w/two chimneys, porch w/six large turned pillars, one over one opening glass sash, interior Christian doors, old wallpapers, six rooms include parlor, kitchen, hallways, master bedroom, nursery, grandfather room in attic, w/family of four & fine collection of assembled furniture & accessories in various scales 1 1/4 to 2" & materials, electrified, late 19th c., modification & some restoration, w/porch & chimneys, 34 x 75", 52" h. (ILLUS.)............................ **2,300**

Late Victorian Oak Doll Dresser

Dresser, oak, a rectangular mirror frame w/serpentine edges swiveling between slender turned uprights above a serpentine splashboard over the rectangular top, case w/three long drawers w/ring pulls, one pull missing, ca. 1900, 15" w., 24" h. (ILLUS.) ... **160**

Living room suite: sofa w/matching upholstered open-arm armchair, coffee table & two end tables; produced to accompany Barbie, hand-finished wood construction, stamped "Mattel - Japan," simple rectangular modern style,

ca. 1960s, sofa 3 1/2 x 9 1/2", 3 1/2" h., the set **121**

Secretary, Biedermeier style, rosewood finish w/gold stenciled trim, four drawers, fall-front, one drawer, mirrored interior, Europe, mid-19th c., 2 5/8 x 4 11/16", 7 1/2" h. **230**

Step-back Wall Cupboard

Step-back wall cupboard, walnut & poplar w/old finish, Gothic arch door panel w/reverse-painted glass in red & white lattice design above three dovetailed drawers, cut-out feet w/scrolled trim, replaced white porcelain pulls, some renailing, 9 x 13 1/4", 19 1/2" h. (ILLUS.)...... **275**

Table, softwood w/old greyish yellow paint w/brown & red striping & flourish, drop-leaf type, 9 1/4 x 15 1/4" w/6 1/8" leaves, 11 1/4" h. **303**

Waffle iron, for toy cook stove, metal, marked "Wagner Mfg. Co. Sidney, O.," 7 1/2" l. **165**

Planet Junior Cultivator

Rare Lightning Half Pint Fruit Jar

FARM COLLECTIBLES

Asparagus Buncher

Asparagus buncher, metal on
wood, came in assorted colors,
adjustable to bunch length,
ca. 1800-1900s (ILLUS.) **$35-50**

Barbed wire stretcher, two-fold
metal blocks w/hook, chain & grab,
Canton, ca. 1850s, rope pull 3 to
5', self locking **20-25**

Calf Weaner

Calf weaner, metal w/pointed spring
units, held on head w/chain,
unmarked, ca. late 1800s to 1900s,
6" inside measurement, 6" l.
springs (ILLUS.) **15-50**

Cant hook, commercial, hook w/no
point, ca. 1700-1900, 18" to 6' **50**

Cider press, top grinder w/wood
slate sides, unknown
manufacturer, ca. 1900, 4' h. **100-200**

Corn husking pegs, wood, hand
carved w/leather finger loop,
ca. 1850s, 3 to 5" **2-5**

Corn Sheller

Planet Junior Cultivator

Corn sheller, excellent metal & wood construction, similar to Sloane-Stanley Museum piece, ca. 1800-1900, approx. 3' h. (ILLUS.) **250-300**

Cradle scythe, grain, wooden & wire collector, fine scythe blade, unknown manufacturer, usable, ca. 1800-1900 .... **100-300**

Cultivator, hand, red or natural handles, w/assortment of attachments, Planet Jr., late 1800s to late 1900s, 36 to 40" h., 4 to 6' l., 12 to 24" wheels (ILLUS.).......... **25-100**

Dung hoe, blacksmith, made from horseshoe, adze-type handle eye, oak handle, ca. 1700-1900 .... **50-100**

Fence wire stretcher, wooden handle, metal jaws & hook, Neverslip, ca. 1850s, 25" to 30" .. **20-35**

Flail, grain, local shop or farmer, natural wood swivel & thong, handle length for user, flail length & diameter for material, ca. 1700-1900 .... **5-50**

Gate weight, cast iron, model of a dove, full-bodied figure w/outspread wings, retains traces of white paint, late 19th c., 9 1/2" l. **1,955**

Grain scoop, wooden, commercially made, all wood, no sparks, ca. 1800s, 12" w., 40" l. **25-35**

Hay knife, saw type, unpainted blade, red or black handle, ca. 1800-1900, approx. 2' l., 4 to 8 teeth **25-50**

Hay probe, farmer-made, common, apple tree branch w/straight & curved prong tip, ca. 1800-1900, 3 x 5' **5-50**

Hay rake, all-wood, a long slender pole w/one end formed into four long gently curved tines joined at their base by two small arched braces, 64 1/2" l............................. **275**

Hoe, horse-drawn for tilling, red, marked "Prout," ca. 1800s **50-250**

Horse bog shoes, blacksmith, all steel, ca. 1800-1900, set of four (ILLUS. of one) **50-200**

Ice pike pole, painted red tip, Wm. T. Wood, ca. 1800-1900s, 2 to 20' (Wm. T. Wood prior to 1906, Gifford-Wood & other manufacturers after 1900) **1-25**

Jack With Screw and Rachet Gear

Jack, screw & ratchet gear, black paint, top hinged to lower 2", Ajax six-ton style, ca. 1900, 12 to 18" (ILLUS.) **25-75**

Ox cart, double axle, blue grey, ca. 1750-1850, 5 x 12' w/pole........ **800+**

Peevee, commercial style, ca. 1700-1900, 18" to 6' (age & size determine price) **5-50**

Horse Bog Shoe

Hand Planter

Wm. T. Wood & Co. Crescent Ice Saw

Peevee, homemade, hook
blacksmith, ca. 1800s, 5' **50**

Pitchfork, common three-tang,
ca. 1700-1900, 4 to 6' handle **5-25**

Planter, corn, hand, unmarked,
ca. 1700-1800 (ILLUS.) **5-25**

Plow, child's toy, farmer-made
w/scrap wood, ca. 1800-1900s,
2' l., 18" handle (ILLUS.) **50-100**

Plow, wood moldboard w/assorted
scrap metal, ca. 1750-1850 (price
depending on attached metal)
.... **100-1,200**

Potato digger, two-horse, marked
"Champion," usable, ca. 1800s . **300-500**

Rake, bull, unpainted, peg teeth
w/collector teeth, unreadable
manufacturer, 5 to 6' l. **25-75**

Rick fork, three-tang, farmer-made,
ca. 1700-1800, 10 to 12' handle ... **25-75**

Ropemaker, homemade, wooden
gears, four-strand, head stock
only, original handle & hooks, not
usable, 2' w., 8" h. **100-150**

Saw, buck, varnished, occasionally
w/red paint, wood spreader varied
from plain bar to unique designs,
tensioning rod from simple
turnbuckle to extremely fancy
device, ca. 1700-1900, in half size
for boys, medium or full **25-300**

Child's Toy Plow

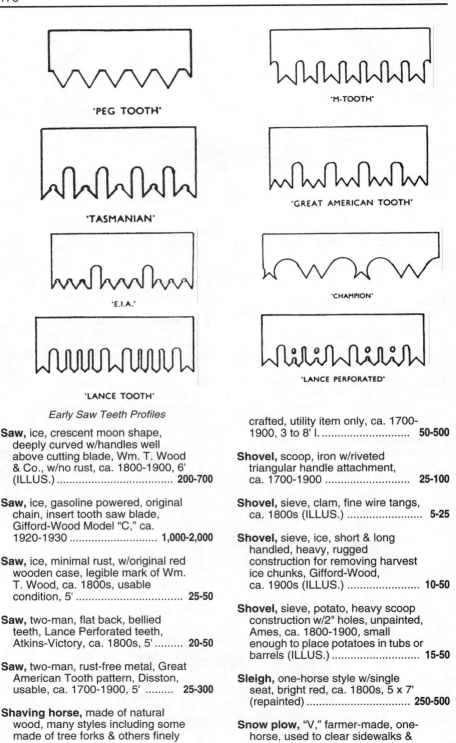

'PEG TOOTH'

'M-TOOTH'

'TASMANIAN'

'GREAT AMERICAN TOOTH'

'E.I.A.'

'CHAMPION'

'LANCE TOOTH'

'LANCE PERFORATED'

Early Saw Teeth Profiles

Saw, ice, crescent moon shape, deeply curved w/handles well above cutting blade, Wm. T. Wood & Co., w/no rust, ca. 1800-1900, 6' (ILLUS.) **200-700**

Saw, ice, gasoline powered, original chain, insert tooth saw blade, Gifford-Wood Model "C," ca. 1920-1930 .... **1,000-2,000**

Saw, ice, minimal rust, w/original red wooden case, legible mark of Wm. T. Wood, ca. 1800s, usable condition, 5' **25-50**

Saw, two-man, flat back, bellied teeth, Lance Perforated teeth, Atkins-Victory, ca. 1800s, 5' **20-50**

Saw, two-man, rust-free metal, Great American Tooth pattern, Disston, usable, ca. 1700-1900, 5' **25-300**

Shaving horse, made of natural wood, many styles including some made of tree forks & others finely

crafted, utility item only, ca. 1700-1900, 3 to 8' l. **50-500**

Shovel, scoop, iron w/riveted triangular handle attachment, ca. 1700-1900 .... **25-100**

Shovel, sieve, clam, fine wire tangs, ca. 1800s (ILLUS.) **5-25**

Shovel, sieve, ice, short & long handled, heavy, rugged construction for removing harvest ice chunks, Gifford-Wood, ca. 1900s (ILLUS.) **10-50**

Shovel, sieve, potato, heavy scoop construction w/2" holes, unpainted, Ames, ca. 1800-1900, small enough to place potatoes in tubs or barrels (ILLUS.) **15-50**

Sleigh, one-horse style w/single seat, bright red, ca. 1800s, 5 x 7' (repainted) **250-500**

Snow plow, "V," farmer-made, one-horse, used to clear sidewalks &

windrowing for ice harvesting,
ca. 1800-1900, 2' h., 4' l., 3' swath
.... **50-200**

Snow plow, "V," one-horse
reproduction for demonstrations,
used to clear sidewalks &
windrowing for ice harvesting,
ca. 1800-1900, 2' h., 4' l., 3' swath   **75**

Tendon, puller, cast iron & painted
aluminum, late 1800s to 1900s, 25"
.... **40-60**

Tractor license plate, Pennsylvania,
1915, one-sided porcelain,
rectangular w/blue ground &
"Penna - 1915 - Tractor" in small
white letters at one end & "E1222"
in white filling the remainder,
"Brilliant Mfg. Co. Philadelphia,
Pa." stamped on back, 6 x 14"
(chips to mounting holes,
manufacturer's defect in white
letters) **132**

Wagon, buggy style, black, single
seat, high narrow wheels,
interchangeable pole or shafts,
ca. 1800s.............................. **250-1,000**

Wagon wheels, single wood w/metal
rim, ca. 1800s.......................... **25-100**

Weed cutter, "Dock," cast iron &
steel, narrow rectangular blade on
wooden handle, unmarked,
ca. 1900s, 40".............................. **10-25**

Shovels: Clam, Ice, Potato

Wheelbarrow, adult, wood, light
weight w/wooden wheel, metal
shod, removable sides, usable,
ca. 1700-1900 .... **100-200**

Windmill weight, cast iron, model of
a rooster, embossed "Hummer
E184," Elgin Wind, Power & Pump
Co., Elgin, Illinois, now on wooden
block base, overall 13 1/2" h.
(pitted) **330**

Winnower, fanning mill, all wooden
gear & crank, complete w/some
screens, ca. 1800s **100-300**

FIREARMS

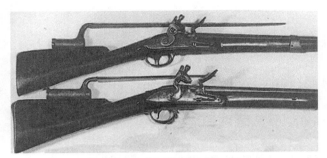

"Brown Bess" & Flintlock Muskets

Carbine, Ball Civil War period model, walnut stock (ILLUS.) **$2,000**

Carbine, Maynard .50 cal. **1,232**

Carbine, Model 1859 Sharps, .52 cal. **1,792**

Carbine, Model 1863 Sharps, .52 cal. **1,904**

Carbine, Sharps, factory conversion to metallic cartridge, faint cartouche on side of stock, 22" blued barrel w/faint "New Model" mark (wear to some stampings, stock w/some dings) **1,430**

Long rifle, Kentucky-type, cherry stock w/brass patch box & hardware, checkered wrist, octagonal barrel, two small side plates w/simple engraving, barrel 48" l. (repairs w/some replacements) **1,100**

Musket, "Brown Bess" flintlock, wooden stock w/refinish & repaired age crack along barrel channel, boldly marked "Tower" & "G.R"

w/crown, barrel shortened to 39" l., brass hardware & butt plate engraved "68," w/bayonet (ILLUS. bottom) **1,210**

Musket, flintlock, wood stock w/old dark patina w/iron mountings & light pittings on lock & breech, three bands & 42" l. round barrel, early, unmarked, one lock bolt missing, w/bayonet, overall 57 1/2" l. (ILLUS. top) **880**

Musket, Parkers Snow & Co. 1861 percussion model, .58 cal., 40" brown barrel, stock w/inspector's mark & cleaned dark finish **1,265**

Musket, Pottsdam percussion model, European walnut stock w/old finish & stamped "F.W." w/crown, 41" round barrel w/"1820" stamp, brass hardware (pieced repair along barrel channel) **495**

Pistol, pepper box percussion model, six-shot, 3" fluted barrels, one chamber w/blown-out opening, frame w/simple scroll engraving & bar hammer, 8" l. **248**

Ball Civil War Carbine

Colt 1849 and 1860 Revolvers

Pistol, S. North flintlock Model 1819, reconverted flint w/later hammer, brass pan & friesian, 10" barrel w/bold inspector's stamps, walnut stock (pieced repair & age cracks in grip) **550**

Revolver, Colt 1849 pocket model, percussion-type, cylinder w/painted engraved stagecoach scene, all serial numbers match, few dents, octagonal barrel 4" l. (ILLUS. bottom) **660**

Revolver, Colt 1860 Army model, .44 cal., reblued finish w/all serial numbers remaining & matching including cylinder, grips w/faint inspector's stamp, 8" barrel w/New York address & cylinder engraved w/scene w/light pitting (ILLUS. top) **715**

Rifle, flintlock Kentucky type w/sighted smoothbore barrel formed in two stages w/beveled lock signed "H. Parker," w/tiger maple full stock, brass mounts including large pierced patchbox engraved w/scrolls & animals, reverse side of butt inset w/three German silver plaques of an eagle, hare & game bird, three brass ramrod pipes & wooden ramrod, 19th c., 56" l. **10,925**

Rifle, Model 1861, percussion-type, .58 cal. **1,000**

Rifle, percussion half-stock, boy's model, curly maple stock w/a poured end cap & nickel silver inlays including dog & deer & escutcheon plates, lock marked "Moore," 24" l. barrel w/brass cap box, overall 39" l. **1,980**

Rifle, Remington Model 6 single-shot, .32 cal., select grade walnut butt stock, case colors on frame, serial number 458793 .... **248**

Rifle, Stevens-Ideal #44, 25 rimfire cal., blued 24" octagonal to round barrel, some case colors left on receiver **220**

Rifle, U.S. Whitney Model 1848, percussion-type, .52 cal., a.k.a. "Mississippi Rifle" **1,904**

Rifle, Winchester Golden Spike commemorative, 30 - 30 cal., original box (box sleeve w/end tears) **303**

Rifle, Winchester Model 1892, lever-action, 25-20 cal., octagonal barrel & full-length magazine tube, barrel 24" l. **495**

Shotgun, Parker Brothers double-barrel model, 12 ga., finely engraved, walnut stock (ILLUS.) .. **1,840**

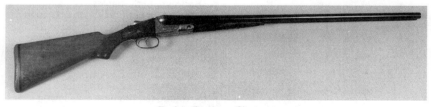

Parker Brothers Shotgun

FIREPLACE & HEARTH ITEMS

Figural Andirons

Andirons, cast iron, figural standing Hessian soldiers, 19th c., 20 1/2" h., pr. **$230**

Andirons, wrought iron, Arts & Crafts style, a looped spade-shaped top on a pair of canted slender uprights on a flat lower crossbar w/S-scroll end feet, square log bar, similar to Gustav Stickley Model No. 314, original patina, early 20th c., 13 x 21", 21" h., pr. **231**

Andirons, wrought iron & cast-brass knife-blade style, Federal, urn-form finials above a flaring support on arched legs w/penny feet, probably Pennsylvania, one andiron stamped "IC," 1780 - 1810, 15 1/2" l., 9 1/2" w., 20 1/2" h., pr. **1,955**

Andirons, cast iron, figural, cast in the half-round, cat w/green glass eyes seated on haunches on a flaring pedestal, American-made, 20th c., 16" h., pr. (ILLUS.) **1,495**

Art Deco Style Andirons

Andirons, brass, steeple top finials, angled tubular legs w/ball feet, 21 1/2" h., pr. (damage & old repairs) **275**

Andirons, bronze & nickeled metal, Art Deco style, flaring feather-form standard on a lobed base w/an iron log support behind, ca. 1930, wear to finish, some oxidation, 23 1/2" h., pr. (ILLUS.) **1,840**

Arts & Crafts Andirons

Andirons, brass, Arts & Crafts style, each formed w/a sinuous standard & flaring foot surmounted by a swirling quatrefoil finial, England, last quarter 19th c., 24" h., pr. (ILLUS.) **1,035**

Andirons, cast brass, Classical style w/gilding & tapering cylindrical red marble columns topped w/small urn-form finials, 28 1/2" h., pr. (restored cracks in marble & one finial bent) **660**

Bellows, painted wood, original red paint w/stenciled & free-hand vintage design in gold, bronze & black, old worn releathering, brass nozzle, 19th c., 18" l. **193**

Bellows, turtle-back type, painted wood, decorated w/cornucopia in black, gold & green on worn red ground, brass nozzle, old leather deteriorated, 19th c., 18" l. **193**

Bellows, turtle-back type, painted wood, original white paint w/smoked graining & yellowed varnish, stenciled & free-hand flowers & foliage in red, green, black & gold, brass nozzle, professionally releathered, 19th c., 17 1/2" l. **358**

Ornately Carved Bellows

Bellows, turtle-back type, painted wood, small rounded tab handles & tapering rounded sides w/original yellow paint decorated w/stenciled & free-hand fruit & flowers, brass nozzle, old releathering, small size, 19th c., 15 1/4" l. (wear, especially on handle) **358**

Bellows, turtle-back type, painted & decorated wood & leather, old red paint w/polychrome floral decoration, tin nozzle, 17 1/2" l. (old leather is torn & valve missing) **303**

Bellows, turtle-back type, decorated wood w/very ornate relief-carved eagle, lions & scrollwork, Europe, 25" l. (ILLUS.) **385**

Fire screen, metal w/tooled interior scene in high relief, man sitting in front of fireplace w/children & woman working in the background, 27 1/2" w., 18 1/4" h. (feet have been soldered & are loose) **220**

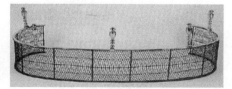

Brass & Wire Fire Fender

Fireplace clock jack, brass, slender cylindrical neck above the wide cylindrical casing for the works above a suspended small hook & round iron suspension ring, marked "Geo. Salter & Co. Improved, Warrented," 19th c., 17" h. **193**

Fireplace fender, brass & wire, a curved form w/brass top rim & five urn-form finials above a vertical wire screen, 19th c., 48" l, 8" h. (ILLUS.) **575**

Fireplace fender, steel & wire w/brass top rail, above a wire screen w/serpentine design, 57" w., 12" h. (some battering & damage) **1,210**

Fireplace fender, cast brass w/marble inserts & ribbon decoration, 69 3/4" l., 7 1/2" h. (minor dent in top rail) **385**

Brass Fireplace Tool Set

Fireplace tool set, brass, double lemon top design andirons, 19 3/4" h., signed "Bailey," ca. 1800, New York, New York, together w/a matching pr. of tongs & a shovel, the set (ILLUS. of part) **2,070**

Hearth fork, wrought steel, decorated w/an engraved geometric design, England or America, late 18th - early 19th c., 15 1/4" l. **115**

FRAKTUR

Fraktur paintings are decorative birth and marriage certificates of the 18th and 19th centuries and also include family registers and similar documents. Illuminated family documents, birth and baptismal certificates, religious texts and rewards of merit, in a particular style, are known as "fraktur" because of the similarity to the 16th century type-face of that name. Gay watercolor borders, frequently incorporating stylized birds, hand-lettered documents, which were executed by local ministers, school masters or itinerant penman. Most are of Pennsylvania Dutch origin.

Birth & baptismal fraktur (Geburts und Taufschein), pen & ink, watercolor & cut paper on laid paper by Frederick Krebs, recording 1804 birth in Northampton County, decorated w/crown, suns, flowers & tulips in black ink w/red, brown & yellow watercolor, cut-outs in gilt paper or w/embossed gilded religious figures, printed format w/"F. Krebs," heavily alligatored frame decorated w/red & yellow stenciled designs on black ground, Pennsylvannia, 15 7/8" w., 12 5/8" h. (fold lines & taped repairs) **$2,420**

Birth & baptismal fraktur (Geburts und Taufschein), pen & ink & handcolored floral detail w/tulips & hearts in red, green & yellow, recording 1820 birth in Union County, Pennsylvania, framed, 18 3/4" w., 16 1/4" h. **743**

Birth & baptismal fraktur (Geburts und Taufschein), printed & handcolored, recording 1798 birth in Montgomery County, printed by Johann Ritter, decorated w/angels, birds & flowers in red, green & pink, framed, 13 1/2" w., 16 5/8" h. (stains & fold line) **94**

Birth & baptismal fraktur (Geburts und Taufschein), printed & handcolored, rectangular, recording 1816 birth in Lebanon County, printed by "Johann Ritter, Reading," signed & dated

"Catharina Nordden 1838," birds, angels & heart illustrations in red, blue, yellow & black, Pennsylvania, framed, 14 3/4" w., 18 3/4" h. (edge wear, damage & stains) **330**

Birth & baptismal fraktur (Geburts und Taufschein), rectangular, printed & handcolored, recording 1817 birth in Berks County, printed by "Johann Ritter, Reading," handcolored angels & birds in yellow, red, blue & black, Pennsylvania, framed, 14 3/4" w., 18 3/4" h. (wear, tears, stains & fold lines) **55**

Birth letter for Elizabeth Ness, watercolor, pen & ink on paper, ornately decorated inscription framed by scrolls, flowers & berries w/three inscribed hearts, attributed to the Manor Township Artist, 1801, 4 1/4 x 6 1/2" **1,150**

Birth letter for Michael Lurich, Burks County, watercolor, pen & ink on paper, four inscribed hearts trimmed in blue w/orange & green flowers, inscription framed w/orange border in lower portion of painting, attributed to Conrad Trewitz, 1778, framed, 8 x 13" **2,875**

Birth record, fine cutwork 'Scherenschitten,' the circular document w/pinked edges & pin- 17 1/2" h. (wear, damage & repair w/one corner poorly restored) **385**

Cutwork 'Scherenschitten' Birth Certificate

Birth record, pen & ink & watercolor on laid paper, recording 1795 birth in Weyenburg township, Northampton County, Pennsylvania, stylized flowers, birds, two angels, heart & center ring w/sawtooth design encircling text, red, green, yellow & black, framed, 22 1/4" w., 18 3/4" h. (stains & some damage repaired) **3,410**

Early Birth Record

Birth record for Elizabeth Wenger, watercolor & ink on wove paper, floral design on one side & top, "Elizabeth Wenger" in large letters w/date of 1795, red, black & yellow w/reddish brown ink, Pennsylvania, minor stains, framed, 10" w., 7 1/2" h. (ILLUS.). **1,760**

Birth Record Fraktur

Birth record for Rahel Haas, pen & ink & watercolor on wove paper, central circle w/text is faded brown & bordered by a wreath of leaves in yellow, orange, green, black & grey, Oley Township, Berks County, Pennsylvania, framed, 10 1/2" w., 12 3/8" h. (ILLUS.) **715**

Book plate, pen & ink & watercolor on wove paper, rectangular, inscribed "Christina Yoder 1828" in red, black & green, new curly maple frame, 3 x 5 1/4" image (stains, edge damage) **413**

Book plate, watercolor on wove paper, stylized tree w/birds on branches, "S.Z.," red, blue, green, yellow & black, frame covers bird at top of tree & date "1823" in bottom right, framed, 5 5/8" w., 6 1/2" h. (minor damage) **165**

Book plate, pen & ink & watercolor on wove paper, a large heart w/pinked edges w/"Maria Christ 1828" in red, green, yellow & black, ink in name is faded brown, framed, 7 5/8" w., 6 7/8" h. (minor wear & edge damage) **220**

Book plate, pen & ink & watercolor on lined paper, "Benjamin Frailich - and - Mary Frailich," & signed "Israel Gorb, Apr. 29, 1868," red, pink, green & black, framed, 6 1/8" w., 8 3/4" h. (wear, tape stain along one edge & edges glued to backing) **330**

Drawing, watercolor on wove paper, stylized bird on branch in black, green, pink, yellow & orange, pen inscription in upper right reads "Pretty Polle Birde," framed, 7 1/2" w., 5 3/4" h. **605**

Drawing, pen & ink & watercolor on wove paper, stylized tulip tree w/a bird on each side, yellow border stripe w/blue, salmon red, green yellow & black, framed, 5" w., 6" h. (minor stains w/tape stains) **935**

Drawing, pen & ink & watercolor on laid paper, stylized floral design in red, yellow, blue & black, bordered by black background paper, framed, 5 1/4" w., 6 3/4" h. (stains, top of flower smeared & some damage from acid ink) **358**

Drawing, pen & ink & watercolor on laid paper, text in large heart w/date "1788" surrounded by stylized floral design w/two birds, red, yellow, green & black, framed, 11 1/2" w., 16" h. (paper is fragile & worn w/tears & small holes) **990**

Drawing, ink & watercolor on wove paper, primitive scene w/bird, flowers & tree in blue, red, yellow & green, back signed "May 15th, 1848 Catrine Gice," framed, 10 3/8" w., 12" h. (fly specks & minor stains) **660**

Drawing, pen & ink cut-out on wove paper, farm yard scene w/very good detail & color w/buildings, people, animals, etc., cut-out vignettes of farm activities & cut-out title backed w/black coated paper, Dutch inscriptions & title dated 1848, rebacked on heavy paper, framed, 18" w., 16 3/4" h. (damage & stains) **1,430**

House blessing (Haus Seegen), printed & hand-colored floral & heart design in red, blue, green & yellow, dated "1785," framed, 18 1/2" w., 21 1/2" h. (damage & portions missing w/old tape stains on repairs in left corner) **385**

Rewards of Merit, watercolor, pen & ink on paper, stylized tulip standing

over inscription, surrounded by thin border, American School, 19th c., framed, 2 x 3 1/2", pr. **1,955**

"Tauf Zettel," printed & hand colored floral design in red, blue, green & yellow on black & white engraving, framed, 8 1/2" w., 9" h. (stains & some damage at fold lines) **220**

Verse, pen & ink & watercolor on laid paper, verse w/"Northumberland County, January 21, 1814," by Martin Brichelle, Pennsylvania, rebacked on paper, framed, 10 1/4" w., 11 1/4" h. (edge tears & slight stains) **605**

Vorschrift fraktur, pen & ink on laid paper, red & black ink, German, framed, 8" w., 5 3/4" h. (stains, edge wear & pencil mark)............. **688**

Vorschrift fraktur, pen & ink & watercolor, decorative name w/flowers & border design in red, yellow, green & black, old black molded frame, 14 3/8" w., 11 3/8" h. (wear, some damage & bits of paper adhering to watercolor surface)...................... **1,210**

Vorschrift fraktur, pen & ink & watercolor, flowers & heart along side of text, red, yellow, green & black, framed, 10 5/8" w., 12 3/4" h. (stains, small holes & tattered edges) **165**

FRUIT JARS

Almy, base marked "Patented - Dec 25 1877," ground lip, original screw-on glass lid, ca. 1877-80, aqua, qt. **$132**

Bee, smooth base, ground lip, ca. 1875-85, aqua, 1/2 gal. (closure missing) **440**

Bodine (F. & J.) Manufacturers - Philadelphia PA, smooth base, ground lip, ca. 1870-75, aqua, qt. (reproduction metal & wire closure)... **88**

F. & J. Bodine Fruit Jar

Bodine (F. & J.) - Philada, smooth base, ground lip, reproduction metal & wire closure, ca. 1870-80, aqua, qt. (ILLUS.) **94**

Brooks (C.D.) - Boston, smooth base, applied mouth, golden yellow amber, qt. **55**

Champion (The) - Pat. Aug. 31 1869, smooth base, sheared & ground lip, correct glass insert & iron yoke clamp, ca. 1869-75, aqua, 1/2 gal. (tiny chip on insert) . **165**

Common Sense Jar - Gregory's Patent - Aug 17th 1869, smooth base, applied mouth, original glass stopper & metal yoke closure, ca. 1870-80, aqua, qt. (small chip on lid)... **825**

Eureka 17 - Patd Dec 27th 1864, smooth base, ground lip, ca. 1865-70, aqua, 1/2 gal. (missing closure)....................................... **66**

Globe, original closure, "23" on base, amber, pt. **110**

Haines's Improved - March 1st 1870, smooth base, applied mouth, correct glass lid marked "Patented March 1870," aqua, qt. (lid wire probably reproduction, some lid stain)... **72**

Rare Lightning Half Pint Fruit Jar

Indicator, smooth base, ground lip, ca. 1875-85, aqua, qt. (reproduction metal lid & neck band, some lip chipping) **440**

Lafayette (in script), original gasket, aqua, pt. **175**

Lightning - Putnam 763 - Trade Mark (on base) smooth base, ground lip, original glass lid embossed "Lightning Pat. April 25, 82," wire bail, amber, 1/2 pt. (ILLUS.) **1,980**

Mason's 2 Patent - Nov 30th 1858, smooth base, ground lip, original zinc screw-on lid, aqua, midget pt. (some lid deterioration, milky bruise on screw thread) **22**

Mason's (keystone) Patent Nov. 30th 1858, original lid, good whittle, lime aqua variation, qt. **143**

Mason's Patent - Nov 30th 1858, smooth base, ABM lip, zinc screw-on lid, ca. 1920-30, deep aqua w/heavy yellowish olive striations, 1/2 gal. **220**

Mason's Patent - Nov 30th 1858 - Dupont (in circle) smooth base, ground lip, zinc screw-on lid, light apple green, 1/2 gal. (minor inside lip bruise) **231**

Mason's S Patent Nov. 30th 1858, shoulder seal, aqua, qt. **10**

Mason's - SGCo - Patent Nov. 30th 1858, w/zinc cap, good whittle, lime aqua, 1/2 gal. **198**

Moore (John M. & Co.) Manufacturers, Fislerville, NJ (in script), also marked "Patented Dec. 3d 1861," jar only, aqua, pt. ... **495**

Peerless, glass lid, iron yoke clamp, lid marked "Patented Feb. 13 1863," aqua, qt. (very light haze)... **165**

Potter & Bodine - Air Tight - Fruit Jar - Philada - Patented - April 15th 1858, cylindrical shouldered bottle w/grooved neck w/ring for wax sealer, aqua, ca. 1860-65, 1/2 gal. (stress crack in ring) **177**

Puritan (The) - I.S. Co. (monogram), smooth base, ground lip, original glass lid in citron, ca. 1880-90, aqua, pt. (iron ring & closure reproductions) **165**

Spencer's (C.F.) Patent Rochester, N.Y., different style lip, aqua, qt. (two under lip chips) **25**

Stone & Co. (A.) - Philada, smooth base, applied mouth w/internal screw threads, original screw stopper embossed "A. Stone & Co. - 2 - Philada," ca. 1860-70, aqua, pt. (V-shaped chip on side of mouth, chips on stopper edge) **149**

Triumph No. 1 Fruit Jar

Triumph No. 1, smooth base, pressed-down wax seal channel, ground lip, remnants of original pressed-on tin lid exist on lip, ca. 1865-75, bluish aqua, 1/2 gal. (ILLUS.) **908**

Union #4, aqua, qt. (1/4" chip on back).. **450**

Western Pride - Patented June 22, 1875, smooth base, applied mouth, original glass lid embossed "Patented June 22, 1875," metal clamp closure, aqua, 1/2 gal. (small rainbow-type bruise on inside applied lip).......................... **77**

Yeoman's Fruit Bottle - Patent Applied For, smooth base, outward rolled lip, ca. 1865-75, aqua, 1/2 gal................................. **50**

FURNITURE

BEDS

Country-style low poster "folding" bed, painted wood, turned headposts flanking a shaped headboard, joined to the footposts by jointed rails fitted for roping & folding, old Spanish brown paint, New England, early 19th c., 52 3/4 x 77 1/2", 33 1/2" h. (imperfections)............................... **$690**

Early Low-Poster Bed

Country-style low-poster bed, painted pine & maple, the pointed headboard between blocked stiles w/flattened knob turned finials & swelled turned & tapering legs, original side rails w/rope holes & low footposts w/flattened knob turned finials over the corner blocks on swelled turned & tapering legs, old red paint, Pennsylvania, early 19th c., 52 x 80", headboard 34 1/2" h. (ILLUS.) **575**

Federal tall poster bed, carved mahogany, the vase- and ring-turned footposts carved w/pineapples above a reeded swelled post w/carved sheaves of wheat continuing to acanthus leaves & carved palmettes on vase- and ring-turned legs, the headposts also vase- and ring-turned but uncarved, all joined by a flat tester frame, 54 x 72", 87" h. **12,650**

Federal tall poster bed, painted, the vase- and ring-turned & reeded footposts joined to the simple turned headposts & shaped pine headboard w/an arched canopy frame, ring- and baluster-turned legs, old red stain, New England, ca. 1820, 48 x 69", 75" h. (minor imperfections)............................... **2,645**

Massachusetts Federal Bed

Federal tall-poster bed, carved mahogany, the square tapering tall headposts centering a scroll-cut pine headboard, the footposts w/waterleaf-carved tapering reeded posts on swag- and leaf-carved urn-form supports on square tapering legs, all legs w/spade feet, w/flat tester, headboard possibly replaced, North Shore Massachusetts, ca. 1795, 59 x 80", 92" h. (ILLUS.) **5,750**

Federal tall-poster canopy field bed, maple, a low peaked headboard flanked by simple slender turned & tapering posts, the footposts w/ring- and baluster-turned posts & square tapering legs, w/an arched serpentine canopy frame, late 18th - early 19th c., 58 1/2" w., 68" h............... **2,000**

Turn-of-the-century bed, brass, elaborately scrolled head- and footboards w/foliate detail, ca. 1900, one small spindle missing, 61" w., 64" h. (ILLUS.).... **2,200**

Ornate Early Brass Bed

Long Wood & Iron Park Bench

Park bench, cast-iron & wood, the long wooden slat back & seat joining the pierced scrolled iron arms above pierced ends of squirrels among leafy vines on short legs of gargoyles ending in paw feet, painted green, George Smith and Co., Glasgow, Scotland, late 19th c., 31 x 98", 33" h. (ILLUS.) **2,070**

Window bench, Classical style, mahogany veneer, the up-curving seat flanked by scrolled ends above four outscrolled legs, New York, 1815-25, old refinish, some veneer cracking & loss, 14 x 39 1/2", 23 5/8" h. (ILLUS.)... **3,450**

Window bench, Classical style, carved mahogany veneer, upholstered seat above a veneered rail on leaf-carved cyma-curved ends joined by a ring-turned medial stretcher, old surface, Boston, 1835-45, 16 1/4 x 48", 17 1/2" h. (imperfections).............................. **2,185**

BENCHES

Bucket (or water) bench, painted pine, a low backrail w/notched corners on a long rectangular board top w/chamfered front corners over an apron w/chamfered ends, raised on tall inset one-board legs w/low arched cut-outs, old worn & weathered grey paint, 19th c., 15 x 52", 31 3/4" h. (some edge damage) **363**

Kneeling bench, poplar, a long narrow board top w/a narrow apron raised on three arched bootjack legs, old brown finish, 7 x 76 3/4".. **220**

Classical Window Bench

CHAIRS

Early Campeche Lolling Chair

Campeche armchair, lolling-type, walnut, tall back w/rolled flat crestrail flanked by stiles continuing down to upcurved seat, small truncated wings at top sides, flat S-scroll open arms on shaped arm supports, inverted-U legs joined by squared & shaped cross-stretchers, old webbing, Southern United States, first half 19th c. (ILLUS.) **8,338**

Chippendale armchair w/wingback, upholstered mahogany, the serpentine crest above the curving wings & outwardly scrolling arms flanking a cushioned seat & upholstered apron, on square molded legs joined by square molded stretchers to the raking rear legs, old surface, surface imperfections, New England, 1780-1800, 48 1/2" h. (ILLUS.) **7,475**

Chippendale country-style side chair, cherry, serpentine crestrail w/flared ears over a loop-pierced splat between raked stiles, upholstered slip seat on square beaded legs, old surface, crewel-worked seat cover in golds & blues, Connecticut, 1770-1800, imperfections, 37 3/4" h. (ILLUS.) **690**

Chippendale country-style side chair, tiger stripe maple, serpentine crestrail w/raked molded ears above a pierced splat, old rush seat & block- and vase-turned front legs joined by a turned stretcher, old refinish, Connecticut River Valley, 39" h. (imperfections)............................. **863**

Chippendale Armchair with Wingback

Country Chippendale Side Chair

Philadelphia Chippendale Chair

Carved Mahogany Chippendale Chair

Chippendale "ladder-back" side chairs, carved mahogany, a serpentine crestrail pierced w/a central circle & scrolls & w/a beaded edge above three matching slats between the raked molded stiles over the trapezoidal upholstered slip seat, on square beaded legs joined by box stretchers, old refinish, probably Philadelphia, ca. 1780, 37 1/2" h., pr. (minor imperfections) **1,725**

Chippendale side chair, carved mahogany, serpentine crestrail w/decorated carved scrolls & flaring ears above a lattice-carved back splat between carved canted stiles over the molded upholstered slip seat accented by pierced brackets & flanked by square molded legs, old refinish, Philadelphia, 1770-85, imperfections (ILLUS.)................. **2,185**

Chippendale side chair, carved mahogany, the serpentine crestrail w/leaf carving & molded ears above the carved pierced scrolled splat flanked by raked stiles joined to the frontal cabriole legs ending in pad feet w/block-turned stretchers, old refinish, missing returns, other imperfections, Massachusetts, ca. 1780, 37 1/2" h. (ILLUS.)........................ **1,380**

Carved Chippendale Side Chair

Chippendale side chair, carved
mahogany, the shaped leaf-, scroll-
and ruffle-carved crestrail flanked
by leaf-carved ears above a
pierced strapwork splat,
gadrooned shoe & trapezoidal slip
seat flanked by wavy stiles, the
shaped molded seat frame below
on leaf-, bellflower-, and scroll-
carved cabriole legs ending in
scroll feet, possibly Southern
United States, crack to crest at
juncture w/splat, 1740-70,
38 1/2" h. (ILLUS.)........................ **4,025**

Chippendale side chair, carved
walnut, serpentine crestrail
w/raked ears above the pierced
splat w/C-scrolls & lattice over the
upholstered compass slip seat
over cabriole front legs ending in
high pad feet, raking rear legs, old
refinish, restoration to stiles,
Boston or Salem, Massachusetts,
1760-80, 38 1/2" h. (ILLUS.)......... **2,185**

Chippendale "Ladder-back" Side Chair

Massachusetts Chippendale Chair

Chippendale side chair, mahogany,
four serpentine pierced horizontal
splats above an over-upholstered
seat & stop-fluted front legs joined
to the raking rear legs by square
stretchers, old dark surface,
Rhode Island, 1775-1810, minor
imperfections, 36 1/2" h.
(ILLUS.) **1,150**

Chippendale side chair, mahogany,
the serpentine crest w/molded ears
above a pierced strapwork splat,
the overupholstered seat raised on
angular cabriole legs joined by
turned stretchers & ending in pad
feet, New England, third quarter
18th c. **1,092**

Chippendale side chair, mahogany,
the serpentine crestrails w/central
piercing & beaded edge above
a scrolled pierced splat flanked
by gently outswept stiles over
the over-upholstered seat, on
square molded legs joined by
square stretchers, old surface,
minor repairs, attributed to
Robert Harrold, 1765-75,
Portsmouth, New Hampshire,
37" h. (ILLUS.).............................. **1,955**

New Hampshire Chippendale Chair

Chippendale side chair, carved mahogany, the oxyoke crestrail w/upswept molded ears above a scroll-pierced vasiform splat & raked stiles over the trapezoidal slip seat, front cabriole legs ending in pad feet on platforms, raked chamfered rear legs, Massachusetts, ca. 1780, old refinish, 37" h.............................. **1,725**

Chippendale side chair, carved mahogany, a serpentine crestrail w/molded ears above a pierced Gothic design splat, molded seatrails w/upholstered seat, cabriole front legs ending in claw-and-ball feet, baluster- and block-turned stretchers joining front legs to rear chamfered raked legs, old refinish, Massachusetts, 1755-90, 36 1/8" h. (minor surface abrasions).................................... **4,255**

Chippendale side chairs, transitional-style, painted & decorated wood, the serpentine oxbow crestrail w/outswept ears centered by a lunette over the vase-form loop-pierced splat over the upholstered slip seat, on square tapering legs joined by flat stretchers, later black paint w/gilt band trim, Newport, Rhode Island, or Connecticut, 1765-90, 37 3/4" h., pr. (repair to a foot) **2,645**

Chippendale-Style Armchair

Chippendale transitional-style armchair, mahogany, the simple oxyoke crestrail w/rounded corners continuing into the inward curving stiles flanking the simple solid vasiform splat, shaped open arms w/scroll-carved hand grips on incurved arm supports, wide needlepoint-covered slip seat, plain curved seatrail over cabriole front legs w/acanthus leaf-carved knees & ending in heavy claw-and-ball feet, canted square rear legs joined to front legs w/a block- and reel-turned H-stretcher, old finish, late 19th - early 20th c., minor wear, 43 3/4" h. (ILLUS.) **275**

Chippendale transitional-style side chair, carved mahogany, the arched crestrail w/rounded corners centered by ornate leafy scroll section centering a flowerhead above the spooned solid vasiform splat, the tapering curved stiles above the upholstered balloon-form slip seat, curved plain seatrail above cabriole front legs ending in claw-and-ball feet, square canted rear legs w/spade feet, old finish, Centennial era, late 19th - early 20th c., 40" h. (ILLUS.) **358**

Transitional Chippendale-Style Chair

Chippendale-Style armchair, mahogany, the serpentined crestrail w/carved leafy scrolls above a pierced leafy scroll-carved vasiform splat flanked by molded stiles, serpentine open arms w/scroll-carved handholds on incurved arm supports flanking the wide overupholstered seat w/a thin gadroon-carved seatrail, cabriole front legs w/leafy scroll-carved knees & ending in claw-and-ball feet, canted square rear legs, old dark finish, early 20th c., 37 1/2" h. (repairs, seat reupholstered) **330**

Chippendale-Style corner chair, a back-scrolled crestrail on a U-form even rail ending in shaped arms w/scrolled handholds above two scroll-bordered vase-form splats pierced w/a central spade design & alternating w/three ring-turned columnar spindles above the square upholstered slip seat, cabriole legs w/scrolled returns & ending in claw-and-ball feet joined by a turned cross-stretcher, old dark finish, early 20th c., 33 1/2" h. (one arm w/age crack)................... **330**

Chippendale-Style side chair, mahogany, the serpentine crestrail w/carved swags above the ornately pierced looping splat flanked by the square slightly flaring stiles above the over-upholstered seat, cabriole front legs w/leafy scroll-carved knees & ending in claw-and-ball feet, square canted rear legs, Centennial-type, old refinishing, late 19th c., 38" h. **440**

Chippendale-Style side chairs, hardwood w/old brown finish, ladder-back style w/four pierced ribbon-form back slats flanked by molded stiles above the upholstered slip seat w/needlepoint upholstery, square molded legs joined by an H-stretcher, early 20th c., 37" h., set of 8... **1,144**

Chippendale-Style wing chair, the tall upholstered back w/a serpentine crest flanked by slightly curved upholstered wings above the rolled upholstered arms, cushion seat above the upholstered seatrail, on mahogany cabriole front legs w/leafy scroll-carved returns & ending in claw-and-ball feet, reupholstered, 20th c., 41" h. **385**

Classical side chairs, brass-inlaid & carved mahogany, a horizontal reverse-scrolling crest board above a pierced flowerhead- and leaf-carved lower rail, upholstered slip seat, on sabre legs, rich patina, nice old finish, New York City, ca. 1810, 32" h., set of 4.............. **5,175**

Baltimore Classical Side Chairs

Classical side chairs, carved mahogany, gently curving & rolled veneered crestrail above a leaf-carved & pierced splat, upholstered slip-seat over a flat veneered seatrail between ring-, knob- and reeded rod-turned tapering legs w/pad feet, Baltimore, 1815-20, imperfections, 34 1/2" h., set of 4 (ILLUS. of two) **805**

Classical side chairs, grain-painted, a curved horizontal crestrail atop stiles flanking a flat lower rail above the caned seat, on klysmos-type legs, original graining in imitation of rosewood w/gold accent striping, northern New England, ca. 1825-35, 33" h., set of 6 (imperfections)....................... **1,380**

Classical side chairs, tiger stripe maple, stepped rectangular curved crestrail above angular-cut vase-form splat above the seat w/curving front rail, on flat Grecian legs, refinished, one branded "A.G. Case," Norwich, Connecticut area, 1830-50, 33 1/2" h., set of 6 (caned seats missing, other imperfections) **3,105**

Country-style armchairs, stained maple, the squared back panel of

tightly woven splint between projecting backswept stiles w/long shaped open arms on baluster-turned arm supports continuing down to form side braces, tightly woven splint seat, simple turned legs w/plain turned double front & side & rear stretchers, splints partially distressed, minor chips to feet, back of stiles worn, late 19th - early 20th c., 34 1/2" h., pr. (ILLUS.) **805**

Country-style "banister-back" side chair, maple, the high scroll-cut crestrail between ring-, knob-, rod- and block-turned stiles w/mismatched turned finials flanking four split-banisters above a shaped base rail over the woven rush seat, knob- and block-turned front legs joined by a ring- and knob-turned front stretcher & plain side & back stretchers, on front knob feet, old refinish, New England, 18th c., 44 1/2" h. **460**

Country-style "ladder-back" armchair, maple & ash, four arched slats joining knob- and rod-turned stiles w/knob finials over long scrolled arms on baluster- and knob-turned arm supports continuing into turned front legs, woven splint seat, double knob-

Woven Splint Armchairs

turned front stretchers & plain
double side stretchers, old painted
surface, restored, probably
Massachusetts, early 18th c.,
45 1/2" h. (ILLUS.).......................... **546**

Early "Ladder-Back" Armchair

New England "Ladder-back" Armchair

**Country-style "ladder-back"
armchair,** painted birch & hickory,
four arched back slats between
sausage-turned stiles w/knob
finials flanked by shaped arms
w/fluted terminals, baluster-turned
arm supports above the woven
rush seat, ring- and rod-turned
front legs joined by two ring-turned
stretchers, double plain side
stretchers, old yellow & red paint,
losses to paint, height reduced,
formerly fitted w/rockers, New
England, 1700-40, 41 1/4" h.
(ILLUS.) **920**

**Early American "ladder-back" side
chair,** maple, tall simple turned
back stiles w/pointed knob finials
flanking five arched slats, woven
rush seat, baluster- and rod-turned
front legs w/knob feet joined by a
double-knob and ring-turned
stretcher, double plain side
stretchers & one at the back, found
in Bucks County, Pennsylvania,
reputed to have belonged to an
early Quaker, old refinishing & rush
seat, late 18th - early 19th c.,
43 3/4" h. **605**

Federal Leather & Wood Armchair

Federal armchair, mahogany, butternut & leather, the ring-turned slender crestrail above the raking leather-upholstered back, downward scrolling open arms on urn-shaped arm supports on a wide leather-upholstered seat over ring- and baluster-turned tapering front legs on peg feet, square back stile legs, original surface & leather, minor imperfections, possibly Portsmouth, New Hampshire, early 19th c., 40" h. (ILLUS.) **1,150**

Federal "lolling" armchair, mahogany, the tall upholstered back w/a serpentine crest above molded open serpentine arms on slightly molded & incurved arm supports joining an over-upholstered seat on molded square front legs joined by square stretchers to the raking rear legs, muslin under-upholstery, Massachusetts, 1785-1800, 43 1/4" h. (minor imperfections) **4,255**

Federal side chair, carved mahogany, the back w/an arched crestrail centered by a narrow tablet w/carved swags & draping on a star-punched background above thin latticework splats carved w/Neoclassical design, over-upholstered seat w/serpentine front seatrail over molded tapering front legs joined to canted rear legs by square stretchers, old refinish, minor repairs, Salem, Massachusetts, 1790-1800, 35 1/2" h. (ILLUS.)...... **863**

Federal side chairs, carved mahogany, a gently arched & stepped crestrail on a square back w/Neoclassical carving on the tablet & beaded edges above reeded & carved criss-cross splats on a curved beaded stay rail over the over-upholstered seat w/bowed front seatrail, on square tapering front legs ending in spade feet joined by square stretchers to the raking rear legs, old surface, Salem, Massachusetts, ca. 1800, 35" h., set of 4 (very minor imperfections) **6,900**

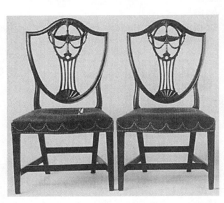

Part of Federal Shield-back Chair Set

Federal side chairs, carved mahogany, shield-back style, the arched & molded crestrail & molded stiles above a carved kylix splat w/festoons draped from flanking carved rosettes, above a pierced splat terminating in a carved lunette at its base above the molded rear seatrail & over-upholstered seat w/serpentine front, square tapering front & canted rear legs joined by flat

Salem Federal Side Chair

stretchers, seats w/old black horsehair, old surface, Rhode Island or Salem, Massachusetts, ca. 1795, four side chairs & matching armchair, armchair w/arm restoration, 37 3/4" h., the set (ILLUS. of two) **23,000**

New York Shield-back Federal Chair

Federal side chairs, carved mahogany, shield-back style w/serpentine molded arched crestrail above a pierced splat carved w/swags, plumes & feathers, the over-upholstered seat below on square tapering molded front legs & gently canted rear legs, one w/repair to crest & patches to back of splat, other w/cracks to splat, New York, ca. 1795, 40" h., pr. (ILLUS. of one) **5,175**

Federal-Style armchair, mahogany & mahogany veneer w/inlay, a spiral-turned & leaf-carved straight crestrail atop backcurved stiles flanking a wide lower back rail w/line inlay, S-scroll open arms on reeded arm supports flanking the wide upholstered slip seat, narrow

slightly straight seatrail between corner blocks above the front legs w/inverted acanthus-carved tops over tapering spiral-turned section ending in knob & peg feet, square canted rear legs, late 19th - early 20th c., 36 1/4" h. **303**

Federal-Style armchair, mahogany, the squared upholstered back w/rounded corners above padded open arms on incurved molded arm supports, overupholstered curved seat, square tapering legs ending in spade feet, old dark finish, early 20th c., 35 1/2" h. **303**

Hitchcock side chair, child's, painted & decorated, a rolled crest above a rectangular splat above the woven rush seat & ring-turned legs, black-painted ground, some of it wood-grained, & gold-leaf decoration, Hitchcocksville, Connecticut, early 19th c., 21" h. (minor surface imperfections) **863**

Hitchcock side chairs, rosewood-grained surface w/the original gilt decoration including an urn centering the cornucopia-form splat, old rush seat, ring-turned legs, original surface, Hitchcocksville, Connecticut, 1830y+s, 35 1/2" h., set of 4 .... **1,265**

French Provincial-Style Armchair

Louis XV Provincial-Style armchair, carved hardwood, the arched serpentined crestrail w/leaf carving continuing to oblong back frame w/serpentine carved medial rail, slender curved open arms on incurved arm supports over the woven rush seat, curved front seatrail w/scalloped rim, simple cabriole front legs w/scroll-carved stretchers, plain turned side & back stretchers, worn brown finish, France, late 19th - early 20th c., 37 1/4" h. (ILLUS.)........................ **138**

Pilgrim Century "Great" chair, turned & painted, the knob- and rod-turned stiles w/knob finials joining three flattened-arch slats & shaped flat open arms ending in a knob handrest above the knob- and rod-turned front legs, simple turned double rungs in from sides & single rung at back, woven rush seat, old red paint, southern New England, late 17th c., 43" h. (imperfections)............................ **4,025**

Queen Anne corner chair, maple, the curved shaped crest continuing to form arms on curved armrests over three ring-turned tapering stiles centered by twin trapezoidal splats, the trapezoidal slip-seat on front cabriole legs ending in a pad foot, New England, 18th c. **1,500**

Queen Anne Corner Chair

Queen Anne corner chair, walnut, U-form crestrail w/raised center continuing to form flat scrolled arms above two wide scroll-cut vase-form splats & three ring-, rod- and knob-turned spindles, upholstered compass seat, front cabriole leg ending in pad foot & three simple turned legs w/pad feet, block-, rod- and baluster-turned cross-stretchers, old refinish, restored, southern New England, 18th c., 29 5/8" h. (ILLUS.) **2,990**

Queen Anne Corner Commode Chair

Queen Anne corner commode chair, maple, U-form back crestrail w/raised center section & continuing to scrolled arms over two slender vase-form splats & three ring- and rod-turned spindles over the upholstered molded seat, deep scalloped aprons, cabriole frontal leg w/deep pad foot, turned & swelled side & back legs, old refinish, minor imperfections, New England, 18th c., 31" h. (ILLUS.).. **2,070**

Queen Anne side chair, walnut, the serpentine crestrail w/upturned ears above a vasiform splat, raked stiles, molded seatrails frame the upholstered seat, front cabriole legs ending in pad feet, joined to rear legs w/block- and vase-turned stretchers, old refinish, die-branded under front seatrail "F. Shaw," Massachusetts, 18th c., 37 1/4" h. (restored, imperfections).............................. **805**

Queen Anne Walnut Side Chair

Queen Anne side chairs, carved walnut, shaped crestrail w/volute-carved ears above a pierced beaker-form splat, upholstered slip seat over scalloped front apron & cabriole front legs ending in trifid feet, turned & canted rear legs, chocolate brown color, old finish, Mid-Atlantic States, ca. 1740, 40" h., pr. (ILLUS. of one).......... **10,925**

Queen Anne-Style side chair, mahogany, the tall back w/an oxyoke crestrail w/rounded corners & tall spooned stiles flanking the tall solid vasiform splat, trapezoidal upholstered slip seat, slightly shaped front seatrail on cabriole front legs w/scroll-cut returns & ending in pad feet, canted square rear legs, old worn finish, early 20th c., 44" h. **83**

Queen Anne-Style wing chair, the high upholstered back flanked by rounded tapering wings above outrolled upholstered arms, cushion seat over the upholstered seatrail, simple cabriole front legs ending in pad feet, square canted rear legs, modern reproduction w/striped velvet upholstery, 46" h. **248**

Salem-type rocking chair w/arms, child's, painted & decorated, the flat crestrail w/round corners decorated w/painted flowers & leaves above canted turned stiles flanking four slender spindles, S-shaped arms on canted, turned arm supports & one spindle over the deeply S-shaped seat, turned front legs joined by turned rung above inset rockers, old blue w/striping & polychrome crest, New England, mid-19th c., 24 3/4" h. (surface imperfections)................. **316**

William & Mary-Style armchair, walnut, the tall back w/an arched & pierced scroll-carved crestrail above a pierced scroll-carved framework centering an oval caned panel, free-standing ropetwist-turned stiles w/knob finials above long shaped open arms ending in scrolled hand grips, wide upholstered seat above a narrow flat carved seatrail on ropetwist-and block-turned front legs joined by an arched, pierced & scroll-carved wide flat stretcher, the front & rear legs joined by a ropetwist-turned H-stretcher, old finish, late 19th - early 20th c., 50" h. (minor edge damage) **275**

William & Mary-Style Side Chair

Windsor "Arrow-back" Highchair

William & Mary-Style side chair,
walnut, the tall back w/arched &
pierced scroll-carved crest rails
above a back panel framed
w/further scroll carving centered by
an oval caned panel, free-standing
twist-turned stiles w/knob-turned
finials above the wide upholstered
seat above a narrow scroll-carved
seatrail above twist- and block-
turned legs joined by a wide
arched & scroll-pierced front
stretcher, the four legs joined by a
ropetwist-turned H-stretcher, old
finish, early 20th c., seat originally
caned, 46 1/2" h. (ILLUS.) **248**

Windsor "arrow-back" highchair,
painted, a stepped crestrail raised
on backswept tapering stiles
flanking three long curved arrow
slats over simple turned arms on
bamboo-turned spindles over the
thick shaped plank seat, tall canted
swelled bamboo-turned legs w/a
front footrest over a high turned
swelled stretcher & matching rear
stretcher, lower side stretchers,
early red paint, very minor surface
imperfections, New England, 1820-
30, 36" h. (ILLUS.) **2,875**

Bamboo-turned Windsor Side Chairs

Windsor "bamboo-turned" side chairs, painted & decorated, the flat crestrail above four swelled bamboo-turned spindles between bamboo-turned stiles over a shaped saddle seat, canted bamboo-turned legs joined by box stretchers, yellow ground w/green & red stenciled leaf & berry decoration on the crestrail & green accents, New England, ca. 1820-30, some repaint, 33 1/4" h., set of 4 (ILLUS. of two) **863**

Windsor "birdcage" side chairs, the back w/two simple turned horizontal crestrails joined by three short spindles above seven simple turned long spindles all flanked by canted bamboo-turned stiles, oblong-shaped plank seat on canted bamboo-turned legs joined by bamboo-turned box stretchers, old refinishing, first half 19th c., 33 1/2" h., pr. **275**

Windsor "bow-back" side chair, painted, slender arched backrail above seven slender turned spindles over the shaped saddle seat, canted bamboo-turned legs joined by a swelled H-stretcher, old worn black paint, late 18th - early 19th c., 38" h. **358**

Windsor child's rocking armchair, painted & decorated, rectangular tablet crestrail decorated w/colored florals & leaves raised on simple turned stiles joined by a narrow medial rail & flanked by simple turned open arms over the thick shaped saddle seat, ring-turned front legs & plain turned rear legs w/simple turned stretchers, mounted on heavy, long rockers, greenish yellow ground w/striping decoration in olive green & black, minor damage, Pennsylvania, mid-19th c., 18" h. (ILLUS.) **3,450**

Windsor "continuous-arm" armchair, painted, the arched slender crestrail continuing down to form flat arms, the back w/seven slender swelled spindles w/two short spindles & a canted baluster- and ring-turned arm support under each arm, a shaped saddle seat on four canted baluster- and ring-turned legs joined by a swelled H-stretcher, green paint, probably

Windsor Child's Rocking Chair

Pennsylvania, late 18th - early 19th c., 39" h. (repairs) **978**

Windsor "continuous-arm" brace-back armchair, painted, the slender arched crestrail curving down to form slender arms w/scrolled grips above numerous slender turned spindles & canted baluster- and ring-turned arm supports, shaped saddle seat, on canted baluster-, ring- and rod-turned tapering legs joined by a swelled H-stretcher, old black paint, New York, school of W. MacBride, 18th c. **2,500**

Windsor "continuous-arm" brace-back armchair, painted, the slender molded crestrail continuing down to form narrow arms above six tall slender swelled spindles & two under-arm spindles & canted baluster-turned arm supports, the shaped saddle seat w/a back projection supporting a pair of flared brace spindles, on baluster- and rod-turned tapering canted legs joined by a swelled H-stretcher, old black over early paint, imperfections, underside left arm repair, branded "E. Swan," Elisha Swan, Stonington, Connecticut, 1755-1807, 39" h. (ILLUS.) **2,760**

Windsor "fan-back" armchair, a narrow serpentine crestrail supported by six short spindles on

Windsor "Continuous-Arm" Armchair

a U-form medial rail continuing to form shaped arms ending in shaped handholds w/canted baluster-turned arm supports & above eleven turned spindles, wide carved saddle seat on four canted baluster- and ring-turned legs joined by a swelled H-stretcher, three old coats of red paint, New England, ca. 1790, 31" h. (minor imperfections)............................... **6,325**

Windsor "fan-back" side chairs, a cupid's-bow shaped crestrail above six swelled spindles flanked by baluster- and ring-turned canted stiles & a pair of projecting back braces, the shaped saddle seat raised on canted baluster-, ring- and rod-turned legs joined by a swelled H-stretcher, 18th c., pr..... **3,100**

Windsor "fan-back" side chairs, painted, shaped crest & shaped incised seats above turned, splayed legs joined by medial stretchers, old black paint, New England, early 19th c., 35 7/8" h., pr. (imperfections) **1,035**

Windsor "fan-back" writing-arm armchair, painted, a small shaped crestrail above five tall slender spindles above the U-form mid-rail continuing at one side to form a wide writing surface w/two small drawers beneath, numerous slender swelled spindles from mid-rail to wide shaped seat over a small drawer, raised on canted bamboo-turned legs joined by a bamboo-turned H-stretcher, old black paint, New England, early 19th c., 42 1/2" h. (restoration to drawers) **4,025**

Windsor low-back writing-arm armchair, country-style, a curved shaped crestrail continuing to form arms ending in knuckled armrests & a wide teardrop-shaped writing surface at one side above a small bowed drawer all raised on simple bamboo-turned spindles, a wide shaped plank seat on canted bamboo-turned legs joined by turned box stretchers, overall worn black paint, Vermont, late 18th - early 19th c. **5,200**

Windsor "rod-back" child's side chairs, painted, a curved crestrail above seven bamboo-turned spindles & a shaped saddle seat over bamboo-turned canted legs joined by stretchers, painted dark red, New England, ca. 1790, 28" h., pr. (minor imperfections) **633**

Windsor "rod-back" side chairs, painted & grained, double crestrails over raked incised spindles, incised saddle seat on splayed, turned legs, old repaint w/gold striping & brown graining on the seats, New England, early 19th c., 33" h., pr. (surface imperfections) **920**

Windsor "sack-back" armchair, grain-painted, the wide bowed crestrail over seven spindles continuing through the medial rail that extends to form scrolled arms on a spindle & a baluster- and ring-turned canted arm support, wide oblong-shaped saddle seat, on canted ring- and baluster-turned legs joined by a swelled H-stretcher, later rosewood graining & yellow outlining, old surface, minor repairs, southern New

Grain-painted "Sack-back" Windsor

Early "Sack-back" Windsor Armchair

England, late 18th c., 38" h.
(ILLUS.) **1,495**

Windsor "sack-back" armchair,
painted, the bowed crestrail over
seven spindles continuing through
the medial rail that extends to form
narrow shaped arms over a spindle
& baluster- and ring-turned canted
arm support, wide oblong saddle
seat, on slightly splayed ring- and
baluster-turned tapering legs
joined by a swelled H-stretcher, old
green paint over earlier black,
imperfections, southeastern New
England, ca. 1780, 38 1/2" h.
(ILLUS.) **3,335**

Windsor "sack-back" armchair, the
bowed crestrail above eight
spindles continuing through a
curved medial rail ending in
shaped arms above a plain spindle
& a baluster- and knob-turned
canted arm support, wide shaped
seat on canted ring-, baluster- and
rod-turned legs joined by a knob-
turned H-stretcher, painted salmon
red & black over earlier green, New
England, ca. 1780, 37 1/2" h. (loss
to feet) **1,840**

Windsor "step-down" side chairs,
the narrow stepped crestrail above
backswept & tapering stiles &
seven slender spindles above the
wide shaped saddle seat, on
canted swelled & turned legs
joined by box stretchers, decorated
w/the original yellow ground paint
w/freehand gold & green
decoration on the crestrail w/light
brown front seatrail & leg
decoration, highlighted w/brown
striping, original surface,
Farmington, Maine, ca. 1820,
35" h., set of 4 (very minor
imperfections) **9,200**

**Windsor-Style "arrow-back"
side chairs,** a flat crestrail
between tapering rabbit ear
stiles flanking the arrow slats
above the shaped saddle seat,
raised on canted bamboo-turned
legs w/an arrow form stretcher
& plain turned side & back
stretchers, old worn dark brown
finish, branded label of I. & J.G.
Stickley, "Stickley - Fayetteville -
Syracuse," New York, early
20th c., 34 3/4" h., set of 6 .... **825**

Queen Anne side chair, carved cherry, the bow-form crestrail w/curved & curled ears on slightly canted flat stiles flanking the vasiform splat & shaped upholstered slip seat within arched rails, on cabriole front legs & square canted rear legs joined by baluster- and block-turned stretcher & ending in pad feet, old & possibly original finish, Massachusetts, 1730-50, 39" h. **2,587**

CHESTS & CHESTS OF DRAWERS

Apothecary chest, pine & walnut, a rectangular walnut top over a case enclosing 32 small square drawers w/white porcelain knobs over two rows of 12 slightly larger drawers w/large porcelain knobs, wire nail construction, refinished, 14 1/4 x 36 3/4", 21 3/4" h. (top board added) **1,375**

Apothecary chest, hardwood w/old dark stain, a rectangular top above a tall case w/six rows of three small drawers each, simple bail pulls, a single paneled long drawer at the bottom flanked by two small square panels, molded apron & short square stile legs w/corner brackets, faint Chinese characters on each drawer, China, late 19th - early 20th c., 22 x 32", 40" h. **770**

Blanket chest, country-style, painted & decorated, six-board construction, the rectangular molded & hinged top opening to a well w/a till & drawer above a dovetailed case w/a molded base on bracket feet, the exterior painted mustard yellow to resemble tiger stripe or bird's-eye maple, brass keyhole escutcheon, lettered in black on the back "G.H.C.," possibly New England, early 19th c., 14 3/4 x 32", 16 1/8" h. (repairs) **431**

Blanket chest, Chippendale country-style, painted & decorated pine, a hinged rectangular top w/molded edges & original bright-cut strap hinges opening to a well & till, the case decorated w/tombstone & diamond panels, flowers & dated "1771," the sides similarly painted, the molded base below hung w/a central pendant on straight bracket feet, Pennsylvania, 22 x 51", 20" h. (top decoration worn, feet shortened) **1,265**

Blanket chest, country-style, painted & decorated poplar, rectangular top w/molded edges & wrought-iron strap hinges opening to a well w/lidded till, the dovetailed case w/a molded base & scroll-cut bracket feet, decorated w/original red graining, early 19th c., 19 1/2 x 45", 23" h. (some foot repair) **1,210**

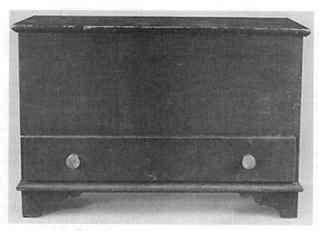

Early Massachusetts Blanket Chest

Blanket chest, country-style, painted pine, six-board dovetailed construction, the rectangular top w/molded edge hinged above a deep well above a molded base raised on bracket feet, original red paint, New England, ca. 1780, 19 x 43 3/4", 26" h. (minor imperfections) **690**

Blanket chest, country-style, painted & decorated poplar, a rectangular lid w/molded edges opening to a well w/a lidded till w/secret compartment over a dovetailed case w/two small drawers at the bottom above a base molding & scroll-cut bracket feet, the sides decorated w/original brown graining & green painted trim & stenciled decoration in gold, white & green including fruit, flowers, lyres & foliage w/"D.R. 1857," similar to the Soap Hollow School, Pennsylvania, 20 3/4 x 46 3/4", 29 1/2" h. (back feet repaired, other minor repair) **3,025**

Blanket chest, painted pine, rectangular hinged top w/molded edges opening to a well w/a lidded, molded till, a single long drawer across the bottom w/old replaced pressed glass pulls, molded base band on shaped bracket feet, old green over old red paint, paint wear on top, western Massachusetts, 18th c., 17 x 45", 31 5/8" h. (ILLUS.) **2,645**

Blanket chest, country-style, painted & decorated six-board style, the rectangular hinges opening to a deep well, solid board ends w/high arched bootjack legs, overall putty-grained finish in quarter-round and half-round designs, New England, 19th c., 39" l **1,700**

Chippendale "block-front" chest of drawers, mahogany, the rectangular thumb-molded top w/a double-blocked front edge above a conforming case of four long blocked drawers on a molded base, raised on scroll-cut bracket feet, old refinish, replaced butterfly brasses, Boston, 1750-90, 19 1/4 x 33", 29 1/4" h. (rear foot missing) **46,000**

Chippendale "Block-front" Chest

Chippendale "block-front" chest of drawers, mahogany, the rectangular top w/serpentine front w/molded edge overhanging a conforming cockbeaded case w/four graduated block-front drawers, molded base, pointed central apron drop & shaped bracket feet, old but not original brasses, restored, Boston, ca. 1770, 19 x 33", 30" h. (ILLUS.) **19,550**

Chippendale "bow-front" chest of drawers, inlaid mahogany, a rectangular molded top w/a bowed front edge above a conforming case w/four long graduated line-inlaid cockbeaded drawers, molded base on short cabriole legs ending in claw-and-ball feet, appears to retain original simple bail pulls, 21 x 41 3/4", 35 1/4" h. (losses to beading, feet replaced & chipped).................................... **5,750**

Cherry Chippendale Chest of Drawers

Chippendale chest of drawers,
cherry, a rectangular top w/molded
edge widely overhanging a case
w/four long graduated beaded
drawers w/simple bail pulls,
molded base on scroll-cut bracket
feet, appears to retain original
brasses, two foot facings replaced,
New England, probably
Connecticut, ca. 1790,
20 1/4 x 31", 31 1/2" h. (ILLUS.)... **4,025**

Chippendale chest of drawers,
walnut, rectangular top w/molded
edges above a pair of molded
overlapping drawers above three
long overlapping graduated
drawers all w/simple bail pulls &
brass keyhole escutcheons,
molded base on ogee bracket feet
w/scroll-cut returns, the front
corners w/reeded quarter columns,
late 18th c., 20 3/4 x 37", 37 1/2" h.
(old worn finish, feet & brasses
replaced, other restoration) **3,025**

**Chippendale country-style chest of
drawers,** maple & birch, a
rectangular top slightly
overhanging a case of four long
reverse-graduated drawers
w/incised beading & diamond inlaid
escutcheons, molded base on tall
bracket feet, replaced oval brass
pulls, varnish over old red wash,
New England, ca. 1790, 17 x 40",
38 3/4" h. (minor restoration)........ **2,185**

Connecticut Chippendale Chest

**Chippendale "serpentine-top"
chest of drawers,** cherry,
rectangular top w/a molded edge &
serpentine front overhanging a

case of four long graduated
beaded drawers w/oval pulls
flanked by fluted quarter-columns,
the molded base on heavy ogee
scroll-cut bracket feet, repair to
front left foot & both rear feet,
Connecticut, ca. 1780, 23 x 41",
37 3/4" h. (ILLUS.)........................ **6,325**

Chippendale tall chest of drawers,
tiger stripe maple, rectangular top
w/a deep stepped cornice above a
case of seven long graduated
thumb-molded drawers w/replaced
butterfly brasses, refinished,
southeastern New England,
ca. 1780, 22 x 36", 64" h.
(restored) **3,220**

Chippendale Tall Chest over Drawers

**Chippendale tall chest over
drawers,** painted pine, a
rectangular molded hinged top
opening to a deep well in a case
w/two false long drawer fronts over
four long working thumb-molded
graduated drawers, molded base
on tall bracket feet, simple bail
brasses appear to be original,
minor imperfections, painted red,
New England, late 18th c.,
18 x 36", 52 1/2" h. (ILLUS.)......... **4,888**

**Classical (American Empire)
country-style chest of drawers,**
birch, a high crestboard w/a flat top

& scroll-cut & rounded corners
above a pair of small handkerchief
drawers w/small replaced round
brasses, the rectangular top above
a single long, deep stepped-out
drawer above ring-, rod- and block-
turned columns flanking three long
setback drawers, ring-turned
tapering legs w/ball feet, replaced
butterfly brasses, old mellow
refinishing, first half 19th c.,
17 3/4 x 37", overall 48 1/4" h. **935**

Paw-footed Classical Chest

paw front feet & turned rear feet,
old refinish, minor imperfections,
possibly Pennsylvania, ca. 1825,
23 1/2 x 45 1/2", 47" h. (ILLUS.).... **920**

Classical chest of drawers, child's,
carved pine, the scroll-carved
splashback centered by a shell
crest & reeded corner posts
flanking an inset narrow
rectangular top w/molded edges
over a pair of small handkerchief
drawers w/turned wood knobs on
the rectangular top above the case
w/a deep long projecting drawer
over two long narrower drawers
flanked by swelled columns, small
tapering turned front feet, turned
knobs on all the drawers, dark
finish, ca. 1840, 19" w., 23" h. **1,200**

**Classical country-style chest of
drawers,** cherry & poplar w/old
cherry red finish, a rectangular top
above a pair of deep overhanging
drawers over ring-turned columns
flanking a lower case w/three long
graduated drawers, simple turned
wood pulls, on ring- and knob-
turned feet, ca. 1840, 21 x 43 1/8',
47 1/4" h. **605**

**Classical country-style chest of
drawers,** tiger stripe maple, a
scroll-cut crestrail w/block ends on
the rectangular top over a case
w/three small shallow projecting
drawers over a long deep drawer
above three long graduated
drawers all w/turned wood knobs,
short turned legs w/knob feet,

Classical Mahogany Chest of Drawers

Classical chest of drawers, carved
mahogany & mahogany veneer, a
flat-topped scroll-ended top
backboard above a row of three
short drawers stepped back on the
rectangular top over a pair of
overhanging deep drawers above
three long drawers flanked by
columns w/a carved pineapple
over leaf bands & a spiral-carved
section, molded conforming base
on heavy knob-, ring- and baluster-
turned tapering legs, replaced
early glass pulls, refinished,
imperfections, North Shore
Massachusetts, ca. 1825,
22 x 42 3/4", 45" h. (ILLUS.).......... **978**

Classical chest of drawers, carved
mahogany & mahogany veneer,
the rectangular top over a long
drawer overhanging a case w/three
long drawers flanked by carved
free-standing columns on a molded
base, simple turned wooden
knobs, acanthus-carved heavy

paneled ends, old finish, probably Pennsylvania, ca. 1830, 19 1/2 x 46", 49 1/2" h. **2,185**

Curly Maple Classical Tall Chest

Classical country-style tall chest of drawers, curly maple, a rectangular top over a pair of drawers over four long graduated drawers flanked by baluster- and ring-turned free-standing columns, molded base on heavy turned ovoid front feet on casters, first half 19th c. (ILLUS.) **715**

Dower chest, painted & decorated, a rectangular top w/molded edges opening to a well, the front decorated w/a large arch-topped rectangular panel centered by a large spread-winged eagle w/shield & banner in its beak,

pinwheels, compass stars & tulips around the bird, in dark shades of umber, black, red & yellow within a red & white border, the background w/a finely sponged black & brown ground, black base molding & scroll-cut bracket feet, light surface cleaning, several spurs replaced, Center County, Pennsylvania, ca. 1814 (ILLUS.) **12,500**

Fine Federal "Bow-front" Chest

Federal "bow-front" chest of drawers, cherry & bird's-eye maple veneer, a rectangular top w/bowed front over a case of four long graduated cockbeaded drawers outlined in cross-banded mahogany around bird's-eye maple, scalloped apron & tall slender French feet, replaced oval brasses, old surface w/minor veneer patching, attributed to Eliphalet Briggs, Keene, New Hampshire, ca. 1810, 20 1/2 x 39 3/4", 38 1/2" h. (ILLUS.)........... **9,775**

Early Pennsylvania Dower Chest

Federal "Bow-front" Chest of Drawers

Federal "bow-front" chest of drawers, mahogany, a rectangular top w/molded edges & a bowed front above a conforming case w/four long graduated cockbeaded drawers w/oval pulls, molded base on slightly canted bracket feet, patches & repairs to feet, New England, ca. 1795, 24 x 42", 33 1/2" h. (ILLUS.)........................ **3,737**

Federal "bow-front" chest of drawers, cherry, a rectangular top w/bowed front above a conforming case w/four long cockbeaded graduated drawers w/oval brasses & keyhole escutcheons, veneered cyma-curved front apron, tall French feet, original brasses, old refinish, New England, early 19th c., 21 3/8 x 41 1/2", 37" h. (surface imperfections)................ **2,875**

Federal Bird's-eye Maple Chest

Federal chest of drawers, birch & bird's-eye maple veneer, a rectangular top w/reeded edges above a case w/four long reverse-graduated beaded drawers w/oval pulls & brass keyhole escutcheons, flat base, raised on baluster- and ring-turned legs w/peg feet, brasses appear to be original, old refinish, imperfections, New England, 1815-25, 19 x 40 1/2", 38" h. (ILLUS.)............................ **2,415**

Federal Curly Maple Chest of Drawers

Federal chest of drawers, curly maple & curly maple veneer, a rectangular top above a case of four long graduated cockbeaded drawers w/oval pulls, valanced apron w/center blocked drop, tall slender French feet, brasses appear to be original, old finish, imperfections, southern New England, ca. 1790, 18 x 39 3/4" h., 37" h. (ILLUS.)............................ **4,888**

Federal chest of drawers, inlaid cherry, rectangular top w/string-inlaid edges slightly overhanging a case w/four long graduated cockbeaded drawers above a double-scallop apron & flaring slender French feet, New England, ca. 1800, 19 3/4 x 42", 38" h (replaced oval brasses, refinished).................................... **2,990**

Federal chest of drawers, mahogany & figured mahogany veneer, the rectangular top over a case of four cockbeaded long graduated drawers & replaced oval brasses & keyhole escutcheons, deeply scalloped apron & tall

flaring French feet, early 19th c.,
20 x 42 1/2", 41" h. (age cracks
in top & ends, minor veneer repair)
.... **2,750**

**Federal country-style chest of
drawers,** cherry, a rectangular top
above a case of four long
dovetailed graduated drawers
w/simple turned wood knobs,
scalloped apron, simple turned
feet, paneled ends, refinished,
early 19th c., 19 3/4 x 40 3/4",
39 1/2" h. **770**

Federal Tall Birch Chest of Drawers

Federal tall chest of drawers, birch,
a rectangular top w/a flaring
molded cornice above a case of six
long thumb-molded drawers w/oval
brasses, molded base on simple
bracket feet, original brasses,
refinished, Concord, New
Hampshire, late 18th - early
19th c., 16 1/4 x 35 3/4" h.,
54 3/4" h. (ILLUS.) **4,255**

Hardware chest, poplar, a thin
rectangular top & sides enclosing
stacks of 35 small drawers w/tiny
knobs, old brown finish, wire nail
construction w/plywood back,
some drawers w/worn tape labels,
5 1/4 x 16 3/8", 16 3/8" h. **330**

Grain-painted Early Mule Chest

**Mule chest (box chest w/one or
more drawers below a storage
compartment),** painted pine,
rectangular top w/molded edges
opening to a deep well above a
single long drawer across the
bottom, on high arched & shaped
bracket feet, original turned wood
knobs, original red & yellow
painting simulating tiger stripe
maple, old dry surface, minor
surface scratches on top, Rhode
Island, 1830-40, 20 x 39 3/4",
36" h. (ILLUS.) **2,070**

**Mule chest (box chest w/one or
more drawers below a storage
compartment),** pine, the molded
rectangular hinged top opening to
a deep well over a single lower
drawer below w/small turned wood
pulls, bootjack ends, the keyhole
escutcheon made from a brass
button impressed w/the legend
"long live the president GW," old
surface, New England, late 18th c.,
17 3/4 x 36 1/4", 32 1/2" h.
(imperfections).............................. **1,265**

**Mule chest (box chest w/one or
more drawers below a storage
compartment),** painted pine,
rectangular hinged top w/molded
edge opening to a deep well above
a pair of long drawers below,
original grain painting resembling
mahogany w/two banded false
drawers at the top over the two
working drawers, four oval brasses
at the top & two each on the
working drawers, molded band
w/simple bracket feet w/painted
banding, old repaint, early 19th c.,
17 1/2 x 21 1/2", 44 1/2" h. (repairs
to feet, scratches on side) **825**

Pilgrim Century chest of drawers,
painted oak, cedar & yellow pine,
a rectangular top w/applied
molding above a case of four long
drawers each w/molded fronts &
chamfered mitered borders &
separated by applied horizontal
moldings, the sides w/two
recessed vertical molded panels
above a single horizontal panel,
deep cove-molded base on turned
ball feet, old red paint,
southeastern New England,
ca. 1700, 20 1/2 x 37 3/4", 35" h.
(minor imperfections)................ **26,450**

Queen Anne chest of drawers,
figured walnut, a rectangular
molded top w/notched corners
overhanging a case w/a pair of
short drawers over three long
graduated drawers flanked by
fluted chamfered corner columns,
the molded base on ogee bracket
feet, appears to retain original rare
openwork brass butterfly pulls &
keyhole escutcheons,
Pennsylvania, 1750-60,
22 x 36 1/2", 34 1/2" h. (patched
to back of top where mirror was
fitted, half of front left foot
replaced) **13,800**

Queen Anne chest-on-frame,
carved & painted pine & maple,
two-part construction: the upper
section w/a rectangular top w/a
widely flaring & stepped cornice
above a band of dentil molding
over a case w/two pairs of small
drawers flanking a deep fan-carved
central drawer w/incised scallops &
overlapping lunettes, over a stack
of four long graduated drawers, all
w/simple bail pulls; the lower
section w/a molded top above a
deeply scalloped apron raised on
short angled cabriole legs ending
in pad feet, New Hampshire,
18th c., 36" w., 56" h. **2,500**

Queen Anne chest-on-frame,
walnut & burl walnut veneer, the
rectangular top above a case
w/four long graduated dovetailed
drawers w/brass teardrop pulls set
onto a molded frame w/arched
apron & short cabriole front legs
ending in duck feet, England, first
half 20th c., 19 14 x 33 1/2",
38 1/2" h. **825**

Queen Anne Mule Chest

**Queen Anne mule chest (box chest
w/one or more drawers below a
storage compartment),** painted
pine, a rectangular top w/molded
edges opening to a deep well w/a
case front of three thumb-molded
graduated false drawers over two
working drawers, molded base on
simple high bracket feet centering
a small shaped pendant, replaced
butterfly pulls, old dark brown
paint, minor imperfections,
probably Massachusetts, mid-
18th c., 17 1/4 x 36 1/2", 46 1/2" h.
(ILLUS.) **3,738**

Queen Anne tall chest of drawers,
carved & painted, a rectangular top
w/a deep stepped projecting
cornice above a case of five long
graduated drawers w/simple
rounded butterfly pulls & oval
keyhole escutcheons, molded
base w/carved beading & dogtooth carving, raised on short
bandy cabriole legs ending in pad
feet, old red paint, New
Hampshire, Dunlap School,
18th c., 35 3/4" w., 48" h............ **40,000**

Queen Anne tall chest of drawers,
maple, the rectangular top w/flaring
stepped cornice over a pair of
small drawers over four long
graduated drawers, molded base
on simple shaped bracket feet,
appears to retain most of the
original brasses, numerous chips &
patches to drawer lips, one inch

Queen Anne Tall Chest of Drawers

Victorian Eastlake Cottage-style Chest

missing on left rear foot, New
England, 1740-60, 19 1/2 x 39",
45 1/4" h. (ILLUS.)........................ **2,300**

**Victorian country-style chest of
drawers,** Renaissance Revival
substyle, walnut, a tall oval mirror
swiveling between a pierced
"wishbone" frame on a short
pedestal above the rectangular top
over a case w/long drawer w/a
raised panel & curved leaf pulls
slightly overhanging three
matching long lower drawers,
bracket front feet, ca. 1875,
18 x 41", base, 43" h. plus mirror .. **489**

**Victorian country-style chest of
drawers,** Renaissance Revival
substyle, walnut, an arched &
scalloped crestboard above a
narrow rectangular shelf above a
pair of shallow handkerchief
drawers w/turned wood knobs &
quarter-rounded bobbin turnings at
the corners, the rectangular top
w/molded edges above a case
w/chamfered front corners & half-
round bobbin-turned drops at the
top corners above four long
graduated drawers w/turned wood
knobs, half-round bobbin turnings
at the bottom front corners flanking
the scroll-cut bracket feet,
refinished, ca. 1870, 18 x 39 1/2",
overall 50 3/4" h............................. **605**

**Victorian Eastlake Cottage-style
chest of drawers,** painted &
decorated pine, the superstructure
w/a notch-cut crestboard w/peaked
center & incised & gilt-trimmed
lines & florettes over a gilt-banded
frame enclosing a rectangular
swivel mirror over decorated
panels & a narrow open shelf
flanked by shaped side uprights
w/gilt-trimmed line-incised florals &
loops, the rectangular top
w/molded edge w/further gilt trim
over a case of four long graduated
drawers painted w/a large round
continuous reserve decorated w/a
lakeside landscape, the reserve
surrounded by a rectangular gilt
band frame w/angled corners &
further stylized gilt florals, on
original brown & orange comb-
grained ground accented w/black,
the top in olive green w/a rose &
gold floral design, original round
ring pulls & paint, on casters,
ca. 1880-90, height loss,
18 3/4 x 38", 76" h. (ILLUS.).......... **978**

Golden Oak Chest of Drawers

Golden Oak "Highboy" Chest

Victorian Golden Oak chest of drawers, the top mounted w/a large squared mirror w/rounded corners within a framework w/a high arched & scroll-carved crestrail & shaped sides & rounded bottom corners swiveling between tall scrolled uprights w/scroll carving across the base, the rectangular top w/a serpentine front over a conforming case w/a pair of drawers over two long drawers, all w/pierced brass pulls, simple cabriole front legs & square rear legs, on casters, ca. 1900, 20 x 44", 82" h. (ILLUS.)................ **403**

Victorian Golden Oak "highboy" chest of drawers, oak, a rectangular top w/molded edges mounted w/a simple wishbone upright support holding an oblong serpentine-framed beveled swiveling mirror, the tall case w/a pair of small serpentine-front drawers over four long drawers, simple turned wood pulls, scalloped apron & short shaped front legs & square rear legs, on casters, ca. 1900, 19 x 34", 66" h. (ILLUS.) **259**

Victorian Golden Oak "highboy" chest of drawers, the rectangular top w/molded edges & incurved sides mounted w/an oblong cartouche-form beveled mirror in conforming scroll-carved frame swiveling between wishbone uprights w/scroll carving along the bottom, the tall case w/a pair of drawers over four long drawers, all w/pierced brass pulls, scroll-carved apron & leaf-carved front cabriole legs & square back legs, excellent condition, ca. 1900 (ILLUS.).......... **850**

Victorian Golden Oak "side-by-side" chest of drawers, a tall narrow rectangular beveled mirror on one side swiveling within a framework w/an arched & scroll-carved crestrail, beside a short scroll-carved top crest over a stack of two small drawers over a small paneled cupboard door, all on a rectangular top w/molded edges over two long drawers, stamped brass pulls, ca. 1900, possibly missing feet (ILLUS.)................. **150-300**

Victorian Golden Oak "Highboy" Chest

Golden Oak "Side-by-Side" Chest

William & Mary chest over drawer,
child's, painted pine, a rectangular
hinged top w/molded edges
opening to a deep well, half-round
edge moldings down the corners &
above the long base drawer
molded to resemble two small
drawers, front & sides w/a red
painted wash & brown free-hand
designs of concentric rings,
demilune & meandering vines, the
drawer painted salmon, red, &
brown, single arch molding in
black, possibly coastal
Massachusetts, early 18th c.,
17 1/8 x 28", 19" h. (minor
imperfections) **9,200**

CRADLES

Bentwood, the arched bentwood
matching head- and footrail above
simple turned spindles w/the side
composed of seven turned
spindles between turned rails, a
slat rail bottom, suspending &
swinging between simple turned
uprights w/knob finials raised on
shaped & arched shoe feet w/a
central drop w/two long rod
stretchers from end to end, ivory
fittings, late 19th - early 20th c.,
41" l., 39" h. **440**

Country-style Painted Cradle

Country-style, painted pine,
rectangular deep mortised frame
w/paneled side slats w/double
almond-shaped cut-outs, hooded
end, found in Amish country, old
worn black paint, 19th c., 31" l.
(ILLUS.) **880**

Rustic style, twig-constructed sides
on a rocker base, unsigned, early
20th c., 22 x 33", 22" h. **55**

CUPBOARDS

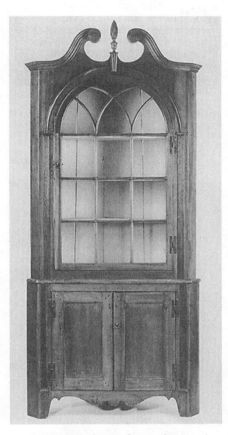

Chippendale Cherry Corner Cupboard

Corner cupboard, Chippendale, carved cherry, two-part construction: the upper section w/a scrolled molded pediment flanking a fluted keystone w/flame finial above a wide arched door w/geometric glazing flanked by reeded columns, opening to three serpentine-shaped painted shelves; the slightly projecting lower section w/a pair of paneled cupboard doors opening to single shelf flanked by reeded columns, scalloped apron on simple bracket feet, old refinish, hardware changes, minor patching, probably Pennsylvania, early 19th c., 17 3/4 x 41 1/2", 95" h. (ILLUS.)... **9,200**

Corner cupboard, Chippendale, poplar, two-part construction: the top section w/a flat top & deep stepped cornice over a wide arched molding w/central keystone above a pair of geometrically glazed cupboard doors opening to two serpentine shelves w/plate rail & spoon cut-outs; the slightly stepped-out lower section w/a pair of raised panel doors w/H-hinges opening to a single shelf, serpentine apron & simple bracket feet, old surface, imperfections, Pennsylvania, late 18th - early 19th c., 25 1/2 x 51", 67" h. (ILLUS.) **3,680**

Corner cupboard, Chippendale-Style, mahogany, two-part construction: the upper section w/a flat top & narrow molded cornice over a lattice-carved frieze band over a tall single geometrically glazed door opening to three shaped shelves; the stepped-out lower section w/a wide single geometrically glazed door opening to a single shaped shelf, molded base & bracket feet, England, early 20th c., 28" w., 72 1/4" h. (ILLUS.)........................... **715**

Chippendale Poplar Corner Cupboard

English Chippendale-style Cupboard

Corner cupboard, Federal country-style, painted poplar, one-piece construction, the flat top over a deep stepped cornice over a pair of tall paneled doors w/double incised vertical bands & cast-iron latch over a pair of shorter matching doors, flat apron & plain bracket feet, worn blue paint, Pennsylvania, ca. 1830, 43" w., 69 1/2" h. (ILLUS.)........................ **5,175**

Federal Tulipwood Corner Cupboard

Corner cupboard, Federal country-style, tulipwood, two-part construction: the upper section w/a flat top over a deep coved cornice over a wide tall 12-pane glazed door w/the three upper panes forming Gothic arches, opening to three shelves; the lower section w/a paneled central drawer flanked by small recessed panels above a pair of paneled cupboard doors w/H-hinges opening to a shelf, serpentine apron continuing to bracket feet, old refinish, some imperfections, probably Pennsylvania, ca. 1830, 19 x 41", 84 3/4" h. (ILLUS.)........................ **3,910**

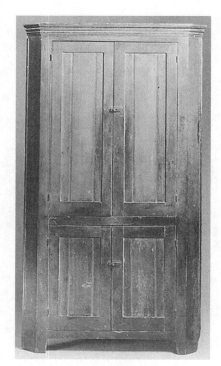

Painted Federal Corner Cupboard

Country Federal Corner Cupboard

Federal One-piece Corner Cupboard

Corner cupboard, Federal country-style, cherry, one-piece construction, a flat top w/a widely flaring deep coved cornice over a dentil band above a pair of tall double raised-panel doors opening to shelves over a pair of shorter raised panel cupboard doors, deeply scalloped apron & bracket feet, old worn refinishing, repairs, edge damage & wear, early 19th c., 52 1/2" w., 85" h. (ILLUS.) **1,045**

Corner cupboard, Federal country-style, pine, two-piece construction: the upper section w/a deep flaring & stepped cornice above a pair of tall, narrow 8-pane glazed cupboard doors w/molded muntins & wooden knob opening to three shelves; the lower section w/a mid-molding over a single cockbeaded drawer w/two wooden knobs above a pair of cross-form paneled cupboard doors w/brass latch, molded base on scroll-cut ogee bracket feet, Middle Atlantic states, early 19th c., restoration, 21 1/2 x 48 1/2", 87" h. **2,415**

Corner cupboard, Federal country-style, cherry, one-piece construction, a flat top w/cove-molded cornice over a pair of tall 8-pane cupboard doors opening to three shelves over a pair of small drawers over a pair of wide paneled cupboard doors, curved apron & simple bracket feet, minor edge damage & age cracks, one pane w/corner crack, old refinishing, first quarter 19th c., 53 3/4" w., 88 3/4" h. (ILLUS.) **2,970**

Corner cupboard, Federal, cherry & tiger stripe maple inlaid, the flat top w/a coved cornice over a narrow arched band w/center block continuing down to two blocks over narrow inlaid tiger stripe maple bands all flanking the arched open front w/three shaped shelves above a slightly stepped-out lower section w/a single raised double-panel door flanked by narrow tiger stripe bands & opening to a single shelf, flat molded base, Mid-Atlantic States, early 19th c., restored, 20 x 41 1/2", 89" h. (ILLUS.) **1,610**

Federal Cherry Corner Cupboard

Large Inlaid Federal Corner Cupboard

Corner cupboard, Federal, cherry, two-part construction: the upper section w/a flat top over a deep coved cornice over a reeded frieze band over a tall 12-pane glazed cupboard door opening to three shelves; the lower section w/mid-molding over a pair of small paneled cupboard doors centered by inlaid rings, molded base on shaped bracket feet, old finish, feet replaced, minor repairs, found in Tennessee, early 19th c., 49 1/2" w., 89 3/4" h. (ILLUS.) **5,225**

Fine Federal Walnut Corner Cupboard

Corner cupboard, Federal, carved walnut, two-part construction: the upper section w/a flat top & deep coved cornice over a narrow tiger stripe maple frieze band over a raised arched molding w/center keystone & serrated inner edge continuing down to tall pilasters flanking the tall arched geometrically glazed cupboard door opening to three shelves; the lower section w/a mid-molding over a pair of drawers above a pair of paneled cupboard doors w/H-hinges, flat molded apron on scroll-cut bracket feet, old refinish, imperfections, probably New Jersey, early 19th c., 22 x 44", 94 1/4" h. (ILLUS.) **8,625**

European Hanging Cupboard

Hanging cupboard, painted, a rectangular top w/a flaring coved cornice over a single paneled door w/scrolled brass keyhole escutcheon, molded base, old dark green paint bordered by red, probably lacks interior drawers, other imperfections, probably Northern Europe, last half 18th c., 8 x 16", 17" h. (ILLUS.) **1,495**

Hanging wall cupboard, country-style, butternut, a rectangular top w/a flat chamfered cornice above a pair of glazed cupboard doors w/recessed panels opening to shelves, on a molded base, refinished, probably New England, 19th c., 11 x 26 3/4", 29" h. **863**

Hutch cupboard, country-style, painted, a flat rectangular top above slightly sloping front framed by molded boards around the two-shelf open upper section above the stepped-out lower section w/a pair of tall flat cupboard doors w/wooden thumb latches, painted red, New England, late 18th - early 19th c., 35" w., 70" h. **2,800**

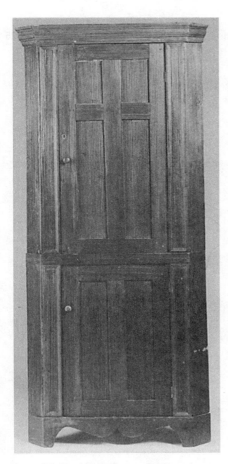

Federal-style Corner Cupboard

Corner cupboard, Federal-Style corner cupboard, poplar, one-piece construction, the flat top w/a deep stepped cornice above a tall cross-framed four-panel door above a lower shorter double-panel door w/overall thin fluting, scappled apron & simple bracket feet, simple turned wood knobs, wear, late 19th c., 22 x 38", 84" h. (ILLUS.).. **1,092**

Hutch cupboard, pine, slant-back style, a flat rectangular overhanging top above a cockbeaded open front w/three shelves above a tall raised panel door w/wrought-iron HL hinges, flat base, old refinish, replaced door, New England, 18th c., 12 3/4 x 29 1/2", 93" h. (ILLUS.)... **1,610**

Hutch cupboard, pine, slant-front style, the flat rectangular top w/a stepped cornice above narrow back-slanting boards framing the open front w/two shelves, the stepped-out lower section w/wide side boards flanking the narrow tall raised panel door w/small wood knob, flat base, old refinish, imperfections, top doors missing, New England, late 18th c., 18 x 37 1/2", 73" h. (ILLUS.)......... **2,300**

Hutch cupboard, poplar, one-piece construction, the wide flat top above wide flat boards framing the open front w/two shelves above the stepped-out lower section w/wide side boards flanking the narrow crude flat cupboard door, one-board sides w/bootjack feet, old dark reddish brown finish, age cracks, top probably cut down, 19th c., 18 x 42", 71 1/2" h. (ILLUS.) **1,430**

Early Pine Hutch Cupboard

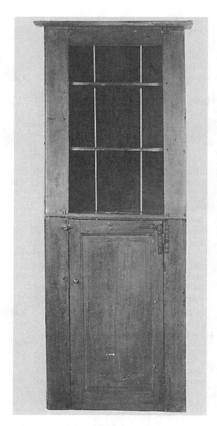

Slant-back Hutch Cupboard

Primitive Hutch Cupboard

Fine Decorated Jelly Cupboard

Jelly cupboard, painted & decorated pine, the rectangular top over a deep coved cornice above a tall narrow paneled & molding-trimmed central door w/original brass thumb latch flanked by tall narrow molding-trimmed side panels, wide double-arched apron, original overall red flame graining, minor damage, 19th c., 16 1/2 x 48 1/4", 63" h. (ILLUS.) **4,620**

Pine Jelly Cupboard

Jelly cupboard, pine, a rectangular top w/beaded edges overhanging a case w/a pair of tall raised &

molding-trimmed double-paneled doors w/wood turn latch & replaced brass thumb latch, slightly scalloped apron & low bracket feet, refinished, strip between doors added, age cracks in top, 19th c., 18 x 43 1/2", 42 1/2" h. (ILLUS.).... **605**

Golden Oak Kitchen Cupboard

Kitchen cupboard, Golden Oak, two-piece construction: the upper section w/a rectangular top w/stepped cornice above a pair of single-pane glazed doors opening to two shelves above a row of drawers w/a long drawer flanked by two small drawers; the lower section w/a cylinder front w/a pull-out work shelf over a tall paneled-front fold-down flour bin beside a square double-paneled door over a drawer, scrolled bracket feet, on casters, ca. 1900, 21 x 37 1/2", 83" h. (ILLUS.) **1,320**

Old Glass-doored Kitchen Cupboard

Fine Cherry Chippendale Linen Press

Kitchen cupboard, oak & pine, two-part construction: the upper section w/a rectangular top over two wide square frosted glass doors w/etched geometric designs opening to a shelf over a row of three small drawers, the center w/a curved-down bottom over incurved sides & a narrow shelf; the lower section w/a wide rectangular top overhanging a case w/a central pull-out work shelf over a large paneled door beside a drawer over a smaller paneled door, flat apron, square stile legs, ca. 1910, 26 x 45", 70" h. (ILLUS.) **345**

Linen press, Chippendale, cherry, two-part construction: the upper section w/a rectangular top w/deep flaring cornice over a pair of tall paneled cupboard doors w/serpentine top molding & opening to three shelves; the lower slightly projecting section includes three long thumb-molded graduated drawers, molded base on scroll-cut bracket feet, old oval brasses, old refinish, repairs, imperfections, probably Pennsylvania, late 18th c., 19 1/2 x 47", 80" h. (ILLUS.) **6,325**

Chippendale Maple Linen Press

Linen press, Chippendale, figured maple, two-part construction: the upper section w/a stepped rectangular top molded above two arched paneled cupboard doors opening to two shelves flanked by fluted stiles; the lower section fitted w/a mid-molding over a pair of drawers over two long drawers, molded base on bracket feet, repairs to feet, right side of cornice repairs, New York or New Jersey, ca. 1780, 23 x 56", 78" h. (ILLUS.) **9,775**

Fine Federal Linen Press

Linen press, Federal, inlaid mahogany, two-part construction: the upper section w/a swan's-neck pediment centering an acorn finial on a conch shell-inlaid support, the field-paneled cupboard doors below each centering a patera inlaid w/a spread-winged eagle clutching a shield beneath two rows of stars; the lower section w/a mid-molding over four long cockbeaded graduated drawers

w/oval brass, scalloped apron & slender tall French feet, front left foot restored, rear foot repaired, finial of later date, repairs at upper hinges, partially illegible inscription on the top of the lower section "My — Salyer (?) 1810, 1810," New York, ca. 1810, 21 x 46 1/4", 93" h. (ILLUS.) **12,650**

Linen press, Victorian, oak, two-part construction: the upper section w/a rectangular top & overhanging cornice above a pair of cupboard doors w/large recessed & gently pointed panels & opening to later shelves, the sides w/knob- and spiral-turned columns; the lower section w/a mid-molding over two pairs of short drawers over a single long drawer at the bottom, molded base on scroll-cut bracket feet, England, mid-19th c., 21 x 53 1/4", 79" h. **4,600**

Scarce Early Pewter Cupboard

Pewter cupboard, Chippendale country-style, pine & poplar, two-part construction: the upper section w/a rectangular top over a deep molded cornice above a pair of 9-pane glazed cupboard doors opening to two shelves over an open pie shelf w/shaped projecting ends; the lower section w/a stepped-out rectangular top over a row of three small drawers w/wooden knobs over a pair of paneled cupboard doors w/wooden turn latches & knobs, molded base on short bracket feet, old refinish, imperfections & repairs, probably Pennsylvania, late 18th c., 21 x 56 3/4", 86" h. (ILLUS.)......... **5,463**

Pie safe, cherry, a rectangular top w/a low three-quarter gallery above a pair of tall three-panel doors each w/a punched-tin panel decorated w/a central diamond framed by four punched circles, one door w/wood knob, a long drawer w/two wood knobs at the base, raised on ring-, rod- and knob-turned tapering legs, three matching tin panels on each end, refinished, 19th c., 18 x 42", overall 60" h. (considerable foot restoration, gallery replaced)........ **1,045**

Pie safe, grain-painted wood, a rectangular flat top slightly overhanging the case w/a single screened door flanked by narrow screened panels, pair of narrow screened panels on each side, raised on tall stile legs, overall grain-painted finish, 19th c., 35" w., 48" h. **850**

Pie safe, painted poplar, the rectangular top above a pair of tall three-panel cupboard doors, a punched tin in each panel in a circle & star design, one door w/simple wooden knob, a single long drawer across the bottom w/two wooden knobs, three panels on each side w/punched-tin panels, tall stile legs, old blue paint over other colors, 19th c., 17 1/2 x 39 3/4", 59" h. (ILLUS.)... **1,540**

Pie safe, painted wood, a flat rectangular top above a pair of tall three-panel doors each w/a punched tin panel in a tulip & vase design, three matching tin panels down each side, raised on short stile legs, painted white, 19th c., 41 1/2" w., 45" h. **850**

Step-back wall cupboard, butternut w/old dark brown finish, two-part construction: the upper section w/a rectangular top w/a deep flaring cornice above a pair of tall double-paneled cupboard doors opening to shelves, the top one w/cut-out for spoons; the stepped-out lower section w/a pair of flush drawers above a pair of paneled cupboard doors, on short double knob-turned feet, found in Cairo, Ohio, mid-19th c., 13 x 49 1/4", 80" h. (most hardware removed) **1,980**

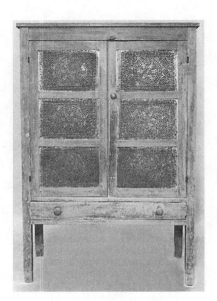

Painted Poplar Pie Safe

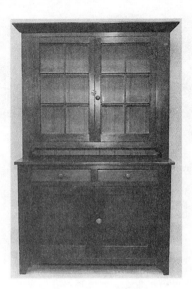

Cherry Step-back Wall Cupboard

Step-back wall cupboard, country-style, cherry, two-part construction: the upper section w/a rectangular top w/a wide flat & flaring cornice over a pair of tall 6-pane glazed cupboard doors opening to two shelves over a low open pie shelf; the stepped-out lower section w/a pair of shallow drawers w/wood knobs over a pair of paneled doors w/a keyhole & wooden knob, flat apron & curved bracket feet, original brass latch in top, replaced wooden pulls, old refinishing, 19th c., 15 1/2 x 54 1/4", 83 3/4" h. (ILLUS.) **3,960**

Painted Pennsylvania Cupboard

Step-back wall cupboard, country-style, painted pine, two-part construction: the upper section w/a rectangular top over a shallow widely flaring stepped cornice over a deep frieze above a pair of 6-pane glazed cupboard doors opening to two shelves over a low pie shelf w/shaped end brackets; the lower stepped-out section w/a row of three drawers w/turned wood knobs over a pair of double-paneled cupboard doors w/wood knobs & a wooden thumb latch, molded apron on heavy ball feet,

yellow paint of later date, chips to cornice, missing right side of mid-molding, Pennsylvania, ca. 1830, 18 x 54", 88" h. (ILLUS.) **7,475**

Early Pine Step-back Wall Cupboard

Step-back wall cupboard, country-style, pine, one-piece construction, the flat rectangular top above a molded edging across the top & down the sides flanking a pair of tall double-paneled doors w/a small square panel over a long rectangular panel over a deep pie shelf, the stepped-out lower section w/further molded edging & a pair of tall paneled doors w/small turned wood knobs, flat base, two shelves in top & three in bottom, old refinish, New England, 1790-1810, 21 x 37 1/2", 86" h. (ILLUS.) **2,990**

Poplar & Curly Maple Wall Cupboard

Nice Walnut Step-back Cupboard

Step-back wall cupboard, country-style, poplar w/some curly maple, two-part construction: the upper section w/a rectangular top over a deep coved cornice above a pair of tall 3-pane glazed cupboard doors opening to two shelves over a low open pie shelf; the lower stepped-out section w/a pair of drawers w/turned wood knobs over a pair of paneled cupboard doors w/a replaced brass thumb latch, tightly scalloped apron on low bracket feet, pieced cornice repair, 19th c., 14 x 45 1/2", 81" h. (ILLUS.).......... **1,595**

Step-back wall cupboard, country-style, walnut, one-piece construction, a rectangular top w/a wide flat & flaring cornice above a pair of 6-pane glazed cupboard doors w/original brass latch opening to two shelves, the stepped-out lower section over a pair of shallow drawers w/small wood knobs over a pair of paneled cupboard doors w/a brass latch, gently scalloped apron on bracket feet w/casters, knobs missing on latches, light blue interior repaint, minor foot damage, old varnish finish, mid-19th c., 16 3/4 x 50 1/2", 81 1/4" h. (ILLUS.) **1,980**

Step-back wall cupboard, Georgian, walnut, two-piece construction: the upper section w/a rectangular top over a narrow flared cornice & a carved dentil band above a pair of 6-pane glazed cupboard doors flanking three central fixed panes all flanked by side rails w/a carved paterae panel above a row of three small raised rectangular panels over an open pie shelf w/scroll-cut brackets; the projecting lower section w/a pair of drawers w/small wood knobs flanked by horizontally incised rectangular panels over a pair of raised panel cupboard doors flanked by long narrow raised panels, molded base on scroll-cut bracket feet, old dark varnish finish, Canada, early 19th c., 12 1/2 x 63", 85 1/4" h. (restoration to top, back replaced by plywood) **4,400**

Step-back wall cupboard,
Neoclassical, inlaid mahogany,
two-part construction: the upper
section w/a pair of flat-topped
rectangular cupboards w/a single-
pane glazed door opening to two
shelves & mounted at the upper
corners w/ormolu bosses flanking
the central set-back rectangular tall
mirror w/a gently arched top &
molded crestrail w/an ormolu shell
& leafy branch mount, the lower
section w/a light rectangular
marble top above a case w/a pair
of banded drawers w/simple pulls
above a pair of banded cupboard
doors w/central oval floral urn
inlays, leafy sprig ormolu mounts
at each upper corner, flat molded
apron on simple baluster-turned
legs, France, early 20th c.,
20 3/4 x 55", 75 1/2" h. **1,265**

Step-back wall cupboard,
Victorian-Style, mahogany,
two-part construction: the upper
section w/a rectangular top above
a deep flaring ogee cornice above
a pair of tall glazed cupboard doors
topped w/a band of applied pierced
scroll carving across the top &
scroll-carved drops at the front
corners; the stepped-out lower
section w/a rectangular top over a
pair of flush ogee-fronted drawers
over a pair of raised panel
cupboard doors w/a band of
applied pierced scroll carving
across the top & flanked by scroll-
carved drops at the sides, molded
flat plinth base, early 20th c.,
12 1/2 x 42 1/2", 86 1/2" h. **935**

Wall cupboard, country-style,
cherry, a flat rectangular top w/no
cornice above a pair of tall paneled
doors w/original brass thumb
latches w/porcelain knobs above a
lower pair of shorter paneled doors
w/matching latches, flat bottom,
refinished, mid-19th c.,
16 1/2 x 461/2", 83 3/4" h.
(porcelain knobs damaged, minor
edge damage) **990**

Wall cupboard, country-style,
painted pine, one-piece
construction, rectangular flat top
over a single wide raised double-
paneled door w/latch & simple

Red-painted Pine Wall Cupboard

wood knob opening to three
painted shelves over a medial rail
& a short two-panel lower door
opening to one shelf, shaped
apron w/short bracket feet, original
red exterior paint, repainted
interior, hardware changes, minor
height & cornice loss, old scraping
to original red, New England, early
19th c., 19 1/4 x 43 1/2", 81" h.
(ILLUS.) **1,093**

Wall cupboard, country-style,
painted pine, one-piece
construction, the rectangular top
w/a molded cornice over a tall
narrow raised panel door opening
to three full shelves & one
contoured shelf over a similar
shorter door opening to a single
shelf, tall wide solid board front
sides, hardware losses & changes,
repainted chrome yellow,
restoration, probably New York
state, early 19th c., 19 x 36", 81" h.
(ILLUS.) **978**

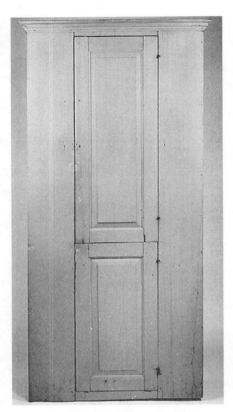

Simple Painted Pine Cupboard

Early Canadian Painted Cupboard

Wall cupboard, country-style, painted pine, rectangular top w/a deep stepped cornice over a pair of wide & tall raised double-paneled doors w/wooden thumb latches at the top, molded base on tall scroll-cut bracket feet, paneled sides, painted blue, restoration, Canada, late 18th c., 21 1/4 x 53 1/2", 71 1/2" h. (ILLUS.) **1,725**

Wall cupboard, country-style, painted pine, the rectangular top w/a deep flaring stepped cornice above a tall narrow case w/two double raised-panel cupboard doors opening to six shelves, molded base on bracket feet, remnants of red paint, New England, late 18th c., 18 1/4 x 38", 79 1/2" h. **4,830**

European Wall Cupboard

Wall cupboard, country-style, painted pine, the rectangular top w/a high arched central section topped by a tall pierced & scrolling crest over flattened side cornices w/turned finials at the front corners, raised panel narrow frieze panels alternating w/rondels over a pair of tall cupboard doors w/single-pane glazed sections w/raised molding borders w/outset corners over matching solid panels in the lower section all opening to wooden shelves, a pair of drawers at the base above a flat apron on heavy ring- and peg-turned legs, old dark painted finish, damage & repairs, Europe, second half 19th c., 16 x 39", 73" h. (ILLUS.)................ **605**

Unusual Early Pine Wall Cupboard

Early Painted Wall Cupboard

Wall cupboard, country-style, painted, rectangular top w/a narrow stepped molding over a wide frieze board w/wooden thumb latch above a pair of tall paneled doors w/a turned wood knob, flat wide apron on slender baluster-turned legs on knob and peg feet, opens to unpainted interior w/two shelves, bluish green worn paint, all original condition & surfaces, Pennsylvania or Ohio, 1835-45, 14 1/8 x 36 1/4", 59 1/4" h. (ILLUS.) **4,600**

Wall cupboard, country-style, pine, one-piece construction, the rectangular top w/stepped-out front corners over a deep conforming flaring cornice above a pair of sliding triple-paneled tall doors enclosing three shelves above a gadrooned molding & a single four-panel hinged door, all flanked by paneled pilasters w/molded capitals & bases, old refinish, remnants of bluish green paint, minor imperfections, southeastern New England, 18th c., 19 1/2 x 37 1/2", 78" h. (ILLUS.)... **9,775**

Wall cupboard, country-style, walnut, one-piece construction, the rectangular top w/a thick slightly overhanging cornice over a single wide double-paneled door w/a brass thumb latch over a medial band & a slightly shorter matching lower door, flat base, old finish, 19th c., 18 x 44", 76 3/4" h. (ILLUS.) **1,375**

Walnut One-piece Wall Cupboard

Wall cupboard, pine, a pair of glazed cupboard doors opening to a single shelf above a pair of recessed-panel doors opening to six shelves, refinished, New England, mid-19th c., 17 3/4 x 39", 81 3/4" h. (some height loss, one pane missing) **1,840**

Wall cupboard, walnut, rectangular top above a pair of short square ornately pierce-carved doors each w/a central floral- or bird-carved cartouche framed by pierced scroll bands above a pair of tall flat cupboard doors w/flat oval two-part central latch, serpentine apron carved w/slender facing dragons, on slender square stile legs, old finish, China, late 19th - early 20th c., 18 x 38", 60 3/4" h. **660**

DESKS

Chippendale slant front desk, curly maple, a narrow rectangular top above a wide hinged slant front opening to an interior fitted w/a row of small drawers above a row

w/two drawers centering a pigeonhole above arcaded & plain pigeonholes, the case w/three long thumb-molded graduated drawers w/butterfly brasses, molded base on scroll-cut bracket feet, old refinish, Massachusetts or New Hampshire, late 18th c., replaced brasses, 17 1/2 x 36", 43 1/2" h. (imperfections) **3,335**

Chippendale slant front 'reverse serpentine' desk, carved mahogany, narrow rectangular top above the wide hinged slant front opening to a stepped interior of small drawers, the central one w/shaping on a case w/four long graduated scratch-beaded conforming drawers above a conforming molded base w/central drop & front ball-and-claw feet & shaped bracket rear feet, old refinish, Massachusetts, 18th c., 22 x 42", 44 1/2" h. (repairs) **5,175**

Chippendale Slant-Front Desk

Chippendale slant-front desk, carved maple & cherry, a narrow rectangular top above a hinged molded slant lid opening to an interior fitted w/a central fan-carved drawer flanked by document drawers & six pigeonholes above four short drawers, the case below w/four long graduated drawers above a central apron pendant, scroll-cut bracket feet, repairs to feet, New England, probably New Hampshire, ca. 1780, 17 1/2 x 35", 41 3/4" h. (ILLUS.) **6,900**

Chippendale-Style Block-Front Desk

Classical Butler's Desk

Chippendale-Style block-front slant-front desk, mahogany, a narrow top above a winged slant lid opening to an interior fitted w/three shell-carved arches above stacks of small drawers separated by arched pigeonholes over small drawers, the case w/four long block-front drawers each w/brass butterfly pulls & keyhole escutcheons, labeled "Museum Reproduction, Authorized by Edison Institute, Dearborn, Mich., Colonial Mfg. Co. Zeeland, Mich.," old finish, early 20th c., minor wear & edge damage, 22 1/4 x 40 1/2", 43 1/4" h. (ILLUS.)........................ **1,375**

Chippendale-Style slant-front desk, mahogany, a narrow rectangular top above a wide hinged slant front opening to a fitted interior above a double-serpentine fronted case w/four long graduated drawers w/butterfly brass & keyhole escutcheons, molded conforming base on short front cabriole legs w/claw-and-ball feet, marked "Maddow Colonial, Jamestown, NY," ca. 1920s, refinished, 16 x 28 1/2", 40" h. **440**

Classical butler's desk, carved mahogany & mahogany veneer, the rectangular top above a drawer opening to a writing surface & a bird's-eye maple interior of eight drawers & six valanced pigeonholes, the case w/three recessed long drawers w/flanking free-standing columns w/acanthus carved Corinthian capitals, on a

stepped plinth base & large ball-turned feet on casters, replaced brasses, old feet, possibly New England, ca. 1825, imperfections, 22 x 45", 48" h. (ILLUS.)................ **920**

Early Cherry Desk on Stand

Country-style desk on stand, cherry, a narrow galleried top shelf above a hinged slanted lift lid w/applied edge molding opening to a compartmented interior set into a base w/a long thumb-molded drawer & flat apron raised on four tall slender square beaded legs joined by box stretchers, original brown paint, central Massachusetts, ca. 1800, 19 x 30 3/4", 47 1/2" h. (ILLUS.)... **3,220**

Country-style fall-front desk,
walnut, a rectangular top above
a large flat hinged fall-front
opening to form a writing surface
w/an interior composed of
pigeonholes & letter slots w/two
small drawers & a secret
compartment, the lower case w/the
long drawers each w/two turned
wood knobs & a keyhole, simple
bracket feet, old finish, 19th c.,
17 x 37", 44 3/4" h. **605**

Federal Lady's "Tambour-front" Desk

Federal Lady's Desk on Turned Legs

Federal lady's desk, carved
mahogany & mahogany veneer,
the rectangular box top opening to
an interior of three drawers & a
writing surface on a base w/a
single long drawer w/two round
brass pulls raised on ring-, knob-
and spiral-turned legs ending in
disk & peg feet on casters, old
finish, probably Massachusetts,
ca. 1825, minor imperfections,
19 1/2 x 29 1/2", 37 3/4" h.
(ILLUS.) **1,093**

**Federal lady's "tambour-front"
desk,** inlaid mahogany, two-part
construction: the upper section w/a
rectangular top above a pair of
tambour sliding doors opening to
four short drawers & two valanced
pigeonholes flanking a central door
opening to two short drawers & a
valanced pigeonhole; the lower

projecting section w/a hinged
writing flap above two long drawers
w/oval brasses & inlaid dies, on
square double-tapering line-,
bellflower-, dot- and lozenge-inlaid
legs ending in crossbanded cuts,
appears to retain original brasses,
Boston, Massachusetts, ca. 1795,
losses to inlay, patches to veneer,
repair to one front leg, 20 x 36 1/2",
43" h. (ILLUS.) **4,312**

Federal slant-front desk, cherry, a
narrow rectangular top above a
wide hinged slant-front
w/breadboard ends opening to a
stepped interior of a central drawer
flanked by eight valanced
compartments above five short
drawers & two shallow drawers,
the case w/four long graduated
drawers above a valanced apron &
slender French feet, New England,
ca. 1800, 15 x 40", 44" h. (replaced
butterfly brasses, refinished,
imperfections) **4,880**

Federal slant-front desk, inlaid
mahogany veneer, a narrow
rectangular top above a hinged
slant front opening to an interior
fitted w/two groups of four small
drawers over arcaded pigeonholes
flanking a center prospect door,
the lower case w/four long drawers
w/banded veneer & stringing inlay,
oval brasses & keyhole
escutcheons, curved apron &
French feet, old surface, original

brasses, New York state, early
19th c., 21 1/2 x 41 1/2", 44" h.
(veneer cracking, loss & patching,
other surface imperfections)......... **2,530**

Federal "tambour" desk, inlaid
mahogany, two-part construction:
the upper section w/a stepped-
back rectangular top above a row
of two long drawers flanking a
short center drawer all above twin
tambour doors flanking a small
plain prospect door all opening to
an arrangement of drawers &
valanced pigeonholes; the lower
section stepped-out w/a fold-down
writing surface over a case of three
long graduated drawers flanked by
banded stiles & raised on ring- and
rod-turned tapering cylindrical legs
w/peg feet, probably Newburyport,
Massachusetts, early 19th c.,
21 1/2 x 40 3/4", 52" h. **4,140**

Federal-Style writing desk, inlaid
mahogany, a rectangular top
above a pair of long drawers
w/inlaid border banding above a
central arched kneehole opening
w/applied fans at corner brackets
flanked by two smaller inlaid
drawers, round brass pulls, worn
blonde finish, 20th c., 30 x 48",
28 3/4" h. **220**

Queen Anne-Style Child's Desk

**Queen Anne-Style child's desk on
frame,** curly maple, two-part
construction: the upper section w/a
narrow rectangular top over a
hinged slant-lid opening to a block-
and fan-carved interior w/three
graduated drawers below; the
lower section w/a mid-molding over
one long drawer above a scroll-cut
apron on cabriole legs ending in
pad feet, butterfly pulls, probably
19th c., 15 x 25 3/4", 38 1/2" h.
(ILLUS.) **6,900**

Queen Anne slant front desk,
maple, a narrow top above a wide
hinged slant front opening to an
interior of valanced compartments
above small drawers, the end
drawers separated by scrolled
dividers, above a case of three
long thumb-molded drawers on a
molded base w/bracket feet &
central drop pendant, old darkened
surface, probably northern Maine,
18th c., 17 1/2 x 35 1/2", 40 1/4" h.
(imperfections)............................. **5,175**

Queen Anne-Style Desk on Stand

Queen Anne-Style desk on stand,
parcel-gilt red-japanned wood, two
part construction: the upper section
w/a narrow rectangular top over a
hinged slant-lid opening to an

interior w/pigeonholes & three small drawers over two long cockbeaded drawers w/teardrop pulls; on a base w/a mid-molding above a narrow apron w/central drop all raised on tall cabriole legs ending in pad feet, decorated overall w/chinoiserie scenes & designs, probably 19th c., chips, 16 1/4 x 21 1/2", 37" h. (ILLUS.)... **2,300**

William & Mary Desk on Frame

Queen Anne-Style Library Desk

Queen Anne-Style library desk, oak, a wide rectangular top w/molded edge above a deep bowed band w/a long conforming drawer w/bail pulls at the front above the kneehole opening, above an incurved band w/a small drawer on each side of the kneehole, raised on heavy cabriole legs ending in paw feet, ca. 1900, 28 x 45", 30" h. (ILLUS.)................ **863**

Victorian plantation desk, walnut & mahogany veneer, two-part construction: the upper section w/a rectangular top w/flaring stepped cornice above a wide veneered frieze band over a full-width two-panel fall-front hinged lid opening to a fitted interior; the lower stepped-out section w/a rectangular top over a single long veneered drawer w/replaced brasses, raised on four ring-, knob-and block-turned legs w/ball feet, mid-19th c., 21 1/2 x 34", 59 1/4" h. (restoration).................. **770**

William & Mary desk on frame, tulipwood & oak, two-part construction: the upper section w/a narrow rectangular top over a hinged raised-panel fall-front opening to an interior of four

compartments, three drawers & a well w/sliding closure above a double arched deep molded front; the lower section w/a mid-molding above a wide molded rectangular top overhanging a deep apron w/a long drawer w/brass teardrop pulls & a diamond-form keyhole escutcheon over the valanced apron, knob- and trumpet-turned legs on shaped flat cross stretchers over turned 'turnip' feet, replaced brasses, old refinish, minor imperfections, probably Connecticut, early 18th c., 15 x 24 3/4", 42 1/2" h.(ILLUS.)   **17,250**

William & Mary-Style writing desk, oak, rectangular top w/molded edges above a case w/a central long drawer w/angular border molding forming a long panel over the kneehole opening flanked by two stacks of three drawers each decorated w/similar molding & panels, each drawer w/a brass teardrop pull, raised on eight baluster-, ring- and block-turned legs joined by low ball-turned stretchers, on ball feet, old finish, early 20th c., 27 3/4 x 59", 31" h. (one piece of drawer molding missing) **495**

DRY SINKS

Painted pine, the rectangular well top w/upright board edging above a case w/a pair of narrow flush-mounted single-board doors, old goldenrod repaint, 19th c., 47 3/4" l., 28 1/2" h. (one bottom board loose, feet gone) **770**

Painted poplar, a high board back w/a narrow top shelf above down-curved sides to the rectangular top well beside a small work shelf at one end over a small drawer, the lower case w/a pair of large paneled cupboard doors w/old cast-iron thumb latches w/brass knobs, old green repaint, 19th c., probably old conversion from cupboard, 18 1/4 x 43 1/2", 52" h. (drawer knob replaced, some edge damage) **770**

LOVE SEATS, SOFAS & SETTEES

Finely Carved Classical Recamier

Recamier, Classical, mahogany, the molded & shaped back rail continuing to a leaf-carved scroll above the scrolled paneled arms w/concentric ringed bosses, above a paneled seat rail & carved paw feet on casters, Boston, old finish, ca. 1825, 65 1/8" l. (ILLUS.) **8,625**

Recamier, Federal, mahogany, a narrow reeded downward curving crestrail above the upholstered back & joining a high & low scrolled end arm w/reeded scrolled framing continuing down to the reeded seat rail, on reeded sabre legs ending in brass paw feet w/casters, probably Boston, early 19th c., 76" l............ **7,475**

Federal-Style Decorated Recamier

Recamiers, Federal-Style, parcel-gilt & ebonized wood, the outscrolled open back rest formed w/turned & paneled slats above a long shaped arm over the narrow rectangular caned seat on slender knob- and ring-turned splayed legs joined by turned stretchers, decorated overall w/Classical designs in gold on black, some wear, ca. 1900, 76" l., pr. (ILLUS. of one)............. **2,875**

Finely Carved Classical Settee

Settee, Chippendale-Style, mahogany, the delicately carved slender triple-arch crestrail above delicate scroll- and swag-carved pierced splats, slender curved open-end arms on incurved arm supports, upholstered spring seat w/a thin serpentine seat rail, slender carved cabriole front legs & square canted rear legs, old finish, early 20th c., 42" l. (one back leg repaired).......................... **770**

Settee, Classical, carved mahogany, the upholstered double-shield-form back centered by a carved spread-winged eagle above a veneer panel, scrolled back stiles above the deep semi-overupholstered seat on a bolection-molded plinth & eagle-carved legs ending in paw feet, formerly fitted w/casters, probably New York City, ca. 1825, 72" l. (ILLUS.)............................... **6,325**

Settee, William & Mary-style, mahogany, triple-back style, the back section w/a high arched & pierced scroll-carved crestrail above a scroll-carved frame enclosing an oval caned panel between free-standing rope-twist stiles w/knob finial, long shaped open-end arms w/scroll-carved hand grips on rope-twist supports above the long upholstered seat on new plywood over the original caning, narrow carved seat rail raised on four rope-twist- and block-turned front legs joined by three wide arched & scroll-carved flat stretchers, long rope-twist H-stretcher joining front & rear legs, early 20th c., old dark finish, 66" l., 50" h. **715**

Settee, William & Mary-Style, oak, the high double-arched upholstered back flanked by shaped upholstered wings above the rolled upholstered arms, long cushion seat above the scalloped upholstered seat rail, raised on onion- and block-turned front legs & square canted rear legs joined by two sets of flattened double-arch stretchers, old worn finish, early 20th c., Europe, 60" l. **935**

Settee, Windsor "arrow-back" style, painted & decorated, the long flat crestrail divided into three sections w/four tapering stiles, seven arrow slats in each section, scrolled end arms above slender turned spindles & canted turned arm supports, long plank seat raised on eight ring-turned tapering legs joined by stretchers w/three central tablets & plain side & back stretchers, the crestrail w/gilt floral sprig decoration & banding on a dark ground, overall dark ground w/gold banding on slats & leaf bands on stretcher tablets, Pennsylvania, 1820-30, 78" l., 36" h. (some old repaint, minor imperfections)............................... **1,093**

Settee, Windsor country-style, bamboo-turned hickory & poplar, a long flat crestrail between turned & flattened stiles w/two other stiles dividing the back into three sections filled w/slender turned tapering spindles, scrolled end arms over turned, canted arm supports & four spindles, long thick plank seat raised on eight canted bamboo-turned legs joined by flattened front stretchers & turned rear stretchers, refinished, first half 19th c., 84" l. (age cracks in seat)... **935**

Settee, Windsor country-style, painted & decorated, the shaped triple-back crestrail raised on three stiles over a pair of long lower rails over numerous knob-turned short spindles, scrolled arms on two spindles & a canted turned arm support over the wide plank seat, raised on eight ring-turned tapering legs joined by turned box stretchers, worn original brown paint w/light green & cream-colored striping & h.p. rose decoration on the crest sections, stenciled label "E.D. Jeffries... Philadelphia, PA," plank seat worn, repaired break in one arm at post, first half 19th c., 73 1/2" l. (ILLUS.) **1,430**

Sofa, Classical, carved mahogany, the long narrow rolled single paneled crestrail above out-scrolled arms w/reeded arm supports punctuated w/carved rosettes, upholstered back, arms & cushion seat, reeded seat rail w/flanking panels of foliate & leaf carving above reeded sabre legs

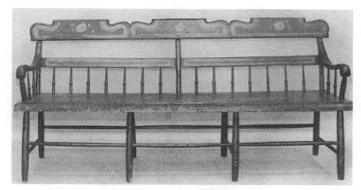

Windsor Country-style Settee

on brass paw feet on casters, old surface, minor imperfections, attributed to the workship of Duncan Phyfe, New York City, 1815-25, 85" l. (ILLUS.)............... **4,600**

Sofa, Classical, carved & veneered mahogany, a gently arched reeded crestrail w/scroll-carved terminals over the upholstered back & flanked by rolled arms w/applied carved frontal shells over the cushion seat & seat rail w/gadrooning on front egg-and-dart-carved feet on casters w/ring-turned rear feet, Baltimore or Philadelphia, ca. 1825-35, imperfections, 84" l. (ILLUS.)......... **690**

Sofa, Classical, mahogany & mahogany veneer, the raised crestrail w/rope-carved top & incurved ends above the upholstered back flanked by out-scrolling arms w/floral & cornucopia-carved arm supports continuing to carved panels & a flat molded seat rail raised on figural dolphin-carved front legs & turned back legs, refinished, reupholstered, first quarter 19th c., 107" l. (ILLUS.)............................ **3,850**

Sofa, Classical-Victorian transitional style, carved mahogany & mahogany veneer, the triple-arch crestrail w/high arched end sections centered by a shell & leafy scroll crest w/each end topped by a pierce-carved scroll crest, crestrail curved down around the upholstered back & arms & terminates in heavy scroll-carved

arms on heavy scrolled front legs, molded serpentine seat rail, reupholstered, some frame damage, ca. 1840, 92" l. (ILLUS.) **743**

Sofa, Federal-Style, mahogany, long narrow crestrail carved w/three drapery- and floral-carved panels over the upholstered back flanked by scrolled closed arms on reeded turned & tapering arm supports & paneled corner blocks, flat seat rail on four reeded, turned & tapering legs w/peg feet, labeled "Hickory, N.C.," 20th c., 80" l. (ILLUS.)......... **468**

Sofa, Queen Anne-Style, walnut, rectangular-framed upholstered back over outscrolled arms, three loose cushions in seat, raised on cabriole front legs ending in pad feet, floral upholstery, England, early-20th c., 76 1/2" l., 39" h. **1,840**

Wagon seat, painted & turned wood, two pairs of arched slats joining three simple turned back stiles, double woven rush seat flanked by turned arms & turned handholds atop the turned, tapering front end legs, shorter center legs all joined by simple turned rungs, old brown paint over earlier grey, New England, late 18th c., 30" l., 15" h. **1,093**

SHELVES

Floor shelves, country-style, painted pine, a rectangular board top above board sides on arched cut-out feet, a board back enclosing

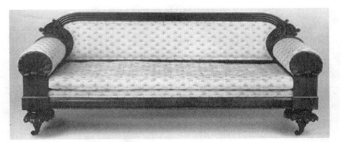

Attractive Classical Sofa

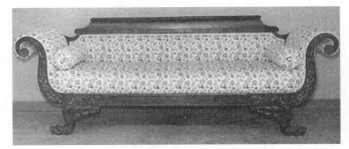

Dolphin-footed Classical Sofa

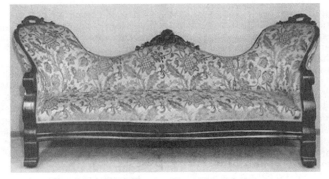

Classical-Victorian Transitional Sofa

Federal-Style Mahogany Sofa

two shelves, old grey paint, square
nail construction, 19th c., 35" w.,
35 1/2" h. **523**

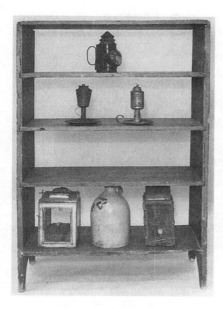

Painted Pine Floor Shelves

Floor shelves, country-style, painted
pine, a rectangular top above
single-board sides w/arched cut-
out feet framing four open mortised
shelves, wooden peg construction,
old green paint, some old renailing,
a bit shaky, open knot holes in one
end, 14 3/4 x 33 1/2", 49 1/4" h.
(ILLUS.) **550**

Floor shelves, painted pine, tall one-
board ends tapering sharply
toward the top & w/arched base
cut-outs, three staggered open
shelves, old red finish, 19th c.,
12 1/2 x 43", 46" h. **935**

Floor shelves, painted poplar, tall
one-board ends w/rounded cut-out
feet & curved top front corners,
four open shelves, brass braces
added to the back, old worn red,
9 1/2 x 26", 50" h. **880**

Hanging shelves, Federal country-
style, mahogany, whale-side
shaped sides supporting four open
shelves, the lower shelf above a
pair of short drawers, New

England, early 19th c., 24" w.,
34" h. **1,000**

Painted Pine Hanging Shelves

Hanging shelves, painted pine, four
open graduated shelves between
deeply scalloped side boards,
square nail construction, old black
paint, mid 19th c., some edge
damage on back, 8 x 29",
34 1/2" h. (ILLUS.) **1,100**

Hanging shelves, walnut, four
graduated rectangular boards
w/rounded front corners joined to
each other w/two simple turned
corner posts & a flat stick at the
back projecting at the top w/a
hanging hole, old worn dark patina,
possibly Shaker, 7 x 24", 19 1/2" h.
(repairs, back post replaced) **495**

Wall shelf, walnut, a narrow
rectangular shelf above a pair of
shallow nailed drawers w/tiny pulls
above a lower backboard all joined
by scalloped tapering bracket
ends, old worn reddish finish,
19th c., 32" l. **550**

SIDEBOARDS

Classical country-style sideboard,
cherry, rectangular top above a
projecting row of drawers w/a long
drawer flanked by shorter drawers
over tall end doors flanking a pair
of central doors each w/double

Virginia Classical Sideboard

punched-tin panels decorated w/pinwheels in ovals within a looped border, the doors separated by four baluster-, rod- and ring-turned columns on a conforming plinth base raised on ring-turned tapering short legs w/knob & peg feet, further tin panels at the ends, Virginia, ca. 1840 (ILLUS.) **6,250**

Classical server, carved mahogany & cherry veneer, rectangular top w/molded edges over a long veneered drawer w/turned wood knobs over a beaded band & a pair of beaded panel recessed tall cupboard doors opening to a shelf, all flanked by veneered squared ogee pilasters on block feet, old refinish, hardware changes, missing top splashboard, minor surface imperfections, Mid-Atlantic

States, 1840-45, 18 3/4 x 40", 40 1/8" h. (ILLUS.) **2,530**

Classical Mahogany Server

Classical sideboard, carved mahogany, the pedimented splashboard w/three urn- and pineapple-carved finials over the rectangular top w/a molded edge over a long drawer flanked by short drawers all projecting over a series of four paneled cupboard doors separated by four free-standing columns resting on blocks above heavy paw feet, round brass drawer pulls, Duncan Phyfe or a contemporary, New York City, ca. 1830, 26 x 79", 58" h. (ILLUS.) **6,038**

Fine New York Classical Sideboard

Federal country-style huntboard, walnut, rectangular top above a deep apron w/a pair of deep beaded-edge dovetailed drawers flanking a narrow matching center drawer, turned wood knobs, on knob-, ring- and rod-turned legs w/ball-and-peg feet, refinished, Southern, first half 19th c., 22 1/4 x 49", 43 3/4" h. (repairs, top replaced) **2,475**

Delicate Federal Server

Federal server, brass-mounted figured mahogany, the rectangular top above two short drawers w/lion head & ring pulls on turned swelled supports joined by a platform stretcher over tapering ring-turned legs ending in brass ball feet, pulls appear original, New York City,

ca. 1800, 18 x 32", 35" h. (ILLUS.) **4,600**

Mahogany Inlaid Federal Server

Federal server, inlaid mahogany, the rectangular top w/a border of lunette inlay above a single long line-inlaid drawer above a pair of central cupboard doors flanked by tall narrow bottle drawers all flanked by reeded stiles & above another border of lunette inlay, a scalloped apron above the square tapering legs, New England, early 19th c., 22 x 38", 41" h. (ILLUS.).. **4,025**

Federal sideboard, inlaid mahogany, the rectangular top w/square corners & banded center above a conforming case w/an inlaid long central drawer flanked by a shorter drawer at each end above single end cupboard doors

Federal Virginia Walnut Sideboard

flanking a pair of central cupboard doors, raised on short inlaid square double tapering legs, replaced butterfly brasses, old finish, Massachusetts, ca. 1790-1800, 27 1/2 x 64", 41" h. (imperfections) **2,990**

Federal sideboard, walnut & yellow pine, rectangular top w/molded edges above cockbeaded case w/end drawers, the right drawer visually divided into two drawers & the left w/two working drawers, flanking a central cupboard door w/cockbeading, raised on four tall slender square tapering legs, old oval brass pulls, old refinish, repairs, Virginia, 1790-1810, 22 x 56", 39" h. (ILLUS.)............... **5,520**

Federal-Style "serpentine-front" sideboard, mahogany veneer, the rectangular top w/a serpentine front above a conforming case w/two long bowed central drawers above an arched opening w/fan-applied corner brackets all flanked by two ranks of three short concaved drawers, oval brasses, pairs of incised bands down stiles, square tapering legs w/pairs of incised grooves & ending in spade feet, first half 20th c., 23 1/2 x 68", 38 1/2" h. **825**

STANDS

Fine Chippendale Candlestand

Candlestand, Chippendale, carved & figured mahogany & walnut, the round top tilting above a slender flaring standard & urn-form support on a tripod base w/cabriole legs ending in claw-and-ball feet, chips to feet, New York City, ca. 1770, 20 1/2" d., 27 1/2" h. (ILLUS.)....... **5,175**

Candlestand, country-style, cherry & maple, a rounded top on a ringed columnar-turned pedestal on a tripod base w/three tapering flat canted legs ending in button feet, remnants of old dark green paint, southeastern New England, late 18th c., 12" d., 25" h. (imperfections).............................. **1,035**

Federal Country-style Candlestand

Candlestand, Federal country-style, birch, the square top above a slender slightly flaring standard on an urn-form support on a tripod base w/spider legs, top stained, slightly warped, northern New England, ca. 1800, 14 1/2 x 15 1/4", 28 1/4" h. (ILLUS.) **1,150**

Candlestand, Federal country-style, mahogany & curly maple, the oblong top w/notched corners in mahogany & tilting above a ring-and baluster-turned curly maple column raised on a tripod base w/three outswept mahogany legs on small ball feet, refinished, attributed to New York, early 19th c., 17 x 23", 26" h. **715**

Fine Federal Candlestand

Queen Anne Candlestand

Candlestand, Federal, inlaid cherry, the long octagonal cockbeaded top w/a central oval inlaid in mahogany veneer panel framed by stringing & set in bird's-eye maple w/crossbanded mahogany border, on a slender vase- and ring-turned post on a tripod base w/widely canted simple cabriole legs w/pad feet, refinished, minor imperfections, possibly New Hampshire, ca. 1810-20, 13 x 18 1/8", 28" h. (ILLUS.)......... **1,955**

Candlestand, Federal, mahogany, the oval top tilting above a vase- and ring-turned pedestal on a tripod base w/cabriole legs ending in arris pad feet on platforms, old refinish, Massachusetts, ca. 1790, 17 x 17", 28 1/2" h. **2,415**

Candlestand, Federal, maple, a rectangular top w/rounded corners on a vase- and ring-turned pedestal on a tripod base w/spider legs, old red finish, New England, ca. 1825, 16 1/2 x 19 3/4", 28 3/4" h. **431**

Candlestand, Queen Anne, cherry, the round top on a baluster- and ring-turned standard on a tripod base w/flattened cabriole legs ending in arris pad feet on

platforms, old refinish, possibly Vermont, 18th c., 15 1/4" d., 25 3/4" h. (ILLUS.)........................ **1,035**

Candlestand, Queen Anne country-style, painted, the small square top on a vase- and ring-turned pedestal on a tripod base w/cabriole legs ending in pad feet, old dark brown paint, New England, second half 18th c., 11 3/4 x 11 7/8", 27 1/4" h. (imperfections).............................. **748**

Candlestand, Windsor, a central candlearm w/a socket at each end adjusting on a screw-turned central post above a round dished platform on a simple turned post on a small thick disk on three tall canted turned legs, old dark finish, candle cups later, New Hampshire, late 18th c., 13" d., 36" h. (ILLUS.).................. **1,840**

Crock stand, painted pine, four rectangular tiers, the three upper tiers w/open fronts & backed by an angled frame board, the bottom tier w/a deep apron & raised on heavy square chamfered legs on porcelain casters, old worn green paint, 24 x 48", 35 1/4" h. **578**

Early Windsor Candlestand

Federal Reading Stand & Canterbury

Reading stand w/canterbury, Federal, mahogany, the rectangular lattice stand above a baluster- and ring-turnd post on a rectangular canterbury base w/pairs of slender turned spindles forming six slots, on casters, labeled "Blanchard and Parson No. 294 North Market Street, Albany," Albany, New York, early 19th c., 14 x 22 1/4", 47 1/2" h. (ILLUS.)... **3,105**

Painted Country Plant Stand

Plant stand, country-style, painted wood, three graduated demi-lune shelves on baluster- and ring-turned supports joined by square rail, old green paint, on casters, probably New England, 19th c., 20 x 40", 39" h. (ILLUS.).............. **1,610**

Washstand, Classical country-style, painted & decorated, the high arched splashback w/lower scroll-cut sides over a rectangular top over an apron w/two drawers w/simple turned wood knobs, on ring-, knob- & rod-turned tapering legs w/peg feet, grain-painted to simulate mahogany except the top which simulates grey marble, minor imperfections, England, ca. 1830, 19 x 36", 40" h. (ILLUS.) **863**

English Classical Washstand

Tiger Stripe & Bird's-eye Maple Stand

Washstand, Classical country-style, tiger stripe & bird's-eye maple, the high scrolled backsplash & scrolled lower sides on the rectangular top over a single long drawer w/a simple turned wood knob raised on rod- and ring-turned supports to the rectangular medial shelf w/block corners on ring-turned short legs w/knob feet, refinished, imperfections, probably Pennsylvania, ca. 1825, 17 x 21 3/4", 29" h. (ILLUS.).......... **1,150**

Washstand, Federal, carved mahogany veneer, a three-quarter shaped low splashboard on the rectangular top above a veneered cabinet door flanked by ovolo top corners & carved columns of leaves & grapes on a punchwork ground continuing to slender ring-turned tapering legs ending in brass casters, paneled sides, narrow cockbeaded drawer below the door w/round pulls, North Shore Massachusetts, ca. 1815-25, 16 x 21 1/2", 35 5/8" h. (old replaced brasses, old refinish, minor imperfections)..................... **2,300**

Fine Portsmouth Area Washstand

Washstand, Federal, inlaid mahogany, corner-style, the pointed arch & shaped splashboard centered by a quarter-round shelf above a round-fronted top w/a pierced basin hole, the edge w/square string inlay, raised on three square supports continuing to an open shelf over a satinwood veneered apron centered by a small drawer, string inlay on the supports & the three outswept lower legs joined by three slender tapering stretchers centered by an inlaid patera, patterned inlay trim, old finish, minor imperfections, Portsmouth, New Hampshire area, ca. 1800, 16 1/2 x 23", 41" h. (ILLUS.)......... **5,750**

Washstand, Federal, mahogany, a tall shaped splashboard w/a narrow shelf above the rectangular top w/a round cut-out basin hole raised on ring-turned & reeded supports to a medial shelf over a shallow drawer w/wooden pulls raised on ring-turned & reeded tapering legs ending in knob feet, school of John & Thomas Seymour, Boston, early 19th c., 22" w., 41" h. **2,070**

Early Federal Corner Washstand

Washstand, Federal, mahogany & mahogany veneer, corner-style, the high arched & shaped splashboard centered by a small quarter-round shelf over the conforming top w/a cut-out round basin hole over the conforming case w/a pair of cockbeaded cupboard doors over a narrow central drawer w/oval brass flanked by two small cockbeaded panels, on square outward flaring legs joined by the loop-pierced stretchers centered by a molded round medallion, replaced brass, old finish, minor imperfections, probably Massachusetts, ca. 1810, 15 3/4 x 22 3/4", 40 3/4" h. (ILLUS.) **690**

Federal Rectangular Washstand

Washstand, Federal, mahogany, a tall three-quarters gallery w/sloping sides & a small quarter-round shelf in each corner above the rectangular top w/a central large pierced basin hole flanked by two small cup holes over a scalloped front apron, raised on four ring-turned posts on a medial shelf over a single long cockbeaded drawer w/a round brass knob all raised on slender ring-, knob- & baluster-turned tapering legs w/peg feet, old finish, replaced brass, minor imperfections, probably Massachusetts, ca. 1815, 14 1/2 x 20", 41 1/2" h. (ILLUS.).... **690**

Washstand, Federal, mahogany & tiger stripe maple, corner-style, the high pointed arch & serpentine-sided splashboard above a quarter-round top w/a round basin cut-out & scalloped shallow apron raised on three square supports to the medial shelf above a row of three small tiger stripe maple-veneered drawers over the three square tapering legs & a central turned & reeded front leg, Massachusetts, early 19th c., 23" w., 39" h. (ILLUS.) **1,840**

Federal Mahogany & Tiger Stripe Stand

Federal "Tambour-front" Washstand

Washstand, Federal "tambour-front" style, mahogany, the top arched & reeded sides centering a retracting tambour top on paneled dies centering a drawer over a cupboard door on turned & reeded legs w/baluster-turned legs on casters, appears to retain original cast-brass hardware, losses to veneer, missing fitted interior, New York City, ca. 1810, 20" sq., 36 1/2" h. (ILLUS.) **1,495**

Painted Victorian Cottage Washstand

Washstand, Victorian cottage-style, painted & decorated pine, the tall splashback w/beveled corners fitted w/two small shelves w/brackets above the rectangular top over a case w/a long drawer w/two narrow oblong brass pulls over a pair of cupboard doors on a molded base, original decoration w/painted decoration of outlined panels & stylized florals w/brown & grey flowers, black striping, etc., wear, some edge damage, ca. 1880, 14 3/4 x 29 1/4", 35 1/2" h. (ILLUS.) **248**

Classical two-drawer stand, curly maple, a rectangular two-board drop above a deep apron w/two round-fronted drawers each w/two small turned wood knobs, raised on heavy rope-twist-turned legs w/ring-turned top & bottom segments & baluster-turned feet, refinished, ca. 1840, 18 1/4 x 23", 28 1/2" h. (top replaced) **825**

Federal country-style one-drawer stand, cherry, a rectangular one-board top over an apron w/a single drawer w/turned wood knob, raised on slender ring- and rod-turned tapering legs ending in baluster- and knob-turned feet, first half 19th c., 20 1/2 x 22 1/2", 30" h. (top reattached & w/plugged holes) **523**

Federal country-style two-drawer stand, cherry & bird's-eye maple, the rectangular top above a deep case w/two graduated drawers w/bird's-eye maple fronts, on spiraled leaf-carved round legs on baluster-form feet on casters, clear lacy glass pulls on one drawer, pressed ribbed knobs on others, refinished, first half 19th c., 17 5/8 x 22", 28" h. **1,100**

Federal country-style two-drawer stand, walnut, a rectangular top flanked by two wide hinged drop leaves over the deep case w/two drawers w/Rockingham-glazed pottery knobs, raised on simple sausage-turned legs, old soft finish, mid 19th c., 18 x 24" plus 11 3/4" w. leaves, 28 3/4" h. **330**

Federal one-drawer stand, country-style, painted & decorated pine, the nearly square top w/shaped corners overhanging an apron w/a single drawer w/a small turned knob, raised on tall square tapering legs, grain-painted in old burnt sienna & ochre, heavy graining wear to top, replaced pull, New England, early 19th c., 18 x 18 1/2", 27" h. (ILLUS.) **1,725**

Federal one-drawer stand, country-style, pine & butternut, rectangular two-board pine top above an apron w/a single drawer, on turned & tapering legs w/bulbous ankles & tall peg feet, imperfections, early 19th c., 19 x 20 1/2", 30" h. (ILLUS.) **805**

Federal one-drawer stand, inlaid cherry, the nearly square top w/line inlay including a center diamond enclosing a pinwheel design & edge banding overhanging the apron w/a single line-inlaid drawer w/round brass pulls, line-inlaid apron & slender tall tapering square legs, crack repair under top, appears to retain original drawer pull, Connecticut, ca. 1800, 19 3/4 x 20 1/4", 28" h. (ILLUS.)... **2,300**

Federal one-drawer stand, mahogany, diminutive size w/an oval top above a small drawer w/turned pull, raised on slender square tapering legs, New England, early 19th c., 13 1/4 x 19 1/2", 27" h. **4,250**

Federal two-drawer stand, country-style, tiger stripe maple & mahogany veneer, rectangular top flanked by two wide drop leaves w/rounded corners over a deep apron w/two mahogany-veneered drawers w/simple turned wood knobs, raised on ring- and baluster-turned tapering legs w/knob feet, imperfections, New England, ca. 1825, 17 x 20", 28 1/2" h. (ILLUS.) **2,990**

Federal two-drawer stand, painted birch & bird's-eye maple, the rectangular top overhanging a deep apron w/two cockbeaded graduated drawers w/bird's-eye maple fronts, the borders stained to imitate inlay, on slender square tapering legs, simple bail pulls & oval keyhole escutcheon appear to be original, New England, ca. 1810, 13 1/2 x 17 1/8", 28 3/4" h. (minor imperfections) ... **2,990**

STOOLS

Classical footstool, mahogany veneer, the high square rounded floral needlepoint top above a deep serpentine apron w/a scalloped & scroll-bordered apron on round bracket feet on casters, ca. 1840, 18 1/2" sq., 16" h. (some edge damage) **220**

Classical footstools, painted & decorated, pillar & scroll style w/pierced seat rails, grain-painted in raw & burnt umber, possibly New York or Pennsylvania, ca. 1830-40, 15 1/2" l., 6" h., pr. (imperfections).............................. **230**

Classical piano stool, mahogany & mahogany veneer, the circular overupholstered top on a conforming veneered base

Federal Grain-Painted Stand

Pine & Butternut Country Stand

Federal Inlaid-Cherry Stand

Federal Country Two-Drawer Stand

bordered in brass beading on a baluster-turned shaft & three scrolled brass-inlaid legs, resting on brass ball feet, possibly Boston, ca. 1825, 11 1/2" d., 20 1/2" h. (imperfections).............................. **633**

Federal footstools, mahogany, the upholstered rectangular seat on horizontally reeded rails joining swelled ring-turned legs on ball feet, old finish, possibly New York City, ca. 1815-25, 9 x 13", 8 1/2" h., pr. (minor imperfections).................... **920**

Gout stool, Victorian, mahogany, a rectangular upholstered top, adjustable ratchet base, on turned feet, England, mid-19th c., 12 x 19" **173**

Jacobean-Style stool, oak, a rectangular expanding top & cubbyhole above a deep canted apron w/panels carved w/double S-scrolls, one side forming a hinged door, on short baluster-, ring- and block-turned legs joined by box stretchers, metal label for Kittinger, 20th c., 14 1/2 x 22 1/2", 20" h. **110**

Windsor Painted Footstool

Windsor footstool, painted pine, the oval top w/incised edge raised on widely splayed bamboo-turned legs joined by turned box stretchers, painted white w/red trim, early-19th c., 9 1/2 x 15", 10 1/4" h. (ILLUS.)........................ **287**

TABLES

Chippendale card table, carved mahogany, the rectangular hinged top w/rounded corners above a deep apron w/a pair of cockbeaded drawers w/butterfly brasses, cabriole legs w/leaf-carved knees & ending in claw-and-ball feet, New York or Philadelphia, 18th c., 36" l. **3,500**

Fine Chippendale Pembroke Table

Chippendale Pembroke table, figured mahogany, the rectangular top w/rounded ends flanked by serpentine-edged drop leaves, a cockbeaded apron drawer at one end w/simple bail pull, on square tapering stop-fluted legs ending in spade feet, appears to retain original brass, minor patches to veneer, sunbleached, Mid-Atlantic States, ca. 1780, closed 20 1/2 x 32", 27 1/2" h. (ILLUS.)... **8,050**

Chippendale Pembroke table, mahogany, a rectangular top flanked by two rectangular drop leaves above an apron w/one end drawer w/replaced brass, raised on four square tapering legs w/inside chamfer joined by a cross-stretcher, old finish, late 18th to early 19th c., 20 x 33" w/9 1/2" leaves, 29" h. (repair to stretcher) **1,540**

Chippendale tea table, carved & figured mahogany, round dished top tilting on a birdcage mechanism above a ring-, rod- and ball-turned pedestal on a tripod base w/cabriole legs ending in claw-and-ball feet, Philadelphia, ca. 1770, 33" d., 28 1/2" h. **14,950**

Chippendale tea table, figured mahogany, a round top tilting above a birdcage support & ring- and baluster-turned pedestal on a tripod base w/three cabriole legs ending in claw-and-ball feet, New York City, ca. 1780, 31 1/2" d., 27 1/2" h. (feet worn & chewed) ... **3,450**

Chippendale-Style tea table, mahogany, the scalloped round top w/carved fans & rings for plates, raised on a turned columnar support above a spiral-twist knob over the tripod base w/cabriole legs leaf-carved at the knees & ending in elongated claw-and-ball feet, old finish, England, late 19th c., 31 1/2" d., 28 1/2" h. **1,045**

Chippendale-Style tea table, mahogany, wide round top tilting on a birdcage mechanism above a ring- and knob-turned column w/gadrooned & reeded sections above the squatty tripod base w/cabriole legs ending in snake feet, refinished, 20th c., 35 " d., 27 3/4" h. (two-board top & birdcage old replacements, top wobbles) **275**

Classical Mahogany Breakfast Table

Classical breakfast table, carved & inlaid mahogany, the rectangular top w/brass inlay in outline &
. stamped brass on the edges of the flanking, shaped drop leaves above one working & one faux end apron drawer, drop pendants at the corners, raised on four ring-turned columns on a rectangular curve-edged platform raised on outswept leaf-carved legs ending in paw feet on casters, replaced pulls, old

refinish, repairs, losses, New York City, ca. 1820-30, 24 x 39", 28" h. (ILLUS.) **2,415**

Classical card table, carved mahogany & mahogany veneer, the fold-over rectangular top w/rounded front corners above a paneled veneered apron flanked by scrolled end panels, raised on a square molded tapering pedestal resting on a quadripartite platform on four scroll- and acanthus-carved feet, attributed to Isaac Vose & Son, Boston, ca. 1825, 18 x 36 1/2", 30" h. (refinished) **3,105**

Classical Mahogany Card Table

Classical card table, carved mahogany, the rectangular hinged top w/rounded corners above a conforming apron w/horizontally reeded corners above a leaf-turned & leaf-carved & reeded pedestal on outswept beaded legs ending in brass paw feet on casters, old refinish, imperfections, New England, 1825, 17 3/4 x 36", 29 5/8" h. (ILLUS.) **805**

Grain-painted Classical Game Table

Classical card table, grain-painted, rectangular hinged top w/rounded corners opening above a simple ogee apron raised on a heavy slightly tapering square pedestal on a cross-form platform base above flattened ball feet, original red & gold graining simulates mahogany, imperfections, Maine, 1830s, 18 x 36", 28 3/4" h. (ILLUS.) **1,093**

Classical Center Table on Ball Feet

Classical center table, carved mahogany veneer, the round top w/rounded edge on a conforming veneered apron w/banded lower edge, raised on a heavy ring- and knob-turned & acanthus-carved pedestal on a tripartite platform on incised ball feet, imperfections, possibly Boston, ca. 1840, 40 1/2" d., 30 3/4" h. (ILLUS.) **1,955**

Mid-Atlantic Classical Center Table

Classical center table, carved & veneered mahogany, round top w/a flat veneered edge over a cockbeaded veneered apron raised on a heavy ring- and knob-

turned pedestal set on a concave-shaped platform on acanthus- and scroll-carved paw feet, w/an additional leaf, refinished, minor imperfections, Mid-Atlantic States, ca. 1825, closed 44" d., 28 3/4" h. (ILLUS.) **1,035**

Classical Center Table on Casters

Classical center table, carved & veneered mahogany, the round top w/rounded edge above a conforming apron w/applied panels & cast-brass beaded edge, raised on a ring-turned & acanthus leaf-carved post on four outswept scrolled & acanthus-carved legs ending in cast-brass cap caster feet, refinished, minor imperfections, probably Massachusetts, ca. 1825, 36" d., 27 1/2" h. (ILLUS.) **8,050**

Fine Classical Center Table

Classical center table, parcel-gilt & carved mahogany, the round white marble top on a conforming apron w/brass & mother-of-pearl-inlaid edge raised on three white marble columns w/gilt carved scroll capitals on gilt carved winged paw feet joined by a tripartite platform w/central rondel, New York City, ca. 1830, 39" d., 31 1/2" h. (ILLUS.) **8,338**

Classical Country Dressing Table

Rare Small Classical Center Table

Classical center table, part-ebonized mahogany, figured round top above a conforming apron fitted w/a drawer, the turned flaring heavy pedestal on a tripartite platform on leaf-carved scrolling feet on casters, patches & veneer losses, Boston, Massachusetts, possibly by Vose or one of its comtemporaries, ca. 1825, rare small size, 24" d., 26 1/4" h. (ILLUS.) **3,737**

Classical country-style dressing table, painted & decorated, the scroll-cut crestboard behind a small rectangular drawer on the rectangular top overhanging an apron w/a single long drawer, raised on slender ring- and rod-turned tapering legs w/peg feet, original red & brown graining simulating rosewood w/yellow foliate designs on the leg corner blocks & overall yellow-painted bordering to simulate inlay, Maine, early 19th c., 17 3/4 x 34", 34 1/2" h. (ILLUS.) **1,150**

Classical Country Work Table

Classical country-style work table, tiger stripe maple, a nearly square top flanked by hinged drop leaves w/rounded corners above a case w/two round-fronted drawers w/pairs of turned wood knobs, raised on a heavy square tapering pedestal on a stepped square base on four belted bun feet on thick short pegs, old finish, minor imperfections, New England, ca. 1820-30, 16 1/2 x 17", 30 1/2" h. (ILLUS.) **1,495**

Classical dining table, carved & veneered mahogany, extension-type, round top w/molded edge over a smooth apron w/thin gadrooned base band raised on a clustered column-form split pedestal ending in four downswept foliate-carved legs ending in paw feet on casters, together w/seven leaves, New York City, ca. 1840, closed 48" d., 29 1/2" h. (ILLUS.) .. **7,475**

Fine Classical Dining Table

Classical library table, mahogany, the wide rectangular top flanked by two hinged drop leaves w/notched & rounded corners above an apron w/a single long drawer w/round brass pulls & turned corner drops, raised on a short bulbous pedestal over four outswept leaf-carved legs ending in brass eagle caps on casters, appears to retain original hardware, New York City, ca. 1830, 39 x 52", 28 1/4" h. **2,875**

Classical Marble-topped Pier Table

Classical pier table, mahogany & mahogany veneer, a rectangular white marble top w/molded edges above the ogee molded apron on two heavy S-scroll supports & a shaped concave platform w/scrolled front feet & turned rear feet, a recessed molded base panel flanked by tapering pilasters, old refinish, imperfections, probably Boston, ca. 1825, 19 1/4 x 40 1/4", 37" h. (ILLUS.)... **2,070**

Classical side table, decorated pine & poplar, a rectangular top w/cut

corners decorated w/a grey marbleized decoration w/brown glazing over the grey base color, molded apron, square molded & tapering pedestal centered on a square platform base w/slightly scalloped apron, mid 19th c., 19 1/4 x 25 3/4", 28 1/4" h. (wear, top braced but loose).................... **495**

Classical Lyre-based Work Table

Classical work table, carved & veneered mahogany, the rectangular top flanked by wide drop leaves w/rounded corners over an apron w/two round-fronted veneered drawers w/early pressed-glass pulls raised on a leaf- and floral-carved lyre-form pedestal on a square platform w/beveled top edge all raised on S-scroll carved feet on casters, probably Massachusetts, ca. 1825, 18 x 19", 28 1/2" h. (ILLUS.)......... **1,610**

Classical-Style games table, mahogany, the demi-lune top w/hinged leaf & beaded edge above a conforming apron w/three blocks above the three front legs w/a ring- and compressed knob-turned section above a reeded tapering section ending in a brass claw w/glass ball foot, fourth matching swing-out support leg, old finish, early 20th c., closed 18 1/4 x 36", 29 1/4" h. **633**

Federal card table, inlaid mahogany, rectangular fold-over top w/ovolo corners & inlaid edges above a conformingly shaped apron centering an inlaid shaped contrasting panel, bordered by stringing w/geometric banding on the lower edge joining four square double tapering legs, the dies inlaid w/panels & stringing continuing to banded cuffs, old finish, probably Massachusetts, ca. 1790, 17 x 35 3/4", 30 3/4" h. (minor imperfections).................... **5,175**

Federal card table, mahogany & flame birch veneer inlay, the rectangular serpentine-edged hinged top w/banded inlay edges & ovolo corners above a conforming top & apron centered by an inlaid birch veneer oval reserve in a rectangular panel, raised on ring-turned & reeded tapering legs w/knobbed ankles & peg feet, imperfections, North Shore, Massachusetts, early 19th c., 17 1/2 x 34 3/4", 29 3/8" h. (ILLUS.) **4,600**

Federal card table, tiger stripe maple, birch & bird's-eye maple veneer, the rectangular fold-over top w/a serpentine front & half-serpentine sides & ovolo corners above a conforming apron w/bird's-eye maple veneer joining quarter engaged ring-turned legs

ending in swelled peg feet, old refinish, New Hampshire or Massachusetts, ca. 1820, 18 x 36", 28 1/2" h. (imperfections)............................. **1,495**

Federal country-style dining table, birch, a rectangular two-board top flanked by deep hinged drop leaves w/rounded corners, the apron raised on swelled turned round legs ending in ring-turned ankles & peg & ball feet, first half 19th c., old red finish, 16 1/2 x 41 1/2" plus 11 3/4" w. leaves, 29 1/4" h. (age crack & edge repair in top, age crack & repair to one leg) **330**

Federal country-style dining table, cherry, a rectangular top flanked by wide hinged drop leaf w/rounded cut corners, one dovetailed drawer in the apron at one end, raised on turned cylindrical legs w/double-knob feet, refinished, first half 19th c., 20 x 42" plus 16 3/4" leaves, 28 1/2" h. (age cracks in top)......... **550**

Federal country-style dining table, tiger stripe maple, the rectangular top flanked by wide hinged drop leaves over a plain apron & six ring- and rod-turned legs w/small bun feet, old refinish, no casters, New England, ca. 1825, 29 x 56 1/2", 28" h. (ILLUS.)......... **3,335**

Massachusetts Federal Card Table

Country Federal Dining Table

Federal Pembroke Table

Federal country-style dressing table, painted & decorated, the scroll-cut backsplash w/shaped ends above the rectangular top over a long narrow drawer in the apron, raised on ring-, knob- and tapering rod-turned legs w/knob feet, the backsplash painted w/a stylized stenciled fruit & leaf cluster in gold & green, the table w/a green & mustard gold grained surface & banding, old replaced opalescent glass drawer pulls, New England, early 19th c., 15 x 32 1/4", 34" h. (some old repaint) **1,380**

Federal dining table, mahogany, two-part, each half of demilune form w/a molded edge & a wide hinged drop leaf, wide plain conforming apron, each half w/four reeded & ring-turned legs w/ball feet, one leg a swing-out support for the leaf, Massachusetts, probably Newburyport, late 18th to early 19th c., open 48 x 90", 30" h. **7,188**

Federal games table, carved mahogany, the rectangular top w/serpentine sides & front w/a hinged leaf over a conforming apron w/flowerhead-carved corner dies on waterleaf-carved reeded tapering legs ending in peg feet, appears to retain old & possibly original finish, attributed to the Haines-Connelly School, Philadelphia, ca. 1810, 18 x 35 3/4", 29 1/2" h. (top warp repairs, repairs to top left rear leg) **2,587**

Federal Pembroke table, cherry, rectangular top flanked by rectangular drop leaves above an apron w/a single end drawer w/wooden knob, raised on slender square tapering legs joined by arched cross-stretchers, old refinish, New England, ca. 1810, open 34 x 38", 29" h. (ILLUS.)...... **1,495**

Federal Pembroke table, inlaid mahogany, a rectangular top flanked by hinged drop leaves w/notched & rounded corners bordered by inlaid stringing, the apron w/a working drawer at one end & a false drawer at the other, each w/stringed inlay & flanked by shaped satinwood corner panels above the square tapering legs, old oval brasses, old finish, probably New York, 1790-1800, closed 19 x 32", 28 1/2" h. (imperfections).............................. **2,990**

Federal Pembroke table, inlaid mahogany, a rectangular top w/gently bowed ends flanked by D-form drop leaves above a conforming apron w/a single line-inlaid drawer at one end, on square tapering legs w/inlaid cuffs, New York, early-19th c., 32" l., 28" h. **5,175**

Federal side table, inlaid cherry, a rectangular top w/tiger maple inlaid edging above an apron w/a single long drawer w/line inlay above a serpentine front apron, raised on square tapering legs w/arched line & geometric inlay, Newburyport, Massachusetts, early 19th c., 21 x 33", 30 1/2" h. **8,050**

Federal side table, mahogany, a rectangular top w/molded edges flanked by D-form drop leaves flanking an apron w/a single long drawer w/replaced lion head brass pulls, raised on a tapering octagonal column over four outswept sabre legs ending in brass paw feet on casters, refinished, early 19th c., 29 1/4 x 79 1/4" plus 9 1/2" leaves, 27 1/2" h. **605**

Unusual Federal Sofa Table

Federal sofa table, figured maple, the rectangular long top w/reeded edges flanked by D-form drop leaves above an apron w/a long cockbeaded drawer w/two oval brass pulls, on slender ring- and rod-turned legs w/knob ankles & peg feet, appears to retain original hardware, probably New England, early 19th c., 29 3/4 x 44 3/4", 29" h. (ILLUS.)............................... **4,887**

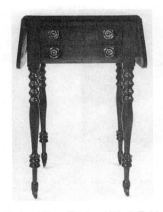

Federal New England Work Table

Federal work table, birch & mahogany veneer, rectangular top flanked by D-form drop leaves over an apron w/two drawers each w/two large round brass pulls, raised on bobbin-, baluster- and ring-turned tapering legs w/knob feet on casters, old finish, imperfections, New England, ca. 1830, 16 3/4 x 19 3/4", 28 3/4" h. (ILLUS.)......................... **748**

Fine Federal Work Table

Federal work table, figured mahogany, the hinged rectangular top opening to a fitted interior w/adjustable writing surface flanked by compartments, the deep case w/two flush drawers w/pairs of round brass pulls raised on slender ring- and baluster-turned supports to a medial shelf w/concave front over short ring- and baluster-turned legs on casters, appears to retain original drawer pulls, patches to veneer, New York City, ca. 1810, 16 3/4 x 20 1/2", 31" h. (ILLUS.)... **4,312**

Federal work table, mahogany & figured mahogany veneer, a rectangular top above a deep case w/figured veneer on the front including two drawers w/original florette & ring gilded brasses, a shallow small writing drawer under

Rectangular Hutch Table

Early Painted Pine Hutch Table

the top to the right side, raised on turned reeded legs w/ring-turned sections at the top & bottom w/peg feet on casters, refinished, ca. 1810-20, 16 1/2 x 21", 30" h. (minor veneer repair, writing drawer missing hinged shelf, age cracks) **1,540**

Hutch (or chair) table, painted pine, the rectangular cleated top w/old red paint tilting above wide sides & closed back over seat w/narrow apron, low cut-out feet, original red surface, minor surface imperfections, New England, early 19th c., 36 x 43", 27 1/2" h. (ILLUS.) **3,220**

Hutch (or chair) table, painted pine, the round top tilting on two cut-out ends joined by a beaded frontal panel continuing to molded shoe feet, red paint over earlier paint, probably New England, 18th c., 31" d., 26 1/4" h. (ILLUS.) **6,900**

Hutch (or chair) table, painted wood, a wide rectangular four-board top lifting above one-board sides w/bootjack feet flanking a lift-top seat compartment, greenish grey paint, early 19th c., 37 x 57". **2,250**

Jacobean Revival side table, oak, the rectangular top composed of two caned panels within a scroll-carved narrow frame & apron w/floret-carved corner blocks above the slender rope-twist-turned legs w/bottom floret blocks on ovoid feet, rope-twist- and block-turned H-stretcher, old finish, early 20th c., 24 x 30", 24" h.......... **176**

Jacobean-Style Dining Table

Jacobean-Style dining table, inlaid walnut, draw-leaf extension-type, the rectangular top w/draw-leaf extensions above an S-scroll-carved apron w/scroll-carved brackets above the bulbous carved cup-and-cover design legs on shaped shoe feet joined by a half-round stretcher, some wear, ca. 1900, 35 x 71 1/2", 31" h. (ILLUS.) **8,625**

Mission-style (Arts & Crafts movement) side table, round top w/inset heavy square legs joined by a flared cross-stretcher base, cleaned original finish, unsigned Gustav Stickley, Model No. 440, 30" d., 29" h. **2,200**

Early Queen Anne Dining Table

Queen Anne dining table, carved & figured walnut, the rectangular top flanked by deep rectangular drop leaves, arched end aprons on cabriole legs ending in paneled trifid feet, appears to retain an old & possibly original finish, warm nut-brown color, Pennsylvania, ca. 1750, closed 17 1/2 x 50 1/2", 28" h. (ILLUS.)............................... **4,887**

Queen Anne dressing table, maple & pine, rectangular top w/molded edges above an apron w/a pair of deep drawers flanking a small shallow central drawer above a deeply scalloped apron w/two urn-turned drops, simple cabriole legs ending in pad feet, rear knee return missing, formerly painted white, New England, 1740-60, 18 1/2 x 34 1/2", 29 1/2" h. (ILLUS.) **3,737**

Queen Anne Dressing Table

Queen Anne mixing table, painted, a rectangular top w/a projecting molded edge enclosing a black marble slab above a deep openwork apron carved w/overlapping circles & diamonds, raised on angular cabriole legs w/scrolled returns & ending in stylized hairy paw feet, painted black, 18th c., 20 x 32 1/2", 28" h. **7,000**

Quality Queen Anne Tavern Table

Queen Anne tavern table, painted pine, oval top widely overhangs a deep apron on splayed ring- and rod-turned tapering legs ending in turned feet, scrubbed top, original red paint on base, minor imperfections, New England,

18th c., 26 3/8 x 35", 26 1/4" h.
(ILLUS.) **14,950**

Queen Anne Small Tavern Table

Queen Anne tavern table, poplar &
turned maple, rectangular top
w/rounded corners above a deep
apron on tapering turned legs
ending in pad feet, repair to top,
top possibly reshaped, New
England, 1740-60, 14 x 19 1/2",
25 1/2" h. (ILLUS.) **2,875**

Queen Anne Tilt-top Tea Table

Queen Anne tea table, mahogany,
wide round top tilting on a vase-
and ring-turned pedestal on a
tripod base w/cabriole legs ending
in pad feet on platforms, refinished,
minor imperfections, probably

Massachusetts, ca. 1760,
33 1/8" d., 27 3/4" h. (ILLUS.) **1,840**

Pennsylvania Queen Anne Tea Table

Queen Anne tea table, turned
walnut, the large round dished top
hinged & tilting & revolving above a
birdcage support, the tapering
columnar pedestal w/urn-form
compressed-ball bottom on a
tripod base w/squatty cabriole legs
ending in snake feet, small section
of stem at top of pedestal replaced,
Pennsylvania, ca. 1750, 25 1/2" d.,
26 1/2" h. (ILLUS.) **6,900**

Queen Anne work table, painted
black walnut, the removable
rectangular plank three-board pine
top supported by cleats w/four
dowels widely overhanging a deep
apron w/a long & shorter drawer on
one side each w/a simple turned
wood knob, on beaded-edge
straight cabriole legs ending in pad
feet, original apple green paint, old
replaced wood pulls,
Pennsylvania, 1760-1800,
32 x 48 1/2", 27" h. (surface
imperfections, cracked foot) **2,415**

Renaissance-Style refectory table,
mahogany, the simple rectangular
top raised on a scrolling standard
carved w/an armorial medallion,

Europe, late 19th c., 39 x 101",
30" h. **2,760**

"Sawbuck" table, painted pine, the
rectangular overhanging top on a
nail-constructed rectangular skirt &
chamfered crossed legs joined by
a turned medial stretcher w/keyed
exposed tenon, old reddish brown
paint, New England, mid 19th c.,
28 x 50", 30" h. (ILLUS.)............... **2,070**

"Sawbuck" table, pine & painted
pine, the rectangular top w/a
natural finish raised on a black-
painted base w/end cross-legs
joined by a flat chamfered
stretcher, each section of legs
w/chamfered edges, late 19th. c.
copy of earlier style, 23 x 48 3/4",
30" h. **880**

Tavern table, country-style, painted
pine, a rectangular top widely
overhanging a beaded apron on
four square chamfered legs
w/molded edges, painted red,
early, 27 x 38 1/2", 26 1/2" h. **2,000**

Tavern table, country-style, pine &
cherry, rectangular overhanging
top on four square tapering beaded
splayed legs joined by a deep
beaded skirt, old refinish,
imperfections, top stains, some
surface loss, two interior 19th c.
braces, New England, ca. 1790,
32 x 34 1/4", 25 1/2" h. (ILLUS.)... **1,265**

Early Country Tavern Table

Painted Country Tavern Table

Tavern table, painted birch,
rectangular top widely overhanging

Early "Sawbuck" Table

a deep apron raised on simple turned & tapering legs, later blue paint, northern New England, early 19th c., 22 x 38", 27 1/2" h. (ILLUS.) **920**

Round Wicker Table with Shelf

Wicker side table, round oak top w/wicker banding on four tightly woven wicker panels framing a lower oak shelf over a tightly woven conforming apron, pointed flaring woven legs, painted white, ca. 1910, 30" d. (ILLUS.) **201**

Rare William & Mary Dining Table

William & Mary dining table, figured walnut, a rectangular top w/rounded molded ends flanked by D-form matching drop leaves over an apron w/a deep drawer at each end, on square chamfered legs &

swing-out gate-leg supports, joined by box stretchers, repairs to drawer fronts, possibly Southern U.S., 1700-30, closed 16 x 44", 31 1/2" h. (ILLUS.) **10,925**

Early William & Mary Dining Table

William & Mary dining table, turned & figured maple, the rectangular top w/gently rounded ends flanked by two wide D-form drop leaves above an apron w/a drawer at one end, swing-out gate-leg supports, baluster- and ring-turned legs joined by block-, ring- and baluster-turned stretchers, on ball feet, restoration, New England, 1730-50, closed 19 x 49", 28" h. (ILLUS.) **3,737**

William & Mary "hutch" or chair table, painted maple & pine, the oval two-board top tilting on a base of two horizontal supports ending in scrolled handholds joining four block- and baluster-turned legs w/a medial seat & box stretchers all resting on turned feet, original Spanish brown paint, southeastern New England, early 18th c., 47 1/4 x 51 1/4", 26" h. (minor imperfections) **20,700**

William & Mary tavern table, maple & pine, the wide rectangular breadboard top overhanging the apron w/a single long drawer w/wooden knob, on ring-, baluster- and block-turned legs joined by square stretchers & ending in

button feet, old refinish, New
England, 18th c., 21 x 33", 27" h.
(minor imperfections).................... **1,610**

William & Mary tavern table,
painted, a wide rectangular top
w/breadboard ends above an
apron w/a single long drawer
w/simple turned pull, on baluster-,
ring- and block-turned legs joined
by box stretchers, worn red paint,
Massachusetts, 18th c., 28 x 38",
28 1/2" h. **3,000**

Small William & Mary Tavern Table

William & Mary tavern table,
pine & birch, the oval top above
a deep canted apron w/a single
drawer raised on canted baluster-
and ring-turned legs ending in
blocks joined by box stretchers
& raised on waisted knob feet,
retains traces of red wash,
New England, 1700-30,
diminutive size, 17 1/4 x 25 1/2",
25" h. (ILLUS.)........................... **12,650**

William & Mary-Style games table,
inlaid wood, the shaped
rectangular top w/bone & ebony
geometric designs, above an apron
w/a single drawer, raised on
turmed legs joined by a cross
stretcher, England, late 19th c.,
32 x 45", 29" h. **3,737**

WARDROBES & ARMOIRES

Provincial Louis XVI Armoire

Armoire, Lous XVI Provincial-style,
oak, the rectangular top w/a widely
flaring curved cornice w/round
corners over a pair of tall cupboard
doors each w/three matching
molded serpentine panels,
rounded paneled front stiles, on
plain feet, France, late 18th to early
19th c., 22 x 44 1/2", 86 1/2" h.
(ILLUS.) **4,025**

Early William & Mary Kas

Kas, (American version of the
Netherlands Kast or wardrobe),
William & Mary style, cherry, pine
& poplar, the rectangular top w/a
high flaring architectural cornice
molding over a pair of two arch-
paneled cupboard doors flanked by
reeded pilasters over applied mid-
molding over a single long bottom
drawer flanked by reeded panels,
molded base on painted
detachable disc & stretcher turnip-
form feet, replaced hardware,
refinished, restored, Long Island,
New York area, 1730-80,
26 1/4 x 65 1/2", 77 1/4" h.
(ILLUS.) **4,025**

Early Canadian Wardrobe

Wardrobe, country-style, painted
pine, rectangular top w/low cornice
overhanging a pair of tall six-panel
cupboard doors & paneled sides
opening to an interior of four
shelves, molded scroll-cut apron &
simple bracket feet, old green
paint, some hardware loss &
changes, shelves added later,
some paint retouched, Canada,
19th c., 16 x 57", 87 1/2" h.
(ILLUS.) **1,495**

Fine Classical Wardrobe

Wardrobe, Classical, mahogany
veneer, the wide rectangular top
w/a deep stepped & flaring cornice
above a pair of large, tall two-panel
doors opening to an interior
w/veneered drawers, molded base
on simple bracket feet, paneled
sides, some small interior drawers
added, other minor imperfections,
Mid-Atlantic States, ca. 1840,
26 x 65", 79 1/2" h. (ILLUS.)......... **3,105**

Wardrobe, Victorian country-style,
painted pine, five-board
construction, a flat rectangular top
above a tall case w/wide front side
boards flanking the central beaded
board tall door w/wooden thumb
latch & white porcelain knob,
original blue paint, late 19th c.,
17 x 41", 71" h. **518**

Wardrobe, Victorian country-style,
walnut, a rectangular top w/a
narrow molded cornice over a
single tall double-panel door

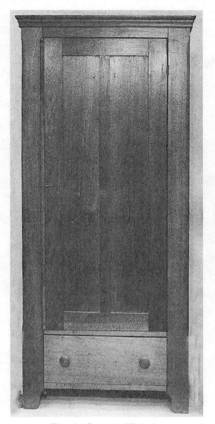

Simple Country Victorian Wardrobe

Victorian Gothic Revival Wardrobe

opening to a fitted rod above a single deep bottom drawer, simple bracket feet, one-board sides, door edge strip w/pieced repairs, found in Missouri, mid 19th c., 17 3/4 x 32", 73" h. (ILLUS.)......... **1,650**

Wardrobe, Victorian Gothic Revival substyle, walnut, the rectangular top w/a deep flaring cornice over a pair of tall cupboard doors w/Gothic Arch panels over a single long drawer at the bottom, scalloped front apron, ca. 1865, 16 x 42", 73" h. (ILLUS.)................ **690**

G

Graniteware Blue & White Swirl Mugs

Graniteware Miniature Tea Set

GLASS

BLOWN THREE MOLD

This type of glass was entirely or partially blown in a mold and was popular from about 1820 to 1840. The object was formed and the decoration impressed upon it by blowing the glass into a metal mold, usually of three—but sometimes more—sections hinged together. Mold-blown glass actually dates back to ancient times. Recent research reveals that certain geometric patterns were reproduced in the 1920s; some new pieces, usually sold through museum gift shops, are still available. Collectors are urged to read all recent information available. Reference numbers are from George l. and Helen McKearin's book, American Glass.

Decanter w/bar lip, Baroque, pontiled base, rare applied bar lip, clear, 7 1/4" h. (GV-8)..................... **$495**

Decanter w/flattened unpatterned stopper, geometric, miniature, ovoid body tapering to a plain neck w/flared rim, clear, 3 1/2" h. (GIII-12).. **495**

Decanter w/pressed wheel stopper, geometric, ovoid body tapering to double-ringed neck w/flattened flared rim, slightly oversized stopper, clear, 1/2 pt., 7 1/2" h., GII-33 (ILLUS. right)....... **209**

Decanter w/stopper, Baroque patt., probably original hollow blown ribbed stopper, clear, 11 1/2" h.,GV-9 (some light interior residue) **209**

Decanter w/stopper, geometric, flared mouth, rayed base, possibly original hollow blown stopper, clear, 10 1/2" h.,GIII-24 (slight light mold impression) **142**

Decanter w/stopper, geometric, large star in ring design around sides w/rows of short ribs above & below, flared folded lip & original hollow blown stopper, clear, 11 1/4" h. (GV-10) **550**

Decanter w/stopper, geometric, ovoid body tapering to a plain neck w/flattened flared rim, original hollow patterned ball stopper, clear, 10 1/2" h., GIII-5 (ILLUS. left) **176**

Blown Three Mold Decanters

Decanter w/stopper, Gothic arch design, bands of Gothic arches above & below a central reserve molded w/"RUM," flared rim w/original compressed hollow blown stopper, clear, 10 3/4" h., GIV-7 (some light amber residue) . **220**

Dish, geometric, shallow round form w/folded rim, clear, 5 5/16" d., 1 1/8" h. (GII-22)........................... **99**

Dish, geometric, shallow round form w/rolled rim, rough pontil, clear, 6" d. (GIII-5).................................... **187**

Model of a top hat, geometric, folded rim, deep sapphire-violet blue, unlisted, 2 3/4" h. (GI-6)....... **1,320**

Pitcher, 3 1/8", miniature, geometric, squatty bulbous body w/widely flaring rim & pinched spout, applied handle, clear, GII-18 (hard to see line in handle) **132**

Salt dip, geometric, cushion foot & flaring squatty body w/low flared rim, clear, 2 1/2" d., 2 1/8" h. (GIII-25) **143**

Salt dip, geometric, wide bell-form top w/flared rim raised on a short flaring pedestal foot, clear, unseen pontil chip, 2 1/4" h. (GII-21).......... **468**

Shakers w/original brass lids,
geometric, cylindrical body
tapering slightly toward top, ringed
base w/pontil, loose lids, clear,
4 1/2" h.,GIII-27 (one w/chip under
lid), pr. 143

Tumbler, geometric, cylindrical
w/fine ribbing around lower half,
clear, McKearin Collection sticker,
3 1/4" h. (GI-?).............................. 303

Tumbler, miniature, geometric,
cylindrical, ringed base, clear,
1 3/4" h. (GII-16)............................ 275

Wine, geometric, flaring cylindrical
bowl w/applied bladed stem &
pontiled foot, clear, 4" h. (GII-19) .. 330

CUP PLATES

L & R-128, round, central large eight-
point star w/bull's-eyes alternating
w/diamonds, band of half-round
shells within rope border, clear, 3
5/16" d. (three scallops missing) ... 55

L & R-130, round, four pointed leaf
cluster in center on diamond point
ground, small pointed leaves rayed
around the border within small
knob rim band, clear, 3 7/16" d.
(mold roughness, two scallops
tipped) 121

L & R-167B, round, plain concentric
rings, smooth rim, clear, 3" d. (light
mold roughness)............................. 132

L & R-197C, round, central
blossomhead surrounded by
delicate band of blossoms &
leaves, looped arch border band,
violet blue (very shallow large rim
chip & underfill).............................. 132

L & R-250A, round, central six-point
diamond point star surrounded by
panels of criss-cross design, outer
border of rounded pod-like devices
(three tipped scallops) 33

L & R-253, round. Roman Rosette
patt., bluish green, 3 1/2" d............ 77

L & R-253, round, Roman Rosette
patt., light bluish green (few
scallops missing or tipped)............ 138

L & R-262, round, four-point central
cross alternating w/four heart-form
double scrolls, outer border of
alternating quatrefoils & fleur-de-
lis, dark blue, 3 1/4" d. (tiny rim
spall, few tipped scallops) 330

L & R-262, round, four-point central
star alternating w/heart-form
double scrolls, border of alternating
quatrefoils & fleur-de-lis, dark
cobalt blue, eight scallops tipped. 143

L & R-262, round, four-point central
star alternating w/heart-form
double scrolls, border of alternating
quatrefoils & fleur-de-lis, greyish
blue, few scallops tipped 715

L & R-277, round, large central three-
arm cross alternating w/diamonds,
leaf sprig & scroll border, peacock
blue (small refracting line, light
mold roughness)............................ 770

L & R-279, round, large multi-petaled
central blossomhead, narrow
border bands, lavender (usual
mold roughness)............................ 413

L & R-279, round w/scalloped rim, a
large multi-petaled central
blossom, simple outer band decor,
light green, 2 7/8" d. (light mold
roughness) 176

L & R-311, round, simple six-petal
star surrounded by bull's-eyes in
the center, band of diamonds in the
border, deep opal opaque (mold
roughness, few tipped scallops) 176

L & R-37, round, large eight pointed-
petal central blossom alternating
w/tiny blossoms in center, diamond
point inner band & palmette
scalloped outer border, opaque
white (mold roughness) 990

L & R-37 round w/scalloped rim,
center eight-petal large blossom
alternating w/tiny blossoms, inner
diamond point band & palmette
outer border, fiery opalescent,
3 1/4" d. (moderately heavy mold
roughness, chip on back rim) 154

L & R-388, round, simple eight-petal
central blossom, diamond point
outer border, opaque white
w/amber flashing (mold
roughness) 418

L & R-390 variant, round, smooth rim, Sunburst patt. center, diamond point border band, medium blue (light mold roughness) 165

L & R-412, ten-sided, open five-point star in center, plain rim, peacock green (several chips & flakes on rim) 715

L & R-440B, round, Valentine patt., lyre border, deep blue, 3 1/2" d. (two scalloped tipped, mold roughness) 165

L & R-440b, round, Valentine patt., lyre border, greyish blue, 3 1/2" d. (small rim spall, few scallops tipped) 110

Two Scarce Colored Cup Plates

L & R-440B, round, Valentine patt., lyre border, medium blue, few scallops tipped, mold roughness (ILLUS. right, with L & R-522) 176

Heart Pattern Cup Plate

L & R-459D, round, Heart patt., loop & dart center, brilliant emerald green, one & one-half scallops chipped, some others tipped (ILLUS.) 605

L & R-502, round, Sunburst center patt., plain border, light green 138

L & R-508, round, starburst center, plain border, peacock blue, 3" d. (mold roughness, one scallop tipped) 176

L & R-522, round, Sunburst patt., plain border, deep reddish amber, two scallops tipped (ILLUS. left) ... 275

L & R-523, round, Sunburst center patt., plain rim, light olive green (one scallop missing, six tipped) ... 121

L & R-524, round, Sunburst center design, plain border, blue (light mold roughness) 198

L & R-530, round, Sunburst patt., amethyst (four scallops missing, few tipped) 154

L & R-531, round, bull's-eye & sunburst center design, plain border, knobby rim, light green (few tipped scallops) 132

L & R-571, round, Queen Victoria design, central small bust of queen w/"Victoria" above, outer border w/a crown at the top & flowering vines around the sides (mold roughness) 44

L & R-610A, round, sailing ship center scene framed by rope band within lacy scrolls, looping scroll outer border, deep blue, 3 1/2" d. (three scallops tipped, mold roughness) 198

L & R-612A, octagonal, steamship center design, scroll & shield border, clear, 3 1/2" d. (mold roughness, few scallops chipped) . 110

L & R-686, round, Harp patt., harp, long leafy branches & a star in center, delicate meandering vine outer border, clear (mold roughness) 66

L & R-80, round, tight ring of hearts in center, leafy undulating vine band & other swirled leaf sprig band, plain rim, light opal, 3 3/4" d. 358

L & R-88, round, small florals around border band, concentric rings in center, opal, 3 3/4" d. (area of underfill, few minor rim flakes) 385

PILLAR-MOLDED

This heavily ribbed glassware was pro-duced by blowing glass into full-sized ribbed molds and then finishing it by hand. The tech-

nique evolved from earlier "pattern mould-ing" used on glass since ancient times but in pillar-molded glass the ribs are very heavy and prominent. Most examples found in this country were produced in the Pittsburgh, Pennsylvania area from around 1850 to 1870, but similar English-made wares made before and after this period are also avail-able. Most American items were made from clear flint glass and colored examples or pieces with colored strands in the ribs are rare and highly prized. Some collectors refer to this as "steamboat" glass believing that it was made to be used on American riverboats, but most likely it was used anywhere that a sturdy, relatively inexpensive glassware was needed, such as taverns and hotels.

Rare Pillar-Molded Candlestick

Candlestick, eight-rib, bulbous tapering ribbed stem topped by a thick applied wafer & a ringed & tooled tall cylindrical socket w/flattened rim, on a short applied stem & wide disk foot, rough pontil, clear, 10 1/8" h. (ILLUS.) **$2,200**

Celery vase, eight-rib, tall tulip-form bowl w/heavy ribbing & flared, scalloped rim, on compressed baluster stem & disc foot, blue opalescent w/presentation gilding between the ribs, polished pontil, 9 1/2" h. **10,230**

Celery vase, eight-rib, tall waisted tulip-shaped bowl w/ferns, grapes & leaves engraved between ribs, applied knob stem & disk foot, clear, probably Pittsburgh, 10 3/4" h. **209**

Celery vase, eight-rib, very tall waisted tulip-form bowl w/scalloped rim, on an applied knop stem & round foot, ground pontil, clear, 10 7/8" h. **193**

Creamer & open sugar bowl, eight-rib, each w/squatty thick heavy ribs forming the body, the creamer w/a high plain neck w/wide spout, applied handle w/curled end, raised on three-wafer pedestal & applied foot w/polished pontil, matching sugar w/wide plain upper sides w/folded rim, matching stem & foot, clear, 19th c., each 4" h., pr. **2,750**

Clear Swirled Pillar Mold Creamer

Creamer, clear swirled pillar mold creamer with applied handle. Cased in opaque white. Check at handle. 5 3/4" h. (ILLUS.) **500-800**

Cruet w/original hollow blown stopper, eight-rib, bulbous ovoid body tapering to a tall slender neck w/arched spout, applied long strap handle w/end curl, rough pontil, clear, Pittsburgh, 9 1/2" h. **275**

Decanter w/bar lip, miniature, eight-rib, tapering conical sides below triple applied rings at the base of the tall neck w/bar lip, polished pontil, clear, 6" h. **330**

Decanter w/pewter jigger top, eight-rib, tapering conical form w/applied rim & hollow strap

BOOT JACKS

Cast iron figural bootjack of a cricket with original paint, ca. 1900, $125. Courtesy of Harry A. Zuber.

Cast iron figural bootjack of a female weightlifter holding a barbell, 10" l., $1,000. Courtesy of Harry A. Zuber.

Ornate cast iron bootjack with floral and scroll designs and an inverted heart in the center, ca. 1880-90, original red paint, 12 1/4" l., $300. Courtesy of Harry A. Zuber.

BOTTLE OPENERS

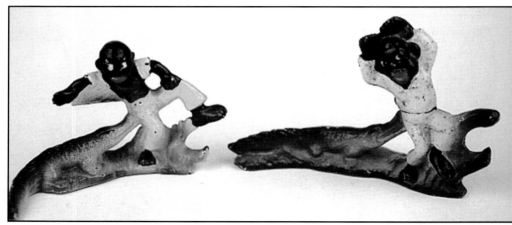

Figural cast iron bottle openers. Left, an alligator biting a black boy, 3" h., $75-150; right, an alligator biting a black boy with his arms raised above his head, 21/4" h., $150-250. Courtesy of Charles Reynolds.

Figural painted aluminum bottle openers. Left to right: Papa Bear, 45/8" h., Mama Bear, 4" h. and Baby Bear, 3" h., each $45-90. Courtesy of Charles Reynolds.

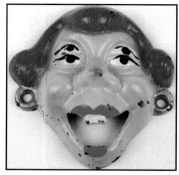

Cast Iron Miss Four Eyes wall-mounted bottle opener, $50-75. Courtesy of Charles Reynolds.

Cast iron Beer Drinker figural bottle opener with original paint, rare, 51/2" h., $1,500+. Courtesy of Charles Reynolds.

BLUE & WHITE POTTERY

Blue and white pottery Basketweave & Morning Glory canisters: Coffee, $325+, Salt, $475+ and Sugar, $325+. Courtesy of Steve Stone.

Blue and white pottery ewer and pitchers. Bottom right: embossed Apple Blossom ewer, 12" h., $450; Bottom left: embossed Plume pitcher, $350+; Top: printed Acorn pitcher, 8" h., $300. Courtesy of Steve Stone.

Blue and white pottery pitchers. Right: embossed Eagle pattern, 8" h., $650+; Left: embossed Lovebirds pattern, 8 1/2" h., $450+. Courtesy of Steve Stone.

Early Father Christmas fold-out two-layer greeting card, $125. Courtesy of Robert Brenner.

An early Christmas postcard showing Santa with a tree standing over a sleeping girl, $50. Courtesy of Robert Brenner.

A group of four counterbalance-style Christmas tree candleholders of tin and lead, the set $120. Courtesy of Robert Brenner.

*Amoy pattern Flow Blue 12" h. water pitcher,
$1,500. Courtesy of Ellen Hill.*

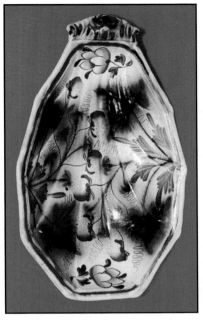

*Gaudy Flow Blue brushstroke relish
dish, $195. Courtesy of Ellen Hill.*

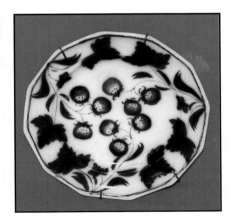

*Brushstroke Strawberry pattern Flow Blue
9 1/2" d. plate, $175. Courtesy of Ellen Hill.*

*Mellor Venables & Co. Gaudy Flow Blue teapot in the
Classic Gothic shape, $900. Courtesy of Ellen Hill.*

FURNITURE

Turn-of-the-century Golden Oak 'side-by-side' chest of drawers, possibly missing the feet, $150-300. Courtesy of DeFina Auctions, Austinburg, Ohio.

Victorian Golden Oak 'highboy' style chest of drawers, ca. 1900, $850. Courtesy Gene Harris Antique Auction Center, Marshalltown, Iowa.

A cherry Chippendale chest of drawers made in New England, ca. 1790, $4,025. Courtesy of Sotheby's, New York.

A Classical country-style combination sideboard and pie safe in cherry with decorative punched tin panels in the doors, Virginia, ca. 1840, $6,250. Courtesy of Green Valley Auctions, Mt. Crawford, Virginia.

Graniteware red and white swirl coffeepot with goose-neck spout and unattached cover, light weight, 8" h., ca. 1960s, $100. Courtesy of Jo Allers.

Graniteware blue and white swirl tea steeper with tin lid, 5" h., $225. Courtesy of Jo Allers.

Graniteware blue and white swirl Columbian Ware teakettle, $625. Courtesy of Jo Allers.

Graniteware Emerald Ware green and white swirl cream can, 91/4" h., $850. Courtesy of Jo Allers.

Mulberry ware Cyprus pattern gravy boat, $150. Courtesy of Ellen Hill.

An 8" h. Mulberry ware Nankin pattern pitcher with a mask spout, $300. Courtesy of Ellen Hill.

A tall ewer in the Wreath pattern of Mulberry ware, $295. Courtesy of Ellen Hill.

PENNSBURY POTTERY

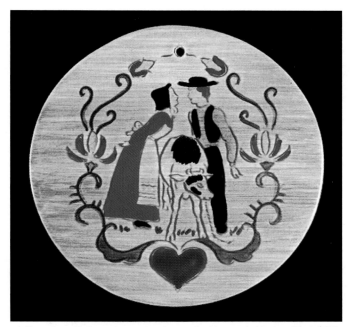

*A Pennsbury Pottery plaque showing an Amish couple kissing, 8" d. $87.
Courtesy of Susan N. Cox.*

*Pennsbury Pottery Amish pattern 71/4" h. pitcher,
$105. Courtesy of Susan N. Cox.*

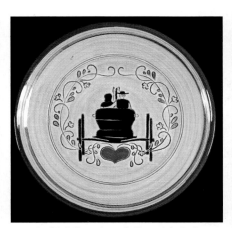

*An 8" d. Pennsbury Pottery plate in the
Courting Buggy pattern, $75. Courtesy of
Susan N. Cox.*

QUILTS

Fine appliqued 'Union' quilt in bright red, white and blue patches with four spread-winged American eagles and shields centering the American flag, white cotton field with overlapping circular quilting; red, white and blue borders, probably Pennsylvania, ca. 1915, 76" sq., $8,050. Courtesy of Sotheby's, New York.

A pieced red, white and blue cotton 'Civil War' quilt based on the American flag. Composed of bright red, white and blue stripes and a star-filled central medallion and star border, scalloped and boxed-diamond quilting, ca. 1865, 88" sq., $12,650. Courtesy of Sotheby's, New York.

An unusual pieced printed cotton 'Kerchief' quilt composed of patriotic printed kerchiefs including one depicting George Washington, American eagles, flags and shields as well as the Declaration of Independence. Large crisscross quilting and printed with the dates "1776" and "1876" in stars, ca. 1876, 92 x 101", $9,200. Courtesy of Sotheby's, New York.

SPATTERWARE

A large grouping of Spatterware handleless cups and saucers, top to bottom, left to right: Peacock pattern with a lilac spatter ground, $2,310; Fort pattern with a blue spatter ground, $600; Peacock pattern with a light green ground, $1,650; Rooster pattern with a blue spatter border, $798; Schoolhouse pattern with blue spatter border, $990; Forget-me-not pattern with blue star spatter, $3,190; Peafowl pattern with a green spatter ground, $495; Mourning Tulip pattern with a dark blue ground, $4,290; Fort pattern with a red spatter background, $1,980; and Thistle pattern with a red and orange rainbow spatter border, $1,870. Courtesy of Garth's Auction's, Delaware, Ohio.

A Peafowl pattern 4" h. creamer with a red, blue and green strawberry or thumbprint design background, professionally repaired, $5,170. Courtesy of Garth's Auctions, Delaware, Ohio.

WATT POTTERY

Watt Pottery 13" d. Dutch Tulip pattern spaghetti bowl, No. 39, $400. Courtesy of Dennis Thompson.

Watt Pottery Rio Rose pattern No. 72 canister, $300. Courtesy of Dennis Thompson.

Nesting mixing bowls in the Tulip pattern by Watt Pottery. Numbers 63, 64 & 65, 61/2", 71/2" and 81/2" d., each $90. Courtesy of Dennis Thompson.

Cow weathervane of gilded molded copper, attributed to Harris and Co., Boston, late 19th c., 33" l, 21" h., $23,000. Courtesy of Skinner Inc., Bolton, Massachusetts.

A jumping horse weathervane of gilded molded and applied copper, probably by A. L. Jewell & Co., Waltham, Massachusetts, second half 19th c., 36 1/2" l., 18" h., $23,000. Courtesy of Skinner Inc., Bolton, Massachusetts.

WINDMILL WEIGHTS

Cow windmill weight painted black and white and embossed with the name "Fairbury," $2,000 to $2,500. Courtesy of Richard S. Tucker.

A barnacle-eye type rooster windmill weight with white and red paint, Elgin Wind Power & Pump Company, Elgin, Illinois, worn paint, 18 1/2" h., $3,500 to $5,000. Courtesy of Richard S. Tucker.

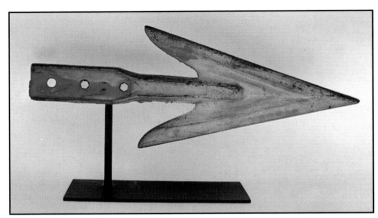

Arrow-shaped windmill weight with old red paint, Leach Windmill Company, Joliet, Illinois, very rare, 25" l., $2,000 to $2,500. Courtesy of Richard S. Tucker.

Boxes:

Rare large wallpaper-covered oval band box. A landscape with a building titled "Castle Garden," signed "Joel Post," early 19th c., 23" l., $3,300. Courtesy of Garth's Auctions, Delaware, Ohio.

Fraktur:

Birth record for Martin Breckall, Pennsylvania, dated 1845, 131/2 x 19", $2,200. Courtesy of Garth's Auctions, Delaware, Ohio.

Theorems:

Fine quality theorem of a basket of fruit, water-color on velvet, dated 1845 on the back; in the original giltwood frame, 11 1/2 x 15", $6,900. Courtesy of Sotheby's, New York.

Wood Sculpture:

Carved wood and painted standing cigar store Indian Princess figure holding a bundle of tobacco leaves. Repainted, but on original base; found in Rhode Island, late 19th - early 20th c., $18,700. Courtesy of Copake Auction, Inc., Copake, New York.

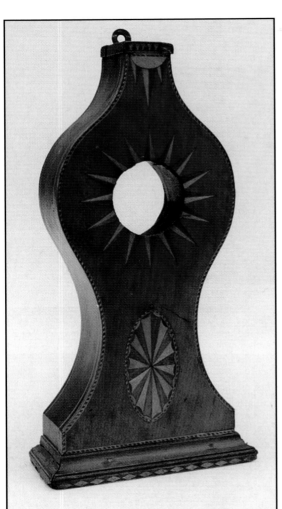

Woodenware:

This rare inlaid mahogany watch hutch features inlaid designs of banding, a starburst around the watch opening and a paterae on the lower body, early 19th c., 11 1/4" h., $3,575. Courtesy of Garth's Auctions, Delaware, Ohio.

handle w/curled end, clear,
Pittsburgh, 9 1/4" h. **303**

Pitcher, 5 3/4" h., eight-rib, opaque
white cased in clear, bulbous
tapering body w/an in-body tweist
tapering to the broad spout,
applied strap handle w/curled end,
check at hande (ILLUS. right
previous column **4,510**

Vase, blue opalescent pillar mold vase
with presentation gliding. Applied
foot, baluster stem and scalloped
rim. Polished pontil. 9 1/2" h.
(ILLUS.) **3,000-4,000**

Blue Opalescent Pillar Mold Vase

GRANITEWARE

Whether you prefer it as Graniteware, Agate Ware, or Enameled Ware, the production was a process of adhering single or multiple coats of enamel to metal. This was done by using high temperatures in a kiln drying system. When completed the items had a glass-like finish. Even though they advertised it as a very durable product, it does chip easily. Production was carried on on a large scale in the United States from the late 1870s through the 1950s. Even today there are a few companies still in existence, but the majority of them are in foreign countries.In determining the values of Graniteware in this price guide the following factors were used— condition, rarity, color, shape, size, age, dated, labeling, and desirability. Values in the listing are based on near-mint condition. Prices will vary according to the condition of the piece.—Jo Allers

BLUE DIAMOND WARE (IRIS BLUE & WHITE SWIRL)

Bowl, mixing, 5" d., 2" h.................... **$75**

Coffee biggin, cov., three-piece, 3 1/2" d., 7 1/2" h. (ILLUS.)........... **1,000**

Cream can, 5" d., 9" h. **575**

Funnel, bulbous, 7 1/4" d., 5" h. **225**

Diamond Ware Mustard Pot

Mustard pot, cov., 2 3/4" d., 4" h. (ILLUS.) **1,000**

Platter, oval, 11 x 14" **300**

Blue Diamond Coffee Biggin

Blue Diamond Sugar Bowl

Blue & White Swirl Mugs

Soup bowl, white interior, 9 1/4" d.,
1 1/2" h. **165**

Sugar bowl, cov., 3 1/2" d., 6 1/4" h.
(ILLUS.) **500**

Diamond Ware Teapot

Teapot, cov., bulbous body, 5 1/2" d.,
6" h. (ILLUS.) **700**

Blue Diamond Vegetable Dish

Vegetable dish, oval, 9 1/2" l.,
7 1/2" w. (ILLUS.) **200**

BLUE & WHITE SWIRL

Baking pan, wire handles, 8 3/4" w.,
12" l. **175**

Bowl, mixing, 10" d., 3 1/2" h............. **100**

Bread raiser, w/tin cover, footed,
16" d., 9 1/2" h. **475**

Chamber pot 10" d., 4 3/4" h. **125**

Coffee biggin, tin biggin & cover,
4" d., 9" h. **800**

Blue & White Swirl Cream Can

Cream can, cov., 5" d., 9" h. (ILLUS.) **275**

Blue & White Swirl Double Boiler

Double boiler, cov., 3 pc.s, 6 1/2" d.,
8 1/2" h. (ILLUS.) **225**

Blue & White Swirl Lunch Bucket

Lunch bucket, oval, wire & wood
handle, 3 pcs., 9" w., 8 1/4" l., 7"
depth (ILLUS.) **600**

Blue & White Swirl Measuring Cup

Measuring cup, 3 1/2" d., 4 1/2" h.
(ILLUS.) **500**

Muffin pan, 12" l. **250**

Mug, miner's, 6" d., 5" h **140**

Blue & White Swirl Railroad Mug

Mug, railroad advertisement,
"C.G.W.Ry." (Chicago and Great
Western Railroad), 2 3/4" d.,
2 3/4" h. (ILLUS.) **350**

Mugs, straight-sided Columbian
Ware, one of a set of 4, 4" d.,
2 3/4" h., each (ILLUS. p. 290)) **125**

Pitcher 6" h., 5" d., convex **300**

Salt & Pepper Shakers

Salt & pepper shakers, 1 1/2" d.,
2 1/2" h., pr. (ILLUS.) **2,400**

Tea steeper, tin cov., 5" d., 5" h. **225**

Teakettle, cov., wood & wire handle,
10" d., 7" h. **300**

Teakettle, cov., wood & wire handle,
Columbian Ware, 10 1/2" d., 7" h. . **625**

BROWN & WHITE SWIRL

Brown & White Swirl Coffee Biggin

Coffee biggin, tin biggin & cover,
3 1/2" d., 7 1/2" h. (ILLUS.) **1,000**

Coffeepot, cov., goose neck,
5 1/2" d., 9 1/2" h. **425**

Dish pan, oval, 14" w., 17 3/4" l.,
7" h. **280**

Brown Swirl Berlin-style Kettle

Kettle, cov., Berlin-style, wood & wire handle, 6 1/4" d., 4 1/4" h. (ILLUS.) **300**

Brown & White Swirl Pitcher

Pitcher, 5" d., 7 1/2" h. (ILLUS.) **500**

Roaster, cov., round, 12" d., 8 1/2" h. **300**

Spoon, 2 1/4" d., 13 1/4" h. **125**

Brown & White Swirl Spoon

Spoon, 9 3/4" l. (ILLUS.) **150**

Sugar bowl, cov., 4 1/4" d., 6" h. **900**

Wash basin, 10 1/2" d., 3 1/4" h. **125**

CHRYSOLITE & WHITE SWIRL (DARK GREEN & WHITE SWIRL)

Chrysolite Berry Bucket

Berry bucket, cov, wood & wire handle, 5" d., 5 1/4" h. (ILLUS.) **375**

Chrysolite Chamber Pot

Chamber pot, cov., 9" d., 6 3/4" h. (ILLUS.) **300**

Chrysolilte Coaster

Coaster, 3/4" h, 3 1/2" d. (ILLUS.).... **300**

Chrysolite Miner's Mug

Mug, miner's, tankard, 4 1/4" d., 5" h.
(ILLUS.) **200**

Pail, water, 9 1/2" d., 8" h.................. **225**

Chrysolite Cream Can

Cream can, w/tin cover, 4 1/2" d.,
7" h. (ILLUS.)................................. **700**

Cuspidor, 7 1/2" d., 4 1/4" h............. **400**

Double boiler, cov............................ **50**

Milk pan, 10" d., 2" h. **75**

Mug, railroad advertisement "C. & N.
W. Ry.," (Chicago & North Western
Railroad), 2 3/4" d., 2 3/4" h. **200**

Chrysolite Pitcher

Pitcher, tankard, 7" d., 12" h.
(ILLUS.) **600**

Chrysolite Skillet

Skillet, 1 3/4" h., 10 1/4" d. (ILLUS.). **300**

Soap dish, hanging, w/insert,
4 1/4 x 6", 3 1/4" h. **250**

COBALT BLUE & WHITE SWIRL

Berry bucket, cov., 6" d., 6" h. **325**

Cobalt Blue Swirl Candlestick

Candlestick, 5" d., 2 1/2" h. (ILLUS.) **950**

Cobalt Blue Swirl Coffeepot

Coffeepot, cov., wooden handle,
5 1/2" d., 9" h. (ILLUS.) **375**

Colander, footed, 9 1/2" d., 3 3/4" h. **300**

Cup & saucer, cup 2 1/4" h.,
4 1/4" d., saucer 6" d. **125**

Cobalt Blue Swirl Dinner Bucket

Dinner bucket, cov., three-piece,
7 1/4" d., 10 1/4" h. (ILLUS.)......... **1,000**

Cobalt Blue Swirl Dipper

Dipper, windsor, 5 1/4" d., 9 1/2"
handle (ILLUS.) **175**

Measurer, 2 3/4" d., 3 1/2" h.
(ILLUS.) **600**

Measurer, 3 1/2" d., 4 1/2" h.
(ILLUS.) **550**

Measurer, 4" d., 6 1/2" h. (ILLUS.) ... **500**

Measurer, 5" d., 8 1/4" h. (ILLUS.) ... **500**

Cobalt Blue Swirl Measurers

Cobalt Blue & White Swirl Muffin Pan

Muffin pan, eight-cup (ILLUS.).......... **385**

Pail, water, 11" d., 9" h. **200**

Platter, oval, 8" w., 12" l **275**

Sugar bowl, open, footed, 4 1/2" d.,
2 3/4" h. (ILLUS. below) **400**

Sugar bowl, cov., 4 1/2" d., 5 3/4" h.
(ILLUS. below).............................. **950**

EMERALD WARE
(GREEN & WHITE SWIRL)

Emerald Swirl Cream Can

Cream can, cov., wood & wire
handle, 5" d., 9 1/4" h. (ILLUS.)..... **850**

Jelly roll pan, 9" d., 1 1/4" h............. **100**

Emerald Ware Plate

Plate, dinner, 9" d. (ILLUS.) **225**

Sauce pan, cov., Berlin-style, 9" d.,
6 1/2" h. **250**

Emerald Swirl Skimmer

Skimmer, 5" d., 11" handle (ILLUS.)   **225**

Emerald Ware Syrup or Molasses Pitcher

Cobalt Blue Swirl Sugar Bowls

Syrup or molasses pitcher, cov.,
3 1/2" d., 6 1/4" h. (ILLUS.) **1,000**

GRAY (MOTTLED)

Candlestick, 6 1/4" d., 2" h. **280**

Canning Jar

Canning jar, 3 1/2" d., 4 1/2" h.
(ILLUS.) **400**

Octagonal Ansonia Clock

Clock, octagonal, Ansonia, works,
one of a kind, 9" d.................... **Priceless**

Cream can, tin cover, mottled steel
ware w/label, reads "EL-AN-GE,"
Boston **225**

Mottled Gray Creamer

Creamer, scalloped rim, pewter trim,
3 1/2" d., 6" h. (ILLUS.)................. **325**

Measuring cup, embossed "1 quart
liquid," labeled "Royal
Graniteware," 4 1/2" d., 6 1/4" h. .. **200**

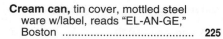

Mottled Gray Melon Mold

Gray Graniteware Teapots

Melon mold, w/tin cover (ILLUS.)..... **45**

Milk can, cov. **120**

Salt box w/original cover, hanging-
type... **245**

Scoop, sugar **45**

Soap dish, hanging, shell-shaped,
5 1/2" w., 2 1/2" h. **100**

Teakettle, cov., 5 3/4" d., 4" h. **200**

Teapot, cov., bulbous body, pewter
trim & cover, 7 1/4" d., 8 1/2" h...... **375**

Teapot, cov., 3 1/2" d., 5" d. (ILLUS.) **200**

Teapot, cov., straight spout,
3 1/2" d., 5" h. **200**

RED & WHITE SWIRL

Baking pan, 10 1/4 w., 15 1/4" l. **2,000**

Red Swirl Coffeepot

Coffeepot, cov., goose-neck,
5 1/4" d., 8 1/2" h. (ILLUS.) **2,000**

Dish pan, w/handles, 16" d., 7" h.
(ILLUS.) **1,500**

Sauce pan, wooden handle, swirl
inside & out, light weight,
ca. 1950s, 13" w., 17 1/2" l............ **140**

Teakettle, cov., light weight,
ca. 1960s, 8" d., 1 1/4" h., 6"
handle.. **80**

Red & White Swirl Dish Pan

SOLID COLORS

Berry bucket, cov., cream w/green
trim, 4 1/2" d., 5" h. **70**

Coffeepot, cov., cream w/green trim,
5 1/2" d., 7 3/4" h. **50**

Colander, footed, solid yellow
w/black trim, 10" d., 5" h. **35**

Ladle, white w/black trim & handle,
3" d., 9" handle **30**

Measuring cup, solid cobalt blue,
3 1/2" d., 4 3/4" h. **70**

Platter, oval, 10" w., 14" l., cream
w/green trim................................... **20**

Teakettle, cov., cream w/green trim,
8" d., 7" h...................................... **80**

MISCELLANEOUS GRANITEWARE & RELATED ITEMS

Bread raiser, tin cover, cobalt &
white mottled, 17 1/4" d., 11" h...... **275**

Chamber pot, cov., blue & white mottled, 8" d., 6 3/4" h. **125**

Cookbook, "Granite Iron Ware," dated 1883 .... **200**

Cookbook

Cookbook, "Granite Ware," dated 1883, 3 1/2" x 5" (ILLUS.).............. **200**

Hot plate, square, green w/yellow legs, ca. 1910, 6 1/4 x 9 x 9 .... **39**

Measuring cup, Shamrock Ware, dark green shading to a lighter green back to dark green, 3 1/2" d., 4 1/2" h. **200**

Mendets Store Display Box

Mendets box, store display (ILLUS.) **150**

Paperweight

Paperweight, stove advertising, gray enamel on cast iron, 2 1/2" d., 3 1/2" h. (ILLUS.)........................... **200**

Pot scraper, advertising, "Nesco and Pot Scraper," pictures Nesco boy holding Royal Granite Enameled Ware, 2 7/8" d., 3 1/2" h. **500**

Sign, advertising, "Nesco Enameled Ware," wooden w/light blue w/cobalt blue lettering, 34" l., 8 1/2" h. **300**

Advertising Sign

Sign, advertising, "Nesco Enameled Ware," wooden, light blue w/cobalt blue lettering, 34" l., 8 1/2" h. (ILLUS.) **350**

Advertising Tray

Tea strainer, blue & white mottled, screen bottom, 4 1/2" d., 6 3/4" h. . **155**

Tray, advertising, paper tip-type, "To the Patrons of Granite Iron Ware," copyright 1884, 7" w., 9 3/4" l. (ILLUS.) **250**

CHILDREN'S ITEMS, MINIATURES & SALESMAN'S SAMPLES

Saleman's Sample Chamber Pot

Chamber pot, salesman's sample, blue & white swirl, 2 1/2" d., 1 3/4" h. (ILLUS.)........................... **500**

Miniature Colanders

Colander, miniature, footed, blue w/white specks, 2 3/4" d., 1 1/4" h. (ILLUS. left) **325**

Colander, miniature, footed, solid blue, 3 1/4" d., 1 3/4" h. (ILLUS. right) **325**

Child's Feeding Dish

Dish, child's feeding, solid blue w/girl & Teddy bear, 1 1/4" h., 7 1/2" d. (ILLUS.) **85**

Miniature Percolator Funnel

Funnel, percolator, miniature, solid blue, white interior, 2 1/4" d., 3 3/4" h. (ILLUS.)........................... **200**

Miniature Tea Set

Grater, miniature, solid light blue,
1 3/4" d., 4 1/2" h. 175

Miniature Gravy Boat

Gravy boat, miniature, solid blue,
white interior, 1 1/2" h., 3 1/2" l.
(ILLUS.) 200

Saleman's Sample Gravy Kettle

Kettle, saleman's sample, gravy,
w/tin cov., 2 3/4" d., 3" h. (ILLUS.)   500

Miniature Molds

Mold, miniature, flutted, blue w/white
specks, 2 1/4" d. (ILLUS.).............   150

Mold, miniature, Turk's head, solid
blue, w/white interior, 2 1/4" d.
(ILLUS.) 225

Saleman's Sample Pitcher & Bowl Set

Pitcher & bowl set, salesman's
sample, gray, bowl 1 1/4" h.,
4 1/4" d., pitcher 2 1/4" d., 2 3/4" h.
(ILLUS.) 500

Tea set, miniature: cov. teapot, four
cups, four saucers, creamer, cov.
sugar, white w/blue design, teapot
3 1/4" d., 5 1/4" h., the set (ILLUS.)
.... 450

Wash basin, miniature, shaded blue
w/floral design, "Stewart Ware,"
4 1/2" d. 125

Wash basin, salesman's sample,
blue & white swirl, 4 1/2" d. 125

Wash basin, salesman's sample,
chrysolite & white swirl, 3 1/4" h. ... 235

K

Figural Dog Reamer

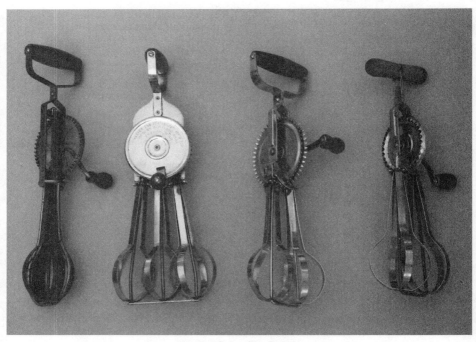

Aurelius Bros. Egg Beaters

KITCHENWARES

COFFEE MILLS

Coffee mills, commonly called grinders, are perfectly collectible for many people. They are appealing to the eye and are frequently coveted by interior decorators and today's coffee-consuming homeowners. Compact, intricate, unique, ornate, and rooted in early Americana, coffee mills are intriguing to everyone and are rich and colorful. Coffee milling devices have been available for hundreds of years. The Greek and Romans used rotating millstones for grinding coffee and grain. Turkish coffee mills with their familiar cylindrical brass shells appeared in the 15th century, and perhaps a century or two later came the earliest spice and coffee mills in Europe. Primitive mills were handmade in this country by blacksmiths and carpenters in the late 1700s and the first half of the 19th century. These were followed by a host of commercially-produced mills which included wood-backed side mills and numerous kinds of box mills, many with machined dovetails or fingerjoints. Characterized by the birth of upright cast-iron coffee mills, so beautiful with their magnificent colors and fly wheels, the period of coffee mill proliferation began around 1870. The next 50 years saw a staggering number of large

and small manufacturers struggling to corner the popular home market for box and canister-type coffee mills. After that, the advent of electricity and other major advances in coffee grinding and packaging technology hastened the decline in popularity of small coffee mills. Value-added features to look for when purchasing old coffee grinders include: • good working order and no missing, broken, or obviously replaced parts • original paint • attractive identifying markings, label or brass emblem • uncommon mill, rarely seen, or appealing unique characteristics • high quality restoration, if not original.—Mike White

BOX MILLS

Box mill, tall wood box w/iron top, cover & handle, w/side crank, top embossed "Arcade Mfg. Co. IXL" (ILLUS.) **$400**

Box mill, tapered iron box, English mill w/porcelainized hopper, marked "Kenrick & Sons Patent Coffee Mill" (ILLUS.) 150

Box mill, wood box w/embossed covered hopper, marked "Logan & Strobridge Pat' Coffee Mill," some damage to box (ILLUS. pg. 304) ... 80

Arcade Mfg. Co. IXL Coffee Mill

Kenrick & Sons Coffee Mill

Logan & Strobridge Coffee Mill

Arcade Coffee Mill

*Sun No. 1085 Challenge
Fast Grinder Coffee Mill*

Austrian Coffee Mill

Box mill, wood box w/handle on top, sunken tin hopper, label reads "Sun No. 1085 Challenge Fast Grinder" (ILLUS.) **140**

Box mill, wood box w/raised iron hopper & tin dust cover, straight handle, Arcade, unmarked (ILLUS.) **150**

Box mill, tapered wood box w/brass hopper, Austrian, 3 1/2 x 3 1/2" top (ILLUS.) **180**

Box mill, wood box w/tin dome & sliding cover, label marked "PeDe Dienes Mokka," 4 x 4" top (ILLUS.) **60**

Box mill, tapered cast-iron box w/brass hopper, marked "T. & C. Clark Co.," England, 4 1/2 x 4 1/2" top (ILLUS.) **250**

Box mill, all iron box w/original paint, raised hopper cover reads "Grand Union Tea Co.," 5 x 5" base (ILLUS.) **750**

Box mill, wood box w/wood hopper & pivoting wood cover, Peugot Freres, 51/2 x 51/2" top (ILLUS.)... **160**

PeDe Dienes Mokka Coffee Mill

Peugot Freres Coffee Mill

T & C Clark Co. Coffee Mill

Parker's National No. 30 Coffee Mill

Grand Union Tea Co. Coffee Mill

Parker's Eagle No. 314 Coffee Mill

Arcade No. 367 Coffee Mill

Box mill, iron top, handle & covered hopper, "Parker's National No. 30," 6 x 6" top (ILLUS. pg. 305) **160**

Box mill, tin hopper & red label reads "Parker's Eagle No. 314," 6 x 6" top (ILLUS. pg. 305) **90**

Box mill, wood box, tin hopper w/partial cover, well-marked "Arcade No. 367," 6 1/2 x 6 1/2" top (ILLUS.) **120**

Box mill, wood box, raised hopper w/pivoting cover, PS&W No. 350 (unmarked), 7 x 7" top (ILLUS.)...... **250**

PRIMITIVE COFFEE MILLS

G. Selsor Coffee Mill w/Pewter Hopper

Box mill, w/pewter hopper, signed "G. Selsor #2" on crank, 7 x 7" top (ILLUS.) **170**

Iron Coffee Mill

Iron mill, post-mounted blacksmith's-type, 5" open hopper (ILLUS.) **350**

SIDE MILLS

Side mill, iron, double grinding gear, Parker Union, unmarked (ILLUS.) . **130**

Side mill, w/sliding cover, "Kenrick & Sons (1815) Patent Coffee Mill" (ILLUS.) **150**

PS&W No. 350 Coffee Mill

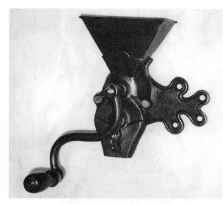

Parker Union Coffee Mill

Kenrick & Sons Coffee Mill

Wilson's Coffee Mill

L&S Brighton Coffee Mill

Side mill, w/wood back, "Increase Wilson's Best Quality No. 3" (ILLUS.) **100**

Side mill, w/wood block, marked "L&S Brighton" (ILLUS.) **90**

UPRIGHT MILLS

1898 Enterprise Mfg. Co. Coffee Mill

Upright mill, cast iron, covered hopper & double wheels, original red paint & decals, 1898 patent date, wheels embossed "Enterprise Mfg. Co, Philadelphia, U.S.A." (ILLUS.) **1,000**

Upright mill, cast iron, single-wheel mill w/wooden drawer & covered tin hopper, on wooden base, Elma, unmarked (ILLUS. pg. 308) **150**

Upright mill, cast iron, spread-winged eagle atop brass hopper, tin catcher, double wheels, original paint & decals, 1887 patent date, wheels embossed "Coles Mfg. Co., Phila. Pa.," model No. 8, eagle replaced (ILLUS. pg. 308) **1,200**

Elma Upright Coffee Mill

LF&C Universal No. 11 Coffee Mill

1887 Coles Mfg. Co. Coffee Mill

Cha's Parker Co. Coffee Mill

Upright mill, cast-iron w/covered
hopper, green w/gold trim, marked
"LF&C Universal No. 11" (ILLUS.).   **320**

Upright mill, cast-iron w/tin drawer,
sliding cover on hopper, double
wheels, original red, blue & gold
paint, 9" wheel embossed "The
Cha's Parker Co., Meriden, Conn.
U.S.A.," model No. 200 (ILLUS.) .. **1,200**

Upright mill, cast iron, spread-
winged eagle perched atop brass
hopper, w/double 11" wheels
repainted red, blue & gold,
replaced drawer, Enterprise No. 4
(ILLUS.) **600**

Upright mill, cast iron, w/wooden
drawer & tin covered hopper,
painted green w/gold trim, 13"
wheel w/gears, embossed "Peugot
Freres 2A, Brevetes S.G.D.G."
(ILLUS.) **450**

Upright mill, cast iron, decorative
   scrolls, w/brass hopper, crank &
   single wheel, black w/gold trim, 15"
   wheel embossed "Parnall & Sons,
   Bristol (England)" (ILLUS.) **1,000**

Parnall & Sons Coffee Mill

Enterprise No. 4 Upright Coffee Mill

"Golden Rule Blend" Wall Coffee Mill

Peugot Freres 2A Coffee Mill

WALL CANISTER MILLS

Wall canister mill, bronzed cast-iron canister w/glass window & cup, embossed canister reads "Golden Rule Blend Coffee The Finest Blend In The World, The Citizens Wholesale Supply Co., Columbus Ohio.," 18" h. (ILLUS. pg. 309) **450**

Universal 0012 Coffee Mill

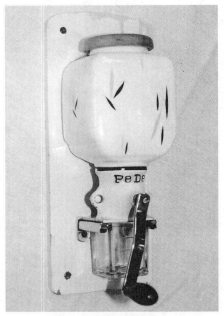

PeDe Wall Canister Coffee Mill

"Kaffee" Leinbrock Ideal DRGM Coffee Mill

Bronson-Walton Holland Beauty Coffee Mill

Wall canister mill, ceramic canister
w/glass cup, marked "PeDe"
(ILLUS.) **130**

Wall canister mill, ceramic canister
w/glass cup & wood backing
board, cannister marked
"KAFFEE," Leinbrock Ideal DRGM
(ILLUS.) **220**

Wall canister mill, steel canister
w/steel cup, green label reads
"Universal 0012 Coffee Mill Pat.
Feb. 14, 1905, Landers, Frary &
Clark, New Britain, Conn. U.S.A.,"
13" h. (ILLUS.).............................. **160**

Wall canister mill, tin lithographed
canister, pictures a young girl
wearing white dress, yellow apron
& bonnet, Bronson-Walton Holland
Beauty, 13" h. including cup
(ILLUS.) **350**

Wall canister mill, steel canister
w/glass cup, embossed "Pat 1891,"
Wilmont-Castle, 15" including
glass cup (ILLUS.)......................... **280**

Wall canister mill, glass canister &
cup, embossed "Enterprise No.
100," 16" h. (ILLUS.)..................... **180**

Enterprise No. 100 Coffee Mill

Wilmont-Castle Coffee Mill

Arcade Crystal No. 3 Coffee Mill

Wall canister mill, glass canister & cup, marked jar, Arcade Crystal No. 3, 18" h. (ILLUS. pg. 311) **350**

MISCELLANEOUS

Box mill, child's, gold painted hopper & crank, labeled "Little Tot," Arcade 21/2 x 21/2" top (ILLUS.)... **90**

Box mill, child's, painted tin, w/brass hopper, 3 x 3" top (ILLUS.)............ **70**

Clamp-on mill, open hopper, original red paint w/label, LF&C No. 01 (ILLUS.) **120**

Electric mill, aluminum hopper & tin catch can, red w/gold trim, Holwick 1/4 horsepower, 27" h. (ILLUS.) **180**

Turkish mill, brass, engraved cylindrical casing w/folding crank (ILLUS.) **50**

Clamp-on Coffee Mill

"Little Tot" Arcade Coffee Mill

Child's Coffee Mill

Holwick Electric Coffee Mill

Brass Turkish Coffee Mill

Landers, Frary & Clark Coffee Mill

Upright mill, miniature, cast-iron w/double wheels, red w/gold trim, embossed "ARCADE," 4" h. (ILLUS.) **150**

Wall mount mill, cast iron, open hopper & cup, repainted red, embossed "Landers, Frary & Clark," No. 001 (ILLUS.)................ **90**

EGG BEATERS

Eggbeaters are pure Americana! No other invention (although apple parers come close) represent America at its best from the mid-19th century to the 1930s or '40s. Eggbeaters tell the unbeatable story of America—the story of demand for a product, competition, success, retreat, failure, faith, and revival.

The mechanical (rotary) eggbeater is an American invention, and ranks up there with motherhood and apple pie, or at least up there where it counts—in the kitchen. American ingenuity produced more than 1,000 patents related to beating eggs, most before the 20th century.

To put it in perspective, try to imagine 1,000 plus ways to beat an egg. Here's a clue, and it's all due to Yankee tinkering: There are rotary cranks, archimedes (up and down)

Arcade Miniature Coffee Mill

models, hand-helds, squeeze power, and rope and water power—and others. If you ever wanted a different way to beat an egg it was (and is) available.

Today, eggbeaters are a very popular Americana kitchen collectible—a piece of America still available to the collector, although he/she may have to scramble to find the rare ones.

But, beaters are out there, from the mainstay A & J to the cast-iron Dover to the rarer Express and Monroe. There is always an intriguing mix, ranging in price from less than under $10.00 to the hundreds of dollars.

—Don Thornton

Items are listed alphabetically by manufacturer

A & J USA Ecko Egg Beater

A & J, ECKO, wood handle, rotary w/apron marked "A&J USA ECKO," on a two-cup measuring cup marked "A&J" (ILLUS.) **$35**

A & J, metal, rotary crank, marked "A&J Pat. Oct. 9, 1923 Made in U.S.A.," 8 1/4" to 10" **10-15**

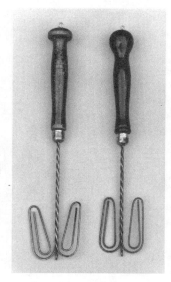

A & J Egg Beaters

A & J, archimedes "up & down" style, marked "Patd Oct. 15 07 Other Pat Pend'g," 9 1/4" (ILLUS. right) **35**

A & J, archimedes "up & down" style, marked "A & J Pat'd Oct. 15 07

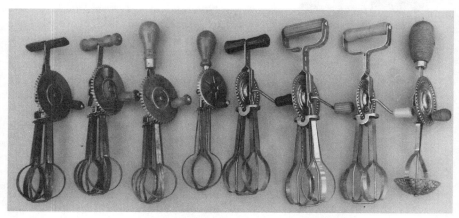

Various Androck Rotary Crank Beaters

Other Pats Pending," 12 1/2"
(ILLUS. left) 35

Androck, Bakelite handle, metal
rotary, marked "Androck," 11"
(ILLUS.) 30

Androck, metal rotary, wood handle,
marked "Androck," 11" (ILLUS.) 15

Androck, wood handle rotary
w/mesh dasher, marked "Another
Androck Product," 12" (ILLUS.) 55

Androck, plastic handle, rotary,
marked "Another Androck
Product," 12 1/2" (ILLUS.) 15

Aurelius Bros., wood handle, rotary
marked "Ideal Mille Lacs Mfg.
(Aurelius," 10 3/4" h. (ILLUS. right) 400

Aurelius Bros., wood handle, rotary,
rare triple dasher, rotary marked
"Master Egg Beater Mfd. By
Aurelius Bros., Braham, Minn. Pat.
Appld. For," 11 1/2" h. (ILLUS. left
center) 400

Aurelius Bros., wood handle, rotary
w/double gearing, marked
"Aurelius Bros., Braham, Minn.
Pat. Nov. 9, 1926," 11 1/2" h.
(ILLUS. left) 45

Aurelius Bros., wood handle, rotary
marked "Favorite Mfg. By Mille
Lacs Lake Spinner Co (Aurelius),"
11 3/4" h. (ILLUS. right center)...... 25

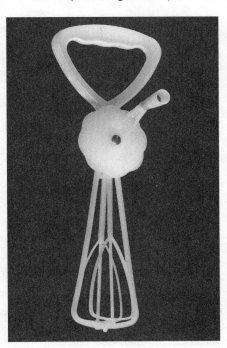

Blisscraft of Hollywood Egg Beater

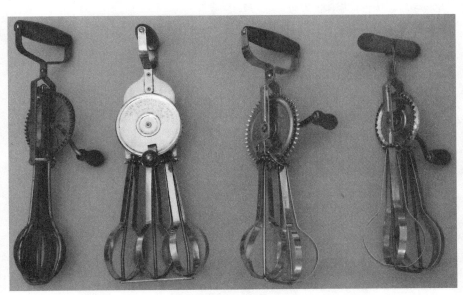

Aurelius Bros. Egg Beaters

Cylone Egg Beaters

Blisscraft of Hollywood, plastic, rotary, marked "Blisscraft of Hollywood Pat. USA Pend.," scarce, 12" h. (ILLUS. pg. 315) **75**

Cyclone, cast iron, rotary marked "Cyclone Pat. 6-25 and 7-16 1901," 11 1/2" h. (ILLUS. center two) **75**

Cyclone, cast iron, rotary marked "Cyclone Pat 6-25-1901 Reissue 8-26-1902," 13 1/2" h. (ILLUS. far left & right) **90**

Dover, cast iron, rotary tumbler model (smaller dashers to fit in glass or tumbler), marked "Dover Egg Beater Pat'd Made in Boston U.S.A.," 9" **80**

Dover, cast iron, nickel-plated, D-handle, rotary marked "Genuine Dover, Dover Stamping Co.," 11 1/4" h. **50**

Dover, cast iron, rotary marked "Dover Egg Beater Patd May 6th 1873 Apr 3d 1888 Nov. 24th 1891

Express Egg Beater w/Fly Swatter

Made in Boston U.S.A. Dover Egg
Beater Co.," 11 1/4" h.................... **50**

Dover, cast iron, rotary marked
"Dover Egg Beater Pat. May 31
1870," 12 1/2" h. **200**

Dream Cream, rotary turbine marked
"The Dream Cream Trade Mark
Whip Manufactured by A.D. Foyer
& Company Chicago," 10" h. **30**

Express, cast iron, rotary w/fly
swatter dasher, marked "Pat. Oct.
25, 1887" only, rare, 11 1/2" h.
(ILLUS.) **1,250**

F. Ashley, archemides, "up & down"
style, marked "F. Ashley Patent
Appl For," 15" **800**

Hand-held, plastic handle, marked
"Patent No. 2906510" **5**

Hand-held, all-wire, unmarked,
13" h. **35**

Holt-Lyon Egg Beater

Holt's Egg beater & Cream Whip (left); Holt-Lyon Side-handle Egg Beater (right)

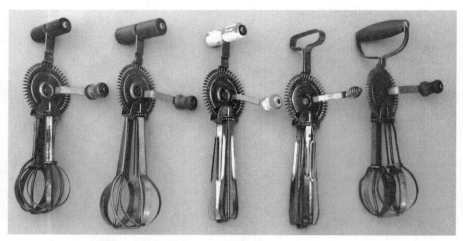

Various Ladd Egg Beaters

Holt-Lyon, cast iron, side-handle, marked "H-L Co.," 8 1/2" h. (ILLUS right p. 317) **225**

Holt-Lyon, cast iron, side-handle, marked "Holt's Egg Beater & Cream Whip Pat. Aug. 22-'98 Apr. 3-00," 8 1/2" h. (ILLUS. left p. 317) **200**

Holt-Lyon, cast-iron propeller, marked "Lyon Egg Beater Albany N.Y. Pat. Sep 7 '97," 10" h. (ILLUS. pg. 317) **120**

Jaquette Bros., scissors-type, cast iron, marked "Jaquette Bros No. 1," 7 1/2" l. **1,100**

Jaquette Bros., scissors-type, cast iron, marked "Jaquette Bros No. 2," 8 3/4" l. **900**

Ladd, metal rotary, marked "No. 0 Ladd Beater Pat'd July 7, 1908 Feb. 2 1915 United Royalties Corp.," 9 3/4" h. (ILLUS.) **15**

Ladd, wood handle, metal rotary, marked "No. 00 Ladd beater Patd Oct. 18, 1921 United Royalties Corp.," 11" l. (ILLUS.) **12**

Ladd, metal rotary, marked "No. 1 Ladd Beater July 7, 1908, Oct, 1921," 11 1/2" h. (ILLUS.)............. **15**

Ladd, tumbler model, metal rotary, marked "No. 5 Ladd Ball Bearing Beater Oct. 18 1921," 11 1/2" h. (ILLUS.) **35**

Ladd, beater held in two-part apron marked "Ladd No. 2," embossed on pedestal jar "Ladd Mixer No. 2," 13 1/2" h. **250**

Monroe Rotary Egg Beater

Monroe, cast-iron rotary, shelf mount, marked "EP Monroe patented April 19 1859," 10 1/2" h. (ILLUS.) **1,500**

P-D-&-Co., cast-iron rotary w/spring dasher bottom w/the word "E - A - S- Y" cut-out on spokes of main gear wheel & marked "Pat Sept. 28 26," 9 3/4" h. **1,000**

S & S Hutchinson, cast-iron rotary (w/Hutchinson cut-out in wheel) marked "Hutchinson New York Pat. apld For," glass apron on bowl embossed "130 Worth St. New York J. Hutchinson S&S Trade Mark," 9 1/2" h. **800**

S & S Hutchinson Rotary Egg Beater

Taplin Rotary Egg Beater

S & S Hutchinson, heavy tin rotary marked "S&S Hutchinson No. 2 New York Pat. Sept. 2, 1913," w/heavy tin apron on ribbed glass

jar embossed "National Indicator Co. No. 2 S&S Trade Mark Long Island City," 9 1/2" h. (ILLUS.) **500**

Taplin, cast-iron rotary, marked "The Taplin Mfg. Co. New Britian Conn, U.S.A Light Running Pat. Nov. 24 '08," 12 1/2" h. (ILLUS.) **45**

REAMERS

Once a staple in the American household during the 1920s-40s, manual juice reamers have again gained popularity as a hot commodity in todays collectible market. Although some wooden reamers date to the mid-1800s, the majority found today were produced during the reamers heyday. They range from American-made Depression glass and pottery to exquisitely painted ceramics and uniquely shaped figurals from far off places like Japan, France, Germany and Czechoslovakia. Lovely silverplate and sterling examples that once graced elegant Victorian tables now command hefty prices. Even the early electric and Deco chrome models of the 1950s have found a collectible niche.

Figural Clown Head Reamer

Ceramic, clown head in saucer, "Sourpuss," 4 3/4" d. (ILLUS.) .. **$100-125**

Ceramic, cream w/yellow & purple flowers & green leaves, two-piece, marked "Universal Cambridge, Ovenproof, Made In USA," 9 1/2" **175-195**

Ceramic, figure of clowns, reamer salt & pepper shakers, 2 1/2" - 3 3/4", marked "Japan" **20-35**

Ceramic, figure of dog, marked "Made in Japan," 4 3/4" h. (ILLUS.) **325-350**

Ceramic, green pitcher w/blue & green flowers & brown trim, w/six matching juice cups, marked "Hand Painted Japan," 8 1/2" h. (ILLUS.) **40-60**

Figural Dog Reamer

Ceramic Pitcher Reamer

Figural Orange Reamer

Ceramic, lustre w/red & yellow flowers, two-piece, marked "Made in Japan," 2" h. **95-125**

Ceramic, model of orange w/yellow & blue flowers & green leaves, "Kiddies Orange Juice," two-piece, marked "Germany," 4" h. (ILLUS.) **125-135**

Crown Ducal Chintz Reamer

Ceramic, sauce-boat shaped, blue chintz/multicolored flowers, marked "Crown Ducal, Made in England," 3 1/2" h., 8" l. (ILLUS.)**350-400**

Ceramic, saucer-shaped, cream, tan & maroon w/blue trim, England, 3 1/4" d **90-100**

Ceramic, white w/multi-colored flowers & gold trim, tab handle, 4 3/4" d. **185-200**

Glass, blue w/white opalescent trim, tab handle, Fry, 4" d. **165-185**

McKee Glass Reamer

Glass, butterscotch, embossed "SUNKIST," marked "Pat. No. 18764 Made in USA," McKee Glass Co., 6" d. (ILLUS.) **850**

Glass, cobalt blue criss-cross, Hazel Atlas Glass Co., 6 1/8" d. **275-300**

Glass, Jade-ite, McKee Glass Co., 6" d. (ILLUS.) **25-35**

McKee Jade-ite Reamer

Jeannette Glass Reamer with Measure

Glass, Jade-ite, two-piece, two-cup measure, Jeannette Glass Co., 6 1/4" h. (ILLUS.)........................... **20-25**

Metal, one piece w/levered handle, marked "Super Juicer," 6" h.......... **30-40**

Metal, "Seald Sweet Juice Extractor," tilt model, w/clamp-on base, 13" h. **60-75**

Metal and glass, amber, "Party Line" cocktail shaker, Paden City, 9 1/4" h. **95-125**

Metal and glass, green bowl & cone, "Mount Joy," green metal base w/clamp, 11" h. **165-185**

Metal & glass, green w/white milk glass bowl, ceramic cone, marked "Sunkist Jucit Refined," electric, 8 3/4" h. **45-55**

Silver Plate Reamer

Silver plate, engraved design, marked "Apollo, E.P.N.S., Made in USA By Bernard Rice's Sons, Inc., 4492, Etchardt, Design Pat'd. Apr 22, '24," 4 3/4" d. (ILLUS.)......... **125-150**

Silver Plate & Wood Reamer

Silver plate & wood, England, 7 3/4" h. (ILLUS.)....................... **175-200**

Wood, hand-held, 6 1/4" l. **30-40**

Wood, hinged, hand-held, 10" l. **40-50**

Little Swan Iron

LAUNDRY ROOM ITEMS

IRONS

What is the spark that inspires an interest in accumulating antique pressing irons? Once the mysterious process is in action, you are changed to the dedicated and possessed individual known as a collector.

One iron is not a collection. It seems lonely by itself. Perhaps it would be happier if others joined it. A collection begins to coalesce.

Most beginners start with common irons. Some remain at the entry level without moving to explore the higher delights of collecting. There is a tendency to acquire only one iron of a type and this is a common mistake. A representative collection should include a range of irons. Look for scarcity, attractiveness, interest and condition; emphasize quality. If you have pride in your collection, insist on the best and don't buy anything broken.

A quest for irons will lead to antiques shows, auctions and flea markets. These are chances to be exposed to various kinds of irons, possibly seeing one that will lead in an entirely new direction. Do not overlook any opportunity to get acquainted with the market. The real education begins by talking to other collectors, reading books and periodicals.

Traditionally, irons are used as book ends and doorstops and they look especially at home on the hearth or mantel. The more decorative pieces are proudly displayed where they can be seen in the entryway, living and dining rooms. Some of the finer irons were originally designed to be shown and admired. Today they still fulfill that purpose as well as they did when originally made a century or two ago.

By collecting irons, you are not only engaging in an absorbing hobby, but you are preserving the cultural and historical interest of antique pressing irons

-Jimmy Walker

Box iron, brass body, swivel gate, Germany **$175**

Box iron, brass body w/lift gate & wood handle, Northern Europe **110**

Belgian Box Iron and Trivet

Box iron, iron body w/brass trivet, drop in slug, wood handle, Belgium (ILLUS.) **750**

Box iron, lift-gate, pierced screw secure uprights, England, 18th c... **150**

Horton's Charcoal Iron Model #7

Charcoal iron, cast iron, Horton's Iron Model #7, patented, late 19th c. (ILLUS.) **85-100**

Charcoal iron, double chimney, marked "Ne Plus Ultra," pat. by George Finn July 9, 1902 .... **275**

Charcoal iron, marked "Queen
Carbon Sad Iron"........................... **400**

Combination iron, cast iron, marked
"Acme Carbon," w/fluter on side of
iron, w/wood handle **350**

Combination iron, charcoal
w/chimney, fluter bed on side,
unmarked **275**

Combination iron, fluter/sad iron
w/wire latch, Charles Anderson
Patent 1871 .... **150**

Electric iron, Art Deco-style,
streamlined body w/black handle &
red & black cord, marked
"Petipoint" (ILLUS.)........................ **175**

Electric iron, General Mills w/steam
attachment.................................... **40**

Fluter, crank, cast iron, w/C-clamp,
marked "Crown" on base, Pat.
Nov. 2, 1875 (ILLUS.).................... **150**

Fluter, crank, marked "American,"
Pat. Nov. 2, 1875........................... **150**

Fluter, mechanical, cast-iron frame
w/double rollers & side crank
handle w/wooden grip, includes
heating irons, clamp, lead inserts &
hand protector, 19th c., the set
(ILLUS.) **250-275**

Fluter, rocking, cast iron, marked
"Geneva Hand Fluter" on rocker,
"Heat This Pat'd 1866" on base
(ILLUS.) **55**

Art Deco Electric Iron

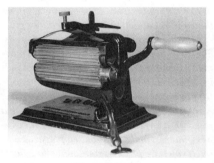

"Crown" Fluter

Fluter with Accessories

Early Sears Fuel Iron

"Geneva Hand Fluter"

Fuel iron, iron base w/round tank mounted on top of iron, wood handle, Sears (ILLUS.)................. 250

Little iron, model of a cross rib, 2 1/2" 50

Little Swan Iron

Little iron, cast iron, figure of a swan, 5" l. (ILLUS.)........................ 700

Polisher, cast iron w/embossed star on top of body, marked "Geneva".. 65

Sad iron, cast iron, coiled handle, marked "Ferris Cold Handle," Pat. Oct. 6, 1891, St. Louis (ILLUS.) 250

Sad iron, cast iron, w/grid-like design on handle & star embossed on top of body, common 15

"Ferris Cold Handle" Sad Iron

Sad iron, detachable handle, bentwood, marked "Bless & Drake" 190

Sad iron, detachable handle, Enterprise, A.C. Williams & others   25

Sad iron, dolphin handle   45

Sleeve iron, 'duck bill' model, marked "Geneva" on body & "GENEVA Pat. applied for" on toe .   450

Tailor iron, cast iron, marked "Sensible" w/removable wood & iron handle, 20 lb. 275

Tailor iron, advertising-type, cast iron, embossed "J. A. Griffith & Co. Baltimore," 3 1/2" 250

LIGHTING DEVICES

ALADDIN® MANTLE LAMPS

The Mantle Lamp Company of America, creator of the world famous Aladdin Lamp, was founded in Chicago in 1908. Like several of its competitors, the Aladdin coupled the round wick technology with a mantle to produce a bright incandescent light comparable to the illumination provided by a 60 to 75 watt bulb.

Through aggressive national advertising and an intensive dealer network, the Aladdin Lamp quickly overcame its competitors to become the standard lighting fixture in the rural American home. From the company's origin until 1926, Aladdin Lamps were produced in table, hanging, and wall bracket styles made mostly of brass and finished in either satin brass or nickel plate.

With the purchase of an Indiana glass plant in the mid-1920s, the Mantle Lamp Company began to make their own glass shades and chimneys, in addition to the manufacture of glass lamp bases. Glass shades, both plain and decorated with reverse painting, were made in a variety of styles. Later, colorful parchment shades were produced in a myriad of colors and with decorations ranging from large, gaudy flowers in the early 1930s to delicate florals and intricate geometrics, sometimes with flocking, from the mid-1930s through the post-war years.

Aladdin kerosene lamps are probably best known for the colorful glass bases made from the late 1920s to the early 1950s. The earliest glass lamps were vase lamps that consisted of a glass vase finished in different colors that had a drop-in brass kerosene font. Later, seventeen different glass patterns were produced and most patterns were offered in a variety of different glass colors. Crystal glass lamp bases commonly came in clear, green, or amber colors, but for a few years crystal bases were produced in ruby red and cobalt blue. The latter two colors are especially prized by collectors.

A translucent to opaque glass called moonstone was produced during the 1930s and was available in white, green, rose, and for one pattern in the late 1930s, yellow. A few styles had white moonstone fonts attached to a black stem and foot. Other lamps had a moonstone font mounted on a metallic base. An ivory to white glass called Alacite is unique to the Aladdin Lamp.

The late 1930s glass formula contained uranium oxide, and the ivory to marble-like appearance sometimes leads to its confusion with the Crown Tuscan glass of Cambridge. With the commencement of the Manhattan Project, this compound was placed on the restricted list and, as a consequence, the glass formula was changed.

Early Alacite lamp bases will glow under a blacklight, whereas later ones will not. The later Alacite lamps also tend toward a white color rather than ivory.

Aladdin kerosene lamps are still being made today. The Mantle Lamp Company left Chicago in 1948 and was absorbed into Aladdin Industries, Inc. In April, 1999, the Aladdin Mantle Lamp Company was formed in Clarksville, TN. The new limited partnership produces kerosene lighting for domestic and foreign markets and supplies/accessories for older lamps.

Aladdin kerosene lamps and their related accessories have been avidly collected over the last thirty years. As a consequence, prices have risen steadily even for the common lamps. Expectedly, condition of the lamp or shade is a very important consideration in determination of value. Glass damage, electrification, or missing parts can seriously depreciate value. By comparison, lamps in mint, unused condition and in the original carton fetch premium prices.
—Thomas W. Small

A

Aladdin Hanging Lamp

Hanging lamp, decorated w/hand painted roses on ball shade, Model No. 6 (ILLUS.) **$4,000-4,500**

Student lamp, original w/functional tank, unelectrified, Model No. 4 (ILLUS.) **7,000-8,000**

Aladdin Table Lamp, Model No. 8

Table lamp, brass finish, No. 8 flame spreader & No. 401 shade, Model No. 8 (ILLUS.) **425-475**

Table lamp, nickel finish, No. 10 flame spreader, Model No. 10 ... **400-450**

Table lamp, nickel plated, No. 6 flame spreader, Model No. 6 ..... **80-100**

Aladdin Student Lamp

Aladdin Table Lamp, Model No. 1

Table lamp, nickel plated w/embossed foot, 1/2 qt. font, Model No. 1 (ILLUS. p. 327)...... **600-700**

Vase lamp, blue variegated, gold foot edge, three feet, 10 1/4"..... **600-650**

Vase lamp, green w/dark green foot edge, model No. 12, six feet, 10 1/4" h. **200-250**

Aladdin Vase Lamp

Vase lamp, peach variegated, gold foot edge, three feet, 101/4" (ILLUS.) **275-325**

Vase lamp, variegated green, gold foot edge, three feet, 101/4"...... **300-350**

B

Table lamp, Beehive patt., clear, Model B **100-125**

Table lamp, Beehive patt., green or amber crystal............................ **125-175**

Table lamp, Cathedral patt., green or amber crystal............................ **150-200**

Table lamp, Cathedral patt., rose moonstone................................ **400-450**

Table lamp, Cathedral patt., white moonstone................................ **350-400**

Table lamp, Corinthian patt., amber or green crystal.......................... **100-125**

Table lamp, Corinthian patt., clear **80-100**

Table lamp, Corinthian patt., white moonstone font w/green, rose or black foot **250-300**

Table lamp, Diamond Quilted patt., green moonstone **250-300**

Table lamp, Lincoln Drape patt., short, amber or ruby crystal w/metal collar at font top **100-125**

Table lamp, Lincoln Drape patt., short, ruby crystal, raised glass collar at font top...................... **900-1,000**

Table lamp, Lincoln Drape patt., tall, cobalt blue, foot top w/circular ring **1,600-1,800**

Table lamp, Lincoln Drape patt., tall, cobalt blue, scalloped ring on foot top **1,900-2,100**

Table lamp, Lincoln Drape patt., tall, ruby crystal, lower value for light ruby, higher for dark **850-1,100**

Table lamp, Lincoln Drape patt., tall, slightly tapered stem, Alacite..... **125-175**

Aladdin Table Lamp, Orientale Pattern

Table lamp, Orientale patt., ivory, green, or bronze enamel, metallic finish (ILLUS.)............................. **125-150**

Table lamp, Queen patt., green, white, or rose moonstone on metallic foot **250-350**

Table lamp, Simplicity patt., Alacite, green or white enamel............... **150-175**

Table lamp, Simplicity patt., rose enamel....................................... **175-200**

Table lamp, Solitaire patt., white moonstone............................ **2,800-3,500**

Table lamp, Venetian patt., clear, fused stem-foot/bowl, Model A .. **350-400**

Table lamp, Venetian patt., clear, green or peach enamel **125-150**

Table lamp, Venetian patt., white enamel....................................... **100-125**

Table lamp, Vertique patt., green moonstone................................. **450-500**

Table lamp, Vertique patt., yellow moonstone................................. **600-650**

Table lamp, Victoria patt., ceramic w/floral decoration & gold bands **600-650**

Table lamp, Washington Drape patt., clear crystal, plain stem, w/or without oil fill **75-100**

Table lamp, Washington Drape patt., clear, green, or amber w/open, thick round stem **100-150**

Table lamp, Washington Drape patt., green or amber crystal, plain stem **100-150**

MISCELLANEOUS

Chimneys, boxed (ILLUS., left pair) each.. **75-100**

    Others, (ILLUS.) each.................. **25-40**

Mantles, boxed (ILLUS., center) each.. **5-15**

Mantles, boxed (ILLUS., left p. 330) each... **75-125**

Mantles, boxed (ILLUS., right p. 330) each.. **40-60**

Matchholder, copper w/accessories & instruction booklet (ILLUS. p. 330) **100-150**

Shades, floral, No. 601F roses **600-700**

Shades, green cased, No. 202 artichoke, No. 204 eight panel **800-1,000**

Shades, plain, No. 201, No. 301, No. 401, No. 501 (for Model No. 11), No. 601 .... **100-125**

Shades, plain, opal No. 205 w/fire polished bottom rim **400-500**

Aladdin Lamp Chimneys

Aladdin Mantles

Shades, reverse painted, No. 601
Log Cabin, No. 616 Gristmill, No.
620 Windmill............................. **300-350**

Shades, reverse painted, No. 616F
poppies, No. 620F roses **800-1,000**

Shades, Whip-O-Lite parchment,
floral, geometric, or scenic, 14" . **150-200**

Wicks, boxed, mounted, (ILLUS., left
stack) each **30-40**

Wicks, boxed, No. 11 & No. 12,
(ILLUS., right center & right) each **10-20**

Wicks, boxed, No. 6, mounted
(ILLUS., left center) each **20-25**

Aladdin Wicks

Aladdin Matchholder

Aladdin Wicks

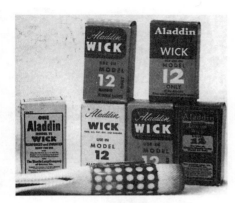

Aladdin Wicks

KEROSENE & RELATED LIGHTING

   Kerosene lamps were used from about 1860 until replaced by electric lighting when it became available. In cities and towns this was generally from about the turn-of-the-century until 1920. Rural electrification occurred in the 1930s or later.Today, kerosene lamps are sought after for their appearance and function. Some owners light them occasionally, while a few enjoy them every night. Certainly experimenting with the lamps can add another dimension to collecting. Try placing lamps strategically—not just to illuminate a room but to create dramatic shadows.If a hanging lamp is the only source of illumination in a room, patterns of light and shadow and perhaps colors will be

Pre-Kerosene Lamps

splayed out on the ceilings and walls. The flickering of an open flame will create shadows in motion which can give a favorite piece of folk art or furnishings, such as a clock or collectible, a different nighttime look. Natural wood finishes which can look flat under incandescent light will glow with a warm sheen to create the mood of a century ago. Most examples shown here are ones that would have been relatively inexpensive when they were made and are compatible with country furnishings. There was tremendous competition and production in the kerosene lamp business. This led to the creation of an astounding variety of lamps and accessories. Because electric lighting was not perfect, kerosene lamps were preserved for emergencies. Thus Americans are blessed with a good supply and an appreciation that will ensure a continuing demand.
— *Catherine Thuro-Gripton*

Note: Lamps do not include burner & chimney, unless otherwise noted.

Polka Dot Pattern Kerosene Hand Lamp

PRE-KEROSENE LAMPS

Hand lamp, pressed waffle design, flared font w/applied handle, burning fluid burner, ca. 1850 (ILLUS., right) 250

Table lamp, free-blown squatty bulbous font above a flared columnar standard, w/whale oil burner, ca. 1850 (ILLUS., left) ... 225-250

Table lamp, pressed Star-and-Punty patt, slightly flared font w/smooth domed top, w/burning fluid burner, ca. 1850 (ILLUS., center) 300-325

KEROSENE LAMPS

Hand lamp, blue opalescent pressed glass, Sheldon Swirl patt., footed
.... 550-650

Hand lamp, blue pressed glass, Whirlpool patt., footed 250-300

Hand lamp, clear pressed glass, Bullseye patt............................. 125-150

Various Kerosene Hand Lamps, Quartered Block Pattern

Hand lamp, clear pressed glass, Polka Dot patt., ovoid font decorated w/opalescent cranberry or ruby dots, applied handle, all above circular domed base, kerosene burner & baluster-shaped chimney w/slightly scalloped rim (ILLUS.) .... **1,550 and up**

Hand lamp, clear glass, Quartered Block patt., w/handle, footed, kerosene burner & "pie crust" chimney, ca. 1880s (ILLUS., far right) **150-200**

Hand lamp, clear pressed glass, Quartered Block patt., w/handle, flat bottom, kerosene burner & "pie crust" chimney, ca. 1880s (ILLUS., center) **150-200**

Hand lamp, clear glass, Ribbed patt., globular font w/applied handle, ca. 1850s-1870s (ILLUS., right front) **125-150**

Hand lamp, clear pressed glass, Ribbed patt., bulbous globular font tapering into flared foot, ca. 1850s-1870s (ILLUS., center front) **75-100**

Hand lamp, clear pressed glass, Ribbed patt., squatty bulbous font, applied handle, ca.1850s-1870s (ILLUS., left front) **75-100**

Atterbury & Co. Kerosene Hand Lamp

Hand lamp, clear pressed glass, squatty ovoid font w/ribbed center ring, tapering to domed foot w/applied handle, patented, marked, Atterbury & Co., ca. late 1860s-1870s (ILLUS.) **75-100**

Hand lamp, milk glass, flared foot below angular font w/handle & wide lip below clear glass top, Collin's burner & milk glass Sun chimney tapering at top, Adams & Company, rare complete (ILLUS.) **1,200-1,500**

Assorted Kerosene Hand Lamps, Ribbed Pattern

Adams & Co. Kerosene Hand Lamp

Hand lamp, tin & glass, painted tin w/handle & removable glass font, w/Columbia burner & cylindrical glass chimney combination, font & holder marked "Bradley's Security Factory Lamp" (ILLUS., left) **250-300**

Adjustable Hanging Kerosene Lamp

Hanging lamp, adjustable, cast iron & glass, elaborately cut-out cast-iron arms holding two lamps, etched glass fonts decorated w/star- and cross-like designs, glass chimneys & glass shades, original finish & shades, ca. 1860s-1880s (ILLUS.) **1,500-2,000**

Mechanical lamp, Wanzer Mechanical lamp, metal base w/forced draft for operation even without a shade, shown w/a 5" d. opalescent Hobnail shade (ILLUS., far right), lamp base only **550-650**

Mechanical lamp, Wanzer Mechanical lamp, metal base w/forced draft for operation even without a shade, shown w/a 5" d. opalescent Hobnail shade (ILLUS., far right), shade only .... **100 and up**

Parlor lamp, milk glass, squatty ovoid shade tapering to slightly flaring rim above squatty pear-shaped bottom, both decorated w/raised & painted flowers, ca. 1880s-1890s (ILLUS.) .... **325 and up**

Kerosene Lamps

Kerosene Parlor Lamp

Parlor Vase Lamp

Parlor vase lamp, globular white glass shade w/hand-painted roses w/cylindrical glass chimney, above baluster-shaped vase w/scroll-cut lip & scrolled handles, all on elaborately scroll-cut footed base (ILLUS.) **375**

Student Lamp

Student lamp, brass & glass, cylindrical chimney w/milk glass shade, original finish & parts, kerosene burner, ca. 1879 (ILLUS.) **600-700**

Student lamp, brass & glass, Manhattan Brass Co., original nickel-plate base & cased green glass shade (ILLUS., center back) .... **450 and up**

Table lamp, clear blown glass, globular font, brass standard on square marble base, or chimney, the appropriate chimneys & burners (as shown here) could easily double or triple the value, ca. 1860s (ILLUS., w/chimney & burner p. 336), lamp w/burner & chimney **225-275**

Table lamp, clear blown glass, globular font, brass standard on square marble base, or chimney, the appropriate chimneys & burners (as shown here) could easily double or triple the value, ca. 1860s (ILLUS., w/chimney & burner), burners & chimney only .... **150 and up**

Table lamp, clear pressed glass, Bullseye & Fleur-de-lis patt., font tapering to baluster-shaped standard, late 1860s (ILLUS.) ... **150-200**

Table lamp, clear pressed glass, Chadwick patt., w/milk glass base **175-200**

Bullseye & Fleur-de-Lis Table Lamp

Corn Pattern Table Lamp

Blown Glass Table Lamps

Table lamp, clear pressed glass, Corn patt., ovoid font tapering to ridge at top w/bulging below burner, glass standard & base, marked w/patent date of 1873, La Belle Glass Company, Bridgeport, Ohio (ILLUS.) **175-225**

Table lamp, clear pressed glass, Corn-in-Shield patt., Oval Band patt. base................................. **175 -225**

Table lamp, clear pressed glass, Daisy and Button patt., glass font w/domed top & angled bottom above paneled standard & base, ca. 1890s (ILLUS.) **100-125**

Table lamp, clear pressed glass, Eyewinker patt., cylindrical font above baluster-shaped standard & base, Dalzell, Gilmore & Leighton Company (ILLUS.).................... **125-150**

Daisy & Button Table Lamp

Gaiety Table Lamp

Table lamp, clear pressed glass, Gaiety patt., angular ribbed font decorated w/opalescent feathered design, cylindrical glass standard on circular base, kerosene burner & baluster-shaped chimney w/scalloped rim (ILLUS.) **425-500**

Table lamp, clear pressed glass, McKee Tulip patt. .... **300 and up**

Table lamp, clear pressed glass, Moon and Crescents patt., w/brass stem & marble base **300-350**

Eyewinker Pattern Table Lamp

Ewing Patent Table Lamp

Table lamp, clear pressed glass, ovoid font above Ewing patent drip catcher above clear glass baluster-shaped standard, ca. 1870s (ILLUS.) **200-250**

Table lamp, clear pressed glass, Quartered Block patt., one-piece, kerosene burner & "pie crust" chimney, ca. 1880s **125-150**

Table lamp, clear pressed glass, Ribbed patt., globular font, columnar standard w/flared ribbed base, ca. 1850s-1870s **125-150**

Table lamp, clear pressed glass, Ribbed patt., inverted pear-shaped font, on baluster-shaped standard, ca. 1850s-1870s **125-150**

Table lamp, clear pressed glass, Riverside Wild Rose patt. **250-300**

Table lamp, clear pressed glass, Sawtooth patt., globular font w/diamond-like pattern on lower half, tapering brass connector, slightly flared columnar milk glass standard & base, includes burner & tall, thin cylindrical chimney (ILLUS.) **300-350**

Table lamp, clear & cranberry opalescent pressed glass,

Snowflake patt., squatty ovoid font in opalescent cranberry, above ribbed clear standard, Hobbs (ILLUS.) **650-750**

Sawtooth Pattern Table Lamp

Snowflake Pattern Table Lamp

Veronica Pattern Table Lamp

Table lamp, clear pressed glass (on inside of lamp), Veronica patt., ovoid font tapering to brass standard on a marble base, Hobbs Brockunier & Company, ca. mid-1860s - mid-1870s (ILLUS.) **150-200**

Cut-overlay Table Lamp

Table lamp, cut-overlay, inverted pear font in white cut to green, tapering brass connector, tapering to slightly flared columnar green alabaster standard & base, (ILLUS.) .... **1,800 and up**

Table lamp, figural, angular etched clear glass font w/star- and cross-like designs, above spelter fisherwoman holding spear w/a basket full of fish at her feet, all on tiered square base, Bradley & Hubbard Mfg., ca. 1888 (ILLUS.)**250-300**

Figural Table Lamp

Empress Eugenie Table Lamp

Table lamp, figural, clear frosted
glass font w/Greek Key design
above spelter bust of Empress
Eugenie (wife of Napoleon III),
ca. 1870s (ILLUS. p. 339) **175-225**

Table lamp, figural, clear pressed
glass font & spelter figure of Mary
& her Lamb.............................. **125-225**

Table lamp, green pressed glass,
Vera patt. **175-225**

Table lamp, marigold Carnival
pressed glass, Zipper Loop patt.
.... **750-850**

Table lamp, Ripley Wedding Lamp,
blue & clear pressed glass, two
matching blue fonts flanking
toothpick holder, above white glass
base.................................... **1,800 and up**

Lightning Rod Balls

These decorative glass ornaments were used to dress-up lightning rods used on the farm structures and homes of rural America. Many were round with embossed designs such as stars or swirls but some were odd shapes. Amber and dark blue were fairly common colors but other rarer colors can also be found. Today there is a serious core of collectors for these fascinating glass objects and values depend on the rarity of the shape and color. Our thanks to Phil Steiner of Weather or Knot Antiques, Wanatah, Indiana for the information and illustrations provided.

An asterisk (*) indicates a piece which has been reproduced.

*Amber mast (ILLUS., top left)......... $600

*Amber RHF (ILLUS., top right)........ 750

Chestnut, milk glass, blue................ 60

Chestnut, milk glass, white.............. 35

Chestnut, red 200-350

*D&S, cobalt blue............................. 200

*Diddie Blitzen, orange, marked "BLITZEN" (ILLUS., bottom left) ... 1,750

Doorknob, milk glass, blue............... 60

Doorknob, milk glass, white 35

Flat quilt patt., grey green mercury (ILLUS., top center) 750

Hawkeye, amber.............................. 250

Hawkeye, bright orange (ILLUS., center middle row)........................ 2,750

Hawkeye, milk glass, blue 85

Hawkeye, milk glass, white.............. 65

Assorted Lightning Rod Balls

Hawkeye, sun-colored amethyst 200

Moon & Star patt., amber (ILLUS., top right) 200

*Moon & Star patt., cobalt blue (ILLUS., bottom left) ....

Moon & Star patt., gold (ILLUS., center) 600

Moon & Star patt., milk glass, flash blue over white (ILLUS., top left) ... 225

Moon & Star patt., milk glass, grey, rare (ILLUS., bottom right)............ 8,500

Moon & Star patt., milk glass, orange, rare (ILLUS., bottom center) 5,000

Moon & Star patt., red (ILLUS., left center) 450

Moon & Star patt., silver (ILLUS., right center) 650

Moon & Star patt., sun-colored amethyst (ILLUS., top center) 150

Onion-shaped, cobalt blue (ILLUS., left center) 2

Plain, milk glass, white, 3 1/2" 25

Plain, "7-Up" green, 4 1/2" 200

Plain, amber, 4 1/2" 45

Plain, cobalt blue, 4 1/2" 80

Plain, flashed orange, 4 1/2" (ILLUS., bottom right) 600

Plain, milk glass, blue, 4 1/2" 35

Plain, milk glass, white, 4 1/2" 25

Plain, red, 4 1/2" 60-100

Plain, sun-colored amethyst, 4 1/2" .. 40

Swirl patt., cobalt blue (ILLUS., right center) 2,500

Various Moon & Star Patt. Lightning Rod Balls

R

Cat & Birds Hooked Rug

Leopard Hooked Rug

Tiger & Foliage Hooked Rug

RUGS - HOOKED & OTHER

HOOKED

Cat & Birds Hooked Rug

Cat & birds, central diamond-form reserve of a seated cat w/perched bird spandrels, worked in gold, terra-cotta, taupe, red & light grey on a black & grey field, American, late 19th - early 20th c., mounted, minor hole, fading, 24 1/2 x 43" (ILLUS.) **$1,265**

Cat & kitten, black animals on white center, surrounded by floral design in black, white, green, yellow, red, blue & brown, backed for hanging, faded colors, wear & repair, 24" w., 29 1/2" h. **605**

Cats & ball of yarn, three cats in white & grey playing w/a ball of yarn against a magenta ground w/blue & white narrow edge stripes, cats named on border "Skeeks," "Shasta" & "Minnie," mounted on a stretcher, 21 x 33 1/2" (wear, minor damage & color bleeding) **468**

Centennial designs, dated 1776-1876, the variegated scrolling border enclosing a foliate reserve, worked in blue, red, brown, camel, taupe, green, purple & grey, backed, 38 x 70 1/2" (minor repairs, staining & fading).............. **460**

Cottage scene, a white cottage w/green shutters, signed "1936 Gussman's Essex N.Y.," worked in green, white, sage, yellow, orange, red & blue yarns, 26 1/2 x 35 1/2" (some fading) **173**

Dog, rectangular w/center off-white oval w/standing black Scottie dog wearing a collar, surrounded by a scalloped black border w/stylized red, blue & green floral spray in each corner, 20 x 31 1/2" **413**

Dog sled scene, rectangular snowy landscape w/two people w/a dog sled team, Grenfell label on reverse, Newfoundland or Labrador, early 20th c., 27 1/4 x 39" (minor fading, staining, very minor losses) **2,185**

Eagle & laurel branches, rectangular, a spread-winged American eagle clutching arrows in brown & white against a blue ground w/white stars & within a shaped oblong reserve w/a wide yellow frame w/red & green laurel leaves & flowers, dark brown outer ground, 38 x 51" (soiling, stains, some overall & edge wear)........... **303**

Geometric design, rectangular w/a center design of triangles & wide ribbons bordered by a circular & oval pattern, worked in shades of brown, blue, & grey on a black field, 27 x 43" (some wear) **495**

Hearts & Floral Hooked Rug

Hearts & floral, heart border enclosing field of large stylized floral design w/a heart in each corner, centering "Hattie," worked in red, sage, taupe, brown, cream & pink yarns on a black field, American, late 19th - early 20th c., minor losses, repairs, minor staining, dry areas, 31 1/2 x 52" (ILLUS.) **1,150**

Horse, central oval reserve w/horse figure worked in beige & brown standing in a grassy green area near a picket fence, blue sky background, surrounded by ivory border w/oak leaves in brown & green, minor wear, 23 1/2 x 37" **275**

Horse & carriage, scene of horse-drawn open carriage & driver w/footman assisting a lady passenger w/parasol, polychrome w/blues & greens, black scalloped border, 27 x 48" (some wear & minor damage) **440**

Leopard Hooked Rug

Leopard, the spotted animal standing in a grassy landscape w/stylized leafage, worked in shades of brown, green & beige fabrics, American, late 19th c., mounted on a stretcher, 26 x 46 1/2" (ILLUS.) **1,380**

Three Bears, the Three Bears, Papa, Mama & Baby, marching in a row dressed in human clothing & carrying their bowl of porridge, multi-colored on a beige ground w/black border, 24 x 40" (minor wear) **550**

Tiger & Foliage Hooked Rug

Tiger, central reserve showing a running tiger w/band borders & surrounded by a striated field w/foliate devices & band borders, worked in green, burnt orange, sage, ecru, red & plum yarns, American, late 19th - early 20th c., backed, minor splits, losses & repairs, very minor wear, 45 x 82" (ILLUS.) **2,415**

Winter landscape, rectangular, detailed snowy scene w/oxen pulling a wagon & a horse & figures in the foreground, a rail fence & horse w/trees in the middle ground & hills & trees in the distance, shades of brown, blue, black, red & green on an off-white ground w/dark narrow border band, 30 x 46" (wear, some fading)......... **715**

OTHER

Braided rug, rectangular w/shaped edges, diamond, heart & circle designs worked in pale blue, teal blue, pink & black, 20th c., 41 x 80" (minor wear) **460**

Drugget-style, rectangular, Arts & Crafts style w/a Native American design w/a stepped diamond in green, orange & black in the center & matching triangular corner designs at each end all on an oatmeal ground, fringed ends, early 20th c., 51 x 83".................... **143**

Penny rug, oblong, composed of multicolored mostly wool circles embroidered in bands into a tan twill ground, initialed "P.P.," late 19th - early 20th c., 23 x 43" (wear, dark stain on one edge)................ **330**

Appliqued Wool Penny Rug

Penny rug, a scalloped border on the rectangular rug, black wool w/chenille background decorated w/appliqued circles of red & pale grey wool & olive velvet highlighted w/black & yellow embroidery, wear to scalloped edge, small holes & wear, 24 1/2 x 35 1/2" (ILLUS. of part) **193**

Woven rag runner, multi-colored thin stripes predominantly blue, brown & white, Pennsylvania, unused, 38 1/2 x 506".................... **330**

Woven rag runner, composed of strips sewn together in a plaid cross-form design in red, blue, green & gold, unused, 14 1/2 x 164" **523**

Miniature Sewing Chest of Drawers

SCRIMSHAW

Scrimshaw is a folk art by-product of the 19th century American whaling industry. Intricately carved and engraved pieces of whalebone, whale's teeth and walrus tusks were produced by whalers during their spare time at sea. In recent years numerous fine grade hard plastic reproductions have appeared on the market so the novice collector must use caution to distinguish these from the rare originals.

Baleen corset busk, long flat slender form engraved w/various geometric designs, plants & a three-masted sailing ship, 19th c., 12 3/4" l. (crack, minor chips, minor insect damage) **$144**

Bodkin, carved whale ivory w/openwork heart-form finial, 19th c., 4 1/2" l. (minor age crack) **1,495**

Busk, engraved whalebone, scalloped end, decorated w/whaling vignettes enclosed by vine borders, flanked w/wreaths, 19th c., 13 1/8" l. (some warping).. **518**

Busk, whalebone, polychrome decorated w/a floral bouquet, potted plant, ship at sea & a basket of fruit & foliage initialed "H.D.R.," heightened w/red, blue, yellow, & green colors, 19th c., 13 1/8" l. **920**

Corset busk, whalebone, long narrow form decorated w/a hot air balloon, an eagle w/American flag, foliate & architectural designs, 19th c., 12 1/4" l. (minor staining, hole) **546**

Scrimshaw Dolphin Jawbone

Dolphin jawbone, one side decorated w/engraved scene of an approaching whale boat, the other side w/two whaleships, one w/boats aboard & the other ship coming about, decorated by two different artists, 19th c., minor losses, particularly to the teeth, 10 1/2" w., 16" l. (ILLUS.) **1,610**

Jagging wheel, handle decorated w/various ships, hearts, flowers, stars & compass rose, 20th c., 4 3/4" l **403**

Jagging wheel, whalebone & walrus tusk, double wheel, w/three-tined crimper, baleen spacers, 19th c., 7 3/4" l. (age crack) **1,840**

Jagging wheel, carved whalebone, shaped open carved handle, 19th c., 7 1/2" l. (losses to wheel).. **978**

Pie crimper, whale ivory, rare three-wheeled crimper w/squared & baluster handle sprouting bird's heads w/fastened pair of crimpers & pricking wheel, handle base incised w/rose blossom & bud stamp, mid 19th c., 8 1/4" l. **5,175**

Pie crimper, whale ivory, stylized carved figure of seahorse w/incised & painted black mane grasping wheel in its forelegs, mid 19th c., 6" l. (age crack)................ **7,475**

Swift, whalebone & ivory, clothespin-type, turned shaft & cup, mounted on a turned mahogany base, 19th c., 19 1/2" h. (minor losses).. **3,450**

Swift, whalebone & ivory, double swift, scribed staves, turned & scribed cup, shaft & clamp, inlaid w/coin silver plaque & rings, 19th c., 16" l. (minor losses & damage) **1,840**

Walrus tusks, one engraved on front w/"Walrus" & images of cannons, a ship & an eagle over a series of American flags, the reverse w/engraved images of two different types of whales & a whaleboat, the second tusk is engraved on the front w/"Tusks," images of crossed swords, a ship, an eagle w/standard & flags, a horse & rider w/the reverse engraved w/two different types of whales, each on circular stepped wooden base, late 19th - early 20th c., approximately 13" h., pr. (ILLUS. p. 348) **3,450**

Ornate Scrimshaw Walrus Tusks

Whale pan bone, rectangular plaque engraved w/a British whaling ship under sail & four whaleboats w/nine whales, supported on a mahogany stretcher, 19th c., 9 x 12 3/4" (some old splits & cracks) **5,750**

Whale's teeth, decorated w/three quarter view of Victorian ladies in elegant dress, 19th c., 3 3/4" l., pr. (age cracks) **489**

Scrimshaw Whale's Teeth

Whale's teeth, each decorated w/incised full-length figure of elegantly attired Victorian ladies, 19th c., 6" l., pr. (ILLUS.) **2,875**

Whale's tooth, decorated w/urn of flowers, 19th c., 7 1/2" l. **1,840**

Whale's tooth, decorated w/whaling scene depicting the vessel working on a pod of whales, two boats away, 19th c., 8" l. (surface wear, minor chips) **2,415**

Whale's tooth, engraved w/a spiraling design of various ships under sail & a whaling scene, late 19th - early 20th c., 6 1/4" l. (stained, minor cracks) **1,093**

Whale's tooth, engraved w/an elegant lady & a seated nude woman, initials "OM," late 19th c., 5 1/8" l. (minor crack, very minor chips) **863**

Whale's tooth, engraved w/an elegant lady, mid-19th c., 7" l. (very minor cracks & chips) **920**

Whale's tooth, obverse decorated w/a framed vignette of a whaling scene w/boats in pursuit, reverse depicting an American whaleship, 19th c., 9" l. (surface wear) **1,725**

Whale's tooth, obverse decorated w/eagle in oval reserve, reverse w/seated Liberty figure, inside curve, a compass rose & initials "TN" outside curve, w/anchor & rope, ocean waves & geometric border, on carved hexagonal mahogany wooden base inset w/four round ivory inlays, 20th c., 5 1/2" h. **1,495**

Whale's tooth, obverse depicting a sailor holding an American flag, reverse depicting a lady wearing a red dress & necklace, holding a rose in one hand & a handkerchief in the other hand, 19th c., 4 1/2" l. (age crack) **633**

Whale's tooth, obverse depicting a ship under sail, reverse w/a flamed scene inscribed "Pacific in a Hurricane" above a leafy garland, 19th c., 8 3/4" l. (age crack) **2,300**

Whale's tooth, obverse w/English ship under full sail, reverse w/a three-masted ship flanked by two entwined leafy borders, & a geometric border around base, 19th c., 6 7/8" l. **1,265**

Whale's tooth, polychrome decorated, an American eagle &

shield above a circular reserve depicting a vessel under full sail, heightened w/red, blue & yellow colors, 5 1/2" l. (age cracks) **1,150**

Whale's tooth, polychrome decorated, obverse depicting a bosun blowing his whistle, reverse depicting a British vessel entering an American port, heightened with red, blue, black & flesh tone colors, 19th c., 8" l **12,650**

Whale's tooth, polychrome decorated, obverse lettered w/"U.S." above an eagle & an American flag, vine & floral border, reverse w/an American ship, both sides, heightened w/red color, 19th c., 4 3/4" l. (age cracks) **2,300**

Whale's tooth, polychrome tooth, obverse depicting a woman among crossed flags & a memorial portrait, flanked by flowers, reverse w/an American eagle & banner above a warship flying an American flag, 19th c., 3 1/2" w., 6 1/4" l. **1,495**

Whale's tooth, snuff box w/brass lid, obverse decorated w/crossed British flags & anchor above a full-rigged sailing ship, reverse depicts a rural village scene, 5" l. **513**

Whale's tooth, decorated w/an engraved figure of Lady Liberty holding an American eagle & an American flag w/the anchor of hope resting at her feet & a garland of leaves encircling the top of the tooth, American, 19th c., 6 1/4" h. (ILLUS.) **1,380**

Whale's tooth, polychrome decorated w/"The Mother of Washington Receiving Marquis LaFayette," early 20th c., 6 1/2" l... **690**

Whale's tooth, decorated w/a reserve of a whaling scene flanked by various whaling implements, rope border, early 20th c., 9 1/4" l. (cracks) **2,760**

Whalebone corset busk, long slender flat busk engraved w/a neoclassical urn w/willow tree, "Love," a ship under sail, coconut tree & lighthouse, polychrome highlights, 19th c., 14 1/8" l. (faded, slightly warped, minor crack) **230**

Scrimshaw Whalebone Ditty Box

Whalebone ditty box, oval, wooden top & base w/eight-finger construction, brass tack decoration, 19th c., minor wear, 3 3/8 x 6 1/8 x 8 1/4" (ILLUS.) **3,105**

Whalebone swift, a bone clamp engraved w/a star & floral design, w/adjustable sliding throat & screw lock, the top of an egg cup design & w/a star & floral design, pieces bound together w/brass pins & cuttyhunk ties (modern), w/a carrying box, polychrome decoration, 19th c., box 3 3/4 x 3 7/8 x 29", 2 pcs. **1,380**

Whale's Tooth with Lady Liberty

SEWING ADJUNCTS

With sewing tools and accessories so popular, collectors in the United States, Canada and England actively search for these small antiques. The wide variety available gives buyers a good selection from which to choose - and allows for plenty of different price ranges too. Be cautious of reproductions - Victorian and Georgian styled sterling thimbles and needlecases marked "Thailand" are found frequently and new pewter thimble holders are sometimes sold as old. A good reference book on sewing tools and accessories is Gay Ann Rogers' An Illustrated History of Needlework Tools, *which can be found in many bookstores. All items listed below are in good condition, minor wear and with no missing parts.*

Bodkin, bone, simply turned, handmade, no design, 3" l............ **$21**

Victorian White Metal Chatelaine

Chatelaine, white metal, four-section w/thimble basket, tape measure,

scissors holder & pin disc, France, late 19th c. (ILLUS.) **595**

Crochet hook, brass, retractable hook in decorative case, England, ca. 1870s **48**

Crochet hook, turned bone, 1880s .. **18**

Darner, black egg shape on sterling handle, Art Nouveau design, ca. 1920s **75**

Darner, blown glass, common shoe form, blue, ca. 1900 .... **65**

Darner, Shaker, mushroom-shaped, checkerboard style design in maple, cherry & walnut **98**

Darner, Shaker, wood ball in socket style, late 19th c., rare **245**

Emery, sterling silver, double-ended cylinder, English hallmarks, floral design, ca. 1880s **125**

Emery, strawberry-shaped, plaid orange fabric w/hand-stitched seeds, ca. 1890s **55**

Hem gauge, sterling silver, complete w/sliding marker, Art Nouveau design, ca. 1920s **95**

Knitting sheath, wood, goose-wing styling, carved initials "T.C.," ca. 1850, 9" l................................. **275**

Knitting sheath, wood, hand-carved date of "1822" near top w/crosshatched design on lower half, England **350**

Lace bobbin, bone w/brass wire-wrapped shaft, England, 1860s..... **89**

Lace bobbin, bone w/pewter "dots" inlaid in shaft (leopard design), England, 1840s **98**

Lace bobbin, solid brass in lathe-turned form, England, 1890s, uncommon..................................... **85**

Lace bobbin, wood w/pewter-banded shaft, England, ca. 1840... **48**

Lace pricking, heavy parchment used for lace pattern, simple

design for 1" wide lace, England,
1840s, 12" l.................................. **39**

Needlecase, bone cylinder w/overall
beaded design, England, 1840s.... **145**

Needlecase, bone, simple lathe-
turned form, England, 1880s........ **50**

Needlecase, bone, Stanhope-type,
opening showing multiple views
from the 1878 Paris Exhibition **145**

Needlecase, bone, umbrella-form
w/fist handle, England, 1870s **165**

Needlecase, figural, wood, carved as
man w/a fish tail, probably
Austrian, late 19th c., rare **195**

Needlecase, ivory, carved overall
w/dragons, China, ca. 1840.......... **115**

Needlecase, sterling silver, fleur-de-
lis designs on embossed case,
France, 1920s **90**

Needleholder, brass, engraved
"Stella," Avery, 1870s.................... **425**

Needleholder, brass, marked "The
Unique," folding-type, Avery,
1870s... **485**

Needleholder, brass, quadruple
casket form, leaf design on front,
Avery, 1880s **285**

Needleholder, figural, brass,
butterfly form, Avery, 1880s **750**

Needleholder, figural, brass, model
of a wheelbarrow, Avery, 1870s.... **950**

Netting clamp, steel, heart-shaped
thumbscrew, England, 1850s **150**

Pin disc, cardboard rectangle,
advertising-type for Prudential
Insurance, scene of mother w/child **12**

Pin disc, cardboard rectangle, scene
of children & dog, ca. 1880........... **120**

Pin disc, Tartanware, heart-shaped,
Scottish, ca. 1880s, 1 1/2" d......... **325**

Pin disc, Tartanware, heart-shaped,
Scottish, ca. 1880s, 2" d............... **450**

Pincushion, figural, brass, model of
a rabbit, ca. 1900, 3" h. **130**

Lady's Leg Pincushion

Pincushion, lady's leg-style, brown
fabric, England, late Victorian, 9" l.
(ILLUS.) **56**

Scissors, gilt over white metal,
figural stork, Germany, 1920s **39**

Early Steel Button Hole Scissors

Scissors, steel, button hole-type,
rachet mechanism, England,
1860s (ILLUS.) **38**

Scissors, steel, figural owl,
Germany, 1920s........................... **49**

Scissors, steel, marked "Sheffield,"
England, late 19th c., w/leather
case, matching set of 3 .... **245**

Scissors, steel, w/embroidered silk
case, China, 1920s...................... **48**

Early Patented Sewing Bird

Sewing bird, brass, 1853 patent
date on wing edge, originally w/two
pincushions (ILLUS. w/top cushion
missing) **375**

Sewing bird, silver plated brass,
1853 patent date on edge of wing,
one pincushion **335**

Sewing bird, steel, simple
streamlined form without detail,
1850s.. **265**

Two-tier Inlaid Sewing Box

Sewing box, bird's-eye maple &
inlaid walnut, two-tiered
rectangular form w/pointed corner
finials & inlaid corner blocks,

drawer in lower tier, American-
made, mid-19th c., minor surface
imperfections, very minor losses to
finials, 6 3/4 x 9 1/2", 7 3/4" h.
(ILLUS.) **374**

Miniature Sewing Chest of Drawers

Sewing box, inlaid walnut, model of
a chest of drawers, rectangular top
w/molded rim topped by two small
heart-inlaid drawers w/pincushion
finials, the case w/three long
drawers w/small metal knobs &
inlaid letters flanked by bands of
inlaid hearts, presentation item
made in 1868 in Concord, New
Hampshire, 8 1/4" w., 12" h.
(ILLUS.) **3,500**

English Lady's Sewing Box

Sewing box, inlaid wood, rectangular w/hinged paper-lined lid opening to a compartmented interior w/wooden & ivory sewing implements, the lower drawer opening to a compartmented interior w/additional implements, case refinished, very minor losses, England, early 19th c., 9 x 12", 5 5/8" h. (ILLUS.).......................... **1,610**

Sewing box, sailor's shell art-type, rectangular, old cigar box w/the top inlaid w/varied large & small seashells surrounding a central pink silk pincushion, small shells form banding on cover & base, American-made, ca. 1910, 6 x 9", 6" h. (ILLUS.)................................... **140**

Sewing clamp, steel, simple rachet-type... **95**

Sewing clamp, wood, Tunbridge ware w/ivory trim, England, ca. 1850, 9" l................................. **265**

Sewing kit, Shaker, folding style, silk, pockets for needle packets, ca. 1920....................................... **60**

Silk winder, glass, medical use, England, 1860s, 2" d. **44**

Silk winder, mother-of-pearl, pillow-shaped, England, 2 1/2" l. **65**

Silk winder, Tartanware, cross-form, Scotland, 1860s, 2 1/2" d. **225**

Stiletto, sterling silver handle w/steel shaft, Art Nouveau design, American-made, ca. 1920s **65**

Tape measure, brass, figural, model of a shoe, marked "Three feet in one shoe," American-made, ca. 1900.. **165**

Tape measure, celluloid, figural, model of a basket w/painted flowers, spring-wind, probably German, 1920s............................. **145**

Tape measure, copper & brass, figural, ornate model of a coffee grinder, manual-wind, Europe, ca. 1900.. **300**

Tape measure, vegetable ivory, pierced design, manual-wind, England, 1860-1890 .... **125**

Tape measure, vegetable ivory w/bone winder, model of a crown, England, 1860s **130**

Tape measure, white metal, figural, model of a clam, marked "A clam w/three feet," ca. 1900.................. **195**

Tatting shuttle, celluloid, pink & green pearlized, American-made, 1930s... **65**

Tatting shuttle, sterling silver, Art Nouveau floral design, American-made, ca. 1920s............................ **235**

Thimble, 14k gold, Ketcham & McDougall, engraved scrolls w/carved rim, early 1900s **155**

Thimble, gold, heavily carved narrow band, Simons Bros., 1890s **195**

Thimble, gold, plain band, unmarked **145**

Shell Art Sewing Box

Thimble, sterling sandwiched over
steel, band decorated w/geometric
designs, marked "Dorcas," 1860s .   **75**

Thimble, sterling sandwiched over
steel, plain band, marked "Dorcas,"
England, 1860s **50**

Thimble, sterling silver, coral
cabochons around rim, unmarked
American, early 1900s..................   **185**

Thimble, sterling silver, impressed
florals on band, Simons, ca. 1900 .   **45**

Thimble, sterling silver, "Salem
Witch," Ketcham & McDougall,
19th c..   **575**

Thimble, sterling silver, souvenir-
type, marked "The Spa," England,
ca. 1870s......................................   **60**

Thimble, sterling silver, souvenir-
type, Washington, D.C. & the
Capitol Building, Ketcham &
McDougall, early 20th c.................   **460**

Thimble, sterling silver w/pale blue
enameled band w/florals, red stone
in top, ca. 1900, unusual **195**

Thimble holder, Mauchline ware, top
w/oval photographic print titled
"View of Marblehead
Massachusetts," made in Scotland,
1860s...   **190**

Thimble holder, mother-of-pearl,
purse-form w/brass chain,
England, ca. 1860s........................   **90**

Thimble holder, velvet, model of a
basket in red w/a white arched
handle, paper label on the base
marked "The Fairy," English, 1860s
(ILLUS.) **145**

Ivory Winding Clamp

Winding clamp, carved ivory, spool
top w/netting knob, Asian, ca. 1840
(ILLUS.) **345**

Basket-form Thimble Holder

SHAKER ITEMS

The Shakers, a religious sect founded by Ann Lee, first settled in this country at Watervliet, New York, near Albany, in 1774. By 1880 there were nine settlements in America. Workmanship in Shaker crafts is an extension of their religious beliefs and features plain and simple designs reflecting a chaste elegance that is now much in demand though relatively few early items are common.

Berry baskets, splint & tin, wide splints angled slightly & flared, joined at the top & base by narrow tin rims, quart, 6 3/8" d., 3 1/2" h., pr. **$242**

Blanket, woven wool, finely woven charcoal w/white & grey wide border stripes, fringed, Sister Mildred Barber, Sabbathday Lake, Maine, 64 x 134"........................... **523**

Box maker's mold, hardwood, a heavy central split post w/side screw clamp handle, one end carved w/a round mold, the other w/an oval mold, old patina, 14 3/4" h. **413**

Buck saw, wood & metal, a wooden H-form frame w/turned wood handles at lower corners, wire brace at the top & thin sawblade at the bottom, old patina, Union Village, Ohio, 26" l. **330**

Bucket, cov., stave construction w/three metal bands, tapering cylindrical form in old blue paint & black bands, black stenciled "28" on side & bottom, the fitted cover w/rounded edges & small turned center knob, interior w/worn light green paint, wire bail handle w/turned wood hand grip, 11" h.... **2,860**

Candlestand, cherry w/old dark red finish, round top on a turned tapering columnar standard on a tripod base w/three flattened cabriole legs ending in snake feet, Mount Lebanon, 19th c., 16 1/2" d., 24 1/4" h. (repaired crack in top) .. **3,080**

Carpenter's scribe gauge, all-wood w/slender turned long end handles, 24 1/2" l. **61**

Cheese colander, tin, wide flat-bottomed pan w/shallow flared sides w/rim handles, the bottom pierced overall w/large drainage holes, 22" d. (split at rim).............. **72**

Cloak cabinet, walnut, a flat rectangular top above a tall case w/a four-panel tall door opening to interior shelves repainted grey over a short lower two-panel doors, slightly scalloped apron & simple cut-out feet, chamfered corners, refinished, Union Village, Ohio, 13 1/2 x 37", 77" h. (repairs, feet have lost height, bottom door replaced, top door repaired) **2,750**

Cloak w/hood, child's, blue wool, machine-sewn, 25" l. (minor moth damage, some wear & soiling) **468**

Coffee boiler, cov., tin, large tapering cylindrical body w/large rim spout & strap handle w/grip on opposite rim, a swing strap handle

Shaker Canterbury Cupboard-Chest

across the top, 16" h. plus swing handle (rust damage, repair) **165**

Cradle, adult-type, painted pine & maple, long rectangular form w/low gently canted sides w/higher sides & headboard at one end, original red wash, dovetailed & nailed construction, possibly Harvard, Massachusetts, 19th c., 33 x 78 3/4", headboard 23 1/2" h. **978**

Cupboard over chest of drawers, refinished pine, rectangular top w/a molded cornice over a pair of paneled cupboard doors w/simple wooden knobs above a case of six long graduated drawers w/wooden knobs, plinth base, Canterbury, New Hampshire, 19th c., 20 x 39 3/4", 72" h. (ILLUS. p. 355) **17,600**

Shaker Deaconess' Desk

Desk, deaconess', butternut & tiger stripe maple, a low backrail over the hinged angled lift top w/molded edges opening to a desk box raised on a simple turned pedestal on a tripod base w/flattened cabriole legs, refinished, Enfield, Connecticut, ca. 1830, 17 x 21 1/2", 29" h. (ILLUS.) **6,900**

Drying rack, walnut, tall rectangular uprights supported on shaped shoe feet & joined by three long rectangular rails, mortised construction, old worn finish, 28" w., 39" h. (one foot replaced) .. **165**

Dust pan, floor-type, tin & wood, the wide, flat U-form tin bottom w/conforming high tapering upright sides w/a slender turned wood upright handle at the back, 34 1/2" l. (some soldered & glued repairs) **330**

Foot warmer, wood & punched tin, oval board top & base w/cylindrical tin sides punched w/pinwheel designs, attributed to Elder Abraham Perkins of the Church family, Enfield, New Hampshire, old tag "Leavitt Collection," 11" l. .. **798**

Grain shovel, wood w/some curl, a wide blade w/squared rim trimmed w/tin edging & rounded upturned back w/long extended handle w/cut-out hand grip, old patina, impressed initials "GMW" for George M. W. Wichersham (1806-88), Mount Lebanon cabinetmaker, 44" l. (rusted tin edge repair) **385**

Harvest table, walnut, long two-board top overhanging a mortised & pinned deep apron on square tapering legs, old soft finish, Union Village, Ohio, 24 x 77", 28 1/2" h.. **2,530**

Harvest table, walnut, long two-board top overhanging a mortised & pinned deep apron on square tapering legs, old soft finish, Union Village, Ohio, 24 x 77", 28 1/2" h.. **2,530**

Hearth brush, a long slender turned handle w/acorn terminal, thick short wood crossbar w/long black bristles, old worn finish, 21 1/2" l. (bristles incomplete) **72**

Harvest table, walnut, long two-board top overhanging a mortised & pinned deep apron on square tapering legs, old soft finish, Union Village, Ohio, 24 x 77", 28 1/2" h.. **2,530**

Jug, stoneware, cylindrical lower white body w/cylindrical dark brown shoulder & small neck w/loop strap handle, the body w/a blue transfer-printed label "Shaker Brand Ketchup - E.D. Pettengill Co. Portland, ME.," 14" h. (minor chips) **880**

Magazines, "The Manifesto," Canterbury, New Hampshire, Vol. XIII, 12 issues, 1893, the set **105**

Measuring stick, walnut, long slender flat stick w/turned oblong knob handle, marked off in 4 1/2" intervals & scratch-carved 1/4", 1/2", 9" & 18", old patina, overall 39" l. **165**

Rocking chair w/arms, child's, turned back stiles w/turned pointed finials flanking the replaced red tape back, open shaped arms w/mushroom hand grips on the baluster-turned arm supports over the replaced red tape seat, simple turned legs w/inset rockers, double front & side rungs, single rear rung, old but not original dark finish, Mount Lebanon, 28 1/2" h. **550**

Mt. Lebanon Rocker with Arms

Rocking chair w/arms, maple, a slender shawl rail across the top of the tall back above four gently arched slats between simple turned stiles, flattened curved open arms w/mushroom hand rests over simple baluster-turned arm supports above the replaced splint seat, simple turned legs inset into rockers & joined by double stretchers at the front & sides, Mt. Lebanon, New York, 1880-1930, repair to two legs, 42 1/2" h. (ILLUS.) **1,265**

Rocking chair w/arms, painted wood, ladder-back style w/four wide gently arched slats & a shawl bar at the top joining the turned stiles, shaped flat arms w/mushroom hand grips above baluster-turned arm supports, replaced blue & grey tape seat, worn down to original finish, No. 7, 40" h. **825**

Early Shaker Armless Rocker

Rocking chair without arms, maple, the tall back w/three gently arched slats joining simple turned stiles w/pointed knob finials above the replaced tape seat, legs inset into rockers & joined by double stretchers at the front & sides, old refinishing, Canterbury, New Hampshire, 1830-40, 40" h. (ILLUS.) **690**

Rug, hooked rag, rectangular w/multi-colored speckled design w/a red & olive green border, attributed to Canterbury, New Hampshire, 23 x 38" **220**

Scarf, silk, square of fine grey silk outlined in a bright blue stripe, Pleasant Hill & South Union Communities, Kentucky, mid-19th c., framed, 30" sq. **1,093**

Sewing box, brown leather, rectangular small box w/brown silk binding & interior, includes steel scissor, silver closure shows three Shaker sisters in relief, 4 1/4" l. **72**

Sewing box, cov., oval bentwood, two finger lappets in the base & one in the cover, the cover w/domed cloth pincushion covered in worn & tattered white & black plaid silk over homespun, light natural varnish finish, Canterbury, New Hampshire, 3 3/4" l. **1,045**

Early Shaker Sewing Steps

Sewing steps, pine & poplar, two steps w/arched sides & a varnished stain, New Lebanon, New York, 1850-75, 13 1/8 x 15 3/4", 15 1/4" h. (ILLUS.) **2,645**

Shawl, woven wool, tiny plaid design in charcoal grey & white w/fringe, Ethel Hudson, Canterbury, New Hampshire, 36 x 74" **66**

Side chair, maple, ladder-back style w/three arched slats between the turned stiles w/ovoid finials, woven tape faded green & tan seat, simple turned legs w/double stretchers at the front & sides, single one at the back, back legs w/tilters, Canterbury, New Hampshire, refinished, 41 1/4" h. .. **1,320**

Side chair, the tall back w/three gently arched slats between the turned stiles w/oblong turned finials, a replaced tape seat in mauve, yellow & sage green,

simple turned legs w/double front & side stretchers & a single rear stretcher, old finish, Perkins Barlow, Mount Lebanon, New York, 40 3/4" h. **770**

Kentucky Shaker Sieve

Sieve, bentwood, rounded shape w/tall pointed back & woven horse hair sieve, old patina, attributed to Pleasant Hill, Kentucky, 9" h. (ILLUS.) **358**

Stand, cherry, nearly square two-board top w/molded edges widely overhanging a narrow apron w/a single drawer w/turned wood knob, slender tall round turned legs, old dark varnish stain finish, 19th c., 18 1/2 x 18 3/4", 27" h. (minor age cracks, one front post w/nailed repair) **330**

Storage box, cov., oval bentwood, three finger lappets in base & one in cover, copper tacks, old refinishing, 9 1/2" l. (minor edge damage on cover) **275**

Storage box, cov., oval bentwood, three finger lappets in base & one in cover w/tack construction, old forest green paint, Sabbathday Lake, Maine, 10 3/4" l. **2,035**

Storage box, cov., oval bentwood, three finger lappets on base & one on the lid, copper tacks, old white repaint over grey, 12" l. (minor age cracks in cover, one w/old plastic wood repair)................................... **495**

Sugar bucket, cov., stave construction w/two interlaced wooden bands, arched bentwood swing handle, old yellow paint, Watervliet, New York, 12 1/2" d., 12 1/2" h. **605**

Tea table, maple, round wide top tilting above a turned tapering pedestal on a tripod base w/flat cabriole legs ending in snake feet, wrought-iron catch, top of column threaded to screw into hinge block, old refinishing, attributed to Watervliet, New York, 19th c., 36" d., 26 3/4" h. **2,310**

Shaker Painted Wall Cupboard

Wall cupboard, painted pine, rectangular top w/rounded edges

slightly overhangs the case w/a single wide flat door w/wooden thumb latch & small wooden knob opening to a single shelf all above a single long narrow bottom drawer, old red translucent stain, minor imperfections, mid-19th c., 8 x 12", 16 3/4" h. (ILLUS.)........... **1,093**

Wall cupboard, painted pine, rectangular top above a case w/a tall recessed panel door opening to two shelves, original turned wood pull & original bittersweet orange wash, Mt. Lebanon, New York, 1830-40, 18 1/4 x 25", 41 3/4" h. (imperfections) **3,220**

Wardrobe, painted wood, rectangular top w/narrow coved cornice above a tall, narrow two-panel door flanked by wide side boards, interior shelves, on simple bracket feet, original bright red wash, probably Canterbury, New Hampshire, third quarter 19th c., 17 1/2 x 48", 83 1/2" h. (hardware changes, only one shelf original) .. **5,175**

Work table, poplar, wide rectangular three-board top widely overhanging the deep apron, on turned tapering legs w/square top posts, mortised & pinned apron, cleaned down to traces of old white paint, Union Village, Ohio, 36 x 61", 28 1/4" h. **2,200**

Yarn reel, wooden, table-clamp base w/slender central shaft supporting an expandable crisscross slat framework, small cup finial, old yellow varnish, Hancock, Massachusetts, 19th c., 20" h. (one member w/damage, one retied)... **143**

STOVES

Over the past several years, much renewed interest in antique stoves has surfaced. From the coveted base-burner beauties to "pot-bellies," steel-jacketed "oak" stoves, cooking stoves, heaters and laundry stoves, these handsome "heavies" are in demand. Like many areas of antiques and collectibles, the market for stoves is thin. It is almost impossible to designate some particular "worth" without several considerations such as economic status, demographics, artistic value, type and age. And although these factors may play a roll in determining a final sale, they do not necessarily "set" the price on a particular stove. Antique stove expert Clifford Boram has supplied us with the following pricing information and photographs.

Art Westminster Base Burner

Base burner, 1890 Art Westminster No. 404, Rathborne-Sard, Albany, N.Y., all cast iron w/mica windows & large rectangular majolica tile on three sides, 13" firepot (ILLUS.) **$22,000**

Base burner, 1911 Wehrle 100, restored, 18" firepot **9,000**

Base burner, 1911 Wehrle 100, The Wehrle Co., Newark, Ohio, restored, 14" firepot **4,000**

Imperial Universal Base Burner

Base burner, 1913 Imperial Universal 50, Cribben & Sexton, Chicago, all cast iron w/mica windows on three sides, nickel plating, restored, 15" firepot (ILLUS.) **4,000**

Base burner, Art Garland 250, ca. 1920, restored **1,250**

Base burner, Art Garland 58, Michigan Stove Co., Detroit, ca. 1910, restored **8,000**

Base burner, Noble Crown, ca. 1920, restored (dismounted from base) **1,300**

Base burner, Radiant Stewart 34,
Fuller & Warren, Milwaukee,
ca. 1900, restored **5,000**

Coal range, 1917 Brilliant Universal,
blue cast iron w/high closet, no
reservoir, good original condition .. **200**

Combination range, 1928
Kalamazoo Peerless, grey & white,
good original condition **875**

Combination range, Globe, grey,
Kokomo, Ind., ca. 1925, good
original condition **150**

Cook stove, 1872 Governor 8,
Chicago Stoves Wks., reservoir &
low closet, good original condition. **325**

Cottage parlor stove, 1842 E.
Ripley's Patent Hinge 2 .... **850**

Gas heater, Jewel, twelve-tube
radiant, no low radiant chamber,
ca. 1889, restored **500**

Gas range, 1924 Quick Meal, grey
four-burner w/canopy & high
closet, unrestored & apart **375**

Gas range, 1929 Magic Chef 39
(Jonquil), four-burner, good
original condition **250**

Gas range, 1929 Roper, four-burner,
one-oven, unrestored **20**

Gas range, 1933 Magic Chef,
American Stove Co., St. Louis &
Cleveland, white porcelain on
sheet iron, six-burner, two-oven
w/high closet, black Bakelite knobs

1933 Magic Chef Gas Range

& handles, good original condition
(ILLUS.) **800**

Gas range, 1938 Magic Chef, white
porcelain on sheet iron, chrome
trim, six-burner, two-oven w/high
closet, restored (ILLUS.) **1,025**

Gas range, 1938 Magic Chef, white
six-burner, two-oven w/high closet,
unrestored & apart........................ **725**

Gas range, Chambers, white four-
burner, ca. 1949, good original
condition **250**

Gas range, Eagle, low-oven style
w/wood side, cream & green,
ca. 1929, unrestored **150**

1938 Magic Chef Gas Range

Gas range, O'Keefe & Merritt, four-burner w/cabinet base, ca. 1929, good original condition **110**

Gas range, Quick Meal, blue four-burner cabinet, ca. 1919, good original condition **925**

Oak stove, 1925 Ideal Heater 417, Gem City Mfg. Co., Quincy, Ill., good original condition **175**

Oak stove, American Oak 214, Keokuk Stove Wks., ca. 1895, restored **300**

Peoria Oak Stove

Oak stove, Peoria Oak 160, Culter & Proctor, ca. 1905, restored (ILLUS.) **600**

Oak stove, Retort 218, Marion, Ind., cased oak w/three mica doors, ca. 1905, restored **2,400**

Round Oak 18-T-31, 1940, good original condition **225**

Round Oak D-18, 1901, complete, unrestored **300**

Round Oak Stove

Superb Peninsular Steel Range

Round Oak D-18, 1904, extra half section, restored, missing standing Indian from top, 18" firepot (ILLUS.) 325

Steel range, 1907 Superb Peninsular w/reservoir & high closet, restored (ILLUS.) 2,000

Templar 27 Todd Stove

Todd stove, 1878 Templar 27, Wm. Resor, Cincinnati, all cast iron w/two mica windows in feed door & side door, incomplete, 27" firebox (ILLUS.) 25

Todd stove, 1908 Acme Wildwood w/sheet-iron jacket, Wehrle/Sears, unrestored condition (no hearth) ... 60

Wood- & coal-burning base heater, Ideal Garland 220, ca. 1898, restored (no urn) 1,300

Wood- & coal-burning range, 1910 Glenwood F 107, cast iron w/high shelf, restored 1,100

Wood- & coal-burning range, 1925 Universal, blue, gas sidecar, unrestored 200

Wood- & coal-burning range, Alpine Bride, black cast iron, ca. 1920, restored 300

Wood-burning range, 1927 Home Comfort AC, high closet, no reservoir, unrestored 50

Magee 88 Range

Wood-burning range, 1880 Magee 88, Magee Furnace Co., Boston, double oven, eight-hole cast iron w/high closet, 8" lids, no reservoir, restored (ILLUS.) 5,500

Simple Tulips in Pots Appliqued Quilt

TEXTILES

BEDSPREADS

Rare Crewel-embroidered Bedspread

Crewel-embroidered linen, large rectangular center panel w/pleated side & end panels, embroidered overall w/scrolled flowering vine design on a linen ground, worked in green, salmon, yellow, navy blue & purple yarns, initialed & dated "E.H. 1804," American, toning, scattered staining, minor fiber loss & wear, 98 x 104" (ILLUS.)........ **$6,900**

Early New England Bed Rug

Hooked bed rug, loose weave butternut-dyed wool ground w/hooked wool floral design in green, cerise & coral, probably northern New England, minor losses, tears, repairs, 70 x 80" **575**

COVERLETS

Jacquard, single weave, one piece, central medallion w/foliage borders, red, olive green, greyish blue & natural white, bottom edge labeled "M. by H. Stager, Mount Joy, Lancaster Co. Pa. Warranted Fast Colors No. 1," 78 x 83" (wear, stains)... **275**

Jacquard, single weave, two-piece, large floral medallions, a vintage grape border, corners labeled "W. in Mt. Vernon, Knox County Ohio by Jacob and Michael Ardner, 1854," reds, gold, navy blue & natural white, 74 x 80" (overall & edge wear, minor stains) **358**

Jacquard, single weave, one-piece, large four-rose center clusters surrounded by a large leafy scroll medallion within a scroll edging & spread-winged eagle spandrels, leafy scroll border w/stylized pineapples in each corner, edge label "Manuf. by H.F. Stager & Son, Fast Colors, Mount Joy, Lancaster County, Penn.," green, navy blue, red & natural white, 76 x 80" (minor stains)................... **550**

Large Medallions w/Pinwheel Borders

Jacquard, double woven, two-piece, leafy stars within scalloped medallions, pinwheel & foliate border, red on white, signed "Berlin - Holmes Co. 1845" w/roosters in corners, minor staining, fiber wear, 66 1/2 x 82" (ILLUS. p. 365) **230**

Jacquard, single weave, two-piece, bands of vintage grape design across the center, tulip borders at ends & leafy vines along sides, corners labeled "Jacob Snyder, Stark Co., Ohio, 1850," navy blue, pink, olive yellow & natural white, 74 x 82" (edge & overall wear, some fringe missing) **495**

Jacquard, double woven, two-piece, large four-rose medallions & a double vintage border, tomato red, navy blue & natural white, 76 x 84" (top edge worn, light stains) **220**

Florals with Eagle Border Coverlet

Jacquard, double woven, two-piece, large four-blossom clusters w/pairs of leaves alternating w/smaller blossomheads, eagle & foliate border, blue & natural white, signed "Caroline L. Mott 1835. French Weaver Waterville," New York, fiber wear, minor repairs & staining, 83" sq. (ILLUS.).............. **920**

Jacquard, double woven, one-piece, rows of large leafy rose blossoms alternating w/bands of small starbursts, leaf & blossom border band, navy blue & natural white, attributed to Enon Valley, Pennsylvania, 19th c., 76 x 86" **165**

Jacquard, single weave, one-piece, central medallion w/corner designs w/horses, eagles, dogs, bust of Grant & "Liberty, Virtue, 1869," wine red & natural white w/an olive green warp in the reds, 76 x 86" (wear, wool yarn missing in some areas) **605**

Daniel Bury Jacquard Coverlet

Jacquard, single weave, two-piece, large star & flower medallions w/wide borders of peacocks standing on domes marked "North America" & "E Pluribus Unum" alternating w/vintage grape borders & baskets of fruit, corners w/stars & signed "Daniel Bury" (1842-47), navy blue & natural white, minor wear & stains, 60 x 88" (ILLUS.) **715**

Jacquard, double woven, two-piece, large urns of fruits & flowers & birds feeding young surrounded by leafy scrolls in the center, a Christian & heathen border, border marked "Piqua 1846," natural white, tomato red, navy blue & royal blue, minor stains, end binding w/wear, 76 x 88" (ILLUS.) **1,540**

Jacquard, double woven, two-piece, geometric floral center medallion, floral border, all corners labeled "J. Craig 2 miles N. East of Greensburg, D.C., IA. 1855," 78 1/2 x 90 1/2" (stains, wear, fringe on one edge) **578**

Dated Coverlet with Urrs & Birds

Jacquard, single weave, two-piece, rows of large oval delicate blossoms surrounded by long serrated leaves & alternating w/small starburst, zigzag blossomhead border, signed "Michael Ruth - John Kaufman - 1838," navy blue, red & natural white, Bucks County, Pennsylvania, sewn-on fringe, 76 x 96" (minor wear & stains) **358**

Jacquard, double woven, one-piece, a central floral medallion w/a vintage border, large floral clusters & long-tailed birds in the corners, narrow scroll & blossom border, corners dated "1852," tomato red & natural white, 89 x 98" (wear, stains & some edge damage)........ **220**

Overshot, double woven, two-piece, summer-winter type, Optical patt. w/Pine Tree border, navy blue & natural white, 75 x 92 1/2" (stains, some wear, no fringe).................... **275**

Overshot, double woven, two-piece, summer-winter type, Snowflake & Pine Tree patt., navy blue & natural white, 19th c. (wear, stains, some edge wear & fringe loss)................ **330**

Overshot, Rob Peter to Pay Paul, Orange Peel patt., indigo, white wool & linen, 19th c., 77 x 79 1/2" . **173**

Overshot, two panels sewn together, woven w/cloverleaf and checkerboards, fringed border, 19th c., 74 x 68"........................... **460**

LINENS & NEEDLEWORK

Blanket, twill-woven wool plaid, initialed & dated "M.M. March the 10 1840," worked in green, rust, sage & yellow yarns, 70 x 81 1/2" . **805**

Blanket, twill-woven wool plaid, initialed "MDC," worked in navy blue & cream yarns, 19th c., 75 x 97" **374**

Needlework family register, silk thread on linen, rectangular w/a wide stylized floral vine border w/the names of the parents & date of marriage in panels at the top above a three-section rectangular register w/columns titled "Names," "Births," & "Deaths," pious verse below w/a one-story house flanked by leafy trees at the bottom, begins w/the marriage of Amaziah Phillips & Lucy Bates in 1809, probably Beverly, Massachusetts, vibrant colors, unframed, 17 x 25" (minor toning, very minor staining) **4,600**

Pillowcases, cotton w/tiny cross-stitching, monogrammed "H.H.F." & dated "1852," 16 x 41", pr. **65**

Pillowcases, embroidered cotton & linen w/crocheted & tatted trim, single size, set of 12 .... **40**

Pillowcases, white, monogramed "H," pr. **18**

Sheet set, padded satin, red couching, "CC," monogram, 108 x 120", together w/four 33 x 42" pillow shams, eyelet trim, 5 pcs. **195**

Sheet set, white padded satin stitch "CC" monogram, Buretto petals, handmade eyelet trim, 96 x 104", together w/four matching pillow cases, 5 pcs. **150**

Sheet set, white w/blue Madeira cut work & embroidery, 88 x 102", together w/four matching pillow cases, 5 pcs. **150**

Long Embroidered Table Rug

Table rug, appliqued & embroidered, rectangular, composed of thirty-two tan & black blocks in a checkerboard design using colored appliques of birds & flowers, framed by flowers & hearts, New England, mid-19th c., minor imperfections, 39 1/2 x 74 1/2" (ILLUS. of part) **4,025**

Early Embroidered Table Rug

Table rug, appliqued, pieced & embroidered wool, the thirteen panel design decorated w/various embroidered & appliqued foliate designs worked in red, green, purple, blue, sage, taupe & white on a black field, New England, first half 19th c., very minor losses, scattered minor fiber wear, minor fading, 30 3/4 x 50 3/4" (ILLUS.) .. **2,645**

Table runner, linen, 6" ecru crocheted edge, 12" corners, 18 x 68" **35**

Tablecloth, ecru filet lace, 72 x 84" .. **55**

Tablecloth, extremely fine drawn work, embroidered dragons center, 80 x 88" **245**

Tablecloth, hand-crocheted white lace composed of squares w/pineapples & fans in each corner, made up of 475 small three inch squares, never used, 72 x 90" **85**

Tablecloth, double damask, woven Blue Willow patt., 92"...................... **75**

Towel, embroidered woven linen, initialed & dated "BC 1828," red embroidery on a cream ground, probably Pennsylvania, 16 1/2 x 56" **86**

NEEDLEWORK PICTURES

Landscape, scene of musicians & two dancing couples in 18th c. dress in a landscape of trees, an oak tree, flowers, a dog, birds & the sun, all petit-point in intricate stitches in shades of grey, blue, gold, brown, black, white & red, good colors, original pine stretcher & molded walnut arch-topped frame, 18th c., 25 1/2 x 35 1/2" (age cracks in frame)................... **1,210**

Birds & urn of flowers, wool & silk embroidery w/a large stylized urn at the bottom issuing stems w/drooping tulips & a large top sunflower flanked by arched stems w/blossoms, a pair of large colorful birds on the branches, worked in green, brown & rose wool & blue, white, pink & yellow silk on a linen ground, probably Pennsylvania, late 18th - early 19th c., 7 x 8 1/2" (ILLUS.) **2,300**

Urn with Flowers & Birds Embroidery

Detailed English Landscape Scene

Landscape scene, needlepoint embroidery on linen w/a detailed landscape showing a lady picking fruit from a tree in the front left, a lady riding in a small open cart in the center, animals, trees, houses, a windmill & a mansion in the distance, all within a leaf border, George III period, England, framed, 33 x 37 1/2" (ILLUS.)....... **3,450**

Moses in the Bullrushes, silk needlework & painting on silk, embroidered in gold, green, blue & brown threads on a painted silk ground w/two maidens & the infant Moses on the seashore & New Haven, Connecticut harbor in the background, in original giltwood & gesso framed w/original reverse-painted black mat w/gilt border & stars & title at the bottom, paper label from back reads "Maria Van Wyck's journal, Litchfield, Conn. June 1808 'spent the day in Embroidery,' Maria Van Wyck born 1794 d. Dec 8, 1831 m. Tunis Brinckerhoff 1814," Miss Patten's School, Hartford, Connecticut, 19 1/4 x 24" (ILLUS.) **23,000**

Mourning picture, silk embroidery on painted silk, worked in shades of green, yellow, beige, cream & blue silk in a variety of stitches including split, satin & chain stitch & French knots w/water-color on silk figures of two maidens in Neoclassical gowns flanking a vine-draped monument atop a plinth inscribed "Sac. to the Memory of Capt. Mayo Gerrish born Nov. 15, 1768 died March 28, 1809 age 41," in original black reverse-painted mat w/gilt trim, Newburyport, Massachusetts, ca. 1818, 17 x 23" **13,800**

Fine Moses in the Bullrushes Picture

Needlework embroidery on silk scene, an oval reserve w/a scene of a woman kneeling in prayer amid neoclassical urns & columns, a brass sequin border, flowering vine outer border, water-color highlights, early 19th c., framed, 13 1/2 x 16 1/2" (toning, minor fiber wear & sequin loss) 259

Peacocks on flowering vines, Arts & Crafts style, silk needlework on linen, a facing pair of detailed long-tailed peacocks perched on forked branches of a tree w/large blossoms & leaves, worked in shades of cream, tan, brown, green, & dark blue, framed, three small tears, early 20th c., 52 x 59"   550

QUILTS

Fine Appliqued Album Quilt

Appliqued Album patt., composed of nine large sections each w/stylized flowering vines or urns of flowers in green & pink calico w/solid red & goldenrod, large leafy blossom stems around border, blind-stitched & whip-stitched w/floss w/some floss embroidery on stems, overall wear, stains, 75 x 80" (ILLUS.) 2,035

Appliqued crib quilt, Oak Leaf variant patt., worked in red, green & yellow calicos on a white ground, 19th c., 28 3/4 x 36" 575

Appliqued Floral Medallion Quilt

Appliqued Floral Medallion patt., composed of six large four-arm stylized floral medallions across the center in pink & green calico w/delicate running flowering vine border, well-quilted white ground, 20th c., 80 x 96" (ILLUS.) 550

Appliqued Flowerhead & Blossom Sprig patt., composed of an arrangement of five large floral clusters w/a large central blossom issuing four blossoms & leaf sprigs, running floral vine border, in olive green calico & solid red & yellow on a quilted white ground, embroidered date & initials "E.S.E. 1855," 85" sq. (overall wear, minor stains) 798

Appliqued Oak Leaf patt., worked in green on a white quilted field, mid-

Rose of Sharon Appliqued Quilt

19th c., 61 x 81" (fading, staining, toning) **316**

Appliqued Princess Feather patt., four large eight-arm pinwheels in salmon pink alternating w/teal green, separated by striped bands & star blocks on a white ground, 75 x 82" (overall wear, some fading & color loss, stains) **303**

Appliqued Rose of Sharon patt., composed of eight large floral clusters alternating w/crossed branch & heart clusters on a white ground, running vine border, worked in green calico & red cotton, second half 19th c., toning, minor fading, very minor staining, 82 1/2 x 84" (ILLUS.) **805**

Appliqued Rose Wreath patt., rose wreath clusters in the center framed by similar running borders, cut corners, worked in red & teal green, mid-19th c., 82 x 84" (fading, very minor staining) **230**

Appliqued Sunburst & Eagle patt., worked in green, terra cotta & red on a white quilted field, mid-19th c., 88 x 90" (fading, staining, minor areas of fiber wear) **230**

Appliqued Sunburst & Rose of Sharon patt., four large scalloped sunbursts w/blossom centers centered by a rose cluster & vining blossom border, four birds on sprigs around the border, worked in red, green & terra cotta on a white quilted ground, mid-19th c., 83 1/2" sq. (very minor staining on back)... **2,415**

Appliqued Tulips in Pots patt., a simple arrangement of nine large three-blossom tulips in small pots in dark green, red & goldenrod on a finely feathered wreath-quilted white ground (ILLUS.) **600**

Ornate Tulips in Pots Quilt

Appliqued Tulips in Pots patt., composed of an arrangement of sixteen blocks w/large three-blossom tulips in small pots all enclosed by sawtooth borders within a wide outer border of birds on branches, trees & stars all on a white ground, in green & red calico, 19th c., minor staining, scattered fiber wear, 92 1/2 x 94 1/2" (ILLUS.) **978**

Pieced Barn Raising patt., Log Cabin variant, composed of various calico & other materials, late 19th c., 68 x 69 1/2" (fading, minor fiber wear) **374**

Simple Tulips in Pots Appliqued Quilt

Pieced Bowtie patt., composed of multi-colored blocks in prints & calico in shades of brown, blue, red & beige on a red dotted ground, 65 x 71" (overall wear & minor stains)... **358**

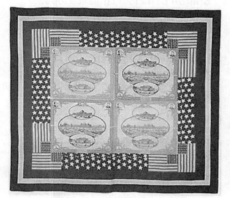

Fine Centennial Pieced Quilt

Pieced Centennial patt., the center w/four large printed fabric reserves w/scenes of various exhibition halls at the 1876 Centennial Exposition, bordered by pairs of American flags & bands of white stars worked in red, white, blue & black, wide border bands, staining, 74 1/2 x 83" (ILLUS.)..................... **748**

Pieced Double Irish Chain patt., composed of blue & pink calico w/a sawtooth border on white, 72 x 80" (wear, small stains, some edge wear & fading to binding).............. **495**

Pieced Grandmother's Flower Garden patt., composed of multi-color print & solid color blocks on a white & yellow ground, 78 x 92" (very minor stains)........................ **248**

Pieced Lone Star patt., composed of blocks of goldenrod, yellow & white sateen, 82 x 84" (minor stains)... **330**

Pieced Miniature Nine Patch patt., composed of small patches in pink, green calico & multi-colored prints on a navy blue ground, 64" sq. (stains, wear, some edge damage) **358**

Pieced Monkey Wrench patt., worked on multi-colored print

blocks on a diamond-quilted white ground, machine-sewn banding, 72 x 84 (overall wear & stains)...... **193**

Sawtooth Design Quaker-made Quilt

Pieced Sawtooth Border patt., wide bands of blue & amethyst w/white sawtooth borders on a khaki field, signed & dated on reverse "Mary Anne Wisner 1841," Pennsylvania, Quaker-made, fading, staining, losses, 95 1/2 x 100 1/2" (ILLUS.). **690**

Pieced Star Medallion patt., composed of nine large star medallions worked in blocks of red, yellow & teal green on a white quilted ground w/a red border band, 75" sq. (overall wear, light stains, small hole in backing) **435**

Early Chintz Trapunto Quilt

Pieced Stars in Hexagons patt., composed of chintz pieces arranged in stars in hexagons forming concentric hexagonal rings, white ground, trapunto technique, blue & red chintz binding, ca. 1850 (ILLUS.)............ **6,325**

Amish Sunshine & Shadow Quilt

Pieced Sunshine & Shadow patt., a large central square composed of multi-colored blocks of wool, crepe, knit, etc., all within a wide purple border, made by Mrs. Hannah King, 1930, Amish, moth damage, spotted fading in border, 80" sq. (ILLUS.) **357**

Trapunto quilt, white on white, embroidered feather border centers a reserve of a basket of fruit & flowers, surrounded by foliate banding, fruit, birds & corner fans, signed "Mary E. Tuutenberg, 1873," 81 1/2 x 83" (old repairs, fiber wear, scattered minor stains & toning) **748**

SAMPLERS

Alphabet, pious verse & inscription, upper bands of alphabet separated by bold vining bands from the short pious verse above another vining band & the lower inscription reading "Ann Cushing is my name with my needle I wrought the same in the 9 year of my age July the 10 1748," Newport, Rhode Island, framed, 7 5/8 x 10 3/4" (ILLUS.) **1,955**

Early Rhode Island Sampler

Alphabets above birds, wreaths & urns, a long rectangular form w/wool needlepoint & silk cross-stitch on woven mesh, a top series of alphabets in various sizes above a lower band of large baskets & urns of flowers, wreaths & a pair of facing birds, signed "Mary J. Mathers," in green, golds, brown, red, blue, purple & yellow, framed, 14 3/4 x 18 1/4" (alphabets faded, stains, some added or repaired wool stitches)................................. **1,045**

Alphabets, inscription & pious verse, the upper two-thirds composed of rows of alphabets above the inscription "Huldah F. Hopkins, Sampler Wrought in the 8th year of her age, Stockbridge July 1812," a short pious verse at the bottom, silk threads in shades of blue, brown & white on a coarse tow linen ground, framed, American, 13 x 18" **468**

Alphabets, numerals, pious verse & landscape, the upper panel of various sizes of alphabets over a row of numerals above the pious verse in tiny letters above the lower panel composed of scrolling grapevines, birds, trees & flowers, a narrow geometric border on

Detailed Early Massachusetts Sampler

Ornate Early American Sampler

three sides all within a wider running bold flowering vine border, signed "Haverhill August 29 Betsey Gage Plummer Born AD 1782 this wrought in the 14 year of her age...," Massachusetts, framed, toning, tack holes, minor staining, 15 3/4 x 19 3/8" (ILLUS.) **10,925**

Alphabets & pious verse, an upper panel of alphabets & a pious verse above a lower panel of geometric designs & flowering plants, a geometric floral border, signed "Harriet French AE7 at Miss Hammonds School Boston," on linen, framed, 11 3/8 x 11 7/8" (toning, fading, scattered staining) **1,150**

Alphabets, pious verse over birds & flowers, the upper panel of alphabets over a pious verse above the large lower panel centered by a large vase w/tall flowering vines flanked by parrots & various fruit, flower & animal designs, all within a running geometric leaf border, signed "Mary Greenleaf born in July the 16 1786," Newbury or Newburyport area, Massachusetts, unframed, toning, fading, minor staining, very minor fiber wear, 16 1/4 x 21 1/8" (ILLUS.) **10,925**

Alphabets & pious verse over florals, the top w/graduated bands

Early Unfinished Sampler

of alphabets over a small pious verse & inscription in a running vine box above a pair of tall-stalked plants flanking a central basket of flowers, a tiny dog in each corner, a narrow running vine outer border, unfinished, signed "Martha A. Grahams Work Done in her 11th years 182...," toning, fading, minor losses & staining, framed, 16 1/4 x 18 5/8" (ILLUS.) **805**

Alphabets & pious verse over flowers, three alphabet panels above a pious verse w/trees, lower panel of birds & floral devices, three sides bordered w/a band of narrow sawtooth & geometric stylized flowers, "Rizpah Farmer born Sept the 26 1797 aged 13 years," mounted on fabric, framed, 17 3/4 x 18 1/2" (toning, fading) ... **1,955**

Flowering vine, potted plants & inscription, upper panel of flowering vine w/bow above a lower panel of a potted flowering plant & flowering vine w/bow flanked by foliate designs, flowering vine border on a dark ground, signed "Lucy Deweys sampler wrought in the eleventh year of her age 1794," unfinished, unframed, 15 1/2 x 17" (toning, fading) **2,070**

Landscape, pious verse & other devices, the upper panel w/various foliate, fruit, animal & regalia designs above a middle panel w/a pious verse, the lower panel w/a scene of a brick house & fence flanked by soldiers, trees & flowering plants, geometric floral border, signed "Eliza matilda Excell AD 13 Pear street 1839," framed, 12 x 15 7/8" (toning, minor fading & staining, scattered minor holes) **1,495**

Pious verse above large building, the two portions flanked by scattered trees, flowers, butterflies & bee skeps, all within a geometric running floral border, silk threads in green, gold, blue, pink, brown, black & white on a homespun linen ground, signed "Emma Husselbee, Brierly Hill, June 18th, 184...," old frame, 21 1/2 x 22" (minor stains, several holes) **935**

Pious verse & floral & bird panel, the upper panel w/a long pious verse above a lower panel w/flowering leafy vines above birds perched on flowering trees, all within a foliate & butterfly border, signed "Jane Oliver 1825 aged 13 years," probably England, framed, 12 7/8 x 19 1/8" (toning, fading, minor staining) **546**

TOBACCIANA

Tobacco was grown, manufactured, sold, and used in all regions of the world. If you are an active shopper you will discover more than 50 different types of tobacco related collectibles and, if you keep at it long enough, at least 50,000,000 different individual items. This guide can be but a hint at the richness of the various hobbies and collections related to tobacco growing, manufacture, selling, and use. Both rare and common items have been included to give you a sampling of items available.Collectibles are second-hand goods and have no fixed price. There is no all-knowing grocery clerk able to stamp each of the world's billions of second hand items with an absolute value. The value of things is determined by who is buying and who is selling and where and under what circumstances a transaction is taking place. There is no "value" except what a buyer and seller agree to. Values in this section are given as a range of wholesale and retail prices likely to be offered and/or paid by pickers, dealers, and collectors of tobacciana.

—Tony Hyman

ADVERTISING & STORE ITEMS

Advertising figure, Admiration cigars, composition Indian vigorously striding w/box of cigars under his arm, S. Fernandez & Co., Tampa, ca. 1940s, 18" h.. $**150-250**

Prince Albert Advertising Sign

Advertising sign, tobacco, " 'You'll Like it Too!' Prince Albert," linen-backed, outdoor sign or indoor banner depicting pipe smoker & Prince Albert can, 4 x 8', excellent condition (ILLUS.)...................... **60-125**

Robert Burns Advertising Sign

Advertising sign, cigar, "Robert Burns 10¢ Cigar," lithographed on tin, 1901-1909, 24" d., very good condition (ILLUS.)...................... **450-800**

Advertising sign, snuff, paper, "Lorillard's Snuff" above handsome red, white, blue & black depiction of snuff taking seniors, reads "Won the Only Gold Medal Awarded on Snuff at the Atlanta Exposition" below, professionally framed, intended for tobacconist's wall, P.Lorillard, New York, ca. 1905-1910, 24 x 32" **300-450**

Cigar box opener, "El Verso Cigars" on one side & "San Felice Cigars" on the other, nickel plated, ca. 1950s, 3" l.............................. **15-30**

Cigar store Indian, full-size, wood, Indian maiden holding bunch of cigars, fair carving by unidentified workman, ca. late 19th century manufacture, repainted before WWII, 5' h. including base
.... **6,000-12,000**

Tobacco container, Bull Durham, cardboard, designed to hold 64 cloth bags of smoking tobacco, intended as display pieces, various cowboy & racist Negro scenes, ca. 1910-1920s, excellent condition, widely reproduced (ILLUS.)..... **400-1,000 and up**

Bull Durham Tobacco Container

Tobacco plug cutter, counter-top, cast iron, figural of an imp, w/original paint, ca. late 1800s, has been reproduced **150-200**

CIGAR BOXES

Between 1860 and 1940, the collectible era of cigar boxes, more than a million and a half different brand names were sold in containers made of wood, tin, cardboard, aluminum, china, glass, and other materials. To qualify as "excellent condition" the inside label should be unmarked or with slight soil outside the image area. The inside paper liner in bottom of box should be present and the outside of the box should be clean; the Revenue stamp may be scratched or removed. A box is not "excellent" if the liner is missing; if words are written in ink on the outside and/or inside of the box; or if there are grease or water stains on the box. Values given are for retail of excellent boxes. Boxes in less than excellent condition retail for 25% to 50% of the prices shown.

Alcazar, nailed wood/cardboard box of 50 cigars in four rows, label depicts famous race horse in full color, ca. 1950s, common, full, excellent condition (some minor external scuffing) **50-75**

Brooks & Co., Tebson/Coronas, standard boite nature box w/interlocked corners, hinges & clasp, collar & no paper label, popular national brand from 1920s through 1960s, near mint condition **3-5**

Corina Larks Cigar Box

Corina Larks, Western shape, sports or other size/shape boxes of 50 cigars, standard boite nature box w/hinges, clasp, collar & no or little inside label, Jose Escalante & Co., New Orleans, ca. 1940s & 50s, common, mint condition (ILLUS.) .. **3-5**

Floradora, nailed wood box of 100 cigars, label depicts bundle of three cigars held together w/pictorial band depicting woman's head, cigars priced at 3/10¢, P.Lorillard, factory 17, Virginia, ca. 1901-1909, excellent condition **50-60**

General U.S. Grant, nailed wood cigar box made to hold 100 cigars in six rows, overall lid & vertical end label, black & white outer label depicts General Ulysses Grant in Civil War uniform, plain white inner label, made by Wescott, Wise & Kent, Binghamton, NY, 1866, signature canceled 1866 revenue stamp in fine condition, handsome end label on an important box made between the war & his presidency (ILLUS. p. 378) **175-300**

Hermann Göring Box with Cigars Made for Sonderanferligung Reichsmarschall Hermann Göring, nailed wood box of 10 large cigars packed in glass tubes, inside label depicts Göring's crest in red & gold, German revenue stamp,

General U.S. Grant Cigar Box

Gildemann cigar factory, Berlin-
Hamburg, ca. 1940s. Excellent
condition **1,000-1,500**

**House of Windsor Palmas or Mark
IV Magnates,** plastic box, either
brown or black, designed to hold
50 cigars four rows deep,
ca. 1970s & 80s, mint condition **3-5**

Merry Christmas, book-shaped
wooden box of 25 cigars packed
two deep, F.M. Howell label
depicts windblown pretty girl in
Santa outfit carrying holly,
unknown western New York
cigarmaker, factory 973, 28th tax
district **60-80**

Metal box, w/top picture frame inset
w/various color pictures, hinges,
clasp & inside mirror, known in
green, red, other colors, w/a wide
variety of subject matter on
pictures from English cottages,
French court scenes, sports, etc.,
held 100 cigars, box used by
variety of Florida & Pennsylvania
factories during 1930s, inside
mirror had label glued on, but
usually removed, excellent
condition (cracked mirror).............   **20-30**

Phillies Perfecto, tin box of 50 cigars
packed four rows high, minor
varieties; made by Bayuk Brothers,
Philadelphia, ca. 1920s & 1930s,
common, mint condition **5-10**

Sam'l Davis 1886, wooden box, held
50 cigars packed in four rows,
w/hinges, often w/a button clasp,
no inside pictorial label, made by
Sam'l Davis, Pennsylvania,
ca. 1950s, mint condition...............   **3-5**

Women's Rights Concha Regalia,
nailed wood box of 100 cigars,
black & white label depicting street
scene w/picketers from Democratic
& Independent parties soliciting
women's attention, John Rauch,
factory 97 in the 6th tax district of
Indiana, ca. 1880, excellent
condition **400-600**

Yellow Kid Reina Victoria, nailed
wood box of 100 cigars, colorful
label depicts the Yellow Kid
smoking a cigar, plus front page of
New York Journal, signed by R.F.
Outcault, ca. 1901-1909, unknown
New York City cigarmaker,
desirable box **600-800**

CIGARETTE DISPENSERS &
ASHTRAYS

Poodle's Head Ashtray

Ashtray, ceramic, three-dimensional figure of poodle's head w/mouth open to receive cigarette, smoke comes out dog's eyes when cigarette left in ashtray, brown & white glaze (ILLUS.) **10-12**

Ashtray, advertising, clear glass w/black imprint "Biloxi Belle Casino" (Biloxi, MS), after 1992, 3 1/4" **3-5**

Ashtray, advertising, amethyst glass w/smooth bottom & white imprint "Hotel Fremont, Las Vegas, Nevada," ca. 1970s, 3 1/2" d. **5-10**

Ashtray, advertising, clear glass, w/red on white imprint "The Fabulous Flamingo, The Showplace of the Nation, Las Vegas, Nevada" & artwork of flamingo w/head lowered, ca. 1947-1967, 4" d. **15-25**

Ashtray, advertising, smoked glass, imprinted in red, "Flamingo Hilton, Las Vegas-Nevada" w/the three flamingos logo, after 1971, 4" d..... **5-10**

Ashtray, ceramic, in shape of the state of New York, w/decals picturing state capitol, state flower & state fish, ca. 1950s, approximately 5"........................... **5-15**

Ashtray, ceramic, three dimensional figure of Ubangi, smoke comes out his pursed lips when cigarette left in ashtray, brown glaze, approximately 7" h., unusual **10-25**

Ashtray, ceramic, multi-colored, shaped as a tobacco leaf w/three dimensional figures of Uncle Sam & Cuban man carrying a giant

Elephant Cigarette Dispenser

cigar, ca. 1920s, approximately 8" l., excellent condition............. **85-100**

Dispenser, cast-iron elephant dispenses cigarette under his belly when tail is cranked, holds approximately one pack in howdah on his back, known in red, black & green, ca. 1920s-1930s, 7" l. (ILLUS.) **50-75**

CIGARETTE LIGHTERS

Evans Ciagrette Lighter/Cigarette Case

Evans cigarette lighter/cigarette case, mother-of-pearl squares, excellent condition, set of 2 (ILLUS.) **75-125**

Dachshund-shaped Figural Cigarette Lighter

Figural, pot metal, shape of a dachshund, made to imitate its much more valuable Vienna bronze counterpart, tag has 1912

patent & is marked "Austria,"
4 1/4" l. (ILLUS.)............................. **????**

Ronson, pocket, Diana model,
ca. 1950s.................................... **10-20**

Ronson, table-type, Queen Anne
model, ca. 1936-1959................... **10-20**

MATCH BOXES & COVERS

Advertising, Bell's Waterproof Wax
Vestas, tin matchbox, w/slip-top &
striker on bottom, litho in blue,
white & tan w/three lines of
lettering, English, ca. 1900-1910,
approximately 2 3/4 x 1 1/2".......... **5-20**

Dewey for President, cover w/photo
of Dewey, ca. 1948...................... **10-15**

First Nite-Life matchcover, set of
famous personalities on standard
covers, colored in pastel, complete
w/original strikers, Diamond Match
Co., 1938, set of 24 .... **20-40**

Girlie matchbook cover, w/original
strikers, "It's great to be an
American" on one side, pin-up girls
by Merlin on the other, Maryland
Match Company, ca. 1940,
excellent condition **3-8**

Lux Super fosforos match box,
cardboard box w/sliding drawer,
label depicts baseball player,
Cuban, ca. 1940s-1950s, good
condition.................................... **10-20**

NBC/CBS stars matchcover,
famous radio personalities on
standard match covers complete
w/original strikers, Diamond Match
Co., 1935, part of set.................... **1-5**

MATCHCOVERS

Airline, "Alaska Airlines, Route of the
Starliners" on front, "24 Years
Serving All Alaska" on saddle,
"Alaska Airlines" on back, map
w/phones inside, dark blue, yellow,
red & white, thirty-strike size **$9-15**

Airline, "American Airlines Inc." w/AA
& outline of plane on back,
"Largest Airline in the United
States" on saddle, "Shell Aviation
Products" w/"Fly Safely with Shell"
on front, red, white & dark blue **8-13**

Airline, "Pan Am 747," pop-up, color
photo of plane interior on front
back, 747 inside, Atlas Match,
1969 .... **23-28**

Airline, "Pan Am" movies set of 50,
New Zealand issue, 1976.......... **135-160**

Airline, "TWA 747," pop-up, white,
Pipo, Japan, 1969, thirty-strike
size, back striker........................... **15-18**

Airline, "United Airlines" on saddle,
"Fly the Friendly Skies of United"
on front & back, blue & white, back
striker.. **3-5**

Buckeye Beer Matchcover

Beer & Ale, "Buckeye Beer" w/bottle
on back & waiter on front, "The
Buckeye Brewing Co., Toledo,
Ohio, Phone AD 7201" on saddle,
green, red & white (ILLUS.)........... **4-8**

Beer & Ale, "Budweiser," "Anheuser-
Busch, Champion Clydesdale
Horses" on back, blank saddle,
color drawing of eight-horse team
on front, red, green, brown, black &
white, forty-strike size, royal flash.. **8-16**

Beer & Ale, "Coors" on back, "Coors
Export Lager" on saddle, "The
Brass Rail, 1518 Champa Street,
Denver, Colo." on front, colorful
waterfall scene w/can & short-
necked bottle inside, yellow, red,
blue & white, forty-strike size, royal
flash.. **10-12**

Beer & Ale, "Falstaff" shield logo
w/"America's Premium Quality

Beer" on front & back, "Falstaff Brewing Corp. St. Louis, MO." on saddle, white, red, yellow & black . **5-8**

Beer & Ale, "Hamm's Beer.... from the land of sky blue waters" on front, "Refreshingly yours" on saddle, ad on back, stock design in white, blue & red........................... **5-8**

Beer & Ale, "Heileman's Old Style Lager, G. Heileman Brewing Co., La Crosse, Wisconsin" on back, "Aged Longer Than Any Other Beer" on saddle, "Cavalier" on front, white, green & yellow **6-12**

Beer & Ale, "Michelob..., period" w/Busch logo on front, "Anheuser-Busch, Inc." on saddle, Michelob shield on back, black, red, white & gold, thirty-strike size.................... **5-10**

Beer & Ale, "Olympia Beer It's the Water" on front & back, "It's the Water" on saddle, "makes the difference" w/"Olympia Brewing Co., Tumwater, Wash., U.S.," on back, black, orange & white **5-8**

Pabst Breweries Matchcover

Beer & Ale, "Pabst Breweries" logo w/"Houtz Tobacco Company, Phone 534, Sunbury, Penna" on front, can w/glass & "Pabst TapaCan" on back, three cans w/"Pabst TapaCan" across sticks, "Pabst TapaCan, Brewery Goodness, Sealed Right In" on inside, dark blue, light blue, red & white (ILLUS.).............................. **25-40**

Beer & Ale, "Rainier Beer, Mountain Finest" on front & back, blank saddle, white, yellow & red, back striker... **5-10**

Beer & Ale, "Red Ribbon Beer" w/bottle & sandwich on back, "Famous Since 1870" on saddle, ad on front, stock design in black, red, silver, yellow & white **8-16**

Beer & Ale, "Schlitz, The Beer that made Milwaukee Famous" on front & back, blank saddle, brown, white, blue & green, front or back striker.. **6-11**

Beer & Ale, "Schmidt's Beer, The Brew that grew with the Great Northwest" on front & back, "Jacob Schmidt Brewing Co., St. Paul, Minn" on saddle, white, red & blue **6-12**

Beer & Ale, "Stroh's & Stroh Light, Official Beers 1982 World's Fair" on front back, red, white & blue, back striker & thirty-strike size....... **5-10**

Beer & Ale, "Stroz, The Orchid of Beers" on back, "Since 1876" on saddle, ad on front, stock design in white, red, pink & brown **5-10**

Blacks, "Coon Chicken Inn, 2950 Highland Drive, Salt Lake City, Phone 7-1062" on back, black bellhop on front, "Famous Coast to Coast" on saddle, gold, red, black, white & pink **28-30**

Blacks, "Cotton Patch, 2720 Midway Drive, San Diego, California" w/mammy on front, "AC. 3-8316" on saddle, "The Bayou Room" on back, map inside, red, white & black **12-18**

Blacks, "Frostop, 22nd Ave & 64th St, Kenosha, Wis" & depicting stylized black face w/large lips w/few teeth & "Man dat sho is good!" on forehead on front, "Star Match Co., St. Louis, MO," black, red & white (ILLUS. p. 382) **23-28**

Blacks, "Hotel Barlow, d.M. Floyd, Manager, Hope Arkansas" on front, "Air Cooled...," on saddle, name w/black man & watermelon w/"Down Where The Watermelon Grow" on back, red, green, white & black **18-23**

Blacks, "Mammy's Chicken Farm 60, W 52nd St, New York" & depicting mammy w/chicken dinner on back, gold, black, red & white **5-8**

Double Mint Gum Matchcover

Black Matchcover

Blacks, "Mammy's" on footer, "Black Mammy" on front & back, "HI. 5-4948" on saddle, "Fine Foods, Cocktails, Capitol Drive at Teutonia, Milwaukee" on back, map inside, white, black, red & yellow, thirty-strike size, back striker **15-20**

Blacks, "Picaninny, Famous for Barbecued Food" & depicting black child w/red lips & name on front, addresses on back, gold, black & red, Lion Match Corporation **18-23**

Blacks, "Sambo's Pancakes" on footer, Indian boy w/tiger on front & back, "they're delightful" on saddle, city list inside, white, red, yellow, green & pink, front or back striker **10-12**

Candy, "Reese's Peanut Butter Cups 1¢" on front, "H.B. Reese Candy Co., Hershey, PA." on saddle, box of 1¢ candies on back, orange, green, white & black **5-8**

Candy, "Tootsie Rolls, America's Favorite Chewy Chocolate Candy" w/boy & girl riding on roll, "Over 240 Million sold last year 1¢ and 5¢ rolls," dark blue, light blue, red, white & brown, full length **7-10**

Chewing gum, "Buy Wrigley's Double Mint Quality Gum," w/dark green arrow, orange, yellow & white, full length (ILLUS.) **5-8**

Girlie, Girlie Matchcover Catalog, No. 200, Marilyn Monroe, drawing on front, thirty-strike size, back striker **17-23**

Girlie, Girlie Matchcover Catalog, No. 247, Domino Club, San Francisco w/reclining nude "Evelyn" on back, blank saddle, thirty-strike size **10-12**

Girlie, Girlie Matchcover Catalog, No. 405, Girlie, black & white photo by Ray Schulz, ca. 1989, giant, full-length **11-20**

Girlie set, Arrow Match Company, Set No. 2 of 5, "Scotty Says!: Go West Young Man," "Always Vote!" "Support The Community That Supports You," "Drive Safely," "Salute America See It First!" drawings, ad on front, Girlie Matchcover Catalog p. 2, ca. 1950, the set **28-30**

Girlie set, Playboy 25th Anniversary, Set of 11, back striker **8-16**

Girlie set, Playboy Club, Set of 17, 20th Anniversary, silver, cities on footer, ca. 1980, back striker **19-25**

Girlie set, Playboy Club, Set of 19, "1961 HMH Publishing Co." on back, back striker, the set **16-25**

Girlie set, Superior Match Co. (Elvgren), Set No. 1 of 5, "A Good Hook Up," "A Live Wire," "Doctor's Orders," "Man's Best Friend," "Sure Shot," ad on front, Girlie Matchcover Catalog p. 26, ca. 1938, the set **20-25**

Political, "Bush for President" w/photo on front, dated Nov. 8, 1988, thirty-strike size, back striker   **3-6**

Political, "Elect Willkie [pop-up], Preserve Your Freedom, Be Thankful You Can Still Do It" on front, blank saddle, "Win with Wendell Willkie" on back, red, white & blue (ILLUS.) **14-25**

Wendell Willkie Pop-up Matchcover

Political, "Goldwater in '64" on front back, white & blue **7-10**

Political, "I Like Ike" on front, "Delaware Citizens for Eisenhower-Nixon, 613 Orange St., Wilmington, Delaware" on back, blank saddle, red, white & blue.. **15-18**

Political, "Kennedy for President" w/photo on front, "Johnson for Vice President" w/photo on back, "Vote Democratic" on saddle, red, white & blue **8-17**

Political, "Nixon Agnew" on front in red & white lettering, elephant on back, thirty-strike size.................... **8-13**

Political, "Ross Perot for President, 1992" on back, "Elect" on saddle, photo of Perot on front, "Vote Nov. 3rd" on footer, red, white & blue **3-5**

Political, "Truman/Barkley Inaugural Dinner" w/photos of both on front, U.S. Seal on back, Mayflower Hotel & names inside, dated January 19, 1949......................... **35-45**

Political, "Win With Wallace" on front, blank saddle, "Vote

Independent American Party" on back, white & dark blue **8-14**

Railroad, "Chicago Great Western Railroad" logo on front, blank saddle, "Ship Via Chicago Great Western Ry." w/circular map on back, red, white, gold & black or black, white, gold & red **5-8**

Railroad, "Litchfield & Madison Railway, The St. Louis Gateway Route" on front, blank saddle, "L&M Engine 201" w/drawing on back, "Daily Co-ordinate Through...," on inside, red, white, gold & black................................. **10-12**

Railroad, "Milwaukee (The) Road, Out in Front" on front, blank saddle, "Route of the Hiawathas" w/photo of electric locomotive on back, "Travel with Pleasure" inside, white, orange, blue, maroon & black **5-8**

Railroad, "Milwaukee (The) Road, Ship and Travel via..." on front, blank saddle, "The Milwaukee Road, America's Resourceful Railroad" w/trains on back, yellow, white, red & black **4-7**

Railroad, "Pennsylvania Railroad" w/streamlined train & "Serving the Nation" on back, "Shortest East West Route" on saddle, "Travel Luxury at Low Fares" w/"The Great All-Weather Fleet" & drawing on front, black, red & white................ **7-10**

Railroad, "Reading Lines, The Wall Street, A Smart..., Modern..., Colorful..., Train...," on front, "The Crusader" w/silver train & "Stainless Steel" on back, "between Philadelphia and New York" on saddle, "Two Famous Reading...," inside, blue, yellow, silver & white **8-13**

Railroad, "Union Pacific Railroad" shield on back, "Dependable Transportation" w/train on front, red, white, blue & yellow............... **5-8**

Soda Pop, "7UP" w/small bottle on front, "Take Some Home" on saddle, "Fresh UP..., 7UP..., It Likes You" on back, green, red, white & black **9-15**

Soda Pop, "Drink Coca-Cola" w/lollipop logo on front, "Drink Coca-Cola" on saddle, "Take home a carton, Get that Refreshing New Feeling" w/a six pack on back, yellow, red, green & brown **8-14**

Pepsi-Cola Matchcover

Soda pop, "Pepsi-Cola, 5¢ Bigger Drink/Better Taste" on front & back, "More Bounce to the Ounce!" on saddle, "Say Pepsi...," inside, dark blue, light blue, red & white (ILLUS.) **8-13**

World's Fair, Knoxville, Tenn., 1982, "Stroh's Light, Official Beer 1982 World's Fair" on front & back, blue, red, yellow & white, thirty-strike size, back striker **6-10**

World's Fair, New York, 1939-40, "Don't Mark Time, 4 Minute Crossings," colorful **7-11**

World's Fair set, Seattle, 1962, Century 21, Boulevards of the World, Coliseum 21, The Gayway,

Monorail, Mt. Rainier, United States Science Pavilion, set of six **25-30**

MISCELLANEOUS

Cigar box, Safety brand, wooden box w/a fine gilded lithographed label inside the lid, a colorful scene of a uniformed male racer & his safety bicycle, exterior sides also illustrated, dated 1901, fair condition **154**

Cigar lighter, cast white metal, figural, a figure of a stocky gentleman wearing a top hat & resembling W.C. Fields stands besides a stone bucket for matches, oil burner in the top hat, on a stepped oblong base, traces of gilt, 5 1/4" h **413**

Cigarette case, sterling silver, obverse enamel decorated w/nautical flags of the alphabet, reverse w/a monogram encircled by a wreath, dated "July 4, 1903," 3 x 3 1/2" (wear, scratches) **920**

"Federal-Style Humidor"

Humidor, cov., inlaid mahogany, Federal-Style, rectangular form w/locked cover over two drawers w/brass hardware, ca. 1900 (ILLUS.) **1,150**

Pipe, carved wood, figural, in the form of two faces, decorated in red, yellow & black paint, late 19th - early 20th c., 24" l. (minor cracks) . **173**

Tobacco box, cov., brass, long narrow oval shape w/two hinged flat covers, a short end one & a long lengthwise one, long cover engraved "E. Ingham 1860," footed, 6 7/8" l. (one foot bent) **193**

Tobacco canister, cov., bentwood, cylindrical w/fitted flat cover, the sides w/the original red paper label printed in black & gold "Velocipede Tobacco Fine Cut" surrounding a scene of a couple on velocipedes, tax stamp for 1868, 10 lbs., 12" h., (some paper loss) **935**

Tobacco cutter, cast iron, countertype, "Brighton," elf thumbing his nose on handle **175**

Tobacco cutter, cast iron, countertype, model of a dog **450**

MISCELLANY

Match safe, brass, figural, in the form of a boy's head sticking out of a folded shirt, marked "Tim & Co., Tim Wallerstein & Co.," late 19th c., 2 3/4" l. **575**

PAPER GOODS

Cigar bands, mounted in album without glue, bands complete w/white tabs at end, more than half are pictorial bands of Presidents, animals, kings, famous persons, etc., approximately 1,000 in set. **100-200**

Postcard, "A Modern Tobacco Factory, Tampa, Fla.," color **3-5**

Postcard Showing A Tobacco Buyer

Postcard, real photo, black & white, shows tobacco buyer, reads "Our Mr. Levy Pres. Enterprise Cigar Co. Buying Havana in Cuba for the Celebrated Lord Stirling & Taking Cigars" (ILLUS.) **10-20**

Poster, L & M cigarettes, featuring Matt Dillon & Miss Kitty from Gunsmoke, reads "They Said It Couldn't Be Done But L&M Did It! - Don't settle for one...without the other!," ca. 1960s, excellent condition **50-75**

PERSONAL ITEMS

Cigar Case

Cigar case, aluminum, holds three cigars, decoration cut into the aluminum along w/inscription "Jamestown, 1907," apparently purchased or received as a prize at the Jamestown Exposition honoring the 300th anniversary of the first colony, 2 1/2 x 4 1/2" (ILLUS.) **30-50**

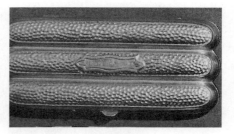

Cigar Case

Cigar case, nickel plated metal, w/space for name or inscription, ca. 1900-1930, 2 1/2 x 4 1/2" (ILLUS.) **15-30**

Cigar case, silver plated, gold wash inside, holds three cigars, minor decoration, ca. 1900-1930, 2 1/2 x 4 1/2" **25-50**

Cigar clipper, brass, shaped like scissors, made in U.S. & Europe, ca. 1890s-1920 .... **25-40**

Cigar Clipper Shaped Like A Man

Cigar clipper, shaped like man sitting on chamber pot, clip cigar by putting it in hole in his stomach, push down on his head & cigar trimming falls into chamber pot, European origin, turn-of-the-century, 6" h. (ILLUS.) **150-400**

Matchbox Grip

Matchbox grip, silver plated, three-sided, device for protecting matchboxes, w/embossed design of the United Brotherhood of Carpenters & Joiners of America, reads "See That This Label Appears On All Wood Work," 1 1/4 x 2 1/4", rare (ILLUS.) **60-100**

Advertising Matchsafe

Matchsafe, nickel plated w/celluloid wrap- around, depicts brewery worker's union label, reads "International Union of the United Brewery Workmen of America ask your Support against Prohibition As it is Detrimental to All," ca. 1920, 1 1/2 x2 1/2", excellent condition (ILLUS.) **150-300**

PIPES & CHEROOT HOLDERS

To be considered in excellent condition, Meerschaum pipes should have no damage & should be smoothly colored, not mottled. The amber or plastic stem should be in place as, ideally, is the case in which it originally came. Briar pipes should show no evidence of reddish colored fill (it looks like clay) to correct blemishes. Pipes should not be dented around the bowl, the result of being banged to loosen tobacco.

Cheroot holder, Meerschaum, w/carving of three nondescript dogs sitting sideways on straight stem, amber bit, approximately 3 1/2" l. (missing case) **35-50**

Cheroot holder, Meerschaum, w/amber stem, three deer w/large three-dimensional carving of antlers in crook of holder, exceptionally carved, ca. 1890-1910, 4 3/4 x 3" in original case, mint condition **50-75**

Cheroot holder, Meerschaum, w/carving of two riders in hunting costume & seven dogs looking for a fox, seen peeking from around the bow, bowl at 45 angle to stem, original fitted wooden case lined w/satin, covered w/split leather, inside marked "Paris," European origin, ca. 1890-1910, approximately 5" l. **250-400**

Pipe, Meerschaum, w/slightly bent amber stem & bit, carved in the form of a hand holding a skull, good detail, stands upright when resting, without case, ca. early 20th c.. **100-175**

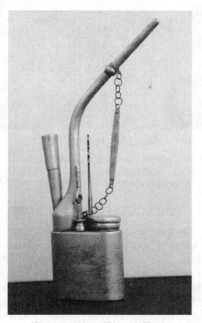

Chinese Water Pipe W/Tools

Pipe, water w/tools, made of paktong, Chinese origin, 20th c., approximately 10" h. (ILLUS.) ... **50-125**

Pipe, Meerschaum, carved w/face of Napoleon, excellent turn-of-the-century likeness, European origin, approximately 6" l. (ILLUS.) **150-300**

Meerschaum Pipe Carved W/Face of Napoleon

Pipe, Meerschaum, w/slightly bent plastic stem, w/two carved bare breasted ladies swooping about garlands of roses, European origin, ca. late 1800s, approximately 6 1/4 x4" (ILLUS.) **400-650**

Pipe, Meerschaum, carved in the form of an elephant w/bead eyes, approximately 14" l. w/plastic bit, no case, Turkish, ca. 1960-1990 **60-150**

Meerschaum Pipe

SNUFF BOTTLES & BOXES

BOTTLES

Agate, brown w/the lighter brown skin cleverly carved in the form of a foo dog incense burner, China **489**

Agate, moss agate of pebble-form carved w/double-gourds in the darker brown of the stone, well hollowed out, green jade branch-form top, China, late 19th c. **920**

Agate, patterned grey & white stone, well-hollowed, stopper of coral-

colored Peking glass, China, late
19th c. **633**

Bamboo, carved in the form of a pair
of peaches, China, 20th c. (no
stopper) **201**

Burnt jade, well-hollowed, fine deep
amber tone, China, late 19th c. **173**

Lacquer, cinnabar lacquer carved
deeply w/a landscape scene
w/children, China, 19th c. **86**

Peking glass, coral color carved w/a
dragon & phoenix, green jade
stopper, China **345**

Porcelain, covered w/a yellow glaze
over an underglaze-iron red
landscape, molded lion mask
handles & a coral-glazed porcelain
stopper, fake Ch'ien lung mark,
China **288**

Porcelain, model of a crab claw
covered in an orange glaze, China **115**

Porcelain, white enameled w/a
cricket on each side, Tao Kuang
mark & period, China..................... **575**

Soapstone, carved in high-relief w/a
pine tree & a horse, China............. **115**

Soapstone, carved in the form of a
Buddha's hand citron w/fine
markings in scarlet & black,
stopper of coral carved in a foliate
form, China, 19th c. **690**

BOXES

Tortoiseshell, carved & decorated
w/Chinese figures, early
19th c., 7/8 x 1 1/2 x 2 1/2" (some
chips & losses) **374**

TOBACCIANA FOLK ARTS

Dish, glass, covered w/cigar bands in
carefully chosen geometric pattern.
ca. 1910-1920, 6 1/2" d., excellent
unfaded condition (ILLUS.)........... **25-50**

Pillow cover, made from satin cigar
ribbons. ca. 1900-1920, value
depends on condition (no less than
excellent is acceptable), the
selection of ribbons & the artistry of
presentation, 2' sq. (ILLUS.)...... **75-250**

Glass Dish Covered w/Cigar Bands

Satin Cigar Ribbons Pillow

Vase, glass, covered w/cigar bands
in random patterns, ca. 1910-1920,
6" h., excellent unfaded condition. **40-60**

TOBACCO PRODUCT TINS

Smoking tobacco tins are among the more expensive tobacco collectibles. Plenty of tobacco tins are worth only a few dollars, but a surprising number are worth more than $100.00 and a significant handful worth $1,000.00 or more. Tobacco tins that are rusty, damaged, or badly scratched have no value. Condition is absolutely vital in the world of tin cans. A can worth $1,000.00 in mint condition may sit on your shelf unsold for years at $100.00 if it has condition problems. To qualify as "excellent condition" the printed surface of the can should be unmarked or with slight soil and/or use wear outside the image area. The revenue stamp *may be scratched or removed. A can is not "excellent" if the image is scratched or if "paint" [ink] is flaking off. Values given are for retail of cans in excellent condition. Cans in less than excellent condition retail for 25% to 50% of the prices shown.*

Alumni Burley Cut, vertical pocket tin in unusual concave configuration, predominantly silver tin with bust of man in cap & gown, United States Tobacco Co., Virginia, approximately 4 x 3 x 1", good condition **700-1,500**

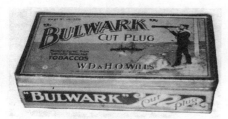

Bulwark Cut Plug Tin

Bulwark cut plug, tin horizontal box, predominantly gold & blue, depicting a sailor looking through a spyglass, made in England by W.D. & H.O. Wills, approximately 6 x 4 x 1 1/2", excellent condition (ILLUS.) **20-35**

George Washington cut plug, tin lunch box, w/wire & wood handle & metal clasp, R.J. Reynolds, Winston-Salem, NC, after 1910, common, approximately 7 1/2 x 4 1/2 x 4 1/2", excellent-mint condition **30-40**

Hi-Plane smooth cut tobacco, vertical pocket tin, lithograph on tin in white on red background w/single engine, near mint condition **25-45**

Hi-Plane smooth cut tobacco, vertical pocket tin, lithograph on tin in white on red background w/China clipper, good condition .... **200-1,000 and up**

Just Suits cut plug, tin lunch box, w/wire handle & metal clasp on end of box, Buchanon & Lyall, New York (div of P.Lorillard, Virginia),

after 1910, approximately 8 x 5 1/4 x 4", common, mint condition **30-40**

Lucky Strike cigarettes, flat tin box called a "Flat Fifties," American Tobacco Company, regularly found in white, green, black, white & Christmas versions, approximately 6 x 4", full, near mint condition **15-25**

Lucky Strike Tin

Lucky Strike (smoking tobacco), small green box w/red circle, some gold trim, "R.A.Patterson Tobacco Co. Rich'd, VA" (div. of American Tobacco Co.), ca. early 20th c., approximately 4 1/4" l., 3" w., excellent condition (ILLUS.) **20-40**

Niggerhair Tobacco Tin

Niggerhair Tobacco, tin can w/bail handle & slip-top lid, black on brown, pictures South Sea Islander w/nose bone, earrings & predominant hair-do, American Tobacco Company, ca. 1920s - 1946 when name changed to Biggerhair, approximately 6 3/4 x 5 1/2" d., common (ILLUS. p. 389) **200-300**

Prince Albert crimp cut (smoking tobacco), vertical pocket tin & other configurations, in various sizes. R.J. Reynolds Tobacco Co., Winston-Salem, North Carolina, ca. 1910 to 1960s, full, near mint condition **5-15**

Prince Albert Now King (smoking tobacco), "Now King" printed under portrait of Albert, most valuable as a vertical pocket tin (but known in other configurations), R.J. Reynolds Tobacco Co., Winston-Salem, North Carolina, ca. 1910s, good condition **200-400**

Rex pipe & cigarette tobacco, vertical pocket tin, Spaulding & Merrick, Chicago (div. of Liggett & Myers), approximately 5 x 2" w., 5" h., excellent condition.............. **50-75**

Stag Tobacco Tin

Stag tobacco, small lightly oval upright pocket tin w/flip-top cover, predominantly red, depicting a large stag, numerous other varieties of Stag are found (ILLUS.) **50-75**

Stanwix Ground Plug Tin

Stanwix ground plug, vertical pocket tin w/flip- top lid, Falk Tobacco Co., Richmond, approximately 4 1/2 x 3 x 1", excellent condition (ILLUS.) **150-250**

White Ash cigar, round woodgrained tin can w/slip-top lid, newspaper-style black & white photo of Snyder in suit & tie is central oval image on can, originally held 50 5¢ cigars upright, made by Snyder in Pennsylvania, a large well-known company, ca. 1930s, approximately 5 1/2" h., common, excellent condition **10-20**

MISCELLANEOUS

Cigar mold, ten cigar size, hardwood, made by Miller, Dubrul & Peters, ca. 1880s through 1920s, common **20-35**

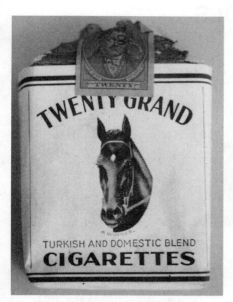

Twenty Grand Cigarette Pack

Cigarette pack, Twenty Grand, paper cup-type package, image on pack depicts race horse, printed brown on white (ILLUS.)............... **5-10**

Cigar Maker's Union Tray

Tray, advertising Cigar Maker's Union & Union, tin 10 1/2 x 13 1/4", ca. 1902-1905 (ILLUS.)............. **150-200**

TOOLS

Nickel Plated Anvil

Anvil, Gem City Elevator Works, nickel plated w/raised cast letters, 3 1/2" l. (ILLUS.) **$125**

Axe, Hibbard, Spencer & Bartlett Co., single bit, marked "Our Very Best," 36" l. 175

Axe, Kelly Axe & Tool Works, Charleston, No. 18722, dated "1912," 7" l. 125

Axe, Kelly Axe & Tool Works, Charleston, No. 33628, single bit, individually registered, 30" l. 115

Axe, Lee, Colt & Anderson Hardware, Omaha, embossed double bit felling axe, ca. 1900, 9" l. 365

Axe, Plumb (Fayette R.), Philadelphia, belt style, marked "O.E.S. 1944," 18" l. 395

Bevel, Craftsman Wood Service Co., Chicago, "12 In 1" bevel w/original card, 6" l. 45

Bevel, Standard Tool Co., Athol, Mass, Stephen Bellows patent square, pat. March 11, 1884, 9" l. . . 550

Brace, Brown & Wells, plated beech w/improved button chuck, 13 1/2" l. 425

Brace, Flather (D.), Solly Works, Sheffield, anti-friction head, "John Bottom" pat., 13 1/2" l. 235

Brace, Morrison (J.H.), pat. Feb. 1, 1898, "The Challenge," intricate gearing, 19" l. (ILLUS.) 745

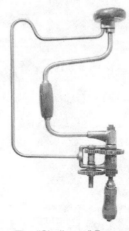

The "Challenge" Brace

Brace, Stanley Tools, No. 2102-10, "Yankee" ratchet, 10" sweep, 10" l.   95

Caliper, Athol Machine Co., Athol, Mass., hermaphrodite w/slide adjust leg, 4" l. 45

Caliper, Smith (E.G.), Columbia, Penna., No. 128, adjustable slide type, 6" l. 85

Caliper, Stevens & Co., Page & Hadley patent Feb. 8, 1870, 4" l. ... 135

Caliper, Union Tool Co., Orange, Mass., quick-adjust, pat. June 13, 1914, 7" l. 45

Caliper, unmarked, "lady-leg" style w/circular joint, 6" l. 1,050

Carpenter's slick, Buck Brothers, 3" w. blade, bulbous handle, 18" l.   145

Chisel, Parr (Geo.), Buffalo, N.Y., heavy socket-framing type, 2" w., 12 1/4" l. 55

Chisel, Swan (James) Co. (The), heavy socket framing, 2" w., 17" l.. 95

Chisel, Witherby (T.H.), heavy socket-framing type, 2" w., 12" l. ... 75

Drill, push-type, nickeled lignum vitae knobs, A. h. Reid 65

Gauge, Peoria Corage Co., Peoria, Ill., rope & twine gauge w/full nickel plating, 5" l. 35

Gauge, Starrett Co. (The I.S.S.), Athol, Mass., No. 45, adjustable depth, extra long body, 10" l. 85

Hammer, Atha Tool Co., No. 20, farrier's tool w/horseshoe logo, 13" l. 45

Hammer, Belknap Hardware Co., Louisville, No. BG 47-7, claw style, 7 oz., 11" l. 65

Hammer, Cheney, Little Falls, N.Y., No. 885, nail-holding claw type w/original handle, 12 1/2" l. 95

Hammer, Heller Brothers Co., Newark, N.J., No. 523, claw type, adze eye, plain face, 16" l. 155

Hammer, Maydole (D.), Norwich, N.Y., ball peen style w/full nickel plating, 2 oz. size, 9" l. 65

Hammer, Maydole (D.), Norwich, N.Y., No. 120, ball peen style w/early imprint, 4 oz. size, original handle, 10 1/2" l. 35

Hammer, Stanley Rule & Level, marked "Stanley's Standard," original decal, 16 oz. size, ca. 1920s-30s, 13 1/2" l. 65

Hatchet, American Ax & Tool Co., Glassport, marked "A.A. & T. Co." on head, pat. April 17, 1900, 15" l. 75

Hatchet, Vaughn & Bushnell, Chicago, Ill., embossed lathing hatchet w/deeply etched logo, 13" l. 75

Level, Davis Level & Tool Co., No. 2, cast iron w/filigree casting, 95% original black Japanned finish, 12" l. (ILLUS.) 695

Level, Goodell Pratt Company, No. 509, open-end style, 18" l. 65

Level, Southington Hardware Co., torpedo-style, mahogany, ca. 1913, 9" l. 55

Level, Stanley Rule & Level, No. 32, graduating w/green paper label on inside of inclinometer dial, pat. April 21, 1863, 28" l. 895

Level, Stanley Rule & Level, No. 41, ornate brass top, pat. June 23, 1896, 3" l. 65

Level, Stanley Rule & Level, No. 93, brass bound mahogany w/original decal, "Sweetheart" trademark, 30" l. 195

Level, Stanley Tools, No. 257, laminated pine, non-adjustable, original box, 24" l. 95

Level, Starrett Co., (The I.S.S.), Athol, Mass., No. 135, hexagon pocket-style, full nickel plating, 3" l. 25

Plane, 26" jointer, "Stanley Rule & Level Co., No. 132," ca. 1877 (old repair to handle) 40

Plane, 6 1/4" compass T-Rabbet, 1 1/2" iron, ca. 1844, "W.H. Pond, New Haven" (mark B-1) 35

Plane, complex molder, Grecian Ovolo w/filet, 1 1/2" iron, ca. 1827, "De Valcourt, 107 Elm, N. York," (mark B-1) 75

Plane, Fulton, New York, N.Y., No. 5320, block style, metallic, pat. March 21, 1893, original box, 5 1/2" l. 115

Plane, hollow No. 18, ca. 1832, "J.W. Farr & Co. N. York" (mark D) 25

Plane, hollow No. 8, ca. 1874, "D.R. Barton, Rochester, NY" (mark F)... 20

Davis Cast Iron Level

Plane, panel plow, screw arm, ca. 1853, "R.W. Booth, Cincinnati, OH" (mark A) 75

Plane, router-type, Stanley Model 71 1/2, patent-dated "10/29/01"..... 95

Stanley Rule & Level Plane

Plane, Stanley Rule & Level, No. 62, low angle block style w/original box, 14" l. (ILLUS.) **2,745**

Plumb bob, Braunsdorf-Mueller Co., brass w/B.M.C. logo, Newark, N.J., 4 oz., 4" l. 75

Plumb bob, Dietzgen Co., Eugene, Chicago, No. 14, surveyor's, brass, 6" l. 45

Early Midwest Plumb Bob

Plumb bob, Leistner (P.), St. Charles, Missouri, millwright's w/reversible tip, 7" l. (ILLUS.) 545

Plumb bob, Wells Screw Products Co., San Francisco, Calif., combination Bakelite reel & plumb bob w/original box, 4" l. 125

Rule, d. & S., Bangor Maine, machinist's bench, marked "O. Beers," 12" l. 95

Rule, Lufkin Rule Co. (The), No. 1206, aluminum zig-zag folding type, flat rolled metal, 72" l. 15

Rule, Sawyer Tool Co., Ashburnham, Mass., No. 4 bench rule w/multiple graduations, 4" l. 25

Rule, Stanley Rule & Level, No. 36, two-fold w/square joint, caliper, 6" l. 75

Rule, Stanley Rule & Level, No. 64, four-fold w/square joint, unbound, 12" l. 185

Rule, Stanley Rule & Level, No. 86, four-fold, ivory & German silver, 24" l. 395

Rule, Stanley Tools, No. 36 1/2, two-fold folding rule w/caliper, 12" l. 45

Rule & level, Stanley Rule & Level, No. 96, "Defiance" zig-zag folding type, 72" l. 55

Saw, Disston (H.) & Sons, Philadelphia, Penn., No. 68, dovetail, 15 1/2" l. 55

Saw, Disston (Henry) & Sons, Philadelphia, Penn., No. 9, double-swivel pruning saw, 21" l. 55

"Young Rip" Hack Saw

Saw, Edison Steel Works (The), Cleveland, Ohio, hack saw, all-steel w/triangular blade & original etching, "Young Rip," 16 1/2" l. (ILLUS.) 85

Saw blades, Clemson Brothers Inc., Middletown, N.Y., No. 1218,

blades w/enameled box marked
"The Star Hack Saw, Clemson
Bros. Inc.," 12 1/2" l. **25**

Screwdriver, Millers Falls Company,
No. 29 X, spiral ratchet type
w/original box, 10 1/2" l. **45**

Screwdriver, Millers Falls Company,
No. 852, permaloid handle, original
box, 10" blade, 16 1/2" l. **35**

Spoke shaves: Herbert (A.E.),
Detroit, Mich., patternmaker's,
solid bronze cast, original box,
ca. 1920s, 3 1/2" l., the set **195**

Tape measure, Stanley Rule &
Level, No. 546, round casing,
vertical reading, marked
"patented," ca. 1947-57, 72" l. **45**

Trammels, unmarked, cast brass in
early-style knurling, marked
w/owner's initials "JBO," 4 1/2" l.,
pr. **115**

Wrench, Billings & Spencer Co.
(The), nut wrench w/graduated
center shaft, pat. Feb. 18, 1879,
6" l. **55**

Wrench, Cellman Wrench
Corporation, No. 91, quick-adjust
style, "Polly, pat. April 17, 1923,"
9" l. **55**

Wrench, Elgin (The), pat. June 8,
1897, 7" l. **25**

Nickel Plated Nut Wrench

Wrench, Ellis, nickel plated nut
wrench w/pivot head, pat. Nov. 3,
1903, 6" l. (ILLUS.) **365**

Wrench, La Gripper Wrench Co.,
Battle Creek, quick-adjust nut
wrench, pat. June 28, 1898, 7" l. **325**

Wrench, North Manufacturing Co.,
O.B., New Haven, Conn., cast iron,
pat. Jan. 9, 1877, 6 1/2" l. **95**

TRAMP ART

Tramp art flourished in the United States from about 1875 into the 1930s. These chip-carved woodenwares, mostly in the form of boxes or other useful items, were made mainly from old cigar boxes although fruit and vegetable crates were also used. The wood is predominately edge-carved and subsequently layered to create a unique effect. Completed items were given an overall stained finish which was sometimes further enhanced with painted highlights. Though there seems to be no written record of the artists, many of whom were itinerants, there is a growing interest in collecting this ware.

Bank, layered rosettes on sides & front, decorative brass tacks securing pyramids, coin deposited in slot drawer is pulled, signed "A.L. 1885," 5" h., 7 1/2" w., 5" deep **$295**

Box, cov., rectangular, a high tapering rectangular stepped pedestal supporting the large conforming box w/stepped sides & a high stepped cover, colored cigar box label inside the cover, late 19th - early 20th c., 10" l., 8" h. **220**

Applied-carving Birdcage

Birdcage, house-shaped w/sculptured & applied bird & flower carvings, metal & wooden grills, ca. 1885, 18" h., 14 1/4" w., 13 1/2" deep (ILLUS.).................... **600**

Box, five pyramids on top w/large pyramids on sides, sits on painted gold footed legs, ca. 1915, 6 1/2" h., 6" w., 3" deep **475**

Box, book-shaped, large heart cut-out on front w/initials "F.S." & dated "1914," 6" h., 6" w., 3" deep........... **395**

Box, cigar box w/applied diamond & circular layered shapes, porcelain button adorns each section, ca. 1900, 6" h., 8 1/2" w., 6" deep . **250**

Box, jewelry, decorated w/brass lion pulls on sides, lock & key lid w/carved wood legend, marked "Alfons Cuns 1908 Marla Maes," web-footed, 6 1/4" h., 13" w., 10 3/4" deep **950**

Rare Box with Acorn Finial

Box, round w/carved acorn finial, built up pyramids around sides, woman's photo under lid, ca. 1890, 7" h., 6 1/2" w., 6 1/2" deep (ILLUS.) **485**

Box, double-pedestal box-on-box, smaller top section w/lift-off top, bottom compartment surrounded by arrowhead-like points, ca. 1910, 8" h., 10" w., 5 3/8" deep **350**

Box, octagonal shape on pedestal, rounded base, pyramid sides w/scored top layer, velvet lining, ca. 1930, 9" h., 7" w., 7" deep **225**

Box, single circular pedestal w/hinged top, flat top layers on pyramids, mirror under lid, ca. 1890, 10" h., 8" w., 6 1/2" deep **500**

Box, simple singular pyramid top on hinges, lined w/blue velvet, six secret compartments slide open on

sides & top, ca. 1920, 14" h.,
17" w., 13" deep **850**

Sewing Box

Box, sewing, painted red, white &
blue, over-painted detailing on
pyramid tops, pincushion top,
printed cigar box label under
fabric-lined lid, ca. 1890,
19 1/2" h., 16 1/2" w., 11 1/2" deep
(ILLUS.) **4,200**

Ziggurat-style Stacking Box

Box, ziggurat-style stacking box
w/pineapple finial, seven drawers
& a lift-out compartment, double-
sided notching w/wave effect,
signed "Miss Lizzie h. Huber,
December 24," ca. 1880,
19 1/2" h., 16 1/2" w., 11 1/2" deep
(ILLUS.) **3,200**

Box, center-type, the ten-sided top
on a pedestal & four shaped legs
w/overall chip-carved raised panel
decoration, northeastern United
States, late 19th c., 33 1/2" w.,
30" h. (imperfections) **1,265**

Boxes, two pagoda-shaped boxes
w/several stacking sections,
painted sandpaper windows,
unique notching style w/pyramids
attached & line-scored, ca. 1910,
12" h., 11" w., 8" deep, pr. **650**

Center hall table, Victorian-style,
scalloped apron w/wood buttons,
built-up pyramids on apron
perimeter, serpentine legs, strong
use of light & dark alternating
woods, ca. 1920, 29" h.,
33 1/2" w., 33 1/2" deep (ILLUS.) . **8,500**

Chest of drawers, drawers
w/crudely attached hearts &
pyramids, metal pulls, scratch-built
from crate wood, full-sized,
ca. 1890, 49" h., 28" w., 14" deep **3,500**

Serpentine-style Clock

Clock, serpentine outline w/light &
dark woods covering plywood
backing, easel stand, ca. 1940,
13 3/4" h., 15 3/4" w., 4 3/4" deep
(ILLUS.) **475**

Clock, house-shaped case w/glass
doors to access clock, incorporates
shingle roof, windows & chimney,
ca. 1890, 25" h., 14" w., 9" deep .. **1,800**

Clock, architectural case w/mirrored
& pyramid-topped wings, flat
layering on spire column, small
clock over archway in center,
ca. 1900, 40" h., 23" w., 15" deep **4,000**

Clock case, miniature house
w/chimney, clock on top, curtains &
crepe flowers in pots below, light &
dark woods, ca. 1930, 13 1/2" h.,
15 3/4" w., 5 3/4" deep **850**

Comb case, dove & horseshoe
design, two smaller heart-shaped
mirrors above & one larger in

Dove & Horseshoe Comb Case

center, two drawers marked with
crosses, dated 1913, 27 1/2" h.,
15" w., 4 1/2" deep. (ILLUS.)........ **3,400**

Crucifix, wood-carved figural Jesus,
footed base, ca. 1920, 26" h.,
12" w. 550

Doll furniture, chair, decorated
w/brass tacks & scalloped rounds
on all edges, ca. 1930, 14" h.,
9" w., 12" deep 750

Doll furniture, miniature dresser
w/seven drawers, glass knobs, top
mirror, signed & dated 1889,
17" h., 9" w., 7" deep. 675

Humidor, circular-box style,
decorated sides lined w/linoleum
on layered feet, ca. 1900, 11" h,
11" w., 7" deep. **1,200**

Inkwell, compartment for two ink
bottles, includes pen & bottles,
3 3/8" h., 6 1/2" w., 4" deep 175

Lamp, pyramid base supports box
w/a column holding light socket,
ca. 1930, 26" h., 6" w., 6" deep 750

Lamp, table-style, octagonal top
w/marquetry design, apron &
center column display different
designs on each side, ca. 1910,
34" h., 32" w., 32" deep **4,800**

Lamp, floor model, carved slender
feet w/narrow stem on three-tiered
pedestal base, scratch-built w/dark
stain, ca. 1930, 68" h., 18" w. **2,800**

Match Safe

Match safe, star decoration on front,
top lifts to insert stick matches held
in open cup in the bottom, painted
gold & silver, 7" h., 4" w., 4" deep
(ILLUS.) 125

Medicine cabinet, scrolling shapes
around front, mirrored door, interior
shelves & glass knob, ca. 1940,
27" h., 20" w., 6 1/2" deep 750

Medicine cabinet, mirrored door
over shelves & drawers, towel bar
at bottom, sides layered
w/diamonds & rosettes, light &
dark woods, ca. 1920, 30" h.,
12" w., 8" deep 900

Music Box

Music box, top crank mechanism
w/porcelain knob, marked "FH,"
plays three different tunes,
ca. 1880, 3" h., 7" w., 6" deep
(ILLUS.) 600

Pedestal stand, flat double-sided
rows dividing areas of squares on
column, painted green, black &
tan, ca. 1930, 25" h., 12 1/2" w.,
12 1/2" deep (ILLUS.) **1,700**

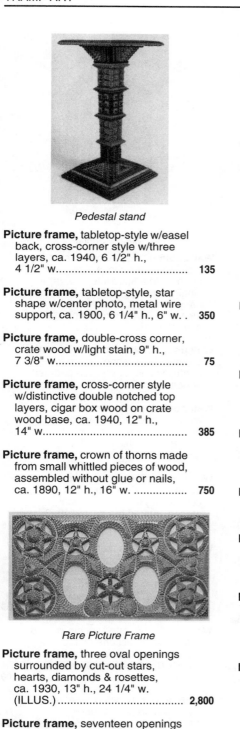

Pedestal stand

Picture frame, tabletop-style w/easel back, cross-corner style w/three layers, ca. 1940, 6 1/2" h., 4 1/2" w... 135

Picture frame, tabletop-style, star shape w/center photo, metal wire support, ca. 1900, 6 1/4" h., 6" w. . 350

Picture frame, double-cross corner, crate wood w/light stain, 9" h., 7 3/8" w... 75

Picture frame, cross-corner style w/distinctive double notched top layers, cigar box wood on crate wood base, ca. 1940, 12" h., 14" w... 385

Picture frame, crown of thorns made from small whittled pieces of wood, assembled without glue or nails, ca. 1890, 12" h., 16" w. 750

Rare Picture Frame

Picture frame, three oval openings surrounded by cut-out stars, hearts, diamonds & rosettes, ca. 1930, 13" h., 24 1/4" w. (ILLUS.)...................................... **2,800**

Picture frame, seventeen openings w/lithographs of saints, adorned

w/porcelain buttons, ca. 1890, 13 1/2" h. 15 1/2" w. **725**

Shield Picture Frame

Picture frame, shield-shaped w/gilt liner, six layers of multiple woods, several geometric shapes topped by a heart, ca. 1915, 14" h., 10" w. (ILLUS.) **650**

Picture frame, eight multiple openings, rectangular shape cigar box pyramids over crate wood, ca. 1915, 14" h., 22" w................... **365**

Picture frame, polychrome finish w/mirror & round crest, two layers, ca. 1940, 19" h., 11" w. (many losses) **350**

Picture frame, double oval opening on rectangular backing, painted top layers, ca. 1910, 14" h., 22" w....... **300**

Picture frame, hearts in each corner w/pyramids in shape of diamonds on all sides, painted gold, ca. 1920, 22" h., 25 1/2" w............ **1,600**

Picture frame, steps & whittled posts, stars & rosettes covering outside walls, open back for access ca. 1920, 29" h. 24" w., 14" deep **2,000**

Picture frame, tulip-shaped corners, balance of frame w/many layered designs of rectangles, rosettes & diamonds extending beyond perimeter edges, ca. 1920, 32" h., 23" w... **3,900**

Picture frame, gold painted
w/fretwork liner of carved hearts &
Polish lettering, bits of mirror in top
pyramids, ca. 1915, 32" h.,
27 1/2" w...................................... **1,900**

Picture frame, topped w/painted
gold cross, top of pyramids
highlighted w/gold paint, contains
religious print, ca. 1910, 33" h.,
22" w... **550**

Two-sided Frame

Picture frame & mirror, two-sided
tabletop-style, mirror on one side,
picture frame on reverse, finger-
like projections around frame
w/heart on top, gold painted base,
ca. 1930, 23" h., 17" w., 7 1/2"
deep (ILLUS.)................................ **950**

Sewing stand, lift-top compartment
lined in felt, large pyramids on
sides w/curved legs & open shelf
on bottom, ca. 1930, 26" h., 17" w.,
11" deep....................................... **1,800**

Shrine, open box w/cross on top,
29" h., 9" w., 10" deep (ILLUS.)..... **400**

Spice cabinet, eight drawers
w/metal pulls, fretwork decorated
top, light layering, ca. 1890, 18" h.,
12" w., 7" deep **775**

Vanity mirror, tabletop-style,
decorated w/hearts & circles,
curved base w/drawer, ca. 1930,
24" h., 16" w., 10" deep **400**

Wall cabinet, diamond pattern
decoration on door w/small
porcelain knob, layered sides,
ca. 1910, 27" h., 15" w., 8" deep .. **1,100**

Simple Shrine

Wall cabinet, shaped crest centering
a swivel mirror above a single door
opening to a fitted interior over a
single drawer, painted & carved,
early 20th c., 7 1/2 x 16 1/2",
29 1/2" h. (repainted, paint wear,
minor losses) **288**

Wall pocket, simple design w/hearts
& center horseshoe, space for
photo in center, open compartment
at bottom, 11" h., 14" w., 4" deep .. **400**

Wall pocket, polychromed-finish
mirror above, drawer & pocket
below, star & rosette accent,
ca. 1880, 23" h., 10 1/2" w., 5"
deep **695**

Wall pocket, mirror in center over
built-out pocket surrounded by
contrasting woods in vertical
stripes, curved top dated "1902,"
30" h., 16" w., 4" deep.................. **675**

Wall pocket, "New York Times,"
deeply layered geometric forms,
scratch-built from crate woods,
named for Sunday-sized
newspaper, 39" h., 31" w., 12"
deep **8,500**

Wall shelf, decorated w/chip-carved
icicle-like projections on top,
mirrored back, curved bottom,
ca. 1900, 11 1/4" h., 17" w., 14"
deep **1,500**

Watch holder, hanging-type, metal
numerals on access door,
11 1/2" h., 7" w., 1 1/2" deep **800**

Rooster Weathervane

Black Hawk Horse Weathervane

WEATHERVANES
& ROOF ORNAMENTS

Weathervanes were widely popular with American farmers at a time when agriculture dominated the workforce of America in the 19th and early 20th centuries. This rooftop adjunct was not only decorative but provided a reliable guide to wind direction from afar. Today farming employs less than 5% of the American workforce but the old adage, "You can take the boy out of the farm, but not the farm out of the boy" still holds true as evidenced by the continued popularity of farm-related antiques. Today valuable old weathervanes adorn walls above fireplaces, in kitchens and family rooms and even on a few rooftops.

As in the past, vanes in the forms of animals remain the most popular with collectors. Farmers sometimes used vanes which represented the stock they raised, so cows and horses were the most common forms, with chickens and pigs also widely seen. Eagles, of course, were popular with the patriotic-minded. Sheep, ears of corn and mules can also be found quite often but more rare are beavers, fish, and wolverines.

Today when you are looking at old weathervanes you are likely to find them with bullet holes since they were popular targets for little boys and hunters of the past. The rarest examples can be found in undamaged condition with an original finish and perhaps traces of original gilding.

In addition to animal-form vanes, beautiful glass-tailed arrow vanes were popular. Found in basically two shapes, rectangular and kite-tail, the framed, colored glass was often etched. The six most common etched designs include: 1. Company names such as Barnett, Electra, Kretzer, and Shinn 2. Fleur-de-lis 3. Moon and comet 4. Star in diamond 5. Hearts and balls 6. Maltese cross What better way to market your company name than perched high atop a few barns around the farming community? In fact, the design of the ball, the arrow and the system was a mark of the company that installed the system. Often

reproduced, an original glass-tail vane should show the stains that result from the rusting of the frame around the glass, unless the arrow frame is of a later example made of aluminum.

—Phil Steiner

Pricing: Current market prices for smaller vanes, dependent on the condition and rarity of form, may run as follows:

ANIMALS:

Chicken, large, in perfect condition .. **$500**

Chicken, small, in perfect condition..   350

Cow, large, in perfect condition.........   375

Cow, small, in perfect condition   225

Ear of corn, in perfect condition ... 1,000

Horse, circus, in perfect condition.....   350

Horse, common, in perfect condition   200

Horse, copper (standing or running), in perfect condition   500

Pig, medium, in perfect condition......   475

Pig, small, in perfect condition   325

Pig, large, in perfect condition, 14" ...   850

ETCHED:

Hearts & balls, 18" - 24"............... 250-350

Maltese Cross, 18" - 24" 250-350

Snowflake, 18" - 24"..................... 150-200

Star in diamond, 18"........................   275

GLASS-TAIL:

(COMPANY NAMES:)

Barnett Systems, red script   375

Plain, kite-tail   150

Plain, rectangular.............................   165

ADDITIONAL PRICE LISTINGS:

Wolverine, sheep, fish, mule, eagle, beaver and the more rare large vanes are valued at $1,000.00 or more. Fascinating, decorative and pleasing to both male and female tastes, weathervanes are majestic reminders of our country heritage.

Arrow Weathervane

Assorted Weathervanes

Arrow, sheet metal, the silhouetted arrow cut w/circles, scrolls, fleur-de-lis & an arrowhead, mounted on a later metal rod & base, some corrosion, late 19th c., 74 1/4" l., 18 1/2" h. (ILLUS.) **1,725**

Bull, molded & gilded copper, full-bodied animal covered in old weathered gilding, mounted on a repaired rod & a later black metal base, third quarter 19th c., 24 1/2" l., 17 1/4" h. **4,887**

Cod fish, gilt copper, New England, late 19th century (a few minor dents), 30" l. (ILLUS.) **1,500-2,500**

Cow, large, standing on end of arrow rod w/arrow point & pierced diamond "King" logo (ILLUS., center) **425**

Horse, circus-type, standing on end of arrow rod w/arrow point & pierced diamond "King" logo (ILLUS., bottom) **475**

Black Hawk Horse Weathervane

Horse, copper, Black Hawk, America, 19th c., verdigris surface, 26" l. (ILLUS.) **800-1,200**

Horse, hackney-type, molded & gilded copper, the full-bodied figure of a running horse w/a zinc head & a cropped tail, w/old gilding,

Cod Fish Weathervane

mounted on a later rod & a black
metal base, third quarter 19th c.,
30 1/2" l., 21" h. **6,325**

Horse, prancing, molded & silvered
zinc, the swell-bodied model of a
horse w/sheet metal ears, ridged
mane & stylized leaf fitted between
its ears, mounted on a rod, third
quarter 19th c., 40 1/2" l., 23" h.
(minor repairs, tail loose) **9,200**

Rooster Weathervane

Rooster, copper, America, 19th c.,
19 1/2" h. (ILLUS.) **700-900**

Rooster, realistically molded silver-
colored body standing on end of
arrow rod w/arrow point & pierced
diamond "King" logo (ILLUS., top
p. 403) **500**

ROOF GLASS

*Roof glass was the creation of a gentleman
from Crawfordville, Indiana in the late 19th
century. Scores of pieces adorned the roof
peak, front porch, front doors and windows
of charming Victorian homes during the
1890s. All of these pieces carried the mark
"Dec. 1, 91," the date of the original patent.*

*A range of colors was available including
dark red, light and dark blue, green opaque
glass, amber, white with a vaseline tint, and
clear, which over the years has often turned
a light purple due to exposure to sunlight.*

*Roof pieces slid into a bent metal (usually
tin) track which was also stamped with the
1891 patent date. Large upside-down "J's"
might be seen standing, some 14" high, at the
outer edges of the roof which was then lined
with arrowhead-shaped pieces about 41/2"
to 6" high. Where two peaks met, a double-
wheel shape sometimes adorned the intersec-
tion. Also common were fan-shaped pieces
that fit in the ninety degree angles of porch
columns. These fans were sometimes used in
groups of four to make a circular window for
a door or hallway.*

*Other unusual pieces included sections
used above doorways and a glass ornament
that was used in conjunction with a large 3'
scrolled brace. This brace elevated itself
above the roof crest arrowhead glass and
held a ball in its center. The ball was designed
in a Dot and Dash design that matched the
pattern of the roof crest glass. This metal
scrolling and the glass ball were not
grounded like a lightning rod system and
served a decorative purpose only.*

ROOF GLASS:
CURRENT VALUES

Upside-down "J" Roof Glass

14" h. Upside-down "J" (ILLUS.) ... **1,000**

WINDMILL WEIGHTS

Windmill weights were manufactured primarily between about 1875 and 1925 for use as counterbalance or governor weights on windmills. Yet, until about 1985, few persons outside the Midwest had ever heard of them. Since that time, they have attracted interest from collectors of folk art and farm equipment as an art form and as a reminder of a way of life which has long since disappeared. This interest has resulted in a dramatic increase in their value and in a like decrease in availability.

Windmill weights, always cast in iron, with two exceptions, can be classified into two categories—counterbalance and governor or regulator weights. The counterbalance weights, which were utilized on vaneless mills as a method of counterbalancing the weight of the windmill's wheels, are primarily figural in form—horses, roosters, bulls, buffaloes, squirrels, spears, arrows, and stars, among others. The governor or regulator weights are primarily non-figural and attract interest primarily from windmill restorers and advanced collectors.

The windmill manufacturers, and farms using windmill weight-type windmills, were concentrated primarily in the Midwest. Hence, the vast majority of weights found today appear in farm sales or in local auctions in Nebraska, Kansas, Minnesota, and the Dakotas.

As with most antiques and collectibles which attract and increase prices, reproductions and artfully repaired weights are now somewhat commonplace. Therefore, weight purchasers should be wary of getting "something for nothing" or of any weights which have new paint or new rust. The following rules should be observed: 1. Don't purchase anything in new paint unless you can remove it to determine age and condition. 2. Avoid weights which have uniform grind marks on the edge. 3. Don't sandblast weights or remove old paint. Patina or surface is acquired through a long aging process by exposure to the elements and is highly regarded by collectors. Removing the paint or sandblasting destroys the character, personality, and historical significance. 4. Don't pass on items because they are not described in a book or because the actual weight or dimensions differ from that indicated in the book. New forms (or variations of known forms) are continually being discovered. Windmill weights were produced at foundries using unsophisticated production techniques (by today's standards). 5. Don't buy a weight because someone says it is rare—it frequently isn't rare or even a weight. I have seen "rare" short-tail horses (the most common forms) and have heard of camels, pigs, and rabbits (which to my knowledge do not exist). 6. Buy the very best you can afford. Don't sacrifice quality, rarity, and condition for price. The great pieces will almost always increase in value while the average or mediocre pieces almost always do not. 7. Lastly, talk to and deal with knowledgeable and reputable dealers. They are generally happy to share their knowledge and enthusiasm.

Values are estimated retail prices and are based upon form, condition and rarity. Prices

Various Windmill Weights

tend to be higher in large metropolitan areas, such as the East Coast.
 —Richard S. Tucker

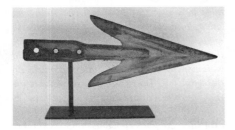

Arrow

Arrow, red paint, w/three small holes in the neck, 221/2 lbs. (including base), Leach Windmill Company, Joliet, Illinois, very rare, 1 3/8 x 25", 9 1/2" h. (ILLUS.) **$2,001-2,500**

Battleship

Bell

Battleship, Monitor, concrete & cast-iron frame & turret, 62 lbs., Baker Manufacturing Company, Evansville, Wisconsin, 12 1/2 (at bracket) x 28 3/4", 8" h., to top of turret (ILLUS.).................... **2,001-2,500**

Bell, rounded corners, 15 1/2 lbs., maker unknown, very rare, some rusting, 2 3/8 x 5 1/4", 5 1/2" h. (ILLUS.) **1,001-1,500**

Bell, Marked "6"

Bell, marked "6," 43 lbs., Breyer Brothers, Whiting & Company, Waupun, Wisconsin, rare, 2 x 11 3/4", 14 1/2" h. (ILLUS.) **3,501-5,000**

Buffalo W/Molded 'Hair'

Buffalo, w/molded 'hair,' 13 1/2 lbs. (without base), maker unknown,

very rare, 1/2 x 16", 10 7/8" h.
(ILLUS.) **3,501-5,000**

Bull, unmarked, 96 1/2 lbs., Fairbury
Windmill Company, Fairbury,
Nebraska, rare, original paint worn
& rust, bull 1 1/2" x 24 1/4", 18" h.,
base 10 x 17 7/8", 3/4" h. .. **2,001-2,500**

Canister

Canister, marked "Fairbanks Morse,"
17 1/2 lbs., Fairbanks, Morse &
Company, Chicago, Illinois, rare,
11 3/4" d. (ILLUS.) **1,001-1,500**

Fairbury Nebr. Bull

Bull, marked "FAIRBURY NEBR.,"
531/2 lbs. (including base),
Fairbury Windmill Company,
Fairbury, Nebraska,
bull 5/8 x 24 1/2", 17 3/4" h., base
9 3/4 x 17 5/8",
3/8" h. (ILLUS.).................... **1,001-1,500**

Cow

Cow, white & black paint,
w/embossed lettering "FAIRBURY"
on side of cow, 54 lbs., Fairbury
Windmill Company, Fairbury,
Nebraska, very rare,
cow 5/8 x 24 3/4", 17 5/8" h., base
9 3/4 x 17 5/8", 3/8" h. (ILLUS.)
.... **2,001-2,500**

Bull

Bull, thick w/separated tail,
unmarked, 71 lbs. (including base),
Fairbury Windmill Company,
Fairbury, Nebraska, rare, rusted,
bull 1 1/4 x 24 1/2", 17 3/4" h.,
base 9 3/4 x 17 5/8", 3/8" h.
(ILLUS.)
.... **2,001-2,500**

Crescent moon, points down,
marked "AA13 - Standard," 14 1/2
lbs., F.W. Axtell Manufacturing
Company, Fort Worth, Texas, rare,
2 1/8 x 10 1/2", 6 1/2" h.
(ILLUS.) **251-500**

Crescent moon, points up, marked
"A13 - SUCCESS," 24 lbs.,

Challenge Company, Batavia,
Illinois, rare, 2 5/8 x 10 5/8",
6 1/2" h. **251-500**

Governor weight, success, D17,
34 1/2 lbs., Hastings Foundry &
Iron Works, Hastings, Nebraska,
8 1/2" d. **100-250**

Crescent Moon

Disc, 40 1/2 lbs., Baker
Manufacturing Company,
Evansville, Wisconsin,
3 x 10 1/4" .... **Under 100**

Heart

Heart, one of two sizes, marked
"The Co. I. Houston Montgomery
PA Patented June 1 1884 April 14
1885," maker unknown, 13 lbs.,
rare, 2 1/4 x 9 1/8", 10" h.
(ILLUS.) **3,501-5,000**

Eagle

Eagle, 13 lbs., maker unknown,
rare, 1/2 x 7 1/8", 15 3/4" h.,
17" h. including lid (ILLUS.) **5,000 and up**

Governor weight, marked "MFG BY
BREYER BROS WHITING & CO
WAUPUN WIS USA," 7 1/2 lbs.,
rare, 1 5/8 x 3 1/4", 5 5/8" h...... **501-750**

Governor weight, model E S262,
17 1/2 lbs., U.S. Wind Engine
& Pump Company, Batavia,
Illinois, 7 7/8" d., 10 1/2" including
bracket..................................... **100-250**

Horse W/Long Tail

Horse, long-tail w/large base, 57 1/2
lbs., Dempster Mill Manufacturing
Company, Beatrice, Nebraska,
rare, base 2 1/2 x 17 1/4",
21 1/2" h. (ILLUS.).............. **2,501-3,500**

Running Horse

Horse, running, smaller version of
two sizes, 33 lbs., attributed to
Benjamin Danforth, Beatrice,
Nebraska, rare, 1 1/2 x 19 1/2",
21 1/2" h. (ILLUS.).............. **5,000 and up**

Horseshoe

Horseshoe, w/bar across middle,
17 1/2 lbs., maker unknown,
11/16 x 8 3/4" (including bracket),
very rare, 10 3/4" h. (ILLUS.) **3,501-5,000**

Letter—B, marked "Hildbreth Iron
Works - Hildreth Neb," 54 lbs.,

Hildreth Iron Works, Hildreth,
Nebraska, very rare,
2 5/8 x 12 3/4" (including bracket),
15 7/8" h. .... **5,000 and up**

Ozark Letter "O"

Letter—Ozark "O," smallest of three
sizes, 28 1/2 lbs., Breyer Brothers,
Whiting & Company, Waupun,
Wisconsin, rare, excluding base,
12" d. (ILLUS.).................... **1,501-2,000**

Letters—CWS

Letters—CWS, 53 lbs. (including
base), Cornell-Wigman-Searl
Company, Lincoln, Nebraska, rare,
weight 1 x23", 10 7/8" h., base
12 x 18", 1/2" h. (ILLUS.).... **3,501-5,000**

Regulator weight, Stover B13,
26 1/2 lbs., Stover Manufacturing
Company, Freeport, Illinois,
2 3/4 x 7" **100-250**

Rooster W/Barnacle-Eye

Rooster, barnacle-eye, white & red paint, 52 lbs., Elgin Wind Power & Pump Company, Elgin, Illinois, paint worn, 2 3/4 x 18", 18 1/2" h. (ILLUS.) **3,501-5,000**

Rooster W/Long Stem

Rooster, long-stem, marked "Hummer E 184" on tail, 9 1/2 lbs., Elgin Wind Power & Pump Company, Elgin, Illinois, 9 1/2 lbs., Elgin Wind Power & Pump

Company, Elgin, Illinois (ILLUS.) **751-1,000**

Rooster, yellow & red paint, marked "10 ft. No. 2" on tail, on red base, 34 lbs., Elgin Wind Power & Pump Company, Elgin, Illinois, 4 3/8 (at base) x 17", 15 3/4" h. **751-1,000**

Rooster W/Large Base

Rooster, large base, red & white paint, marked "Hummer" on tail, 48 lbs., Elgin Wind Power & Pump Company, Elgin, Illinois, paint slightly worn, 4 3/8" (at base) x 17", 17 3/4" h. (ILLUS.) **1,501-2,000**

Rooster

Rooster, small mogul, one of three
sizes, 60 lbs., 4 3/4 x 18 1/2",
18" h. (ILLUS.).................... **3,501-5,000**

Rooster

Rooster (A20)

Rooster, duplex (A20), red & white
paint, 64 lbs., Elgin Wind Power &
Pump Company, Elgin, Illinois,
paint worn, 2 1/2 x 19", 191/4" h.
(ILLUS.) **3,501-5,000**

Rooster, duplex, thick, red & white
paint, 100 1/2 lbs., Elgin Wind
Power & Pump Company, Elgin,
Illinois, rare, paint worn,
4 3/8 x 19", 19 1/2" h.
(ILLUS.) .... **5,000 and up**

Woodmanse Rooster

Rooster, Woodmanse, large, 63 lbs.,
Elgin Wind Power & Pump
Company, Elgin, Illinois, some rust
& paint worn, 3 3/4 x 18",
19 3/8" h. (ILLUS.).............. **1,001-1,500**

Rooster W/Screw Leg

Rooster, screw leg, 64 lbs., Elgin
Wind Power & Pump Company,
Elgin, Illinois, rare, 3 1/4 x 17 1/2",
20" h. (ILLUS.).................... **5,000 and up**

Shield

Shield, decorated w/stars & stripes, 16 lbs. (including base), attributed to Challenge Wind Mill & Feed Mill Co., Batavia, Illinois, rare, excluding base, some rust & paint worn, 1 3/8 x 7 1/4", 8 3/8" h. (ILLUS.) **2,501-3,500**

Spear

Spear, embossed letters read "New Century Sauk Centre Minn," 34 1/2 lbs. (without base), maker unknown, rare, 2 x 15 1/4", 11" h. (ILLUS.) **2,001-2,500**

Spear, marked "MODEL - 1912," 39 lbs., Challenge Company, Batavia, Illinois, rare, 3 1/2 (at rear bracket) x 35 3/4", 14" h. (ILLUS.) **3,501-5,000**

Spear, marked "Model 1913," 39 lbs., Challenge Company, Batavia, Illinois, 3 1/2 x 35 3/4", 14" h. **1,001-1,500**

Squirrel

Squirrel, 35 1/2 lbs., Elgin Wind & Pump Company, Elgin, Illinois, 3 (at base) x 13 3/4", 17" h. (ILLUS.) **3,501-5,000**

Spear Model 1912

Halladay Star

Star (C24)

Star, Halladay, five-pointed star, 38 1/2 lbs., U.S. Wind Engine & Pump Company, paint worn & some rusting, 2 3/4 x 14 3/4", 2 3/4" (ILLUS.).......................... **501-750**

Star, (C24), five-pointed star w/remnants of white paint, 38 1/2 lbs., Flint & Walling Manufacturing Company, Kendellville, Indiana, rare, some rusting, 2 3/4 x 14 3/4", 14 3/4" h. (ILLUS.).............. **1,001-1,500**

WOOD SCULPTURES

American folk sculpture is an important part of the American art scene today. Skilled wood carvers turned out ship's figureheads, cigar store figures, plaques and carousel animals of stylized beauty and great appeal. The wooden shipbuilding industry, which had originally nourished this folk art, declined after the Civil War and the talented carvers then turned to producing figures for tobacconist's shops, carousel animals and show figures for circuses. These figures and other early ornamental carvings that have survived the elements and years are eagerly sought.

Indian Princess with Cigars & Leaves

Cigar Store Indian Brave

Cigar store figure of Indian brave, standing looking to the side, wearing a cape, breeches & loincloth, extended arm missing, fine carving, good paint, late 19th c., 88" h. (ILLUS.) **$24,150**

Cigar store figure of Indian Princess, standing wearing a colorful skirt, sash & breeches, high colorful feathered headdress, holding a roll of cigars in one hand & holding aloft a bunch of tobacco leaves in the other, on original base, repainted, found in Rhode Island, late 19th - early 20th c., over 7' h. (ILLUS.) **18,700**

Cigar store figure of Indian Princess, standing wearing colorful buckskin skirt, one leg raised resting on rock, one arm raised holding a cut plug of tobacco, tall flared headdress, trimmed in red, green, yellow, blue & brown, late 19th c. (ILLUS.) **5,500**

Indian Princess with Tobacco Plug

Figure of a European soldier,
carved & painted, the stylized
standing figure in uniform w/a
domed helmet, one arm to his side,
the other meant to hold a lance, a
rifle slung over his shoulder,
leather medal & shoulder straps,
light painted jacket & dark pants,
velvet bed roll, early 20th c.,
22 1/2" h. (minor imperfections) **374**

European Figure of an Angel

Figure of an angel, carved & painted
stylized figure wearing an off-the-
shoulder gown & drapery, one arm
aloft w/hole for a missing trumpet,
probably northern Europe, 19th c.,
minor losses, repairs, 28" h.
(ILLUS.) **2,185**

Carved Figure of Father Time

Figure of Father Time, stylized
carved giltwood figure of an
emaciated elderly man wearing a
toga-like robe, one arm aloft
holding an hourglass, standing on
an oblong mound base, American,
mid-19th c., old repaint, repair to
ankles, paint loss, loss of
headdress, minor insect damage in
base, 16" h. (ILLUS.) **460**

Figure of female saint, carved
standing & wearing classical robes,
one hand holding a long sword
upright, naturalistic coloring on
face & hands, golden paint on
robes, Europe, 18th c. (ILLUS.
p. 416) **6,037**

European Female Saint Carving

Figure of Madonna of the Sea

Figure of Madonna & Child, carved oak architectural-type figure of Madonna of the Sea, standing w/a rose wreath on her head, holding the Infant Jesus in one hand, supporting an anchor w/the other, Europe, late 19th c., age cracks, some losses, 51" h. (ILLUS.) **3,450**

Crowned Madonna & Child Figures

Figure of Madonna & Child, carved & painted figures w/the Madonna wearing a red robe & brown gold-trimmed cloak & w/a tall flaring ornate gold crown, holding the crowned Infant Jesus w/gold globe in one hand & holding a sceptre in the other, on an ornate scroll- and angel-carved base, Europe, 18th or 19th c., 30" h. (ILLUS.) **5,060**

Figure of mermaid, gilded wood, carved buxom female figure wearing a diadem w/tail curled, mounted on rod attached to shaped painted wood base, 19th c., 15 x 16 1/2" **1,495**

Carved Model of a Chamois

Model of a chamois, the standing
animal w/the front legs resting on a
raised rock, a tree stump support,
its head erect w/upright short
curled horns, polychrome
decoration, Europe, 19th c.,
contemporary base, minor cracks,
paint loss, craquelure, repair to
antler, 24 1/2" h. (ILLUS.)............. **1,150**

Model of a dog, carved wood,
recumbent figure of dog w/head
up, inset glass eyes & tail back,
painted black & brown, ca. 1900, 8
1/8" l., 3" h. **1,035**

Model of a horse, carved full-bodied
figure of brown horse, free
standing w/white 'stockings' &
horsehair tail, late 19th c., 26" l.,
23" h. **6,325**

Model of a monkey, carved &
painted, seated on a tall columnar
rockwork base, wearing a large red
hat & yellow & red smock, holding
out in one hand a shallow round
red dish, brown fur & green base,

probably France, late 19th c.,
65" h. (minor imperfections) **10,925**

Wall plaque, carved & painted eagle
wall plaque w/attenuated wings
grasping a long banner w/stars in
its beak, ca. 1900, 43" l., 8 1/4" h. **14,950**

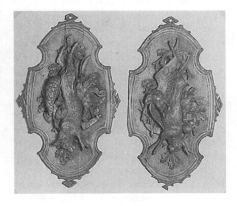

Ornate Carved Wall Plaques

Wall plaques, carved limewood,
oblong cartouche form carved in
full-relief w/hanging game trophies,
one w/a hare, birds, leaves &
powder horn, the other w/a fox,
birds, leaves & a powder horn,
molded edges, minor damage,
probably Europe, late 19th c.,
24 x 42", pr. (ILLUS.).................... **3,450**

Whirligig, carved & painted wood,
flattened bearded figure of sailor
boy w/rotating arms held straight
out from his sides, wearing a blue
shirt w/white collar & white trousers
w/red belt, ca. 1900, 14 1/4" h. **517**

Whirligig, carved & painted wood,
mustached Hussar figure dressed
in full uniform, fitted w/rotating
paddle arms, painted black, blue,
white & gold, mounted on wood
base, 13 1/2" h. (one arm loose) .. **3,450**

WOODENWARES

The patina and mellow coloring, along with the lightness and smoothness that come only with age and wear, attract collectors to old woodenwares. The earliest forms were the simplest and the shapes of items whittled out in the late 19th century varied little in form from those turned out in the American colonies two centuries earlier. A burl is a growth, or wart, on some trees in which the grain of the wood is twisted and turned in a manner which strengthens the fibers and causes a beautiful pattern to be formed. Treenware is simply a term for utilitarian items made from "treen," another word for wood. While maple was the primary wood used for these items, they are also abundant in pine, ash, oak, walnut, and other woods. "Lignum Vitae" is a species of wood from the West Indies that can always be identified by the contrasting colors of dark heartwood and light sapwood and by its heavy weight, which caused it to sink in water. Also see KITCH-ENWARES

Bowl, burl, deep rounded sides on small footring, refinished, 4 1/4" d., 1 3/4" h. (ILLUS. right) **$193**

Bowl, turned burl, of circular form w/incised top & sides, old mellow surface, America, 19th c., 5 1/2" d., 3 1/2" h. **374**

Bowl, ash burl, oval w/well-shaped cut-out rim handles, good figure, thin sides, old finish, dark stain, age crack & wear in bottom, 7 7/8 x 8 7/8", 2 3/4" h. (ILLUS. left) **2,640**

Bowl, burl, simple deep rounded sides w/a dark finish rubbed to a mottled shine, 9" d., 3 3/4" h. **330**

Bowl, turned & painted, an incised 1 1/4" rim band & beaded sides, incised line at base, original red-painted surface, 19th c., 12 3/4" d., 4 1/4" h. (minor imperfections) **920**

Bowl, ash burl, good figure & soft varnish finish, pronounced rim w/irregular notch w/worn edges, minor hairline crack, 13 1/2" d., 6" h. **660**

Bowl, turned burl, large deep oblong form, 19th c., 13 x 16", 6" h. (rim losses) **230**

Bowl, burl, deep-sided oblong form w/recessed hand holds, ca. 1900, 17" l., 4" h. **3,450**

Bowl, ash burl, widely flaring rounded sides, worn patina, 17 1/4" d., 4 3/4" h. (small holes at flaws in burl) **605**

Bowl, turned, sharply tapering flaring sides w/small round bottom, exterior w/old worn light blue paint, interior heavily worn, 16 3/4 x 17 1/2", 5 3/4" h. **358**

Bowl, burl, 19th c., 19 5/8" d., 6 3/4" h. (crack, minor rim chips).. **1,265**

Bowl, turned maple, wide w/incised rim & base, painted ivory, American, 18th c., 25 1/8" d., 9 1/4" h. (minor rim chips & paint wear) **1,955**

Bucket, stave construction, cylindrical form w/two wide bentwood bands w/finger lappets, natural patina, old ink inscription on bottom "Given to Gertrude h. Taylor by Augusta Bates Taylor in the Spring of 1922," 11 1/2" d., 8 1/4" h. **165**

Two Early Burl Bowls

Bucket, stave construction w/two black steel bands, the exterior w/worn red graining, white interior, wire bail handle w/diamond attachments & a turned wood hand grip, 7 1/2" d., 6" h. (bottom steel band replaced) **220**

Butter churn, stave construction, painted blue, late 18th - early 19th c., 8 3/4" d., 26" h. (paint wear) **374**

Butter paddle, ash burl, one-piece w/flat tapering handle w/end hook & wide shallow angled oval bowl, scrubbed finish, 9" l. **369**

Butter paddle, burl, bird's head handle, wear & handle has glued break, 8 1/2" l. **160**

Cake board, carved walnut, three lozenge-shaped molds of a dog, a soldier on horseback & a flower-filled vase, impressed mark of J. Conger, New York, 19th c., 13 x 17" **805**

Cake box, cov., maple, circular form w/inset lid & handle stenciled w/a band of stylized flowers & leafage on yellow ground, together w/a copper milk pail molded w/figure of a standing cow **2,070**

Candle dryer on stand, painted, the stand w/two carved arms w/carved drying holes on the vase- and ring-turned pedestal, on a carved round base, original bluish green paint, New England, 19th c., 22" h. (minor paint wear) **575**

Carrier, octagonal, painted red w/four hexagonal compartments & one central square shape, shaped fixed handle, late 19th c., 12 1/2" d., 4" h. (minor paint loss) . **575**

Compote, inlaid pierced wood, staved construction w/turned & carved decoration w/brass bands, 8 1/2" d., 8 " h. **633**

Cookie board, cherry, rectangular, chip-carved w/a walking bear in a landscape, branded "B.R.," inscribed in ink "B. Raber," 5 x 7 7/8" **193**

Cornucopia, wood, carved spiraling & graduated turned horn w/rope-twist border painted a red-gold color, late 19th c., 13 1/2" l., 12" h. **460**

Corset busk, carved, the long flat board decorated on one side w/pinwheels, hearts & geometric designs, the reverse inscribed "Mary Harlow," 19th c., 13 1/2" l. (minute cracks & a chip) **201**

Cuspidor, turned wood w/incised line decoration, 15 1/4" h. (damage, repairs) **403**

Dipper, bentwood, deep wide slightly tapering cylindrical sides w/copper tacks at the side seam, inset angled baluster-turned pointed side handle, old brown finish, 7 1/2" d. plus handle...................... **193**

Dough box on legs, rectangular deep box w/canted sides & a one-board top, raised on an inset canted apron w/corner blocks continuing to canted ring- and rod-turned legs w/knob feet, poplar w/cherry finish, 19th c., 20 3/4 x 35 3/4", 27 1/2" h. **413**

Early Dough Box on Stand

Dough box on stand, pine & ash, a rectangular lift-off top w/braces above a deep canted dovetailed box w/a mid-molding over the base w/arched canted apron & four block-turned legs, old refinish, possibly New England, late 18th c., imperfections, 22 x 45", 25" h. (ILLUS.) **1,840**

Drying rack, painted poplar, three-section, three flat slender rails joining the tall flat uprights, old worn greyish yellow repaint,

attributed to the Shakers, 19th c.,
each section 35" w., 56" h. **193**

Flagon, cov., painted maple & elm,
cylindrical stave construction
w/sapling binding, the lid w/a
locking mechanism, probably
northern Europe, early 19th c.,
13 1/2" h. (paint wear, minor
losses, insect damage)................. **805**

Pease Turned Wood Jar

Knife box, bentwood, ash &
chestnut, the low rectangular form
w/rounded corners & center divider
w/raised turned handhold, old
varnish finish, 8 1/2 x 13" **138**

Knife box, inlaid rosewood,
rectangular w/canted shallow sides
inlaid w/ivory bands up each
corner & w/an inlaid ivory
rectangular panel centering a large
diamond on the long sides, deeply
scalloped central dividing handle
topped by an arched ivory grip,
probably New England, 19th c.,
13 1/8" l., 5 1/4" h. (very minor
cracks, minor inlay loss) **2,300**

Rare Turned & Incised Wood Goblet

Goblet, turned & decorated, the wide
bell-shaped bowl w/molded rim, on
a bulbous knop stem & round disk
foot, heavily incised decoration
w/panels of animals & Royal crest
between religious verses, England,
late 18th - early 19th c., 8 1/4" h.
(ILLUS.) **9,200**

Grain measure, cylindrical stave-
constructed double-type w/two
replaced metal rings, old sage
green paint, 10 3/4" h. **99**

Grain measure, round bentwood,
steel bands w/cast-iron handles,
old patina, branded "Danial
Cragin...Wilton, N.H.," 14 1/2" d.,
8" h. **83**

Jar, cov., bulbous tapering flat-
bottomed container w/a short
flared neck & low domed cover
w/acorn finial, curly wood w/old
finish, attributed to Pease of Ohio,
late 19th c., minor age cracks,
6 1/2" h. (ILLUS.)........................... **825**

Rare Decorative Knife Box

Knife box, inlaid walnut, a deep
canted rectangular base w/inlaid
band, teardrops & center stars
fitted w/an end drawer w/ivory pull
below the dovetailed upper tray
w/canted sides & a scalloped rim,
arched center divider w/turned bar
over cut-out hand hole, old soft
finish, 19th c., 9 3/4 x 14", 8" h.
(ILLUS.) **5,060**

Knife box, mahogany, rectangular w/canted sides & dovetailed corners, center divider w/a high scroll-cut handle w/oblong cut-out hand hole, old finish, 10 x 14 1/2" . **358**

Leather worker's vise, chestnut, the base w/a tapering rectangular block supporting flattened uprights on two sides which curve at the top to form the vise, one side w/inset handle for adjusting vise opening, old patina, Shaker, Union Village, Ohio, 28" h. **116**

Pantry box, cov., round w/nailed construction & swing handle, original red-painted surface, 19th c., 10 7/8" d., 7" h. (chip on top & bottom, paint wear) **546**

Fine Mahogany Pipe Box

Pipe box, mahogany, hanging-type, tall slender form w/high arched backboard w/hanging hole above the shaped rim & front w/a large heart cut-out, a small drawer at the bottom, molded base, late 18th c., American, imperfections, 18" h. (ILLUS.) **1,380**

Pitcher, cov., painted fir, cylindrical stave construction, sapling-bond, the cover w/a locking mechanism, painted red, probably northern Europe, early 19th c., 13 1/2" (imperfections) **1,380**

Spice chest, butternut & poplar, w/arched back for hanging, eight drawers w/recessed circular knobs, ca. 1870, 5 x 11", 18" h. **350**

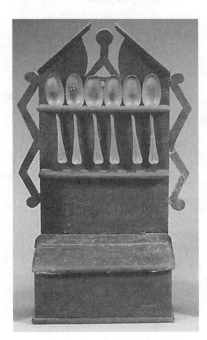

Early European Spoon Rack

Spoon rack, painted pine, hanging-type, the tall backboard w/a peaked cut-out top & cut-out zigzags down the sides flanking two pierced bands for spoons above a slant-lidded lower compartment w/cotter pin hinges, old dark green paint, probably Europe, late 18th c., together w/six pewter spoons, rack 5 5/8 x 11 1/2", 24 3/4" h., the group (ILLUS.) **920**

Storage box, cov., bentwood, painted pine, oval w/deep sides & finger lappet construction, upright rounded end handles, flat board top w/central brace w/cut-out hand hole, American, 19th c., cracks,

Large Bentwood Storage Box

minor losses, paint wear,
19 3/4 x 26 3/4", 14 3/8" h.
(ILLUS.) **1,495**

Sugar bucket, cov., stave
construction w/tapering cylindrical
sides w/two wooden bands, flat
fitted cover & bentwood swing
handle, worn old red repaint over
brown, 14" d., 14" h. **385**

Sugar bucket, cov., stave
construction w/two tacked wooden
bands, alternating staves of dark
walnut & light pine, flat fitted cover,
wire bail handle w/turned hand
grip, old patina, 6 5/8" h................. **193**

Tea bin, cov., painted poplar, the
hinged cover w/canted corners
above a conforming box, old red
paint & transfer w/"A&P" logo &
Greek key border, late 19th c.,
17 x 18", 30" h. (imperfections) **403**

Tub, stave constructed, low
cylindrical sides wrapped w/two
wide pointed lappet bands, painted
w/two shades of old green paint,
impressed mark "C. Whitney,"
19th c., 17" d., 6" h. **220**

Watch hutch, carved & decorated, a
D-form shelf w/a stepped &
scalloped edge supporting a
miniature tall-case clock case
w/short legs w/claw-and-ball feet
supporting a projecting base below
the tall rectangular box w/a painted
rectangular reserve on the lower
front below the round watch face
opening decorated w/delicate
notch-carving below a crest w/a
pair of pierced turret finials flanking
a spread-winged eagle on ball,

painted blue & grey w/gilt
highlights, Europe, 19th c.,
3 3/8 x 12", 10" h. (no backboard,
paint wear).................................... **1,265**

Rare Inlaid Watch Hutch

Watch hutch, inlaid mahogany,
Federal style, a tall flattened
baluster-form case w/molded inlaid
base & edge banding, the lower
front inlaid w/a large paterae, the
upper case w/a round opening
surrounded by inlaid starburst rays,
molded small top w/inlaid semicircle & spearpoints, hanging loop
at top, minor edge damage &
veneer loss, early 19th c.,
11 1/4" h. (ILLUS.)........................ **3,575**

Yarn swift, wooden table clamp-on
style, a wrought-iron thumbscrew
supporting a slender central shaft
w/expanded crisscrossed slats &
small cup top finial, old dark brown
patina, 19th c., 20" h...................... **193**

Yarn winding reel, floor model, hard
& soft woods, splayed simple
turned legs supporting a heavy
rectangular block supporting a tall
slender tapering post w/four long
lower crossbars & four short upper
crossbars, the bars each joined by
angled pairs of long slats, old black
paint, 54 3/4" h. **220**

WRITING ACCESSORIES

INKWELLS & STANDS

For the last 7,000 years, mankind's history has been written in ink of one kind or another. The continuing fascination with containers designed to hold this essential fluid has escalated greatly during the past twenty years.

Inkwells of all types, designs and makers have become increasingly difficult to find as collectors discover the immensely wide variety of inkwells, inkstands and ink containers. Entire collections may be formed of a particular type such as figurals featuring a human, insect or animal figures. Many collectors specialize in glass, wood or bronze while others seek the elusive pewter or art glass well, travel well or perhaps the most difficult category, the tiny, miniature wells designed for the desk of a child.

Pricing of the following inkwells and stands is drawn from flea markets, antiques shops and auctions..

Bronze stand, an oval figural rockwork base w/a realistic figure of a partridge standing atop one end, a round cov. inkwell at the other end, a dished pen tray in the front base, brown & multi-colored patina, Europe, early 20th c., 14" l. **$345**

Bronze well, a squatty bulbous form tapering to a low hinged cover, Oriental design of overall cast stylized dragons in endless loops, inside of cover marked "MF & Co. Viking," Marshall Field & Co., Chicago, early 20th c., 3 3/4" h. (no liner) **98**

Cameo glass well, domed straight sided yellow glass container overlaid in white & cut w/a design of wheat & small five-petaled flowers on leafy stems, applied silver collar & compressed spherical silver monogrammed cover marked by Gorham Mfg. Co., glass probably by Stevens & Williams, ca. 1890, 4 1/2" h. **1,150**

Staffordshire earthenware well, white head painted black w/numbered sections above three wells surrounded by blue scrolls, rectangular base stamped "By F. Bridges, Phrenologist," 19th c., 5 1/2" h. **747**

LAP DESKS & WRITING BOXES

Lap board, pine & walnut, portable rectangular board w/a half-round cut-out for the user's waist, the board composed of alternating strips of pine & walnut w/an impressed rule, strips mounted on a paper backing so it can be rolled up for storage, side braces w/brass clips keep it rigid when in use, old shipping label on the back reads "U.S. & Canada Express - 112 Canal St. - From Boston, Mass.," attributed to the Shakers, 19 1/2 x 36" **220**

Fine Mahogany Writing Box

Writing box, mahogany, rectangular case w/hinged slant lid opening to a compartmented two-drawer interior w/whalebone & ivory pulls, applied carved base band, old surface, minor cracks, 19th c., 14 1/4 x 17 1/2", 7" h. (ILLUS.)...... **920**

CLUBS, ORGANIZATIONS & NEWSLETTERS

Bottle & Openers
Figural Bottle Openers Club
Nancy Robb
3 Ave. A
Latrobe, Pennsylvania 15650

Just For Openers
John Stanley
3712 Sunning Dale Way
Durham, North Carolina 27707

Ceramics

Blue & White Pottery
Blue & White Pottery Club—
Secretary
224 12th Street NW
Cedar Rapids, Iowa 52405
Club dues: $12/year
For free introductory brochure, call:
(303) 690-8649

Red Wing
Red Wing Collectors Society, Inc.
P.O. Box 14
Galesburg, Illinois 61402-0184
(309) 342-1601

Watt Pottery
Watt Collectors Association
P.O. Box 184
Galesburg, Illinois 61401
Club dues: $10/year

Watt Pottery Collectors
Dennis Thompson
P.O. Box 26067
Cleveland, Ohio 44126-0067
(216) 235-8548

Christmas Collectibles
Golden Glow of Christmas Past
Robert Dalluge
6401 Winsdale Street
Golden Valley, Minnesota 55427
Club dues: $20.00/year

Graniteware
National Graniteware Society
P.O. Box 10013
Cedar Rapids, Iowa 52410
(319) 393-0252

Irons
Iron Talk
P.O. Box
Waelder, Texas 78959
Club dues: 425.00/year; $30.00/year
outside United States

Kitchen Collectibles

Kollectors of Old Kitchen Stuff (KOOKS)
Carol Bohn
501 Market Street
Mifflinburg, Pennsylvania 17844
Send long self addressed envelope for
information.

The National Reamers Collectors
    Association (NRCA)
Bobbie Zucker
1 St. Eleanoras Lane
Tuckahoe, New York 10707
(914) 779-1405
or
Debbie Gillham
47 Midlane Court
Gaithersburg, Maryland 20878
(301) 977-5727

Lightning Rod Balls
Wather or Knot Antiques
15832 S.C.R. 900 W
Wanatah, Indiana 46390
(219) 733-2713

Trade Cards
Trade Card Collector's Association
The Advertising Trade Card Quarterly
P.O. Box 284
Marlton, New Jersey 08053

Tools
The Early American Industries
Association
For more information & a book list, write:
John S. Watson, Treasurer
EAIA
P.O. Box 143
Delmar, New York 12054

The Missouri Valley Wrench Club
H. Klein, President
832 Ash Street
Granville, Iowa 51022

Midwest Tool Collectors Association
Rt. 2, Box 152
Wartrace, Tennessee 37183-9406
(614) 455-1935

Ohio Tool Collectors Association
P.O. Box 261
London, Ohio 43140
(614) 852-3180

Rocky Mountain Tool Collectors
2024 Owens Court
Denver, Colorado 80277-1910
(303) 988-5053

AUCTION HOUSES

Barberiana
Anthony J. Nard & Co.
US Route 220
Milan, Pennsylvania 18831
(717) 888-9404

Ceramics
Historical & Commemorative Wares
Collector's Sales and Service
P.O. Box 4037
Middleton, Rhode Island 02842
(401) 849-5012

Stoneware
Bruce & Vicki Waasdorp
P.O. Box 434
Clarence, New York 14031
(716) 759-2361

Decoys
Decoys Unlimited
Theodore S. Harmon
2320 Main Street
West Barnstable, Massachusetts 02668
(508) 362-2766

Guyette & Schmidt, Inc.
P.O. Box 522
West Farmington, Maine 04992
(207) 778-6256 or (207) 778-6266

Furniture, Fine & Decorative Art
Christie's
502 Park Avenue
New York, New York 10022
(212) 546-1000

Garth's Auctions
2690 Stratford Road
Box 369
Delaware, Ohio 43015
(614) 362-4771or (614) 548-6778

Skinner, Inc.
357 Main Street
Bolton, Massachusetts 01740
(508) 779-6214

Sotheby's
1334 York Avenue
New York, New York 10021
(212) 606-7000

Lightning Rod Balls
Russell Barnes
P.O. Box 141994
Austin, Texas 78714
(512) 835-9510 (please call between
8:00 to 10:00 p.m. CST)

Tools
Barry Hurchalla
RD2, Box 558
Botertown, Pennsylvania 19512

Richard Crane
63 Poor Farm Road
Hilsboro, New Hampshire 03244
(603) 478-5723

Bud Brown
4729 Kutztown Road
Temple, Pennsylvania 19560

Tom Witte
P.O. Box 399
Front St. West
Mattawan, Michigan 49071
(616) 668-4161

FURTHER READING

*Books are organized alphabetically by
category*

Baskets

Johnson, Frances. *Wallace-Homestead
Price Guide to Baskets*, Second
Edition. Radnor, Pennsylvania:
Wallace-Homestead Book
Company, 1989

Lawrence, Martha R. *Lightship Baskets
of Nantucket*. West Chester,
Pennsylvania: Schiffer Publishing,
Ltd., 1990

McGuire, John. *Basketry—The Shaker
Tradition*. Asheville, NC: Lark
Books, 1988

McGuire, John E. Old New England
Splint Basket and how to make
them. West Chester, Pennsylvania:
Schiffer Publishing, Ltd., 1985

Schiffer, Nancy. *Baskets*. Exton,
Pennsylvania: Schiffer Publishing,
Ltd., 1984

Teleki, Gloria Roth. *Collecting
Traditional American Basketry*. New
York, New York: E.P. Dutton, 1979

Ceramics

Bennington Pottery
Barret, Richard Carter. *Bennington
Pottery and Porcelain*. New York,
New York: Crown Publishers, 1958

Blue & White Pottery
Alexander, M.H. *Stoneware in the Blue
and White*. Paducah, Kentucky:
Image Graphics, Inc., 1993 reprint

Harbin, Edith. *Blue & White Stoneware
Pottery Crockery. Identification and
Value Guide*. Paducah, Kentucky:
Collector Books, 1977

Harbin, Joseph, M. & E. *Blue & White
Pottery*. 1973

McNerney, Kathryn. *Blue & White
Stoneware*. Paducah, Kentucky:
Collector Books, 1995 reprint

Sanford, Steve & Martha. *The Guide to
Brush-McCoy Pottery*. 1993

Pennsbury Pottery

Henzke, Lucile. *Pennsbury Pottery*.
West Chester, Pennsylvania:
Schiffer Publishing, 1990

Myers, Esther. "Pennsbury Pottery,"
American Clay Exchange (January
30, 1986

Cox, Susan N. "Pennsbury Pottery
Pictorial," *American Clay Exchange*
(June 15, 1985)

Company catalogs and invoices from
1960 through 1965.

Redware Pottery

Mcconnell, Kevin. *Redware—America's
Folk Art Pottery*. West Chester,
Pennsylvania: Schiffer Publishing,
Ltd., 1988

Rockingham Pottery

Brewer, Mary. *Collector's Guide to
Rockingham—The Enduring
Ware—Identification & Values*.
Paducah, Kentucky: Collector
Books, 1996

Children's Dishes

Lechler, Doris Anderson. *English Toy
China*. Marietta, Ohio: Antique
Publications, 1989

Lechler, Doris Anderson. *Children's
Glass Dishes, China, and
Furniture*, Vol. 1., Paducah,
Kentucky: Collector Books, 1986

Lechler, Doris Anderson. *Children's
Glass Dishes, China, and
Furniture*. Vol. 2., Paducah,
Kentucky: Collector Books, 1986

Lechler, Doris Anderson. *Toy Glass*.
Marietta, Ohio: Antique
Publications, 1989

Lechler, Doris Anderson. *French &
German Dolls, Dishes and
Accessories*. Marietta, Ohio:
Antique Publications, 1991

Christmas Collectibles

Brenner, Robert. *Christmas Past*,
Exton, Pennsylvania: Schiffer
Publishing, 1985

_____. *Christmas Revisited.* Exton, Pennsylvania: Schiffer Publishing, 1986

_____. *Christmas Through the Decades.* Atglen, Pennsylvania: Schiffer Publishing, 1993

Decoys

Huxford, Bob & Sharon. *The Collector's Guide to Decoys.* Paducah, Kentucky: Collector Books, 1990

_____. *The Collector's Guide to Decoys, Book II.* Paducah, Kentucky: Collector Books, 1992

Kangas, Linda & Gene. Decoys, Paducah, Kentucky: Collector Books, 1992

Kerosene Lamps

Thuro, Catherine, M.V. *Oil Lamps: The Kerosene Era in North America.* Des Moines, Iowa: Wallace-Homestead Book Company, 1976

Thuro, Catherine, M.V. *Oil Lamps II: Glass Kerosene Lamps.* Toronto, Ontario: Thorncliffe House, Inc., 1983

Kitchen Collectibles

Coffee Mills

MacMillan, Joseph. *The MacMillan Index of Antique Coffee Mills.* 1995

White, Derek and Michael, *Early American Coffee Mills.* 1994

Egg Beaters

Thornton, Don. *Beat This, The Eggbeater Chronicles.* Sunnyvale, California: Off Beat Books (to order send $24.95 to Off Beat Books, 1345 Poplar Ave., Sunnyvale, CA 94087 or call (408) 737-0434)

Rugs

Kopp, Joel and Kate. *American Hooked and Sewn Rugs—Folk Art Underfoot.* New York, New York: E.P. Dutton, 1975

Sewing Adjuncts

Muller, Wayne. *Darn It! The History and Romance of Darners.* L-W Book Sales: 1995 (to order, send $22.25

to Darn It!, P.O. Box 903, Pacific Palisades, CA 90272)

Zalkin, Eselle. *Zalkin's Handbook of Thimbles & Sewing Implements.* Willow Grove, Pennsylvania: Warman Publishing Co., 1988 ($24.95)

Tobacciana

Alsford, Denis. *Match Holders.* Exton, Pennsylvania: Schiffer Publishing

Hyman, Tony. *Handbook of American Cigar Boxes.* Pismo Beach, California: Treasure Hunt Publications (to order, send $25.00 to Tony Hyman, P.O. Box 3028, Shell Beach, CA 93448)

Martin-Congdon, Douglas. *Tobacco Tins.* Exton, Pennsylvania: Schiffer Publishing

Storino, Louis. *Chewing Tobacco Tin Tag.* Exton, Pennsylvania: Schiffer Publishing

Tools

Barlow, Ronald S. *The Antique Tool Collector's Guide to Value.* El Cajon, California: Windmill Publishing (to order, contact the publisher at 2147 Windmill View Rd., El Cajon, CA 92020)

Tramp Art

Cornish, Micheal, and Clifford Wallach. *They Call it Tramp Art.* Columbia University Press, 1996

Windmill Weights

Lindsay, T. *A Field Guide to American Windmills.* Norman, Oklahoma: The University of Oklahoma Press, 1985.

Simpson, Milt. *Windmill Weights.* 1985 (out of print)

EXPERT INFORMATION FOR BUILDING YOUR COLLECTION

Antique Trader's Antiques & Collectibles
Price Guide 2000
Edited by Kyle Husfloen
This annual description and value guide provides up-to-date descriptive and pricing information for thousands of antiques and collectibles in hundreds of the most sought after and popular categories. New or hot catagories include collectibles buttons, children's books, figural bottle openers, costume jewelry, bootjacks and Czechoslovakian collectibles.
Softcover • 6 x 9 • 912 pages
1,500 b&w photos
AT2000 • $15.95

American Stoneware
by Don & Carol Raycraft
An excellently researched book on every aspect of stoneware: history, manufacturers' marks, forms, pricing and collecting techniques. Hundreds of photos aid both beginner and expert in identification and valuation.
Softcover • 6 x 9 • 160 pages
4-page color section
AMST • $16.95

Petretti's Coca-Cola Collectibles Price Guide
10th Edition
by Allan Petretti
The new "Petretti numbering system" gives buyers and sellers a standard way to identify the exact collectible they want to buy or sell. The detailed index helps you quickly locate any item by type. In the image identification system index, simply look up your Petretti number and get the exact page where the item is located.
Hardcover • 8-3/4 x 11 • 648 pages
5,676 b&w photos • 324 color photos
AT5765 • $42.95

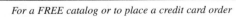

For a FREE catalog or to place a credit card order

 Call **800-258-0929** Dept. ACBR

M-F, 7 am - 8 pm • Sat, 8 am - 2 pm, CST
Krause Publications • 700 E State St., Iola, WI 54990 • www.krausebooks.com

---

Shipping and Handling: $3.25 1st book; $2 ea. add'l. Call for UPS rates. Foreign orders $15 per shipment plus $5.95 per book.
Sales tax: CA 7.25%, IA 6%, IL 6.25%, PA 6%, TN 8.25%, VA 4.5%, WA 8.2%, WI 5.5%

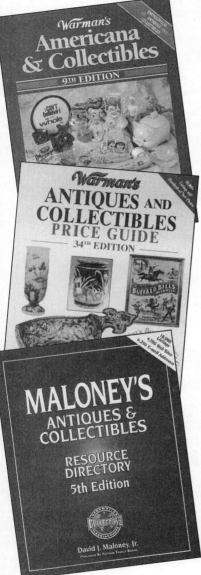